SECOND EDITION

Educating Immigrant Students in the 21st Century

What Educators Need to Know

Xue Lan Rong

Judith Preissle

CORWIN PRESS

A SAGE Company

For information:

Corwin Press
A SAGE Company
2455 Teller Road
Thousand Oaks, California 91320
www.corwinpress.com

SAGE Ltd.
1 Oliver's Yard
55 City Road
London, EC1Y 1SP
United Kingdom

SAGE India Pvt. Ltd.
B 1/I 1 Mohan Cooperative
  Industrial Area
Mathura Road, New Delhi 110 044
India

SAGE Asia-Pacific Pte. Ltd.
33 Pekin Street #02-01
Far East Square
Singapore 048763

Printed in the United States of America

Library of Congress Cataloging-in-Publication Data

Rong, Xue Lan.
  Educating immigrant students in the 21st century : what educators need to know / Xue Lan Rong, Judith Preissle. — 2nd ed.
      p. cm.
  Updated ed. of: Educating immigrant students.
  Includes bibliographical references and index.
  ISBN 978-1-4129-4094-8 (cloth)
  ISBN 978-1-4129-4095-5 (pbk.)
  1. Immigrants—Education—United States. 2. Children of immigrants—Education—United States. 3. Educational anthropology—United States. 4. Educational sociology—United States.
  I. Preissle, Judith. II. Title.

  LC3731.R66 2009
  371.826'912—dc22

2008021402

This book is printed on acid-free paper.

08 09 10 11 12 10 9 8 7 6 5 4 3 2 1

Acquisitions Editor:	Dan Alpert
Associate Editor:	Megan Bedell
Production Editor:	Appingo Publishing Services
Cover Designer:	Karine Hovsepian

Contents

Acknowledgments

We are grateful for the one-semester leave awarded by the School of Education to Xue Lan Rong and the assistance from the PUMS 5% Extraction System at the University of Minnesota Population Center. Our doctoral students and colleagues provided invaluable aid. Yongmei Li and Paul Fitchett helped us with formatting tables, graphs, and references. Dongjin Kim gathered many resources for us. Several people provided critical readings of various chapters: Liv Thorstensson, Janice Fournillier, Esperanza Mejia, Fuad Elhage, and Khalil Dirani. Their comments strengthened our arguments, but any remaining errors are our own. We have depended on the attention and support of our spouses, Cong Yuan and Mark Toomey, and of our loving siblings—Bing and Alice, Rob and Frankie, also known as Pete.

PUBLISHER'S ACKNOWLEDGMENTS

Corwin Press wishes to acknowledge the following peer reviewers for their editorial insight and guidance:

Paul Englesberg
Professor of Education
Western Washington University
Bellingham, WA

Claude Goldenberg
Professor of Education
Stanford University
Palo Alto, CA

Norma Gonzalez
Anthropologist and Associate Professor of Education
University of Utah
Salt Lake City, UT

Sabrina Mims
Professor of Education and
  Director of the Los Angeles Accelerated Schools Center
California State University
Los Angeles, CA

Andrea F. Rosenblatt
Associate Professor
Barry University
Miami Shores, FL

About the Authors

Xue Lan Rong, Professor at the University of North Carolina, Chapel Hill, is a first-generation immigrant whose native language is Chinese. As a classroom teacher, teacher educator, and educational sociologist, she has more than 25 years of teaching experience in public schools at various levels in the United States and China. Her expertise in immigration-related educational issues comes through two kinds of experiences. Her first-hand experience is based on a long-time working relationship with immigrant children, their parents, and their ethnic communities. This book is a reflection of her own experience as an immigrant teacher in and out of the classroom, as a consulting expert in developing curriculum and programs, and as an immigrant researcher, in dialogue with the academic community. She obtained her research experience via sociological, demographic, and pedagogical training. She has continually published in major sociological and educational journals and presented at national conferences on the topics of generation, race and ethnicity, national origins, gender, social class, and educational attainment and achievement of immigrant children since 1988, when she finished a dissertation on immigration and education at the University of Georgia.

Judith Preissle, Professor at the University of Georgia, is a graduate of Indiana University, a teacher educator, and an educational anthropologist who brings a dual insider-outsider perspective to issues of education and immigration. She is a native-born citizen of the United States whose forebears arrived on the continent in the 18th and 19th centuries. She is also one of the many internal migrants of the 20th century, who grew up moving around the country and attending schools in six different states. Beginning her educational experience teaching social studies and language arts to 12-year-olds, she has worked at the University of Georgia since 1975, teaching the social foundations of education, qualitative research methods, and educational anthropology to an increasingly diverse population of graduate and undergraduate students. She has published widely in these areas, with special concentration on research design and ethics and gender and minority education.

Introduction

Since we published our first book on educating immigrant students (Rong & Preissle, 1998), the United States has entered a new era of immigration, and the U.S. government, the general public, and immigrant communities are facing new challenges because of new demographic, political, social, and educational environments. An estimated 17 million immigrants entered the United States between 1990 and 2005, and the number of immigrants and their children reached more than 70 million, accounting for more than 20% of the U.S. population. This group is more diverse than ever before in terms of race, ethnicity, language, religion, education, social class, and reasons for and the process of immigration. However, a third of the current newcomers came from Mexico alone, and Mexican immigrants were likely to come from rural areas and earn minimal wages in the United States. Economic conditions and job outsourcing have created hostilities among some local residents toward newcomers, and government reaction to the 9/11 tragedy has created a harsh political climate for immigrants, especially those who are undocumented and/or from countries perceived by Americans as unfriendly.

A series of legislative attempts to manage relationships with migrants has further aggravated the hostile environment in many local communities. Both legal and undocumented immigrants face limitations on social supports such as food stamps and health care as well as arrests at their jobs, indefinite detention, and deportation. The United States has, nevertheless, failed to adopt either national or state policies or provide any systematic government agencies to oversee and support immigrants' adaptation and adjustment. The current "sink or swim" philosophy and practice are devastating for many immigrants.

In this new text, we provide educational policymakers and administrators at various levels with the information needed to project school enrollment and staff recruitment and development, as well as plan curriculum and program construction and reconstruction. Knowledge of immigration, immigrants, and the history of U.S. immigration and immigrants' schooling provides the nation's educators with understanding, insight, and perspectives on the new immigration movement and on how our society and schools can adapt effectively to the changes.

CONTENT OF THE BOOK

In this book, we focus on the education of immigrant students. Eight chapters examine immigration and how it interacts with race-ethnicity, nationality, gender, immigration generational status, social class, and residential location. Three interrelated approaches guide us: we explore the current information on immigrant children, their families, and their schooling; we examine the factors that influence children's linguistic transitions and educational attainments; and we explain why the educational experiences of immigrant students differ both among themselves and from those of other students. Our goal is to stimulate dialogue on this topic at local, regional, national, and international levels.

The first four chapters are an overview of immigration and education in the United States and a summary of the most current information available on the socioeconomic, demographic, linguistic, and educational characteristics of U.S. immigrant children and adolescents aged 5–18. Chapter 1, "Immigration and U.S. Schools," is an overview of who current immigrants are, how they compare to previous immigrants, and what the immigrant experience in schools has been and why. Chapter 2, "Immigrant Children, Their Families, and Their Environments," examines the sociodemographic profiles of current immigrants—adults and children—in terms of how they differ from one another and where they settle in their new country. Chapter 3, "Learning English and Maintaining Heritage Languages," focuses on the status of immigrant children's language proficiency—English acquisition and the retention or attrition of native languages. Chapter 4, "Educational Attainment," compares the educational achievement of immigrants and their native-born children and grandchildren with that of other U.S. students.

The next four chapters focus on current immigration from different geographic areas: Latin America, Asia, Africa and the Caribbean, and the Middle East. These four chapters are Chapter 5, "Immigrant Children From Asia"; Chapter 6, "Black Immigrant Children From the Caribbean and Africa"; Chapter 7, "Immigrant Children From Latin America"; and Chapter 8, "Immigrant Children From the Middle East." In Chapters 5 through 8, we consider the education of Asian, Black, Latino, and Middle Eastern children in four domains: characteristics of the children themselves, attributes of their families, immigration-related characteristics such as language status, and the attributes of their neighborhoods and schooling environments. Each chapter follows a similar format: a sketch of the immigration history of people from the region, followed by a sociodemographic profile of immigrant children 5–18 years old and their parents in the domains we detailed.

The educational attainment of immigrant children is presented in reporting the information on school enrollment, enrollment in private and public schools, and school completion rates, focusing on school drop-out rates. Data are cross-tabulated by the major nationalities of a regional group. We explain the differences in life and schooling between immigrant children and native-born as well as the variations among the nationality groups in frameworks of established theories. The last section of each chapter outlines the special needs of immigrant children from that region of the world and offers recommendations for educators, policymakers, and parents. This section also considers implications educators can draw from their experience working with immigrant children of particular racial-ethnic groups or nationalities, and whether these apply to educating other immigrant children.

In using a common framework for Chapters 5 to 8, we place multiculturalism and pluralism in a historical, comparative, and international context. These four chapters serve as case studies, inviting readers to compare the experiences of one group to the other groups and thereby to consider how each group relates to other groups and how all groups relate to the effect of immigration on schools and communities. We believe that both the similarities and differences among the various nationality groups require tailoring educational policies and practices to local situations.

Throughout the book, we make comparisons based on grouping the U.S. population in several different ways. The general population and the general school-age child population mean everyone, and these two categories include immigrants. In many other places we distinguish four generations of immigrants: 1st generation, the foreign born; 1.5 generation, foreign-born children who arrived in the United States at 5 years old or younger; 2nd generation, the children of one or two foreign-born parents; and 3rd generation, U.S.-born children with U.S.-born parents. We use the four-generation structure selectively to show population transformation and language transition, and many comparisons are based on only two or three generations.

RACE, ETHNICITY, AND GROUPING HUMANS

The U.S. Census Bureau organizes information on people by categories such as age, sex, socioeconomic status, educational attainment, citizenship status, race, and ethnicity. None of these categories has absolute boundaries. All involve fallible human judgment, and many are controversial. However, these categories can provide useful information about a particular segment of the population and also facilitate comparative understanding of inter- and intragroup relationships.

Race, for example, is a way of categorizing people that human biologists and population geneticists no longer find to be accurate when classifying human beings biologically. Variations in skin color and blood type, for example, are found among human groups everywhere around the globe, and all human genetic variation can be found in Africa. Most importantly, traits once believed to vary together consistently have been found to be distributed unevenly across human populations. See the American Anthropological Association's commentary on race at http://www.understandingrace.org/ for more detail on the discredited biological theory of human race.

Because of the association of race with the geographic distribution of recent human ancestry around the globe, and the historical inequities associated with this geographic ancestry, some scholars have advocated the term "social race" (Harris, 1999; Omi & Winant, 1994). Social race is the assumed geographic origins of individuals' forebears based on such visible traits as skin color, facial features, and such. The social race attributed to a particular individual may or may not match the geographic origin of that individual's recent ancestry. Race, then, in our usage is a social category used to roughly identify people whose forebears came to North America from Asia, Africa, Europe, and other regions of the world. Race is important to continue tracking in the 21st century United States because of the ongoing and contemporary effects of historical racism, discrimination, and prejudice. Because race is associated with ancestry, race is inextricably tied to ethnicity—the cultural characteristics associated with stable human communities—including language, customs, religion and other symbolic systems, and social organization in preferred familial, economic, and political arrangements. Ethnic affiliations may be national, regional, linguistic, religious, and such, and people have often married and procreated within ethnic groups, which accounts for much genetic similarity within groups. However, because humans have consistently procreated across group boundaries, the human genetic pool is continuous. In this text, we use the phrase race-ethnicity or racial-ethnic to denote individuals' affiliations with ancestral groups.

Recognizing these subtleties of classification and their charged political connotations, the U.S. Census Bureau has recently made a number of changes in the system used (see http://www.census.gov/Press-Release/www/2001/raceqandas.html). First, people self-select their racial-ethnic identities on the presumption that individuals are most knowledgeable about their own forebears. Second, the groups designated as "racial" groups are coterminous with the geographic locations of forebears: White (presumably of European or Middle Eastern ancestry); Black or African; Asian, Native Hawaiian, and other Pacific Islanders; and indigenous North Americans, Native Alaskans, and Native Americans. Third, in 2000, the U.S. Census Bureau added an open-ended option to its racial categories that permits people to indicate multiple races. Fourth, only two groups are designated by the U.S. Census Bureau as "ethnic": one is Hispanic or Latino, and the other is non-Hispanic or non-Latino (U.S. Bureau of the Census, 2001a, 2001b). Latino is the more inclusive term, referring to those from Latin America; Hispanic refers to Spanish-speaking individuals who have migrated to the United States from Central or South American countries colonized by Spain, or even from Spain itself. We follow U.S. Census Bureau usage for these terms, using them more or less interchangeably in this book (see Chapter 7 for more information on these ethnic categories).

We agree with S. Lee (2005) and Singer (2002) that race has continued to play an influential role in the equality of opportunity in many spheres of U.S. society. Racism has played a significant historical role in the disproportionate numbers of Black and Hispanic children living in poverty compared to White children. Major differences in educational services and achievements as well as in economic, employment, social, and health trends across race are persistent, and this partially explains why various government agencies have been collecting data on race to document these trends. Laws, policies, and programs designed to prevent racial discrimination, such as the Civil Rights Act and hate crimes laws, have also required these data. Finally, we have also incorporated information from research based on data and information sources other than the 2000 decennial census, which may use different definitions of categories and different classifications for data analyses.

HOW THE SECOND EDITION DIFFERS FROM THE FIRST

Our second edition is a rewritten and updated version of the 1998 book, with new data and more than 85% of the text rewritten. The new book has the following changes and additions:

1. We have updated the information in the 1998 book with data from the 2000 census, 2005 American Community Survey, 2005 Current Population Survey, and so forth. We also use recent data from the National Center for Educational Statistics and other agencies to compare the demographic, social, economic, language, and academic characteristics of immigrants aged 5–18 among 28 nationalities that have significant numbers of immigrant children. We also compare information from 2000 to the 1990 data to reveal consistent or changed trends.

2. All chapters in this book have been rewritten to reflect conceptual developments in the recent research literature published since 1997. We have sketched the immigration history of each of the four major immigrant groups and noted variations among their major nationalities in Chapters 5–8. The theoretical framework of this book stresses the syntheses of additive and subtractive models, framed on the discussion of segmented assimilation (selected assimilation or acculturation) explanations vs. classic assimilation explanations. Compared to the 1998 book, the literature cited and data used in analyses in this book are more

comprehensive, and sections on findings, interpretations, applications, and recommendations have been enhanced in each chapter. We make recommendations for professionals on how to use knowledge about the immigrants in their own communities to make informed decisions about programs and practices, including assessment approaches, accountability measures, parent-involvement programs, and strategies targeted to specific immigrant groups.

3. Our new chapter, "Immigrant Children From the Middle East," was added both to reflect a shifting trend in immigration from this region of the world and to address the difficulties faced by Middle Eastern immigrants because of the events of recent decades.

4. Some components included in our first edition are stressed and enhanced in this revision. Socioeconomic status, immigration status, gender, and undocumented immigrant family status are considered in analyses and discussions in most chapters. Although this book focuses on children who are foreign-born, the influences of immigrant generation are introduced whenever necessary. For example, children's English attainment and heritage language retention and attrition are studied along the four-generation structure we discuss in the first section of this introduction.

KNOWLEDGE BASE

We have used two sources of knowledge for this book: empirical research studies and conceptual material from the literature. The empirical studies comprise two categories: primary data we have analyzed ourselves and secondary data we cite from other researchers' studies. Primary data are quantitative aggregated data or individual data from U.S. government agencies, mainly the U.S. Bureau of the Census and the National Center for Educational Statistics (see Sources of Information, pp. 293–295). Secondary data are material cited from empirical research conducted by others: quantitative studies conducted by demographers, sociologists, and social psychologists and qualitative studies conducted by anthropologists, other ethnographers, psychologists, and educational researchers. The conceptual material from the literature includes theoretical frameworks, policy formulations, and other position statements, and anecdotal accounts from participants. These come from many literatures: the philosophy and psychology of education, demographic studies, critical sociology, cultural anthropology, critical race theory and identity studies, multicultural theory, and many subfields within educational research. From time to time, we also draw from our own lives, experiences, education, and teaching.

DATA

Data from the decennial census of 2000 are our primary sources for information on a wide range of children's characteristics. The long form of the decennial census asked questions about various social, economic, and household characteristics, many relevant to children. Although other data about children are available through government, nonprofit, and private organizations, the information in this report is uniquely important. Unlike school-based data, the census provides comparability across the nation, at the state and local levels, and across decades, enabling us to underscore trends over time and identify the commonalities and differences among subgroups.

The sample size, complexity, and stability of the questionnaire used by the Census Bureau allow detailed analysis of race-ethnicity and nationality by gender, generation, and many other segments in population at the local, state, and national levels for two points (1990 and 2000) in time. Researchers report great variation within each racial-ethnic group. Because we work with such a large census database, we can examine adequate information on immigrant children for each subgroup. Thus, this book provides a rare opportunity to create a detailed picture of children in the United States as they changed between 1990 and 2000.

INFORMATION LIMITATIONS

The data we present in this book must be interpreted cautiously. First, our findings are a sketch of immigrant children aged 5–18 in the United States in 2000. Just as any sketch—selective in its hues, strokes, focus, and perspective—it is likely to be simplified and incomplete because it is a representation of a subject, immigration in this case, that is too rich and elusive to be rendered in images grouped by classifications of race and Hispanic origin. Therefore, although we focus on trends, we point out the exceptions whenever we can. Moreover, this sketch can be seen as a snapshot of the population in April 2000. However, the population has changed because of the continued heavy immigration since 2000.

Second, we believe it is hard to separate the effects of various conditions from each other by simply taking each at face value. Instead, we should see how these conditions relate to one another. These conditions, and the domains we specify in the first section of the introduction, are intertwined; their associations reveal complex relationships far beyond the conventional understanding of the effect of a simple item. Just as pictures arrayed in a kaleidoscope are variable and colorful, the impact of various combinations of the conditions in the four domains changes with the year of entry, the length of residency, country of origin, and other attributes.

OUR GUIDING QUESTIONS

In addition to addressing basic questions about the nature of the new immigration and characteristics of new immigrant children, we grapple with many of the questions in the national discourse about educating immigrant students, a hotly contested topic in recent years. Here are common concerns:

1. What does the U.S. school-age population look like at the beginning of the 21st century? What will it look like in the year 2020? How has this school-age population changed between 1990 and 2000, between 2000 and 2005, and how will it change between 2005 and 2020? What do these changes mean to schools and communities?

2. What challenges do schools face as they try to come to grips with new immigration-driven student demography? What should schools do to encourage the integration of newcomers with the longer-term immigrants and the ones who are established? What role can communities play in helping culturally diverse children do well in school? How will schools cope with declining federal and local supports while still effectively integrating immigrant children into U.S. society? How should schools and communities deal with those who arrive without governmental authorization?

3. What are the promises and problems, challenges and opportunities when society and its schools deal with practical and policy issues on the education of large numbers of immigrant students with enormous diversity? What are differences between temporary and long-term solutions, simplified and more comprehensive solutions? What have been common agreements and disputes, dilemmas and paradoxes, surrounding school and classroom practices and the laws and policies on the education of immigrant children?

4. With the arrival of unprecedented numbers of immigrants from Asia, Latin America, and the Caribbean over the last several decades, we must reexamine the role social race plays in children's acculturation. Rogers (2006) emphasizes that the United States is confronting the challenge of incorporating a steady, substantial stream of non-White, non-European voluntary immigrants into its society.

How are non-White immigrant children making choices in their acculturation? How does racism complicate or limit the assimilation and acculturation patterns of non-White minorities in the United States? Will racism make this process as difficult for these newcomers as it did for Africans in U.S. history? How will U.S. schools integrate the newcomers? What roles will non-White immigrant children play in 21st-century U.S. life? Because over the past three decades, the majority of immigrants have been non-Whites, responses to these questions will help educators think profoundly about how to support newcomers in becoming Americans.

1

Immigration and U.S. Schools

T he United States is in the midst of a wave of immigration. Immigration has been one of the most critical demographic factors in this country in the past three decades, with no sign that it will slow down in the near future. Since 2000, immigration to the United States has reached the highest level ever. More than 7 million people entered this country in the first five years of the 21st century, surpassing the peak decade of immigration in 1910–1919, when 8.9 million immigrants entered the country. More than 1 million arrivals per year have been estimated since the late 1980s, of both legal and undocumented immigrants. Because of these high immigration rates, approximately half of the 35.2 million foreign-born population in the United States arrived between 1990 and 2005. Forty-seven million U.S. residents older than age 5 currently speak a language other than English at home, an increase of 15 million (and up 47%) from 1990.

Although all countries have experienced immigration, no country in the world has maintained such a high immigration rate over such a long period of time as has the United States. From 1820, when the U.S. government started to keep records of immigration, 78 million newcomers have settled in this country. Except for Native Americans and those compelled by enslavement or annexation, everyone today in the United States is either an immigrant or the descendant of immigrants. In 2005, about one in four Americans was either an immigrant or a child of immigrants, and about eight in ten Americans identified themselves with either single or multiple migrant ancestries. Immigration currently accounts for more than 40% of population growth in the nation.

Immigration has had a profound impact on the U.S. economy and society. The successful adaptations of each wave of immigrants and their children depend on the society's response to newcomers, and especially on the effectiveness of the U.S. educational system. Educating immigrant students in the United States has always been a contested issue (Tyack, 1974), and the social and political changes in the nation in the past 40 years have complicated matters. A rapidly swelling immigrant population with vast economic, social, ethnic, cultural, linguistic, and religious diversities only increases these challenges. Recent globalization also provides a new context for immigration that, in many ways, differs from the contexts in the past. Contemporary transportation and communication technologies allow people to move between countries and continents with unprecedented frequency and speed, and permit them to maintain economic, social, and political ties in two or more societies. Human mobility in this globalization context not only calls into question how permanently immigrants may be leaving their society of birth behind, but also transforms how they build new economic, social, and cultural lives in the societies in which they choose to settle (Ray, 2002). Educational reform in the United States, including changes in thinking about and attitudes toward educating immigrant children, must also consider the impact of globalization as well as transnational migration (M. Suarez-Orozco, 2001).

In this chapter, we provide a sketch of the immigration movement in the United States and a brief historical review of policy on the education of immigrant children. Throughout U.S. history, fluctuations and changes in patterns of immigration have occurred. A review of these changes fosters comparative awareness and understanding of the waves of immigration, provides a historical perspective on contemporary trends, and sheds light on U.S. schools' adaptability to such changes. Comparing current trends with past trends for how educational systems work with immigrant children may also suggest necessary changes in our present and future practices in education.

IMMIGRATION AND IMMIGRANTS: THEN AND NOW

In this section of the chapter, we examine different waves of immigration in terms of their countries of origin. We also consider the timing of peaks of immigration activity.

Where We Come From

According to demographers (e.g., Martin & Midgley, 2003, 2006), U.S. ancestry is categorized several ways (see Figure 1.1, "Who We Are and Were and Where We Came From").

1. *Colonists*: European colonists laid the framework of the society that later became the United States in the early 17th century at Jamestown, Plymouth, and other sites along the eastern seaboard of North America.

2. *Involuntary Americans*: Two kinds of coercion were used to incorporate people into U.S. society. One was the incorporation of Native American, Native Alaskan, Spanish, and French populations as the boundaries of the U.S. expanded westward, including the annexation of Hawaii and Puerto Rico. The other type of coercion was the shipment of slaves from Africa, whose descendants composed 19% of the U.S. population in 1790. An estimated 600,000 involuntary Africans had been brought into the country by the slave trade before the 1808 abolition of the importation of slaves; the majority of the Black population in the United States (35 million in 2005) traces descent to these slaves.

3. *Immigrants*: Here we define *immigrant* to mean a noncitizen, classified by the federal government as an alien, who has voluntarily moved from one society to another and intends to stay in a host society on a long-term basis.

Four Waves of Immigration

Immigrants have entered the United Sates in different economic, political, and social climates and under different laws and policies; consequently immigration has varied considerably in magnitude, composition, and means. Scholars (see Martin & Midgley, 2003) have argued that these various factors combined to create four major waves of immigration: the first three were each marked by a peak followed by a trough. The fourth wave began in the mid-1970s and still continues.

Figure 1.1 indicates that the first wave of immigrants arrived between 1790 and 1820 and consisted mostly of English-speaking immigrants from the British Isles (Martin & Midgley, 1994). The second-wave of immigrants (1849–1850s) were predominantly Irish and German settlers who arrived when the United States was undergoing rapid industrialization and expansion. The third wave (1880–1914) brought more than 20 million foreigners to the United States. Most of these were southern and eastern Europeans who found manufacturing jobs in large cities. Immigration in the 20th century was interrupted first by World War I and then, in the 1920s, by numerical country quotas designed to maintain the dominance of northern Europeans in the country's ethnic balance. For example, the 1924 National Origins Act established quotas favoring immigration of northwestern Europeans. The Great Depression and World War II further suppressed the immigration flow in the 1930s and 1940s. The fourth and current wave of migration began with immigration reforms in the 1952 McCarran-Walter Act and the 1965 Immigration Act, which eliminated country-by-country quotas.

FIGURE 1.1 Who We Are and Were and Where We Came From

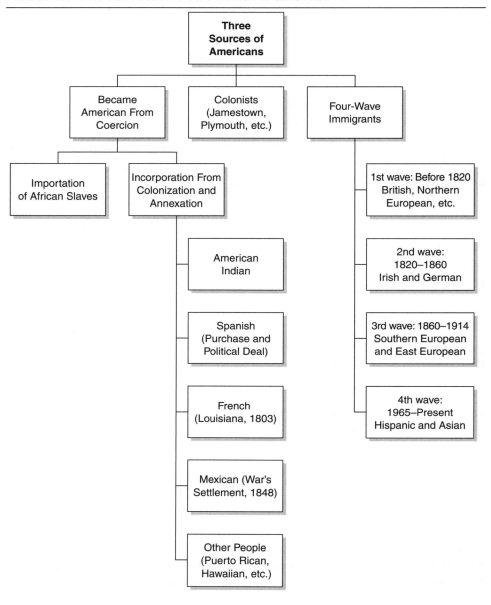

The 1965 Immigration Act and its 1976 amendments paved the way for the fourth wave of immigration, the largest ever in U.S. history. From 1970 to 2005, about 29 million immigrants entered a postindustrial and service-oriented U.S. society. A majority of newcomers were from Latin America, particularly Mexico, or Asia. The influx of Latino and Asian students has been particularly dramatic in the West, Southwest, and Northeast of the United States, where in some districts Spanish- and Asian-language-speaking students comprise a large proportion of the school population. Fourth-wave immigration has also swept rapidly beyond the coastal, gateway states and spread into states experiencing new growth in immigrants, including some intermountain Western states such as Nebraska, Utah, and Iowa. Southern states such as Georgia, North Carolina, South Carolina, and Tennessee, which had a tradition of low or almost no immigration, have also seen unprecedented expansion. This wave of immigration has resulted in the emergence of many multiethnic communities; it has substantially changed the racial and ethnic mix in most urban schools in the South as well as in some rural Southern schools, which have a long-established racial pattern of only Black and White students (Johnson, 2001). Because the immigration rate accelerated at the beginning of the 21st century, we anticipate that for years to come, fourth-wave immigration will continue to change the size of the U.S. population, the proportion of immigrants from different areas of the world, and the racial-ethnic composition of the U.S. population.

Martin and Midgley (2003), however, have pointed out many similarities between third-wave and fourth-wave immigration. They argue that, during both periods, the U.S. economy was undergoing fundamental restructuring, from agriculture to industry in the early years of the 20th century and from service to information at the start of the 21st century. They believe that both waves brought people from countries that had not previously provided large numbers of immigrants, and they emphasize that questions about the nation's common cultural bonds such as language, religion, and culture have arisen for the second time. We see these questions especially playing out in educational policy.

IMMIGRATION AND SCHOOLING

U.S. schools have been the most important social institution for absorbing newcomers; few public institutions have been as directly affected by high levels of immigration as the nation's schools. However, the task of integrating new groups of people into U.S. society has become increasingly challenging. In 2005, approximately 11 million school-age children were considered children of immigrants; this population is about one-fifth of the total number of U.S. school-age children. Among the children of immigrants, about 3 million were born outside the United States. Roughly 17 million school-age children spoke a language other than English at home, and more than 3 million children reported problems in speaking English. Because a large proportion of immigrant children live in urban areas, urban public schools in low-income neighborhoods are expected to educate the majority of them. U.S. schools have traditionally been expected to provide education and many other services to immigrant children with a view to integrating them fully and rapidly into U.S. society (Montero-Sieburth & LaCelle-Peterson, 1991). Two basic arguments frame the struggling process of immigrants' settlement in the

United States and their children's schooling. These arguments center on who is an American, how to become one, at what pace and price, and who will pay for the transition. Learning English has been a central issue in debates of this kind. The two major prescriptions for the education of immigrants in U.S. society over the past century have been, first, classic assimilation and, second, pluralism. The assimilationist aims to quickly eliminate ethnic boundaries, while the pluralist aims to accommodate them (Cornbleth & Waugh, 1995; Viadero, 2000). Accordingly, Takaki summarizes two different visions of the United States: a melting pot with a single American identity (Schlesinger, 2002) and a pluralistic cultural democracy (Takaki, 2002).

To better understand the evolution and impact of many influential ideas on and practical approaches to immigrant students' education, we subsequently provide a historical perspective of the major social views and educational philosophies of how immigrant children should be educated in the United States. This indicates how the balance between these competing influences on education has changed over time. Prior to reviewing these changed and changing views, we consider the variations in U.S. immigration policies and their influences across many political and social domains; these developments are inextricably linked to educational policy on immigrant children's education.

Shifting Immigration Laws and Policies

U.S. immigration laws and policies have shifted over time, reshaping the immigration experience and reconstructing the racial and ethnic composition of immigrants. The United States has opened wider doors to, or imposed restrictions on, immigrants whose countries of origin were regarded favorably or unfavorably at the time. In the first century of the country's existence, 1780–1875, a laissez-faire policy permitted government at all levels and many private companies to bring immigrants to the United States freely. However, the explicit racial criteria in the Naturalization Act of 1790 limited *citizenship* to white Europeans. Although African Americans successfully challenged this law after the Civil War, this policy had been a citizenship criterion for most non-European immigrants for more than 150 years.

Until 1890, immigrants from northern and western Europe predominated, but by the turn of the 20th century, the majority of immigrants came from eastern, central, and southern Europe. The Chinese Exclusion Act of 1882, the Gentlemen's Agreement of 1908, and the 1924 Oriental Exclusion Act significantly reduced immigration from Asian countries. The Immigration Act of 1924 greatly reduced the total number of immigrants and established quotas that favored northern and western European migration and restricted the entrance of Asian immigrants and other people.

This pattern was changed by the McCarran-Walter Act of 1952, and especially the Immigration Act of 1965, which opened up large-scale immigration from Latin America, Asia, and the Pacific Rim. The 1965 act abolished the national-origin quotas that had limited most legal immigration to those coming from Europe, and each country was put on a relatively equal footing with a limit of 20,000 immigrants annually. This law gave priority to those immigrants who had family ties or possessed wanted skills. Since the mid-1960s, the main flow of legal immigration has been from Asia and Latin America, accompanied by an influx of undocumented immigrants from Mexico, the Caribbean, and many other countries throughout the world.

The changes in immigration laws since the 1950s have had many outcomes. For example, Figure 1.2 illustrates the impact of the various immigration waves and changes in immigration laws on the racial-ethnic makeup of the U.S. population. In 1790, when the first U.S. census was collected, the population was categorized as 60% British, 19% African, and 21% others, including both Native American and non-British European. In 2000, the U.S. population was categorized as 68% non-Hispanic White, 14% Hispanic (of any race), 13% African Americans, and 4% Asian. The fourth wave of immigration has changed the United States from a largely biracial society to a multiracial and multiethnic one, with several racial-ethnic groups of considerable size.

FIGURE 1.2 The Race-Ethnic Composition of the U.S. Population in 1790 (top) and 2000 (bottom)

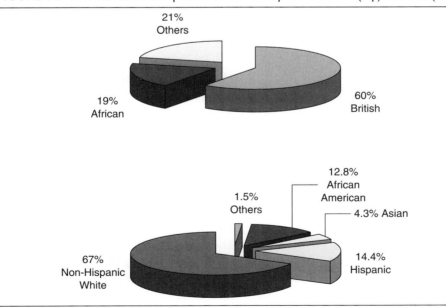

SOURCE: U.S. Bureau of the Census (2003a, 2007d).

Two other notable immigration laws are the Immigration Reform and Control Act of 1986 (the Simpson-Mazzoli Act) and California Proposition 187. Neither law accomplished what it was intended to do; however, their major components have had a lasting and profound impact on popular thinking about—and political campaigning for—immigration reform. The 1986 federal law, intended to reduce illegal immigration to the United States, criminalized the act of knowingly hiring an illegal immigrant and established financial and other penalties for those employers. The law also provided for the legalization of some, offering a one-year amnesty program for illegal immigrants who had already worked and lived in the United States up to January 1982. As a result, 2.7 million undocumented immigrants were granted green cards in the late 1980s and early 1990s.This law established two precedents: first, punishing employers who hire undocumented immigrants, although how well this law has worked is questionable; and, second, offering amnesty, or legal means, for undocumented immigrants who meet certain criteria to remain in the United States. In contrast, California's Proposition 187, passed in 1994, became a state law through popular referendum. It attempted to deny schooling and medical care to undocumented immigrants. Although the main part of Proposition 187 was struck down by the California Supreme Court, it was and is still used, though in more or less different versions, as a sample referendum by many states and local governments in an attempt to limit low-income, undocumented immigrants' access, especially that of Mexicans, to public institutions and aids.

After the September 11 attack on the World Trade Center in 2001, debate about immigration intensified. The INS (Immigration and Naturalization Service) was abolished and divided into several agencies under the Department of Homeland Security in 2003. Most INS functions now fall under the newly created Bureau of Citizenship and Immigration Services (BCIS). We use this new acronym throughout this book. In addition to habitual worries about immigrants suppressing the U.S. labor market for native-born Americans, weakening cultural unity, and threatening the nation's monolingual, English-only practice, the most heated topics after 9/11 include blocking visa requests for international students, enhancing border control to prevent the entry of undocumented immigrants, and detaining and deporting large numbers of undocumented immigrants, some of whom have lived in the United States for decades. The majority of the children of undocumented immigrants have been born in the United States, and they are U.S. citizens on the basis of their birthright (Capps, 2005); however, even they have become targets of a growing nativism.

Although many people agree that terrorism aimed at the United States is a real threat and that both aggressive and defensive measures should be taken to combat it, some argue that no solid evidence shows that the preceding defensive measures are legally valid or practically effective. They claim that some of these efforts reduce U.S. competition in the global economy. For example, the restrictions on admitting international students to U.S. universities have driven many international students to Western

Europe, Canada, and Australia (Mueller, 2004). Furthermore, groups advocating civil liberty rights argue that the historical response to external threat has been internal repression and that the country has not achieved more safety by ignoring the Constitution, the rule of law, and the liberty of its inhabitants (Adelman, 2002; Chemerinsky, 2006). As in former eras, immigration has become a volatile issue in the United States in the early years of the 21st century.

Social and Political Changes

Unlike the previous three waves of immigrants, fourth-wave immigrants have been arriving in a post-civil rights era. The United States is different in several ways from the society that hosted the first three waves of immigrants. First, the structural factors and contexts of immigration today are different from those of the past because of the profound impact of the civil rights movement. Significant changes continue to occur in the nation's major political, judicial, social, and educational institutions. Powerful national organizations and many grassroots groups, those supporting immigrants' rights and those composed of immigrants themselves, have been vocal and active. These politically well-connected groups advocate the preservation of native languages and cultures and the maintenance of ethnic boundaries. Consequently, nativist rhetoric, arguing for the return to a more homogeneous United States, has been challenged. A growing populace asserts the benefits of ethnic identity conservation and of preserving home languages for communicating within families and communities.

In addition, the promotion of a global, free-market economy has led to a reconceptualization of previous immigration theories. The "push and pull" theory (E. Lee, 1966), which attributes people's decisions for moving geographically to individuals and families, no longer fully accounts for migration to postindustrial societies. Instead, international labor market redistribution theories provide more comprehensive explanations for global human geographic movements (Bloom & Brender, 1993; Martin & Widgren, 2002; C. Suarez-Orozco, 2001a). Globalization, and the consequent redistribution of wealth, capital, and technology, shift populations among nations. Permanent cultural boundaries give way, thereby creating dynamic pluralistic global societies. No longer isolated by geographical location, rapidly developing technologies in transportation, communication, and information dissemination allow fourth-wave immigrants opportunities for transnational exchange combined with continuing ties to their indigenous social networks. Sojourner and transnational migration are changing the stereotypic view of immigrants as permanently severed from their original social worlds and uprooted from their motherlands. Sojourners move from their home countries for employment elsewhere, but return home often and expect eventually to return permanently. Transnational migrants move from country to country as employment opportunities arise. The experiences of the sojourner and the multiple-destination migrant, in a process of transacculturation, are replacing what was once viewed as a one-way adaptation concept, acculturation, and they are blurring the lines between what are the country of origin, the destination country, and other host countries—especially for how social, economic, political, and personal resources are deployed (Brittain, 2002). We believe that 21st-century educators need to recognize that previous assimilationist practices are obsolete, given these new patterns in immigration experiences. Because immigration is itself a major feature of current globalization, it is important to understand in what ways these new international contexts are changing how immigrant children and their families are adapting to their experiences.

Transnational migration affects people differently because of their pre- and postmigration social class, their race-ethnicity, their country of origin, and the conditions of their exits; these differences result in considerable inequities, complicated for immigrants to the United States because of the intolerance rooted in xenophobia, racism, and classism pervasive in this society. Moreover, differences in culture, dress, language, political ideology, and religion have been polarizing agents in the status afforded an immigrant population; historically, immigrant groups have been demonized and unfairly blamed for economic, social, and political crises (Ravitch, 1974; Tyack, 1974). While less affluent immigrants have been labeled as social burdens, middle-class migrants are deemed "crossovers" or "job takers." Immigrants from the Eastern Bloc and non-Western nations have often been viewed as subversive because of the politically dissonant history between the United States and their countries of origin. Worse, policies have been enforced to segregate these groups from the majority of society. Infamously, Japanese Americans were detained in internment camps during World War II because of xenophobic, and unfounded, fears about these "permanent aliens" and "enemies within." Displaced and isolated, these immigrants and lifelong U.S. citizens were forcibly removed from their homes and families and lost their land, businesses, and other family belongings. This left an indelible mark on their lives and permanently damaged their children's memories (Chemerinsky, 2006; James, 1987; Pak, 2002). Moreover, religious affiliation continues to perpetuate stigmatization among immigrant arrivals. From the Irish-Catholics in second-wave immigration to the more recent Muslim immigrants, persecution over faith and attributed fanaticism has been common throughout the nation's immigration history.

Eighty years ago, the former President Herbert Hoover dismissed New York Congressman Fiorella La Guardia, an Italian American, by claiming that "the Italians are predominantly our murderers and bootleggers"; Hoover recommended that La Guardia "go back to where you belong," because "like a lot of other foreign spawn, you do not appreciate this country, which supports you and tolerates you" (Martin & Midgley, 1994, p. 19). Fortunately, this kind of overt statement from politicians or policymakers is regarded today as repugnant, although similar anti-immigrant attitudes are represented in more subtle language.

Changes in Immigration Demographics

Because of the effects of a globalized economy, the United States has attracted different types of immigrants than those who arrived in the past. Fourth-wave immigration brought the most diverse population ever to the United States: people with a variety of business, administrative, political, academic, and artistic skills from diverse cultural, linguistic, religious, political, and socioeconomic backgrounds. A very high percentage of Asian Indians, for example, came with postbaccalaureate degrees, English fluency, and the sophistication to function well in a western society. They were able to quickly begin entrepreneurial, scientific, engineering, and other professional careers. Others, however, with less education, fewer skills, and an uncertain legal immigration status, have encountered numerous barriers to surviving in this country. Fourth-wave immigrants also have included a large number of refugees who have suffered psychological traumas both in their home countries and during the emigration journey. These diverse backgrounds are reflected in various settlement patterns (occupational, residential, etc.) and in immigrants' differential adjustments in the United States. Such differences also affect their children's linguistic transition, schooling behaviors, and educational achievements. Hence, the increase in size and diversity of the fourth wave requires sufficient knowledge to understand the complexities within the immigrants' experiences and the wide range of needs (linguistic, curricular, instructional, counseling, to name a few) to which the federal and local governments and educational institutions have been expected to respond.

The different immigration policies we have discussed have brought different immigrants into U.S. social contexts that have changed and continue to change. Keeping this contextual change in mind, we now turn to the two major models for incorporating immigrants into U.S. society introduced previously: classic assimilation and pluralism.

MODELS OF IMMIGRANT INCORPORATION

Classic assimilation and pluralism are differing models for how best to integrate immigrants into the U.S. system. In this section, we assess how they have evolved over time and how they are related to two different, but common, models of practice in working with immigrant students: the additive approach and the subtractive approach.

Classic Assimilation

Research on immigration and education was once dominated by the classic assimilation model, which advocated the elimination of ethnic identity and the reconstruction of an "all American and English only" immigrant identity. It predicted a straightforward, upwardly mobile progression into U.S. society when "foreigners" completed their transformation. Classic assimilationists hold that the key to immigrant assimilation is immigrants' perseverance and willingness to succumb to a national identity. This "rugged individualist" mindset endorses self-motivation and self-sufficiency. Classic assimilationists believe that each successive generation residing in the United States will improve its socioeconomic status as children and their families become more familiar with U.S. culture, the English language, and major U.S. institutions, including schools. This perspective postulates higher educational and occupational attainments for each successive generation in the United States, although rates and paces might vary for various groups (Glazer, 2002; Schlesinger, 2002).

Throughout the history of U.S. immigration, a consistent undertone has been the fear that the "alien element" would somehow sabotage the institutions of the country and cause them to disintegrate. Playing on these nativist fears, extreme assimilationists have directed heated rhetoric and resources toward combating these alleged alien elements of evil (R. G. Lee, 200; Portes & Rumbaut, 1996). In the late 19th century, the nation was perceived to be threatened by the third-wave immigration that brought an unprecedented number of people to the United States from southern, central, and eastern Europe. These new immigrants were thought by many to be too alien and backward to adapt to the United States. Educators were not immune to this perception. Strongly influenced by the educational philosopher Ellwood Cubberley early in the 20th century, the nation's schools took a hard line in the years during and immediately following World War I in seeking the assimilation of new immigrants from southern and eastern Europe. Cubberley (1909) believed that Americanization required breaking up immigrant groups or settlements, assimilating and amalgamating these peoples into an American "race," and implanting in their children the Anglo-Saxon conceptions of righteousness, law and order, public decency, and popular government. The communal nature and cultural habits of many of the regional, ethnic, and religious communities in the United States had little value in Cubberley's vision of a truly "Americanized" nation. In Cubberley's view, immigrants were passive, usually illiterate, servile, and often lacking in initiative; their coming had weakened the national "breed" and was threatening the virtue of U.S. politics and government. Given this crass formulation of the issue of immigration, a kind of ruthless assimilation was prescribed so as to preserve "our national character." Employers and organizations like the Young Men's Christian Association (YMCA) and other community agencies followed Cubberley's lead (Stewart, 1993). So-called "citizenship education" was an attempt to inculcate Anglo-Saxon and Protestant values into these immigrants. Nevertheless, the worst fears of the assimilationists have been discounted by what occurred. The third-wave immigrants increased and prospered, as did their children and grandchildren (cf. Handlin, 1951; Howe, 1980), following the patterns of the two previous waves. However, heritage languages and cultures have been preserved in many ethnic communities, and the 20th century witnessed the development of a hybrid "mainstream" U.S. culture, which has also been refined and redefined as a more inclusive concept. The United States now appears to rest comfortably in the hands of the descendants of the third-wave of immigrants, those once considered to be exerting fearful "alien" influences (Portes & Rumbaut, 1996).

Pluralism

What we label the pluralism model is a collection of somewhat different approaches to immigrant incorporation, but all of them share a vision of a heterogeneous, rather than a homogeneous, U.S. society. Pluralism models include selective assimilation, segmented assimilation, accommodation without assimilation, and pluralistic assimilation, and all of them have been developed to represent actual instances of immigrants' adaptation to a host country (e.g., Gibson, 1988; Olsen, 1997; Portes & Rumbaut, 1996; Portes & Zhou, 1993; Suarez-Orozco & Suarez-Orozco, 2001). The pluralism model accounts for the variety in objectives, processes, or outcomes found among different immigrant communities. Immigrant adaptation in this model is viewed as a multidimensional and multifaceted process with micro-level variables such as race, class, gender, and age interacting with macro-level contextual variables such as laws, policies, the socioeconomic and political environment, immigration history, and the reception in communities where the immigrants settle. Furthermore, adaptation varies across people because of the interaction of premigration factors with postmigration conditions. All of these contribute to children's adjustment to their surroundings and affect their initial and continuing adaptation to the host society. This complex pattern often serves to predict educational achievement and attitudes toward schooling for immigrant youth. Pluralism emphasizes societal obstacles (i.e., xenophobia, racism, low socioeconomic status, etc.) that hinder immigrant acculturation. Pluralism has evolved from debates about whether the cultural characteristics of the immigrants themselves or the social structures of the receiving society (Vermeulen, 2000) are more important to immigrant adjustment. The more recent theory of segmented assimilation (Perlmann, 2000) is the idea that incorporating immigrants into society depends on the interplay of who immigrants are, the history of their experience, and the nature of the society receiving them. Segmented assimilation supporters contend that recognition of community resources and support, in addition to institutional changes in schooling and society, are required to facilitate the needed assimilation (Zhou, 2001).

Segmented assimilation theories claim that critical race theories and pedagogy have likewise served to elucidate glaring inequalities (such as class, education, and labor hierarchies) that frequently result in a systemic deprivation among minority groups (Nieto, 1995; Ogbu, 1987). In reaction to such inequities and the prejudice and discrimination accompanying them, first- and second-generation immigrants sometimes develop patterns of overassimilation—a form of rapid Americanization (Gibson, 1988; Grant & Rong, 1999; Portes & Rumbaut, 2001; Portes & Zhou, 1993). This is characterized by an adoption of U.S. materialistic popular culture and adversarial youth subcultures that interferes with academic achievement and fosters underage labor, excessive extracurricular activities, teenage pregnancy, and substance abuse. Moreover, these behaviors are frequently followed by a rejection of the native culture and decreased parental influence.

Assessment of Classic Assimilation and Pluralism

Neither the classic assimilation nor pluralism models have been fully realized in the United States. Although extreme assimilation advocates the rejection of immigrants' roots and evinces a disdain for whatever immigrants cannot change or disguise in themselves, ethnic affiliation often persists among second- and third-generation Americans, long after the language and knowledge of the "old country" have been lost (Farrell, 1980). On the other hand, the earlier pluralists' insistence on maintaining group identity assumes that ethnic boundaries remain fixed and overlooks divisions within ethnic groups. Historical evidence reveals that, in an open, heterogeneous society such as the United States, people work, make friends, and marry outside their ancestral communities. In addition, they develop increasing commonalities with other Americans with lengthier U.S. residency and more generations (Martin & Midgley, 1994).

Classical assimilative practices have been criticized for supporting the hegemony of the elite through the melting pot approach, at the expense of the variety of diverse cultures and social norms that reflect, and have always reflected, the reality of U.S. society (Tuan, 1998). Such practices contribute to a decline in educational attainment for immigrant populations. Likewise, assimilation has come under attack for overemphasizing the importance of the national society while failing to recognize the strengths and optimism within immigrant communities. In response, recent assimilation models not only focus on institutional barriers, but also seek to champion the solidarity of ethnic communities that act as agents of change to provide social, cultural, psychological, and economic capital for immigrant minorities (Stanton-Salazar, 1997).

Though seemingly very different, both models of immigrant incorporation share a common understanding that immigrant groups have suffered persecution, isolation, and stigmatization (Gordon, 1964; Lieberson, 1980; Park, 1928; Pedraza, 1990). Both posit that the acquisition of the host country's language, an understanding of its laws, familiarity with its customs, and other basic assimilative steps should be attained by immigrants.

The literature we have cited indicates that these models of immigrant incorporation have evolved in the last two decades and reveals gaps between early and later scholarly work on the goals and means of language education, cultural adjustment and adaptation, and citizenship education. However, schools throughout the past century have found themselves in a pendulum swing between these models of classic assimilation and pluralism (Schnaiberg, 1999). Next, we turn to schools and their practices with immigrants.

SCHOOL PRACTICES

As we have emphasized previously, educating immigrant children has always been a challenging task for U.S. schools. Because immigrant students bring with them different life experiences and beliefs, cultural communication patterns, languages, and educational traditions, their immediate addition to U.S. schools places strong demands for reform on many public education systems. U.S. public education, however, has strongly rejected conserving and maintaining the native language and cultural values of immigrant children; the preference for emphasizing Americanization in curricula and instruction aimed at socializing immigrants to the norms of the dominant culture can be traced to the country's genesis.[1] The objective then, and in the early years of the federal period, was indoctrination—achieving unity through homogeneity; many taxpayers saw, and many still see, non-Western backgrounds as detrimental to both U.S. national identity and educational standards. However, when integration means Anglicization, schools have been likely to conflict with immigrant parents and communities, especially when the loss of native languages and cultures is involved.

Accommodating immigrant students' needs has never been easy or trouble-free for immigrants or for U.S. schools. Educators struggle to reach some philosophical consensus for policymaking and battle for the finances and other resources to support their efforts. Moreover, school plans, curriculum changes, and outreach actions are often criticized by both immigrant advocates and assimilationists. Pluralists believe that immigrants' optimism, work ethic, and cultural and linguistic resources not only enrich the United States' national heritage, but also enhance its status in an increasingly globalized world by providing new talents, contemporary skills, and increased trade that fuel economic expansion (Bischoff, 2002; Huntington, 2004). Immigrant advocates claim that U.S. schools have failed to meet immigrant children's special needs; their dissatisfaction is represented by the lawsuits that almost every city has pending, charging local governments with having provided inadequate and inappropriate language services for immigrant students. In many assimilationists' views, however, schools have already

---

1 However, the existence of bilingual schools (Norwegian, German, etc.) in the Northeast and Midwest during the early and mid-19th century shows the relative permissive local educational policies with regard to eliminating native language education (see Chapter 3 for more details).

succumbed to immigrant communities' demands, jeopardizing the English language acquisition of these children as well as the unity and cultural identity of local communities. Though both classic assimilationists and pluralists seek acculturation to U.S. society, classical assimilation advocates what has been called a subtractive practice in comparison to pluralism's additive approach. Subtractive practice emphasizes immigrant children's deficiencies, whereas additive practice builds on immigrant children's unique qualities.

The subtractive practice is prevalent throughout schools and social institutions. It associates immigrant children with multiple "handicaps to progress" within mainstream society. Its proponents emphasize English-only instruction, rapid Americanization, and a monocultural approach to assimilation. Rather than reforms within the social system, it recommends a corrective curriculum that devalues belief structures outside the mainstream. As a result, it dismisses the influence of ethnic cultures and discredits the authority of parents as well as the support systems of ethnic communities. These beliefs remain in vogue among policymakers, the mainstream media, and the general public.

The assimilation-versus-pluralism debate is played out in many facets of U.S. life. However, in recent years, pluralism has gained momentum as educators and educational scholars have sought to champion the additive model of acculturation. They have asserted that community input and family agency are useful tools in assimilating immigrant youth. Supporters of the pluralism model have posited that promoting mutual respect and cooperation between schools and immigrant communities, and including immigrant families in school decision making, help children to maintain a healthy identity as well as social and psychological well-being (Valenzuela, 1999).

Still, the 29 million immigrants—including 5 million or more children—in the fourth wave of immigration entering the United States since 1970 have posed serious challenges to all major U.S. institutions. For example, the 2000 census reported approximately 10 million school-age children (aged 5–17)[2] who speak a language other than English at home, compared to 6.3 million in 1990 and 4.6 million in 1980. The core of the challenge of contemporary immigration to the U.S. educational system is that a large percentage of newly arrived immigrants demand a variety of sophisticated services, including multicultural curricula and bilingual instruction. However, many of today's desperately low-income refugees and undocumented immigrants need to learn basic survival skills to cope in U.S. society, and the needs of these immigrants are often very different from those of the native-born, or even from many other immigrants in the same cohort.

Unfortunately, because of budget restrictions from federal and local governments, the effects of the No Child Left Behind (NCLB) legislation, and other factors, teachers and administrators may lack the training, space, and other resources to accommodate the needs of so diverse a group of

---

2 Our study is based on school-age children (aged 5–18).

students. Generally speaking, suburban districts are being forced to make difficult changes and adjustments, but they have the capacity to cope and adapt to the challenges posed by immigration. The greatest difficulties are reported in already stressed urban school districts and some rural areas that must find ways to serve both immigrants and the native-born from a diminishing resource base. Overcrowded classrooms, heightened social tensions, fierce controversies over curricula, and substandard instruction provided by inexperienced teachers have been the result (McDonnell & Hill, 1993).

In summary, the emergence of a fourth wave of immigrants in the wake of the civil rights movement has been accompanied by unique political and social developments (Muller, 1994). Tacitly followed practices of Americanization are no longer met with ambivalence. A larger proportion of U.S. citizens share nonmainstream heritages than ever before. These groups are leading campaigns to preserve their native languages and cultures within schools and the greater society. As the size of this diverse citizenry grows, immigrants are having a greater political and policy impact on U.S. society. The non-European background of the majority of immigrants challenges traditional U.S. school practices of monolingualism and monoculturalism. Accordingly, nativist ideologues have responded with measures to ensure structural segregation; this has led to more heated and widely publicized debates (Contreras, 2002; Garcia, 1995; Jo & Rong, 2003). However, the consolidation of movements for pluralism remains strong. In the 1982 Supreme Court ruling *Plyer v. Doe*, an attempt to ban undocumented Mexican immigrant children from attending local schools in Texas and Florida, the court ruled that immigration status could not be used to determine children's enrollment. Even more recently, immigrant community groups, in conjunction with the California Teachers' Union, successfully overturned 1994's Proposition 187, an attempt to limit the health care options and schooling privileges available to undocumented immigrant groups.

Throughout this examination of fourth-wave immigration and education, we consider the varying perspectives and approaches of educators and policymakers to addressing the needs of different immigrant groups. In the next chapter, we turn to the children of the fourth-wave immigrants—who the children are, what the circumstances of their lives are, and what this information may mean for educational policies and practices.

2

Immigrant Children, Their Families, and Their Environments

Having addressed in Chapter 1 the nature of current immigrants to the United States, in this chapter we turn our attention to the characteristics of school-age immigrants, aged 5–18. These youngsters are the focus of this book. To respond proactively and strategically to the educational, social, and physical needs of the rapidly growing number of immigrant children, policymakers, educational practitioners, immigrant advocates, and stakeholders require accurate and timely information about the characteristics of immigrant students locally and nationally, their individual and collective preimmigration experiences, and their acculturation to U.S. society.

With the demands on school districts with large numbers of immigrants, one difficulty in policymaking and planning—let alone implementing—a variety of services for immigrant children and their families is the lack of available information about recent immigrants and their children. Immigrant students have limited visibility in governmental education documentation at all levels because neither federal nor state educational agencies count immigrants as a separate group. Immigrant children with other characteristics such as limited English proficiency (LEP), learning or physical disabilities, giftedness, or various social disadvantages are included as part of these groups. Furthermore, for most policymakers, immigrant education is focused on helping students learn English, and immigrant education policy centers on English language acquisition policy. When McDonnell and Hill (1993) interviewed state officials, every interviewee, regardless of role, position, or political ideology, equated the two. These researchers claim that this myopic policy is the product of judicial and legislative actions—the mandatory requirement of aiding LEP students—although adequate education of immigrant children requires a wide range of other services. Immigrant invisibility in official documentation and data, along with narrowly defined school policies, contribute to educators' lack of reliable estimates of immigrant student numbers, awareness of their social and demographic characteristics, or knowledge of their special needs.

To address educators' needs for accurate and current data, this chapter presents sociodemographic characteristics of school-age immigrant children. This information is grouped into four topical domains: the demographic, social, and health characteristics of these children; attributes of the families they live with, including the socioeconomic status of parents and their household living arrangements; what we call the "newcomer," or immigration-related, features of these children and their families; and the racial, language, and socioeconomic characteristics of their neighborhoods and school environments. We chose the elements in these four domains because of their well-documented effects on children's lives and their availability from decennial census data and other reliable information sources. Information about their language resources, the attrition and retention of their native tongues, and English acquisition are addressed in Chapter 3.

Discussing the main issues in these four domains, we show similarities and differences between two groups—immigrant children and children in the general population—across racial-ethnic groups. (As we have noted elsewhere, by "general population" we mean all children, regardless of immigration status.) At the end of the chapter, we suggest what the patterns in these profiles of immigrant children mean for educators, and we identify effective practices in working with immigrant students.

IMMIGRANT CHILDREN

Who are the immigrant children now attending U.S. schools? In this section, we consider what the U.S. census indicates about the characteristics of these youngsters: first, their racial-ethnic affiliations and which immigrant generations they represent, and second, indicators of the state of their health and of the distribution of disabilities among them.

Racial-Ethnic Affiliation and Immigrant Generation

The intersection of immigrant generation with racial-ethnic affiliation produces a mosaic profile. Table 2.1 shows that, among all U.S. children age 5–18 in 2000, fewer than 5% were foreign-born, about 14% were

TABLE 2.1   U.S. Children 5–18 Years Old by Race and Ethnicity and Immigration Status, 2000

	All Children	Immigrant Generations		Child of	Native
		1st	1.5	Immigrant	
All Children	100	2.2	2.5	13.6	81.8
(N)	(2,694,073)	(58,376)	(67,416)	(365,206)	(2,203,075)
Non-Hispanic White	100	0.6	0.6	5.1	93.7
(N)	(1,776,174)	(10,745)	(10,812)	(89,619)	(1,664,998)
Hispanic	100	7.1	9.1	45.3	38.5
(N)	(403,633)	(28,756)	(36,601)	(182,790)	(155,486)
Black	100	1.3	1.1	7.1	90.5
(N)	(365,857)	(4,677)	(3,933)	(26,046)	(331,201)
Asian	100	12.3	14.0	57.0	16.7
(N)	(112,044)	(13,733)	(15,674)	(63,883)	(18,754)
Other	100	1.3	1.1	7.9	89.8
(N)	(36,365)	(465)	(396)	(2,868)	(32,636)

SOURCE: Data from PUMS 5% of the 2000 Census (U.S. Bureau of the Census, 2003a), compiled by authors.

Note: Percentages do not total 100 because of rounding for generation subgroups.

children of immigrant(s), and more than 80% were children from families without recent immigration history. However, among ethnic-racial groups the picture is very different. Although the overwhelming majority of non-Hispanic White children and Black children were from families without recent immigrant history, only about one-sixth of Asian children and two-fifths of Hispanic children were from families of long-term residence. European White children were least likely to be in any of the immigrant generations, and Asian children were the most likely to be in one of the immigrant generations: well over half of Asian children in the United States were children of immigrants. The distribution of Hispanic children among these generational groups was more even. Nearly two-fifths of Hispanic youngsters had no recent immigration experience, but almost half of them did, being children of immigrants, with the remaining being immigrants themselves. Educators may thus need to focus more on the children of immigrants as well as on the transitional period from the second to third generation when working with Hispanic children. In contrast, because well over four-fifths of Asian children were first or second generation, their most compelling educational needs would involve language and culture.

When we compare the racial and ethnic composition of immigrant school-age populations with the total school-age population, Figures 2.1A and 2.1B reveal two drastically different worlds. Only about a third of all U.S. school-age children in 2000 were affiliated with minority groups, compared to over four-fifths of immigrant children. Among the total population of school-age children, two-thirds were non-Hispanic Whites; the remaining one-third had about equal proportions of Hispanics and Blacks, with Asians and others accounting for about one-twentieth of the total. The distribution by race and ethnicity among the foreign-born school-age population, however, was very different: over half the children were Hispanic, nearly one-quarter were Asian, and the remaining one-quarter was divided among non-Hispanic Whites, Blacks, and others. This difference suggests that policies designed for the total school population, including policies for all minority children and for all immigrant children, must take into account these kinds of differential distributions of immigrant generation, races, and ethnic groups. Although U.S. schools have become more and more diverse, an increasing proportion of minority students, especially within the immigrant minority, are Hispanic students. The Hispanic population has been the fastest growing group, accounting for more than half of the number of school-age immigrant children and almost two-thirds of the number of immigrant minority children. However, these variations within the immigrant child population are far beyond the kind of diversity many school districts have anticipated, especially those in the new gateway states.[1] Because of the differing needs for language education and cultural accommodations among these groups, educators must expect to plan for the best fit for the kinds of immigrant students in their particular states and school districts.

Health and Disabilities

Are immigrant children healthier or unhealthier than the general school-age population? What role do race and ethnicity play in immigrant children's health? Findings have been mixed in the few empirical studies with national scope that address these two questions (Ruiz-de-Velasco & Fix, 2002). Although some studies have reported that new immigrants have better health because of their healthier birth conditions, better diet habits, and more stable family structures (e.g., Shields & Behrman, 2004), other reports differ. Based on data from the National Longitudinal Study of Adolescent Health, Fuligni and Hardway (2004) reported better health of foreign-born youth as compared to U.S.-born adolescents of the same ethnicity: although only 9% of immigrant adolescents were in fair or poor health, this percentage rose to 11% for the second generation. The percentages of those in either fair or poor

---

1 The "traditional gateway" states (California, New York, Texas, Florida, Illinois, and New Jersey) have historically hosted large foreign-born populations; "new gateway" states (also labeled "new growth" states by demographers) are states such as North Carolina, Georgia, Iowa, and Utah, which have tripled or quadrupled their immigrant populations in the last 15 years (see Passel & Suro, 2005).

FIGURE 2.1A   Total U.S. Children 5–18 Years Old by Race and Hispanic Origin, 2000

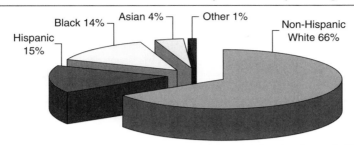

SOURCE: Data from PUMS 5% of the 2000 Census (U.S. Bureau of the Census, 2003a), compiled by authors.

FIGURE 2.1B   U.S. Foreign-Born Children 5–18 Years Old by Race and Hispanic Origin, 2000

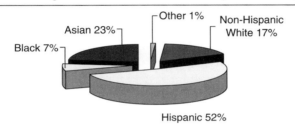

SOURCE: Data from PUMS 5% of the 2000 Census (U.S. Bureau of the Census, 2003a), compiled by authors.

health vary across race and ethnicity. For example, 8% of third-generation White adolescents reported being in poor or fair health, but 12% of African American and 13% of Latino adolescents reported being in poor or fair health. Fuligni and Hardway also reported differences in health for adolescents of various national origins within these broader racial-ethnic categories.

Reardon-Anderson, Capps, and Fix (2002), using information from the 1999 National Survey of America's Families (NSAF), reported that children of immigrants (foreign-born children and U.S.-born children with immigrant parents) are more than twice as likely as children of native-born parents to be in "fair" or "poor" health. Moreover, the children of immigrants suffer declines in health more rapidly as they age than do native-born children. Differences in health outcomes between children of natives and those of immigrants also widen in the low-income population: here, 12% of the children of immigrants age 5 and younger are in fair or poor health, compared with only 5% of the children of natives; for children age 12–17, these figures are 19% and 9%, respectively.

The long form of the Decimal Census Data 2000 collected limited information about the population's health, such as information on children's physical disabilities (one or multiple limitations in mobility, personal care, hearing and visual, etc.) and learning-related disabilities (e.g., difficulties in remembering). Table 2.2 reveals three noticeable patterns.

TABLE 2.2   Physical Characteristics of U.S. Children 5–18 Years Old by
Race, Ethnicity, and Immigration Status, 2000

	All Children (2,694,073)	Immigrant Children (125,792)
% of Children Who Reported Physical Disabilities (One or Multiple Limitations in Mobility, Personal Care, Hearing and Visual, etc.)		
All Children	3.0%	5.1%
Non-Hispanic White	2.4%	3.5%
Hispanic	4.2%	5.8%
Black	4.5%	5.4%
Asian	3.0%	4.4%
% of Children Who Reported Learning-Related Disabilities (Difficulties in Remembering, etc.)		
All Children	4.4%	2.2%
Non-Hispanic White	4.5%	2.1%
Hispanic	3.4%	2.1%
Black	5.0%	2.2%
Asian	2.2%	2.3%

SOURCE: Data from PUMS 5% of the 2000 Census (U.S. Bureau of the Census, 2003a),
   compiled by authors.

First, although immigrant children are more likely than all children to
have physical disabilities, they are less likely to have learning-related disabilities. This pattern is consistent across the race and ethnic groups with
one exception (noted subsequently).

Second, the gap between all children and immigrant children in learning-
related disabilities varies significantly across race-ethnicity: regardless of
race or ethnicity, the learning-related disability rates for all children are
double the rate for immigrant children (4.4% vs. 2.2%). However, the gaps
between the rates for all Black and White children versus the rates for Black
and White immigrant children are wider than they are for Hispanic children: 5.0% vs. 2.2% for Black children, 4.5% vs. 2.1% for White children, but
3.4% vs. 2.1% for Hispanic children. Among Asian children, learning-
related disability rates are similar for immigrants and the overall Asian
population of children. We consider how these patterns may be interpreted
in a subsequent section on the health insurance situation for immigrant
children and their families.

Third, among children of all generations, Black and White children had
higher rates of learning-related disabilities than Hispanic and Asian children.
This finding is consistent with the findings from other studies (e.g., Losen &

Orfield, 2002). However, among immigrant children, the variation in learning-related disabilities rates is small. Asian immigrant children actually had reported the highest rates of learning-related disabilities, though the difference between the rate for Asian immigrant children and all U.S. immigrant children is 0.1%.

FAMILIES AND SURROUNDINGS

Despite its significance for policy and practice, the well-being of immigrant children is rarely studied systematically on a national scale. In this section, we present key indicators of the general circumstances of their lives. These indicators fall into four areas: (a) family location, (b) family economic condition, (c) family living arrangements, and (d) parents' education. To elaborate on the children's lives, we have adopted information on such factors as parental occupation and possession of health insurance from resources other than our own analysis of census data.

Where Children Live

The inner city is one of the most likely locations for newcomers to live. In most inner-city environments, schooling conditions are substandard, poverty levels are high, and neighborhood resources are scant compared to suburban and other areas. We consider that inner-city residency in most cases is an adverse contributing factor to children's education and well-being. Table 2.3 indicates that, nationally, about one of eight children lived in an inner-city area in 2000, but immigrant children were twice as likely to live in inner-city areas compared to all children. Although Black children (both total and immigrant) were most likely to live in an inner-city area, the widest gap between all children and immigrant children was found for non-Hispanic White children: only about one-twentieth of all non-Hispanic White children lived in an inner-city area, but almost one-quarter of their immigrant counterparts did. In other words, although non-Hispanic White immigrant children were as likely to live in the inner city as Hispanic and Asian immigrant children, White children as a whole were less likely to live in the inner city compared to other children.

Furthermore, immigrant children were more likely to live in apartments than nonimmigrants. According to the American Community Survey (U.S. Bureau of the Census, 2006), about 70% of native-born respondents owned the houses they occupied compared to less than half of the foreign-born population (Reardon-Anderson, Capps, & Fix, 2002).

Economic Conditions

In this section, we briefly review the economic situation for immigrants in the United States, emphasizing variations across race and ethnicity and continuing to highlight information from Table 2.3. Poverty has increased since 2000: 2% more of the U.S. population was living at or below the poverty level in 2004 than in 2000. About 37.2 million people were poor in 2004, 5.6 million more than in 2000. However, a much higher percentage of

TABLE 2.3   Characteristics of Families and Living Environments of U.S. Children 5–18 Years Old by Race, Ethnicity, and Immigration Status, 2000

	All Children (2,694,073)	Immigrant Children (125,792)
% of Children Who Lived in Inner Cities		
All Children	13.1%	26.0%
Non-Hispanic White	6.3%	24.7%
Hispanic	24.3%	24.6%
Black	31.0%	38.0%
Asian	21.8%	26.5%
Poverty Rates (% of Children Who Lived in Household in Poverty)		
All Children	14.8%	27.1%
Non-Hispanic White	8.8%	18.9%
Hispanic	26.2%	33.2%
Black	30.5%	25.7%
Asian	14.0%	19.7%
% of Children Who Lived in Household With Total Family Income at or Higher Than 75th Percentile		
All Children	18.4%	10.7%
Non-Hispanic White	22.9%	23.2%
Hispanic	7.2%	3.9%
Black	8.0%	8.3%
Asian	24.4%	17.6%
% of Children Who Lived in Households With Two Parents		
All Children	72.8%	80.4%
Non-Hispanic White	79.2%	87.0%
Hispanic	70.3%	78.3%
Black	41.9%	60.7%
Asian	83.8%	86.2%

% of Children Who Lived in Households Without Father		
All Children	21.5%	13.3%
Non-Hispanic White	15.7%	9.6%
Hispanic	22.3%	13.7%
Black	51.1%	31.2%
Asian	11.4%	9.7%
% of Children Who Lived With Parent or Household Head Having Fewer Than Four Years of School		
All Children	1.5%	8.9%
Non-Hispanic White	0.2%	1.8%
Hispanic	6.7%	12.5%
Black	0.9%	3.6%
Asian	5.3%	7.9%
% of Children Who Lived With Parent or Household Head Having at Least a High School Diploma		
All Children	80.8%	53.7%
Non-Hispanic White	89.1%	84.3%
Hispanic	50.0%	31.7%
Black	75.2%	68.8%
Asian	81.1%	75.3%
% of Children Who Lived With Parent or Household Head Having at Least a Four-Year College Degree		
All Children	23.0%	22.7%
Non-Hispanic White	27.7%	41.7%
Hispanic	8.7%	8.2%
Black	11.5%	20.9%
Asian	39.6%	41.5%

SOURCE: Data from PUMS 5% of the 2000 Census (U.S. Bureau of the Census, 2003a), compiled by authors.

U.S. children live below the poverty level than the general population. The 2000 census indicates that about 11.3% of the entire U.S. population was living in poverty, but about 15% of U.S. children age 5 through 18 lived in poverty, and 17.6% of children under 18 years old lived in poverty (U.S. Bureau of the Census, 2005). Immigrant children are even more likely to live in poverty than other children. More than one of four immigrant children lived in poverty in 2000, compared to one of seven of all U.S. children.

We use two indicators in this chapter to consider the economic conditions of families of immigrant children and of all children regardless of their immigration status: the percentage of children who lived in poor households in 2000 and the percentage of children who lived in households with total family incomes at or higher than 80% of U.S. households. These two indicators represent the two extremes of U.S. families' economic standing, and the comparison between the two ends can be helpful for studying economic conditions in poverty-related research. The data shown in Table 2.3 indicate several patterns. First are patterns about the poorest segments of our society. In 2000 White children were least likely to live in households below the poverty level regardless of their immigration status. Asian children were the second least likely to live in poverty regardless of their immigration status. Although immigrant children were more likely to live in poverty than all children across racial-ethnic groups, Black immigrant children were less likely to live in poverty than all Black children. Black children had the highest poverty rates among all children, and Hispanic children had the highest poverty rates within the immigrant population. Among all children nationally, one of seven children lived in poverty; however, one of three Black children lived in poverty. Among immigrant children, more than one of four children lived in poverty, and Hispanic children were more likely to live in poverty than other immigrant children.

Three points can be made here about children who lived in the most affluent segments of our society. First, within both the general school-age child population and the immigrant child population, economic conditions vary by race and ethnicity. In 2000, Asian and White children were most likely to live in more affluent households. This pattern also occurred among immigrants. Second, across racial-ethnic groups gaps in affluence remain between the immigrant child population and the general child population. This gap is minimal for White children and Black children, moderate for Asian children, but substantial for Hispanic children. Finally, although Hispanic and Asian immigrant children were less likely to live in affluent households than the general child population of these two groups, White and Black immigrant children were actually slightly more likely to live in affluent households than all Black and all White children.

These data support several observations. First, the effect on income of race and ethnicity seems larger than the effect of immigration. Black children are 3.5 times more likely to live in poverty than White children, and Hispanic immigrant children were 6 times less likely to live in affluent households than White immigrant children. Income differences between immigrants and the general population in 2000 were significantly smaller than income differences across racial and ethnic groups. Second, comparing immigrant children's economic conditions to those of the general child population is a way to observe economic mobility, particularly evident among Hispanic and Asian families. Although compared to the general child population, immigrant children were more likely to be poor and less likely to be affluent, this pattern varied for White and Black children. White immigrant children were slightly more likely to live in affluent households than all White children, and a reversed mobility occurred for Black immigrant children: Immigrant Black children were slightly more likely to live in affluent households and were much less likely to live in poverty than the general Black child population.

Family Living Arrangements

Researchers have identified family living arrangements—parents' presence in the home—as a factor in child psychological, social, and academic development, and research evidence indicates that parents' social and economic collaborations in a household contribute to children's well-paced socialization and academic growth. Children who live in single-parent families tend to have emotional and schooling problems, and children who live without fathers may further suffer from economic hardship (Carrasquillo, 1991; Jayakody & Chatters, 1997). In this chapter we consider both factors, the presence of both parents in a household and the presence of fathers in the home. Table 2.3 shows two noticeable patterns. First, immigrant children were more likely to live in households with two parents and more likely to live in households with a father than the general school-age child population. This pattern held consistently for all racial and ethnic groups; however, differences between immigrants and the general child population were larger for Black children. In 2000 Black immigrant children were far more likely than the total population of Black children to live in households with two parents and with a father present. Second, although nationwide fewer than three-quarters of all children lived in a household with both parents, this also varied by race and ethnicity: Asian children were most likely to live with two parents, and Black children were least likely to live with two parents. Asian children were least likely to live in a household without a father; more than one of seven White children, more than one of five Hispanic children, and more than half of all Black children lived in households without fathers.

Parental Education

We have used three indicators for the educational attainment of parents: completion of at least four years of school, receipt of a high school diploma, and completion of a four-year college degree. The differences in educational attainment not only reflect the effect on their education of adult immigrants' socioeconomic status in both native and host countries, but also the general educational conditions and the population's educational attainment level in immigrants' native countries. The data on education in Table 2.3 are somewhat polarized in comparing immigrant parents with the general adult population: immigrant parents were more likely than all parents to be at the top and bottom attainment categories. First, at the precollegiate level, adult immigrants were less likely than the general population as a whole and the general population within each racial-ethnic group to have completed four years of school or to have received a high school diploma. The differences between immigrant groups and the overall groups in completing at least four years of school were present for all racial-ethnic groups, but most pronounced for Hispanics. Likewise the gap between immigrant Hispanics and the general population of Hispanics in receiving a high school diploma was larger than for other ethnic-racial groups.

For completion of a four-year college degree, the attainment pattern is more complex. College completion rates in 2000 were about the same for parents of all children and for parents of immigrant children. However, White, Black, and Asian immigrant children were more likely than children in their overall groups to have parents who had completed college. The gap for Hispanics is minimal and in a reversed direction: the overall population of Hispanic parents was slightly more likely to have graduated from college than were immigrant Hispanic parents.

When we consider the effects of race and ethnicity, the data indicate that Hispanic children were more likely than all other children to live in households where parents had not completed four years of school and had not received a high school or college diploma. Asian children were more likely than other children to live in households with parents who had completed four years of college; however, Asian children, both total and immigrant, were also more likely than Black and White children to live in households where parents had not finished at least four years of school. This is one indication of the polarization in educational attainment patterns mentioned previously.

Parental Occupations

Holtz-Eakin (2004) has reported the different occupations that native and foreign-born Americans held in 2003, including positions the foreign-born population had by race and ethnicity. Hispanic immigrants were least prevalent in management and professional occupations but most prevalent in service occupations, where they could be considered overrepresented compared to the general population and the native-born population. For all people in the United States that year, about 15% of the adult population was in management and 20% in professional occupations. The percentage of native-born Americans in these types of occupations was higher than for foreign-born Americans. However, foreign-born Europeans and Asians were more prevalent in management and professional occupations than the total native-born population. Whereas 23.5% of Hispanic immigrants were in production, transportation, and material moving, 16.9% were in construction, extraction, and maintenance, and 2.5% were in farming, fishing, and forestry, the percentages for the total U.S. population in these occupations were 13%, 9.4%, and 0.6%, respectively. We consider this information on parental occupation to be consistent with immigrant parents' patterns of educational attainment.

Health Insurance

Researchers (e.g., Reardon-Anderson, Capps, & Fix, 2002; Ruiz-de-Velasco & Fix, 2002) have used many factors to explain why children in immigrant families have more health problems compared to children in native families: low income households, segregation within poor neighborhoods, high levels of overcrowding in immigrant homes, and more limited access to Medicaid and other forms of health insurance because of their parents' noncitizen status and types of employment in low paying and part-time jobs in service or construction industries. We believe the lack of adequate insurance to be a major contribution to the status of immigrant health and well-being. Although immigrant adults were at least twice as likely to lack health insurance as native-born Americans (34% vs. 14%), immigrant children were also twice as likely as their native-born counterparts to lack health insurance (20% vs. 9%). The 1999 National Survey of America's Families indicated that the uninsured rates for both immigrants and native-born were lower for children than for adults because of the supplementary state health plans for children only (Capps, 2001; Shields & Behrman, 2004).

Summary

Our analyses of family locations, resources, living arrangements, education, and occupation show enormous and complex demographic and socioeconomic disparities between the immigrants and the general population across racial and ethnic groups. Although both race-ethnicity and immigration status have adverse effects on children's living conditions, immigration status may have a less adverse effect than race-ethnicity. The data reveal large discrepancies across racial-ethnic groups, but the gaps between the immigrant and the general populations within race-ethnicity are relatively moderate. However inequitable it is, socioeconomic conditions of immigrant children and adults across race and ethnicity are generally congruent with socioeconomic conditions across race and ethnicity in the general population.

CHARACTERISTICS OF IMMIGRANT FAMILIES AND CHILDREN

We have addressed several major socioeconomic characteristics of school-age immigrant children and their families and compared characteristics of immigrant children with the general school-age child population. We now focus on several immigration-related factors that reportedly play roles in children's education and acculturation. We first address the language situations in children's households. Then we consider the length of U.S. residence as well as age of arrival in this country. We end with a brief discussion of the citizenship status of these children, a topic we have addressed in Chapter 1.

Language Situations in Immigrant Households

Table 2.4 presents data on the percentage of children who speak languages other than English at home and reveals significant differences across race-ethnicity, immigration status, and the combination of the two. Although over 17% of all school-age children in the United States in 2000 lived in households where foreign languages were spoken, the rates varied from around 5% among White and Black children, to almost 60% among Asian children, and to almost 70% for Hispanic children. Eight-five per cent of immigrant children spoke languages other than English at home. This percentage was highest among immigrant Hispanics, but still very high among immigrant Asians and non-Hispanic Whites (76%). Less than half of Black immigrant children lived in a household where a language other than English was spoken. This may be because a large number of Caribbean Black immigrants had come from countries where English was the official language (e.g., Jamaica, Trinidad and Tobago) and the majority of African immigrants in the United States were from English-speaking countries such as Nigeria, Ethiopia, and Ghana.

To represent the language environment where a child lives, the U.S. census has for decades used the "linguistically isolated" household as an indicator in the decimal census long form. People have been asked if the household in which they live has someone aged 14 or older who speaks English at least "very well." Although many immigrant children live in bi- or multilingual households, a "linguistically isolated" household is one where very few or no child-parent interactions occur in English. Because homes are the first place where most young children develop their language abilities through spoken interactions with adults, children who grow up in linguistically isolated households may need to look for resources in school, the community, and society at large to develop their English proficiency. Table 2.4 presents information on the English-speaking situation in U.S. households. It indicates that, in 2000, one of three immigrant children lived in a linguistically isolated household, including one of four non-Hispanic White immigrant children, slightly less than one of three Asian immigrant children, and over two of five Hispanic immigrant children. More than 860,000 school-age immigrant children—including 560,000 Hispanic children—lived in linguistically isolated households, according to the 2000 census survey.

The percentage of children who live in households where a language other than English is spoken is an indicator for schools of how many languages are spoken locally. However, the percentage of children who live in linguistically isolated households provides information to schools on

TABLE 2.4   Immigration-Related Characteristics of U.S. Households for Children 5–18 Years Old by Race-Ethnicity and Immigration Status, 2000

	All Children (2,694,073)	Immigrant Children (125,792)
% of Children Who Spoke a Language Other Than English at Home		
All Children	17.3%	84.9%
Non-Hispanic White	5.3%	76.0%
Hispanic	69.3%	95.0%
Black	5.8%	48.4%
Asian	58.3%	80.5%
% of Children Who Lived in Linguistically Isolated Households		
All Children	4.5%	34.4%
Non-Hispanic White	0.7%	24.9%
Hispanic	20.7%	42.8%
Black	0.8%	13.1%
Asian	18.6%	29.3%
% Household Heads Who Were U.S. Citizens		
All Children	91.6%	31.5%
Non-Hispanic White	98.2%	34.2%
Hispanic	63.9%	24.5%
Black	94.5%	42.7%
Asian	70.7%	41.7%

SOURCE: Data from PUMS 5% of the 2000 Census (U.S. Bureau of the Census, 2003a), compiled by authors.

designing, planning, and implementing programs for ELL students who may not be able to develop oral English proficiency in their homes. Furthermore, the ability to speak English plays a large role in how well people can conduct daily activities such as communicating with public officials, medical personnel, and other service providers. Living in linguistically isolated households may also mean to the children that no adults in their households are able to help them regularly in such necessary activities as grocery shopping, banking, and visiting physicians. Schools should be prepared to provide information aiding linguistically isolated families to connect them to comprehensive community services.

Length of U.S. Residency and Age at Arrival

Immigrants generally have made progress socially, politically, and economically with lengthier residence in the United States. According to the American Community Survey (U.S. Bureau of the Census, 2006), length of residency affects the immigrant's economic well-being in home ownership as well. Although persons who immigrated before 1970 have higher home ownership rates (77%) than natives (69%), only 18% of recent immigrants lived in their own homes in 2005. Foreign-born Americans, as a whole, are 1.6 times more likely to be living in poverty than natives (22.9% vs. 14.4%). Although people who immigrated to the United States prior to 1970 are less likely than the native-born to be classified as poor (10.8%), recent immigrants are more than 2.5 times as likely to be living in poverty (37%) as native-born. Recent immigrants are also more likely than the native-born to receive public assistance income (5.7% vs. 2.9%). The rates drop significantly for immigrants who have been in the United States for five or more years. Longer-term residents also speak better English, know more about U.S. educational institutions, and are more likely to be U.S. citizens. Immigrants who have been in the U.S. longer are likely to have more influence on their children's education through involvement in educational legislation, school Parent Teacher Associations (PTAs), and the like. Schools in locations with concentrations of newcomers may need to provide services, including various sources of information, to orient the immigrant families not only to the new school and community but also to the new state and country. Immigrant children who arrive in the United States as preschoolers adjust more easily to the U.S. educational system, with a smoother transition to English, and a familiarity with U.S. schools from the start of their educational careers.

Table 2.5 reveals the challenges that U.S. schools face: in 2000, almost half the immigrant children had been in this country for five or fewer years, a pattern consistent across race and ethnicity. Furthermore, the majority of these children had arrived at young ages. Nationally, more than half of immigrant children had come to the United States as preschoolers, and an additional 30% had entered the country before reaching middle school. Across racial-ethnic groups, the majority of immigrant children arrived in this country at a very young age. This means that elementary schools around the country have been meeting the majority of the newcomers. However, in 2000, 16.4% of immigrant children were older than 10 years of age when they first entered this country. Almost half a million immigrant children came to the United States old enough for middle or high school. Given the English fluency required to undertake academic tasks, and the different sociocultural environment in U.S. secondary schools, this kind of transition poses a severe challenge for older newcomers as well as for their educators.

TABLE 2.5   Immigration-Related Characteristics of U.S. Foreign-Born Children 5–18 Years Old by Race and Ethnicity, 2000

	0–5	6–10	11–15	16 and Above
Years in U.S.				
All Children	47.3%	34.0%	16.5%	2.3%
Non-Hispanic White	53.6%	32.2%	12.8%	1.5%
Hispanic	45.3%	35.3%	17.4%	2.0%
Black	53.8%	29.8%	14.3%	2.0%
Asian	44.6%	34.0%	17.9%	3.5%
Age of Arrival				
All Children	53.4%	30.1%	14.5%	1.9%
Non-Hispanic White	50.2%	32.4%	15.5%	2.0%
Hispanic	56.0%	29.0%	13.2%	1.8%
Black	45.7%	32.8%	19.2%	2.4%
Asian	53.3%	30.1%	15.0%	1.6%

SOURCE: Data from PUMS 5% of the 2000 Census (U.S. Bureau of the Census, 2003a), compiled by authors.

Note: Percentages may not total to 100 because of rounding of subgroups.

Citizenship

The privileges and the benefits of being a U.S. citizen are many, but the data in Table 2.4 indicate that in 2000 less than one-third of immigrant children were living in a household headed by a U.S. citizen. At over two-fifths, the proportion is higher for Black and Asian immigrant children and, at about one-quarter, lowest for Hispanic children. To explain the varied citizenship rates for immigrants from various countries, Martin and Midgley (1994) have proposed that distance to the United States and affiliation of countries of origin with the United States are two of the most influential factors on naturalization rates. People who have migrated from a long distance and/or who have fled their countries for political reasons have the highest rates of naturalization. In contrast, people from countries historically and geographically closest to the United States have the lowest rates of naturalization. For example, of the Canadians and Mexicans admitted with immigration visas from 1970 to 1979, fewer than one in six had become citizens by 1992. Most immigrants from Western Europe also tend not to take U.S. citizenship. In contrast, four out of five Vietnamese and almost two of three Filipino and Chinese immigrants arriving between 1970 and 1979 had become U.S. citizens by 1992.

Summary

In 2000, the majority of immigrant children lived in households where a language other than English was spoken, and a third of them lived in linguistically isolated households. Hispanic children were more likely than other children to live in households where a language other than English was spoken and to live in linguistically isolated households. In 2000, the majority of immigrant children were recent arrivals who had come to the United States at a young age. Half entered the country as preschoolers, and a third arrived at elementary-school age. Although only one of three immigrant children are U.S. citizens, the proportion is higher for Black and Asian children and significantly lower for Hispanic children. Each of the demographic characteristics we have discussed thus far in the chapter affects the educational experience of immigrant children, and some of these factors interact to result in even stronger influences.

THE COMPOUND EFFECTS OF DEMOGRAPHIC FACTORS

The combined effects of socioeconomic factors on many aspects of children's lives compound the influence of individual elements. Based on 2000 census data, Rong's study (2006) explores the compounding effects on poverty of race and ethnicity, immigration, and inner-city residency. Table 2.6, adapted from Rong, indicates a clear pattern that in 2000 children who lived in the inner city, regardless of whether they were immigrants, were more likely to be in poverty than people who live elsewhere; moreover, immigrant minority children who lived in inner-city areas were more likely to be in poverty than immigrant children who lived elsewhere. Variations do occur in this general pattern of poverty and inner-city residency, depending on race and ethnicity. By far, more Hispanic immigrant children lived in poverty than other children, regardless of where they lived. Hispanic immigrant children who lived in inner cities had a 50% greater chance of living in poverty than White immigrant children. The largest gap in poverty rates by types of residency was among Asian immigrants. Asian immigrant children who lived in inner-city areas were twice as likely to live in poverty as Asian immigrant children who lived in the other areas. The poverty gaps by inner-city residency for White and Hispanic children were substantial but smaller than for Asians. The difference in proportions of inner-city children in poverty for immigrant and native Blacks is minimal.

Inner cities not only harbor the largest proportion of the poorest immigrant children, but they also have the largest proportion of the poorest native-born children. Table 2.6 also shows the poverty gaps by inner-city residency for native children in 2000 whose families have no recent immigration history; however, variations occur among racial-ethnic groups.

TABLE 2.6   U.S. Children's Poverty Status[1] (in percentage) by Race-Ethnicity, Immigration Status, and Residency in Inner-City Areas in 2000

		At or Below Poverty Level[1]				More Affluent than 75% of the Population			
		Immigrants		Natives[2]		Immigrants		Natives[2]	
	All	Inner City	Other Areas	Inner City	Other Areas	Inner City	Other Areas	Inner City	Other Areas
All	14.8	33.1	25	24.5	12.2	6.8	12.0	15.0	19.6
White	8.8	25.8	16.7	9.3	8.7	14.5	25.9	27.6	22.0
Black	26.2	27.0	25.9	35.9	29.9	7.1	8.9	5.8	8.2
Hispanic	0.5	38.3	31.7	33.3	20.9	3.1	4.3	7.2	11.3
Asian	14.0	30.3	15.8	13.7	10.9	8.9	20.6	25.4	27.0

SOURCE: Data from PUMS 5% of the 2000 Census (U.S. Bureau of the Census, 2003a), compiled by authors. Table adapted from Rong (2006).

Note: Percentages may not total to 100 because of rounding of subgroups.

1 The census poverty index ranges from 1 to 500, with people at 100 or lower defined as at or below poverty level. PUMS 5% 2000 indicates that people at 500 of the poverty index are better off economically than 75% of the U.S. population. Because the poverty index takes the number of family members into consideration and focuses its attention on the lower economic stratum of the population, it is a better indicator of people's economic condition than total family income. For details of the definition and the formula for the calculation, see Technical Documentation, Summary File 3, 2000 Census Population and Housing, U.S. Bureau of the Census, 2002.

2 Native children are defined as U.S.-born children with two U.S.-born parents. These are third- or higher-generation children whose families do not have a recent immigration history.

White and Asian children who lived in areas other than inner cities were less likely to live in poverty than Black and Hispanic children. Although the relationship of poverty to inner-city residency is clear and persistent, this pattern is stronger for Hispanic children than for other native-born children. At least one of three native-born Hispanic children who lived in inner-city areas in 2000 was poor, as compared to one of five Hispanic children living in poverty in other areas. The differences in poverty rates between inner cities and other places were smaller and varied for Asian children and White children. For Black children, although the poverty rate was high in general, the difference in poverty between children who lived in inner cities and children who lived elsewhere was moderate, suggesting that Black children are more disadvantaged by race regardless of where they live.

Table 2.7 indicates further the compound effects of race and ethnicity, immigration, inner-city residency, and poverty on children's lives when considering their parents' living arrangements, parental education, children's disabilities, and rates of living in linguistically isolated households. Table 2.7 shows that poor, inner-city immigrant children are less likely than such children who live elsewhere to live in a household with two parents. Rong (2006) reports that such children are also less likely than their counterparts who live elsewhere to live in a home with a father and to have parents with a college education. Inner-city immigrant children are also twice as likely to report physical disability as other children. Rong (2006) reports that indicators of language proficiency, however, do not appear to differ much for immigrants between inner cities and elsewhere: percentages are comparable for such factors as children who live in linguistically isolated households, children who do not speak English very well, and children who speak a language other than English. English proficiency is comparable for immigrants who live in the inner city and immigrants who live elsewhere. Instead, poverty appears to affect all aspects of children's lives more than residential location. Inner-city immigrant children whose family economic status is in the top category are more likely to live with two parents than immigrant children in poverty, much more likely to live with a father, and much more likely to have a parent with a college education.

Race and ethnicity play important roles in children's living conditions. Black immigrant children, regardless of their residency, were much less likely in 2000 to live with two parents than were other immigrant children. Hispanic and Asian immigrant children who were poor and lived in inner cities were more likely to have parents who did not complete eight years of school than were White and Black children. Although rates for Hispanics and Asians were somewhat comparable, inner-city, White, immigrant

TABLE 2.7   Selected Socioeconomic and Demographic Characteristics of U.S. Population 5–18 Years Old by Race-Ethnicity, Poverty Level, Inner-City Residency, and Immigration Status, 2000

| | At or Below Poverty Level[1] | | | | More Affluent Than 75% of the Population | | | |
| | Immigrants | | Natives[2] | | Immigrants | | Natives[2] | |
	Inner City	Other Areas	Inner City	Other Areas	Inner City	Other Areas	Inner City	Other Areas
% of Children Who Live With Two Parents in Each Subcategory								
All	66.8	72.5	17.1	34	86.1	91.9	85.2	91.9
White	78.1	78.6	32.9	43.6	92.2	93.8	89.6	92.9
Hispanic	62.7	73.4	20.6	29.2	82.6	86.9	80.2	86.8
Black	43.3	43.3	11.9	16.6	67.1	83.5	67.9	78.8
Asian	79.9	75.4	21.7	30.7	88.6	93.4	85.6	87.5

% of Children Who Live With Parent or Household Head Who Has Not Completed Eighth Grade							
All	20.4	21.3	2.2	1.6	4.0	2.1	0.2	0.1
White	6.6	6.3	1.2	0.9	1.3	0.4	0.1	0.0
Hispanic	21.7	25.9	5.4	3.9	11.8	8.8	1.0	0.4
Black	11.4	9.0	2.4	3.0	1.7	0.4	0.5	0.3
Asian	28.6	17.5	1.0	1.8	2.3	0.9	0.0	0.2
% of Children Reporting Physical Disabilities (One or Multiple Limitations in Mobility and Personal Care, Including Hearing, Vision, and Speech Impairment, etc.)							
All	6.1	5.4	6.3	5.0	5.3	2.9	2.0	1.7
White	5.2	3.6	5.9	4.7	4.9	2.0	1.6	2.6
Hispanic	6.7	5.8	7.5	5.3	8.1	5.4	2.7	2.1
Black	5.6	6.3	6.1	5.6	6.1	4.0	3.4	3.0
Asian	5.4	4.9	3.4	4.8	4.8	2.5	1.3	1.8
% of Children Who Live in Linguistically Isolated Households							
All	47.3	48	3.2	1.5	17	12.7	0.3	0.1
White	51	46.3	0.9	0.7	13.6	7.8	0.1	0.1
Hispanic	50.4	51.4	14	8.8	29.4	19.9	2.9	1.2
Black	20.7	24.9	0.2	0.2	4.3	3.4	0.2	0.1
Asian	47.3	43.6	6.4	1.9	16.6	15	0.4	0.3

SOURCE: Table adapted from Rong (2006).

1 The census poverty index ranges from 1 to 500, with people at 100 or lower defined as at or below poverty level. PUMS 5% 2000 indicates that people at 500 of the poverty index are better off economically than 75% of the U.S. population. Because the poverty index takes the number of family members into consideration and focuses its attention on the lower economic stratum of the population, it is a better indicator of people's economic condition than total family income. For details of the definition and the formula for the calculation, see Technical Documentation, Summary File 3, 2000 Census Population and Housing, U.S. Bureau of the Census, 2002.

2 Native children are defined as U.S.-born children with two U.S.-born parents. These are third- or higher-generation children whose families do not have a recent immigration history.

children who were poor were more likely to be living in linguistically isolated households than other children, and Rong (2006) reports that the highest percentage of children who did not speak English very well in 2000 were Asian inner-city immigrant children.

Rong (2006) concludes that census data reveal a bleak picture—a lack of resources affecting many aspects of poor children's lives. However, until the impact of the concentration of poverty on the native-born population is taken into consideration, the severity of the lack of resources in inner-city areas for immigrants may not be evident. As previously emphasized, inner cities not only host the poorer immigrant population, they also host the largest proportion of the poorest native residents. Family configurations among the poor also vary in the inner cities: in 2000 over 70% of all U.S. children lived in families with two parents but less than 20% of poor, inner-city, native-born children lived with two parents; in contrast, 34% of poor native-born children who lived elsewhere and almost 93% of affluent children who lived elsewhere lived in households with two parents.

These patterns are even more striking when taking race and ethnicity into consideration: in 2000 only 12% of economically disadvantaged Black native-born children who lived in the inner city lived with two parents; in contrast, the percentage of those living with two parents among affluent Black children who lived in areas other than the inner city was almost 80%, and for White children that rate was about 92%. The joint effect of poverty and immigration also contributes to these patterns. Native-born Hispanic children who lived in inner cities and in poverty were more than ten times as likely to have parents without eight years of education than native-born Hispanic children who lived in areas other than the inner city. However, immigrant, inner-city, poor Asian and Hispanic children had the highest percentage of parents without eight years of education: more than one of four Asian children and one of five Hispanic children who lived in poverty had parents with less than eight years of school. This is four times greater than for the inner-city, native-born Hispanic children, regardless of where they lived. Here the pattern appears more strongly connected to ethnicity than to place of residence because an even larger proportion of Hispanic immigrant children in 2000 who lived in areas other than the inner city had parents who had not completed eight grades; presumably this is connected to the concentration of Hispanic immigrants in certain occupations, as we have discussed previously in the chapter.

As we have also already noted, inner-city residency by itself is not strongly connected to language, but poverty is. Inner-city immigrant children who lived in poverty in 2000 were almost three times as likely to live in a linguistically isolated household as affluent, inner-city immigrant children and four times more likely to be linguistically isolated than affluent immigrant children who lived elsewhere. Rong (2006) reports similar patterns for the percentage of children who did not speak English very well in 2000. Among inner-city, poor, immigrant children, 47% were reported to lack English proficiency: 55% of Asian children, 48% of Hispanic children, and 43% of White children. However, only 21% of affluent, inner-city immigrant children reported the same problem, and among affluent, immigrant children who lived in areas other than an inner city, only 15% claimed a lack of fluency in English. We move now from comparing inner-city immigrants with those who live elsewhere to considering the qualities of the neighborhoods and schools immigrants inhabit and attend.

Immigrants' Neighborhoods and Schools

Neighborhoods have instrumental value for new arrivals, especially for people whose language, customs, or tradition set them apart from the majority population because immigrant communities usually have a concentration of newcomers from the same region or even the same country. Using data from 1990 and 2000 censuses, Logan (2003) claims that concentrated immigrant settlements arise and are maintained because they meet newcomers' needs for affordable housing, family ties, familiar cultures, and such. A concentrated immigrant settlement often serves as a network that provides immigrants with job information and employment opportunities. This network may supply newcomers easier access to social, legal, and other services such as shopping and getting medications. Furthermore, settlements can be a convenient channel for government at all levels to communicate with immigrants through their community networks to deliver services as well as collect information. Neighborhood and community influence children's growth, their socialization, educational and occupational aspirations, as well as their health and safety. Bartel (1989) mentions that the neighborhood residential cluster also may enhance ethnic group identity, hence increasing immigrants' sense of security and helping them resist racial discrimination.

Although ethnic communities and immigrant concentrations have these positive qualities and provide networks for people in coethnic and immigrant groups, immigrant-ethnic clusters are usually called ethnic enclaves—often viewed as a form of neighborhood segregation, reflecting housing problems and social and racial dissonance (Logan, 2003). One of the issues concerning many educators is the linguistic isolation of children in many immigrant neighborhoods, which often makes acquisition of a new language more difficult. Eighty-five percent of children in immigrant families speak a language other than English at home, and 34% live in linguistically isolated households where no one over the age of 14 has a strong command of the English language.

In the contemporary United States, immigrant residence may also vary by social class. Bartel (1989) found that the best-educated immigrants are most likely to disperse, and the least educated are most likely to cluster. Better-educated immigrants have higher rates of internal migration, and their geographic movement reduces spatial concentration, in contrast to the absence of a tendency toward dispersion among the foreign-born population as a whole.

We believe that a well-integrated neighborhood, with people from different racial-ethnic, socioeconomic, and cultural-linguistic backgrounds, is an ideal human environment for children's social and intellectual growth.

Although diverse communities have challenges in developing cohesion and civic participation (see Putnam, 2007), diverse groups also can be more creative and productive (see Page, 2007). The community that hosts the school as well as the school itself should foster the widest diversity and participation from all sectors. In this section, we describe the neighborhoods the typical immigrant is likely to live in, and we then discuss the schools that work with large numbers of immigrant students. Because the census data we have compiled do not address these issues, we report data from studies that focus on these matters to provide a more complete profile of immigrant children.

Residential and Linguistic Segregation From Natives

Logan (2003) compared decimal census data of 1990 and 2000 to generate a national overview of the racial-ethnic and immigration-related characteristics of U.S. neighborhoods: the percentage of foreign-born and the percentage of persons (5 years and over) who speak a language other than English in their homes. Logan's study poses two questions about immigrants' residential patterns: How different are the neighborhoods where Whites and members of minority groups live in terms of racial, immigrant, and linguistic segregation? How different are the neighborhoods where natives and immigrants live in terms of racial, immigrant, and linguistic segregation? The answers to these two questions indicate the degree of neighborhood integration or separation among these groups.

Based on the comparisons between Whites and other groups, Logan (2003) found two major neighborhood characteristics. First, the average White or Black was more likely to live in a neighborhood with a small percentage of foreign-born or bilingual neighbors, but the average Hispanic or Asian was more likely to live with neighbors who were foreign-born and bilingual. Logan's report indicates that the average White in a metropolitan area has a moderate exposure to immigrants and languages other than English, though these exposures grew between 1990 and 2000 because of the rapid increase in the immigrant population in the United States during that 10-year period. Logan observed that the average White lived in 2000 census tracts where about 15% of the neighbors were foreign-born and just under a quarter spoke languages other than English at home. Blacks lived in neighborhoods with somewhat higher levels of newcomers and people who spoke a language other than English (20.3% and 27.6%, respectively). Hispanic and Asian neighborhoods were markedly different—nearly a third of the average Hispanic or Asian person's neighbors were immigrants, and they were much more likely to hear languages other than English in their neighborhoods. Hispanic immigrants were the most likely to live in a neighborhood where the majority of residents spoke a language other than English.

Second, although natives tend to live with natives and immigrants tend to live with immigrants, this varies by racial-ethnic group. Whites and, to a lesser extent, Blacks, were more likely than Asians and Hispanics to live in homogeneous neighborhoods. Nonimmigrant Hispanics and Asians were more likely to live with immigrant and bilingual neighbors than average Whites and Blacks. Furthermore, average Hispanic and Asian immigrants were also more likely than Whites to live with neighbors who were foreign-born and bilingual. Most noticeable is that the average Hispanic lived in a neighborhood where more than half the residents spoke languages other than English.

Logan (2003) asks a further question about how these different neighborhood characteristics varied between natives and immigrants because the difference between these two groups may indicate diminishing spatial segregation as immigrants assimilate. Logan notes that some researchers believe that the racial concentration and segregation of Asians and Hispanics may be attributed to their large shares of foreign-born members. He comments that the prevalent view is that this segregation is a temporary phenomenon and that the second generation would shift substantially to less segregated, more mainstream locations, a process described as spatial assimilation or social mobility. The speculation was that U.S.-born Asians and Hispanics would live in areas much more similar to those of White natives. However, Logan found little support for this speculation in his findings,

Logan (2003) analyzes immigrants' as well as natives' settlement patterns for exposure to the White majority and concludes that neighborhood characteristics seem to be much more a matter of people's race and ethnicity than of their nativity. Whites, regardless of whether they were native or foreign-born, lived in neighborhoods where Whites were a clear majority. This majority shrank between 1990 and 2000 because of the growing presence of immigrant minorities throughout the United States. Members of minority groups experienced neighborhoods different from those where Whites lived. The average minority person lived in a neighborhood where the majority of residents were not White. For example, in 2000 the average Black person lived in neighborhoods that were one-quarter non-Hispanic White. For the average Hispanic or Asian person, the percentages of White persons in their neighborhoods were 32% and 45%, respectively. However, the difference in neighborhood segregation between natives and immigrants within racial-ethnic groups was modest with the native-born among Blacks and Hispanics experiencing minimally more Whites in their neighborhoods than their foreign-born counterparts. However, Asian natives and immigrants lived in neighborhoods with about the same percentage of White neighbors. In general, average White immigrants still lived in neighborhoods in which two-thirds of the neighbors were White, but average Black and Hispanic immigrants lived in neighborhoods where about a quarter of the neighbors were White. These residential patterns of segregation are mirrored in U.S. schools, to which we turn next.

School Segregation

More than 80% of U.S. children are schooled in public schools in school districts where the children reside. Schools located in inner-city neighborhoods often work with children who are members of minority groups, immigrants, and poor. Based on the 1989–1990 and 1999–2000 Common Core Data (CCD) that have been collected annually by the National Center for Education Statistics (NCES), Logan (2004) reports the cumulative percentages of students of each racial-ethnic group by the percentage of minority group members in the schools that they attended and shows how these percentages shifted between 1990 and 2000. Logan's study reveals the racial and economic segregation of U.S. public urban schools. Logan (2004) points out how extreme the differences are across groups in the racial-ethnic composition of schools for non-Hispanic Whites, Blacks, Hispanics, and Asians. For example, in 2000 about 90% of non-Hispanic White children were in public schools in which less than 50% of the students were minorities, and less than 2% of White children were in schools in which more than 80% of the students were minorities. On the contrary, less than 30% of Black students were in schools in which more than 50% of the students were White, but about half of Black students were in schools in which more than 80% of the students were minorities. In 2000, 6.8% of White students were in schools with no minority students, and 13.2% were in schools in which less than 1% of the students were minorities. Conversely about 40% of Blacks and Hispanics attended schools where over 90% of the students were minorities.

Data from the Condition of Education (National Center for Education Statistics, 2006) indicate that U.S. public schools have also been segregated by economic status, and segregation is aggravated by the inner-city locations of schools and the concentration of minority students. First, nationally in 2005, 41% of fourth-graders were eligible for free or reduced-price lunches; 24% of non-Hispanic White students were eligible, but 70% of Black students and 74% of Hispanic students were eligible. Students who lived in suburban areas were least likely to be eligible for free or reduced-price lunches, and students who lived in inner-city areas were most likely to be eligible for free or reduced-price lunches. The inner-city location of schools increases free or reduced-price lunch eligibility rates 14% for the total student population with 1% increase for White students, 5% for Black students, 6% for Hispanic students, and 9% for Asian students. The same data also show how race and ethnicity intersect with poverty in U.S. schools. Although about 10% of inner-city White fourth-graders were educated in schools in which more than 75% of the students were eligible for free or reduced-priced lunches, almost 30% of inner-city Asian students and over 60% of inner-city Black and Hispanic students were in schools in which more than 75% of the students were eligible for free or reduced-priced lunches.

What we have shown in this section of the chapter is that immigrants are disadvantaged by neighborhood and school segregation. However, the combination of immigrant status, race and ethnicity, and inner-city locations significantly aggravates these disadvantages. Furthermore, Logan (2003) concludes that residential separation falls mainly along racial and ethnic lines: White Americans tend to live in neighborhoods that are overwhelmingly White; members of minorities live in neighborhoods with other minorities. Asian immigrants—to a degree—and Black and Hispanic immigrants—to an even greater extent—live separately from the metropolitan White population, and this division is not as much attributable to their immigrant status. Immigrants typically live in neighborhoods where about 30% of the residents are immigrants and an even larger proportion of their neighbors speak a language other than English at home. Immigrants live in neighborhoods very similar to those of native-born in the same racial or ethnic group. The results from Logan's study are consistent with those from other studies (e.g., Kent, Pollard, Haaga, & Mather, 2001; Orfield & Yun, 1999). Furthermore, because the majority of immigrants to the United States are members of minority groups, and because a large portion live in the inner city, these elements in immigrants' neighborhoods and school environments should be considered when studying immigrant children's education and social development.

Logan (2003) also cautions that immigrant neighborhoods may be "permanent" transitional places if the current large immigration movement continues. Most newcomers may move on elsewhere after the initial settlement and adjustment period; however, the next cohort of newcomers from the same race-ethnicity and nationality groups come to fill the vacancies.

Summary of Immigrant Children's Demographics

Using U.S. Census 2000 data and other sources, in this chapter we have provided focused information on immigrant children and their surroundings. Comparisons between immigrant children and the general child populations suggest several patterns:

- With a few exceptions, immigrant children experienced more social and economic disadvantages than the native-born.
- They were also more likely to be poor and to live in inner-city areas, and to live with parents who had not completed either four years of school or high school.
- Immigrant families were more likely to locate in racially, ethnically, and linguistically segregated neighborhoods and less likely to have health insurance.
- Compared with the general school-age population, immigrant children in general and within each racial-ethnic group were more likely to have physical disabilities.

However, exceptions occur in this general pattern of disadvantages. Immigrant children were less likely than other children to have learning-related disabilities and were more likely to live with two parents. Immigrant children were more likely than others to live with parents who were four-year college graduates. With the polarization in parental education we have discussed previously, immigrant parents comprise both the least and best educated adults in the nation. Furthermore, the differences between immigrant children and all children varies across race-ethnicity. For example, Black immigrant children were less likely to live in poverty than other Black children, regardless of their residential location, while Hispanic immigrant children were less likely to live with parents who were college graduates. Moreover, the sizes of the differences are also variable across race-ethnicity. For example, White immigrant children were almost four times more likely to live in the inner city than the general White population; the differences between Hispanic immigrant children and all Hispanic children were minimal. Also, Black immigrant children were twice as likely as all Black children to have parents who were college graduates, but the difference in parental college education was minimal between immigrant Asian children and all Asian children.

But most important, we have shown the vast diversities in children's social and economic environments across race-ethnicity. Although the data we have presented show the disadvantages that immigrants experience, differences between immigrants and the general population within race-ethnicity are relatively moderate compared to the enormous demographic and socioeconomic disparities across race-ethnicity both in the immigrant population and in the general population. White children were much better off than all children, and White immigrant children were less disadvantaged than all other immigrant children. Hispanic and Black immigrants were the most disadvantaged. This means that, in most cases, the socioeconomic status of immigrant children and adults by race-ethnicity parallels the socioeconomic status of these groups in the general population.

IMPLICATIONS FOR EDUCATION

Constructing immigrants' social and economic profiles is critical for making sound social and educational policies and planning effective strategies for working with immigrant students. The immigrant children's profiles presented in this chapter indicate the depth and breadth of the social and economic conditions affecting the quality of children's lives; these effects may have been overlooked by policymakers and educators around the country for years. Based on the material presented this chapter and on existing research literature, we offer several suggestions for policymakers and practical steps for U.S. schools to improve the life prospects of immigrant children. Before proceeding to our recommendations, however, we consider how immigrant children's difficulties are similar to or different from other children's, and whether the policies that serve other disadvantaged children can effectively serve immigrant children and their families.

Researchers have argued that, in many ways, the needs of the children of immigrants are the same as those of other vulnerable, low-income children; therefore, efforts to support the positive development of all disadvantaged youth would address a wide range of challenges facing immigrant children as well. A wide range of strategies can mobilize policy support for vulnerable children, both inside and outside the immigrant community and across immigrant generations (see Kaufmann & Lay, 2004; Novelli & Goyer, 2004; Shields & Behrman, 2004). However, policy researchers have also pointed out that educators need to understand the strengths and vulnerabilities of specific immigrant groups and, hence, how to meet unique needs of immigrant children and their families. Shields and Behrman (2004) stress that current strategies aimed at addressing poverty in general are not always appropriate for the immigrant population, as their situation differs in several ways from that of the native-born poor. For example, policies that promote increased employment and enhance marriage may be inappropriate for immigrant families in poverty; immigrants tend to have higher employment rates and more intact families than other poor people. Zimmermann and Tobin (1995) analyzed a national sample of metropolitan census tracts in 1990 to compare family conditions in concentrated poor neighborhoods occupied primarily by foreign-born households with those primarily occupied by nonimmigrant households. The researchers found that the primarily immigrant-occupied poverty areas exhibited lower degrees of "underclass" indicators such as rates of public assistance use, unemployment, and female-headed households, even though these immigrant residents tended to have lower average educational attainment levels than the native-born in poverty. Instead of efforts to help poor immigrants increase their employment rates and stabilize their families, policies need to help them deal with low education levels and lack of access to support and programs due to their citizenship status and undocumented ambiguity. Providing resources to improve their English language skills is also critical.

Many scholars have also reported optimism and high motivation among low-income immigrants for improving their families' economic conditions: Immigrant families come to the United States for work, and they work hard. They expect their children to do the same (Galster, Metzger, & Waite, 1999). The strong motivation for social mobility and immigrants' optimism should be taken into account for developing sound policies and effective working strategies.

Some educational researchers have argued that policies and practices that do not work well for native-born disadvantaged children may not work well with immigrant children, either. For example, educational researchers have argued that NCLB, a mainstream, standardized educational practice with a one-test-fits-all assessment, relies on a decontextualization model that ignores the social and economic variations in the student population and the complex realities in schools; therefore, schools cannot meet children's personal, social, cultural, and community-based needs (Valenzuela, 2005). Moreover, focusing on high-stakes tests, many teachers take a reductivist approach in an instructional and test-driven curriculum not responsive to students' academic backgrounds, learning styles, and life experiences. NCLB-centered schools can be particularly difficult for newcomer students because of the requirements for rapid English acquisition and quick cultural adjustment (Velasco, 2005).

MAJOR EMERGING ISSUES

As the data we have presented suggest, schools should make distinctions among the various groups of students, acknowledging the realities of children's lives and recognizing their special needs accordingly. We synthesize the needs of immigrant children and families with the following five emerging issues.

Race Issues

A notable change in fourth-wave immigration is the shift in immigrants' racial-ethnic composition. Three of four immigrants come from Latin American, Asian, and Caribbean countries, and fewer and fewer are from Europe. Although most immigrants must overcome the linguistic and cultural challenges of being newcomers in an unfamiliar land, the majority of contemporary immigrants to the United States face an added challenge: within the context of persistent racial discrimination, these new immigrants join the U.S. "minority" groups and are confronting the same educational and employment hurdles as native minorities. Census data and other sources indicate that the socioeconomic disparities experienced by the foreign-born have more to do with minority status than with place of birth. When immigrants and native-born are compared within the same racial-ethnic group, the disparities between native-born and foreign-born are relatively small. Although immigrants have historically endured the suspicion of being unable to "assimilate," much evidence indicates otherwise: various groups have developed a variety of strategies to battle the racial and social inequality in schooling, employment opportunities, and political participation with "immigrant resources" to achieve social and economic mobility. Policies that address racial equity and inequality will help newcomers resist structural barriers. Multicultural education for pluralistic tolerance will also help society to develop a constructive social atmosphere, as well as support children in developing healthier social and cultural identities.

Poverty Issues

Educators should understand that the poverty level among new immigrants may be partially explained by a changed economy. Since the 1980s, the United States has shifted from an industrial economy to a service-based economy. The many well-paid industrial jobs that fit immigrant skills have gradually disappeared. This shift in the economy has had a negative impact on income levels and has reduced the chance for occupational mobility for recent immigrants. Also, poverty is not merely a matter of money; poverty has a deeper and more complex effect on people's lives, limiting access to employment, housing, education, public transportation, health care, and other resources (Hook, 2003).

Inner-City Residency Issues

As some scholars (e.g., Waldinger & Bozorgmehr, 1996) have indicated, although immigrants revitalize some inner-city areas, U.S. inner-city schools serve a disproportion of both immigrant and native-born minority students who come from low-socioeconomic backgrounds. Rong (2006) has reported that immigrant children who live in inner cities are the most recent immigrants, poorer, less educated, and not citizens. Inner-city children are also less likely to live in two-parent families. To meet the needs of these immigrant students, inner-city schools that serve large numbers of immigrant students may need to reset their priorities somewhat differently as they consider balancing the needs of newcomer and native-born minority students. For example, because inner-city neighborhoods are more likely to be the first settlement location for newcomers, inner-city schools need programs to help these children to adjust quickly to different social, language, and schooling expectations, especially for 11–18-year-old immigrant children who are middle or high school age. Inner-city schools may also need to help newcomers' families locate information to access the federal, state, and local benefit and service programs for which their children are eligible. Those programs usually are familiar to native-born, low-income city residents, whom schools can enlist for help with such matters.

Moreover, policymakers and educators need to understand the risks for immigrant children associated with both inner-city residency and a concentration of poverty. Because today's U.S. inner cities are dominated by racial-ethnic minorities, new immigrants, and the poor, Zhou (2003) emphasizes four risk factors facing immigrant inner-city children; they may be: (1) socially and linguistically isolated from mainstream, English-speaking U.S. society; (2) losing motivation and immigrant optimism because of direct exposure to ghetto cultures and indirect experience with a materialistic mainstream culture through television; (3) devastated by poor living conditions, unsafe streets, and economic distress; and (4) handicapped by inadequate and turbulent schools vulnerable to overcrowding, a high dropout rate, a high rate of below-grade level enrollment, and a problem with English. Sound policies and workable school plans must address these risk factors.

Undocumented Immigration Issues

Approximately 3 million children, including 2 million U.S.-born children, live in families with undocumented parents. Passel (2006) describes a complicated situation for "mixed families," composed of U.S. citizens, legal immigrants, and undocumented persons. Passel estimates that 14.6 million people lived in "mixed" or "nonmixed undocumented" families, including 4.9 million children. Of these, about 3.1 million children—64% of all the children in the mixed families—were U.S. citizens born here; about 1.8 million of the children in these families were not born here and therefore were undocumented. In many mixed families, some children were born in the United States, but others were not—or one of the parents was born here, or a legal immigrant, but the other parent was not. Policymakers and educators must be aware of these complicated family situations and realize that children in these families sustain greater hardships than children in legal, low-income newcomer families. In particular, undocumented families comprise a higher percentage of immigrants in the new gateway states, but these states have limited experience and infrastructure for aiding the settlement of newcomer families. We recommend that officials in new gateway states assess the newcomer populations in their areas and consult with more experienced educators and policymakers elsewhere.

The Policy Context Issue

Many people believe that only nationwide policies can provide adequate leadership and resources for a nation that has dealt with such a huge immigrant influx for such a long duration. Scholars (e.g., Singer, 2002) have argued that, although the United States has always regulated the quantity of immigrants admitted to the country, it has done little for immigrants once they have arrived. The assumption is that the foreign-born will make their way with assistance from family and friends. However, adapting to a diverse nation is challenging to immigrant newcomers as well as established residents. A large number of immigrants who are minorities and inner-city residents are not doing well. Despite heated debates and endless discussions, the United States is the only industrial country that has no national policies to aid newcomers' settlement: the federal government does not have a dedicated settlement or integration policy, but only limited expenditures for immigrant-related programs other than those for refugees. For the most part, federal assistance for immigrant integration programs has been created ad hoc and only modestly funded. Through programs such as the refugee resettlement program and the Adult Education/ESL program, the federal government spent a combined $1.6 billion in FY 1999—a small amount, given the current levels of immigration and the targeting of much of this funding for refugees, who comprise only about 10% of the foreign-born (Fix, Zimmermann, & Passel, 2001).

In addition to relatives and friends, immigrants rely largely on local programs and organizations, funded by a number of sources, including private foundations and state and local governments. Some organizations have developed around target issues, such as the 1986 legalization program, or in response to a hard-hitting problem within immigrant communities, such as the 1996 welfare reform. Others may have been stimulated by federal funding from programs such as the Emergency Immigrant Education Program or the Refugee Resettlement Program (Singer, 2002).

In summary, these five issues highlight the pressing needs of immigrant children and their families. They suggest the two categories of recommendations that we discuss next.

RECOMMENDATIONS FOR SCHOOLS

We make two categories of recommendations for schools. First are suggestions for educational practices and school programs, and second are suggestions for outreach efforts.

Educational Practices and School Programs

Schools need to have a positive and progressive educational philosophy and take an additive approach when they work with immigrant students. The wide diversity in immigrant students' environments and life experiences requires educators to specify knowledge, skill, and affective competencies that build on each student's strengths, knowledge, and cultural identity. Educators must develop and use assessments that reflect high expectations, and they must evaluate progress on an individual basis. Educators must develop skills in cross-cultural understanding and communication to create effective nurturing learning environments. Furthermore, educators are responsible for becoming aware of and countering particular stereotypes that immigrant youth may face during and after school hours. Forming alliances with immigrant families and drawing on what Moll and Gonzáles (2004) call local "funds of knowledge" provide schools themselves with additional resources. Schools must also provide educational opportunities for adult immigrants, especially language instruction. This assists immigrant children by potentially improving the economic status of their families and giving parents skills to enable them to help their children do well in school.

Researchers (e.g., Shields & Behrman, 2004) also caution educators about what immigrant children need at different ages. The programs offered in schools should consider meeting children's various needs at various schooling levels (Coll & Szalacha, 2004; Fuligni & Hardway, 2004; Takanish, 2004).

Birth to age 8. It is important to involve parents and children to obtain early learning experiences that can be extended into kindergarten and the early elementary grades. Programs such as Head Start, Smart Start, Early Start, and some special programs for ELL learning, as well as some general special education programs for learning-disabled children, might benefit many immigrant children. However, children in immigrant families have had a tendency to not participate in any of these programs.

Middle childhood. During this period, it is critical to help children understand how experiences with racism and discrimination and perceptions of diminished life opportunities can influence the paths of their academic futures and career aspirations; such understandings will help them cope with the barriers they may encounter. Children start to develop a strong self-consciousness and sense of identity during this period, and it is important for schools to develop programs with parents to help children maintain respect for parents and preserve connections to their cultural heritages during these years.

Adolescence. For immigrant teens and adolescents to negotiate the difficult passage to adulthood, schools need to have programs focusing on helping students finish school, acquire useful work skills, postpone parenthood, and keep physically and mentally healthy. These programs should provide resources and empower students to overcome barriers of unsafe neighborhoods, family poverty, lack of health insurance, inadequate access to health care, and such. Educators should be especially alert to receiving newcomers who are middle or high school age. Learning English speedily can be hampered when youngsters are grappling with new vocabulary and knowledge in reading assignments in all subjects, especially in science and social studies. They must also adjust to U.S.-style schooling and school social life, including peer pressure and the antischool culture typically formed in U.S. inner-city schools (e.g., Fordham, 1996).

Schools' Outreach Efforts

As we have emphasized previously, schools have historically been one of the most important U.S. social institutions to absorb newcomers; therefore, schools must provide comprehensive services to immigrant children and their families beyond the conventional responsibilities of education. Because many schools in urban areas are the only public places to gather people together, schools usually need to play multiple roles in the community: informing the public, advocating for various groups, coordinating community efforts, and mediating conflicts. In many cases, schools become the liaison between immigrants and their surrounding communities. For example, schools can help recent immigrant parents integrate into the broader community by helping established residents and immigrant communities get to know each other through introducing information on new immigrants to the local population, as well as organizing educational and cultural programs that involve native-born and immigrant residents. Schools may also introduce newcomers to established immigrant communities through setting up adult literacy programs and immigration information centers. Schools can inform newcomers about the services and resources for which they may be eligible, as well as informing social agencies and local businesses of the newcomers' arrival. These efforts will promote immigrants' understanding of the host society and its major institutions and, therefore, help them adjust to the new society. These efforts all benefit immigrant children's schooling.

In addition to these general outreach efforts, we identify two areas that deserve special attention from schools.

1. *Working With Community Organizations.* Schools need to work with various organizations in the community, so they must understand the functions of these organizations. Immigrant-led organizations often are the point of first contact for new arrivals. For many newcomers, these organizations remain anchor institutions for families needing assistance in a variety of spheres. Community organizations can serve as a bridge between formal establishments—such as schools or hospitals—and immigrant newcomers, who may have limited English language proficiency or little experience in dealing with U.S. bureaucracies. Research has shown that certain children living in the inner city are able to do well, despite adverse conditions, because of the availability and accessibility of community-based resources such as after-school tutoring, children's programs in local libraries, and other educationally-oriented programs that serve children (Heath & McLaughlin, 1993; Zhou, 2003). Policy researchers (see Shields & Behrman, 2004) emphasize a variety of after-school activities run by collaborations between school districts and community-based organizations in immigrant communities. These programs have expanded their efforts to enhance students' academic backgrounds while reinforcing the children's cultural values and heritage. Community-based family literacy programs can improve immigrants' English skills by working with children and parents together, especially for children who live in linguistically isolated households. Schools should take the initiative to promote and provide resources for these programs. In many circumstances, schools are in a position to assume a leadership role in facilitating communication among parents, teachers, students, and other parties involved, building the understanding and trust among all parties that can better guarantee the quality of these programs.

Some of these programs can be offered through Supplemental Educational Services in schools in high poverty areas and areas with concentrations of newcomers. Supplemental Educational Services, including tutoring and after-school services, may be offered through providers in public or private sectors; they must be approved or certified by credible agencies such as public schools, public charter schools, local education agencies, educational service agencies, and faith-based organizations (U.S. Department of Education, 2003). Schools and school districts should take active roles to notify the parents of eligible children about the availability of the services and provide information about the approved providers, as many newcomers may be unaware of these programs.

2. *Working With Social Services.* Social workers in schools need to help immigrant children find available resources to improve their family economic conditions, health care, and language learning. Though children in immigrant families experience higher poverty rates and more hardship, they are less likely to receive public assistance than other low-income children. For example, children of immigrants are about half as likely as other children to participate in Medicaid, a gap that has widened in recent years. Changes in the federal welfare law in 1996 made most noncitizens ineligible for Temporary Assistance for Needy Families (TANF) and Medicaid during their first five years in the United States and also restricted their eligibility for food stamps. Although these restrictions do not apply to children who were born in the United States to immigrant parents because those children are citizens entitled to all benefits enjoyed by other citizens, the restrictions on parents have had a chilling effect on family participation in the programs. As we have noted previously, undocumented parents are even less likely to apply for these benefits and attend the programs on behalf of their U.S.-born children from concern about their own legal status. An Urban Institute report indicates that young children of immigrants are less likely than other children to be in center-based child care, potentially limiting their preparation for schooling (InFocus, 2005). Schools also can serve as advocates and resource centers to encourage social service agencies and other institutions to strengthen their bilingual staff and to work with community-based organizations to enhance outreach efforts to facilitate greater access to benefits for eligible children in immigrant families (Shields & Behrman, 2004).

RECOMMENDATIONS FOR EDUCATORS AND CONCERNED CITIZENS—TAKING POLICY STANDS FOR SOCIAL JUSTICE

Schools must advocate sound social policies for immigrant children and their families. People who work with immigrant children also must transcend their traditionally defined duties to advocate for immigrant and other disadvantaged children, both as educators and as responsible citizens. Current debates about immigration are deeply divided between those advocating tight border control and restrictive immigrant admissions and those advocating policies to provide economic and social aid to needy immigrant families. Based on our own findings and the results of other researchers' works (e.g., Hook, 2003), we believe the latter may be a more workable strategy that targets education and training, identifies barriers, and helps to reduce the obstacles to employment, especially for immigrant mothers, and to educational attainment among all immigrant parents. Hook suggests that, in some instances, reform may require changing the incentives for states and/or employment and training providers to address the training needs of immigrant workers who do not speak English and have low levels of education and literacy.

Policy researchers also have found that more work supplementation strategies are needed (Neightingale & Fix, 2004). These strategies include living wage initiatives, wage supplements, and stronger worker support, including child care and parental leave, as well as assistance in acquiring additional skills and making career changes. Social benefits such as health insurance and housing subsidies would also help more working families live above the poverty line. Public policies can be improved to fill the gap in immigrant worker benefits not provided by employers. These types of initiatives are consistent with and reinforce "work first" policies, as they are centered on employment, supporting workers' efforts to retain and upgrade their employability. Perhaps the most prominent proposal is the Immigrant Child Health and Improvement Act that may be taken up as part of the delayed reauthorization of the Temporary Assistance for Needy Families (TANF) block grants.

In spite of the sentiments stirred by heated immigration debates, state and local educational leaders need to advocate progressive policies and allocate funding to resist the "nested inequalities" in terms of resources, ensure that newcomers get the assistance they need, and enable the established community to participate fiscally and socially in the process (Books, 2004; Singer, 2002). Schools should make every effort to ensure that children in immigrant families have access to the resources they need to help them stay on positive pathways to success (Shields & Behrman, 2004). Especially in new regions that are increasingly experiencing an influx of immigrant newcomers, educators should rise to the occasion proactively to assist immigrants, thereby improving children's life chances as well as supporting the well-being of their regions.

Furthermore, educators and schools should also take a stand in resisting the increase in school segregation. Schools with concentrated poverty are linked to many variables that affect a child's overall chance to be successful: parent education levels, availability of advanced courses, teachers with credentials in their subject areas, instability of enrollment, dropouts, untreated health problems, lower college-bound rates, and many other important factors. Orfield and Yun (1999) stress that the nation's largest program of compensatory education, Title 1, has had great difficulty achieving gains in schools where poverty is highly concentrated. Immigrant children ought not be educated in schools that are racially, linguistically, and socially segregated.

In conclusion, because of the increasing numbers of immigrants, including large portions of undocumented immigrants, the nation is split on what policies should be retained or developed for handling immigration issues and working with the immigrant population. In these circumstances, the task of educating immigrant children certainly becomes more difficult and complex, resolutions have to be more inventive, and, once again, the schools are the frontline for incorporating immigrants into U.S. society. In Chapter 3 we turn to the special challenge of language acquisition and retention among immigrant children.

3

Learning English and Maintaining Heritage Languages

The rapid increase in immigrant students has required schools to provide for their language transition. The vast majority of immigrant students who have come from non-English-speaking countries do not speak English at home; however, the policies, curricula, and staff of U.S. educational systems are persistently monocultural and monolinguistic.

In this chapter, we focus on immigrant students' linguistic transitions. We acknowledge the complexities of language use and acquisition; however, we believe linguistic transition is one of the central issues to understanding immigrant student education. Workable policies require updated and accurate information from large populations. In this chapter we examine children's language transition as represented in established educational research and in parental responses to the 2000 census survey long form. We begin by reviewing the changes in U.S. language education policies as well as the patterns of language use among U.S. immigrants, especially their use of heritage languages—the languages they bring from their home communities—and then consider their second-language adaptation: English acquisition. We also compare the characteristics of heritage-language speakers across various states for 1990 and 2000. In the second part of the chapter, after summarizing our findings, we make five major recommendations for improving school practices in this area and conclude with how educators can take stands on this issue.

LANGUAGE PATTERNS AND POLICIES

The 2000 U.S. census counted over 2.4 million foreign-born children from ages 5 to 18. More than three-quarters of them came from countries where English is neither the dominant nor official language. The English Language Learner (ELL) population in U.S. schools includes not only foreign-born children, but also children born in the United States of recent immigrants. Many of these children speak languages other than English at home, and some of them live in households where no person over 14 can speak English very well. Although we focus this chapter on foreign-born children, we include comparisons across generations to show patterns of language transition.

In 2000, over 47 million people aged 5 and over reported speaking a language other than English at home. The number of heritage-language speakers increased 47% from 1990 to 2000 (31.8 million in 1990) and over 100% from 1980 to 2000 (23.1 million in 1980). Although the population aged 5 and over grew only by a quarter from 1980 to 2000, the number who spoke a language other than English at home more than doubled. The percentage of heritage-language speakers in the U.S. population in 2000 was 18%, up from 14% in 1990 and 11% in 1980, and 9.3 million children aged 5–18 in 2000 spoke languages other than English at home, an almost 70% increase from 1990.

According to the 2000 census, of the 3,786,841 ELL children aged 5–18, 64% were born in the United States and about 36% were foreign-born children. The number of ELL students enrolled in U.S. public schools increased by 65% between 1994 and 2004. Latinos constituted the majority of ELL children in the nation (65.6%). California had the largest proportion of the ELL students in 2003–2004 with nearly 30%; Texas, Florida, New York, Illinois, and Arizona divided another 30% among them, while the remaining 40% of ELL students were spread across the rest of the country. In some new gateway states, the ELL student population increased very rapidly. For example, the ELL student population grew four- and fivefold in North and South Carolina, Georgia, and Kentucky between the 1993–1994 and 2003–2004 school years, and about 80% of all these ELL students reported Spanish as their heritage language. Finally, ELL children in new gateway states were twice as likely to live in poor families as compared to children who spoke only English or spoke English very well (National Center for Education Statistics, 2007).

Acquiring fluency in English is crucial for immigrant children's academic success; however, maintaining the ability to communicate in home languages with people in family and community is also necessary for immigrant children's cognitive development, psychological well-being, and healthy socialization. Children who speak two or more languages competently have an advantage in the global economic market, and bi- or multilingualism benefits the United States' cultural exchanges, international trade, and national security. Nevertheless, language policy in the United States has been highly politicized; as a result, many of these policies have been unsuccessful in ensuring the proper education of immigrant children for any purpose (Kubota, 2004).

Public sentiment behind U.S. immigration and language policies has often been polarized: advocates for bilingualism want to preserve and revitalize heritage languages and cultures, and advocates for assimilation press for the cultural "melting pot" with English-only practice. Bilingualism has a long tradition in North America, dating back to pre-colonial times and continuing to the present (Wiley, 2002). Before the 1850s, German bilingual schools flourished in the United States, and Spanish-English and French-English bilingual schools were also present in the Southwest. However, school-related English-only laws aimed at German Catholics were passed in 1889, shortly after German immigration peaked in the United States (Wiley, 2002). Educational language policies from the 1850s to the 1950s were closely tied to the immigration and educational policies described in our preceding chapters and also reflected intra- and international political and economic circumstances. For example, before World War I, German immigrant communities in some Midwest states taught both English and German to their children, including children not of German ancestry. After a U.S. Supreme Court case (*Farrington v. Tokushige,* 1927) found in favor of immigrant communities over the wishes of the territorial governor before World War II, Chinese, Japanese, and Korean languages were taught in Hawaiian public schools. However, World War I brought an end to the English-German bilingual education programs. English-Japanese bilingual education programs fared no better during World War II.

In 1970, the U.S. Supreme Court ruling in the *Lau v. Nichols* case favored the Lau family, and 12 other Chinese-American students, who sued the San Francisco school district. Crawford (1991) maintains that *Lau v. Nichols* has greatly boosted bilingual education in the United States. Three types of bilingual programs were proposed at that time: (1) transitional bilingual education; (2) bilingual-bicultural education; and (3) multilingual-multicultural education (Wang, 1995). The bilingual educational policy known as the Lau Plan was aggressively enforced from 1975 to 1981 in nearly 500 school districts, mostly in the southwestern United States (Crawford, 1991). However, the spread of bilingual education has met with increasing resistance since the 1980s. The best way to provide children with the transition from home languages to English has become a polarized political battlefield affected by nativism, xenophobia, and ethnocentrism. California's 1998 Proposition 227 and the current movement there for English-only instruction, led by California millionaire Robert Unz, are forceful and orchestrated efforts against bilingual education. The English-only initiative is currently spreading rapidly through the United States. Over 20 states have passed official English laws, and over a dozen other states have comparable versions of similar legislation pending (Tse, 2001). The push for English-only education has been increasing as federal and state support and funding for bilingual education dwindles.

Our position is that language shifts and English acquisition parallel the history of immigrant adaptation to U.S. culture, society, and economy. According to Portes and Rumbaut (1996), language in the United States—and perhaps in some other nations also—has a meaning broader than the instrumental value of communication. English has become the symbol of commitment to Americanization; the acquisition of unaccented English and the dropping of native languages represent the test of an immigrant's patriotism. Language homogeneity has come to be seen as the cornerstone of collective identity. Immigrants are compelled to speak English well, but also to speak English only, as a prerequisite of social acceptance and integration. Nieto (1995) has argued that bilingual education is threatening to the status quo because it has the potential to empower traditionally powerless and subordinate groups and affect their and their family members' Americanization process

We believe language transition, in the development of proficiency in English, may involve either the loss or maintenance of bilingualism for children of immigrant families. Scholars who study how children develop proficiency in English believe English learning is neither merely a technical skill nor manageable in isolation. Instead, they see English language learning and transitions of children as a holistic and lifelong process continuously formed and reformed by interplay among three activities: acquisition of English, retention of the heritage language, and attrition of the heritage language. They contend that learning English and learning and maintaining heritage languages are affected by many uncontrollable factors such as place of birth, age of arrival, length of U.S. residency, years of schooling in the first language, social class, parental education, and such (Heath, 1986; Jiobu, 1988; Rubinstein-Avila, 2007).

Other researchers (e.g., Cummings, 1989; Lessow-Hurley, 2003; Lindholm-Leary, 2001) also emphasize the interplay of linguistic environments (including household languages, the extent to which households are linguistically isolated, neighborhood language diversity, etc.); the availability of resources for learning English (the English-speaking environment and neighborhood linguistic segregation, the quality of English-as-a-Second-Language or bilingual education programs, etc.); the sociocultural environment of the community (racial, ethnic, linguistic, and economic segregation); and language politics at local and national levels. All of these factors contribute to a child's linguistic adaptation and must be studied. Depending on the circumstances of a child's transition from monolingual proficiency (either in English or in the heritage language) to bi- or multilingual proficiency, different outcomes may result: true bilingualism, pseudo-bilingualism (preferring either English or the heritage language), or alinguisticism, which is lack of competence in either language. Without studying language transition as a whole, we cannot fully comprehend why some immigrant children learn English more effectively than others, and, more important, how children's linguistic adaptation is related to their academic success as well as their healthy social and psychological growth.

Heritage-Language Patterns

The majority of immigrants to the United States in the last 100 years did not speak English when they first arrived; they learned English afterward. This is true today. The 2005 American Community Survey (U.S. Bureau of the Census, 2006) indicates that the following heritage languages are spoken at home by the U.S. foreign-born population: 16% speak English only, 46% speak Spanish, 18% speak Asian or Pacific Island languages, and 17% speak Indo-European languages other than English. However, the task of educating English speakers is becoming more complicated for U.S. schools. Not only has the percentage of immigrants from non-English-speaking countries been increasing rapidly, but also has the variety of the languages immigrant children speak. More than 400 languages are reported to be spoken in U.S. schools. That is, most languages in the world have been spoken by U.S. students, and more than 70 languages are spoken by at least 10,000 students in the United States.

Table 3.1 shows the top five languages that most children spoke at home in 2000. About 6.5 million children spoke Spanish, and more than a quarter of a million children spoke Chinese.[1] French, Vietnamese, and German were also spoken by 180,000 or more children. The majority of non-Hispanic White and Black children spoke English at home—95% and 94%, respectively. The most common heritage languages among non-Hispanic White children were Spanish, German, French, Russian, and Arabic, and the most common heritage language spoken among Black children was Spanish. However, French Creole, Amharic, and Cushitic were also spoken as heritage languages by considerably large numbers of Black children. The most common heritage languages spoken at home among Latino children were Spanish and Portuguese, with a variety of other languages spoken by less than 0.02% of Latino children. The heritage languages most frequently spoken at home among Asian children were Chinese (11%), Vietnamese (8.5%), Korean (6.5%), Tagalog (3.3%), and Miao (3.3%).

Language variations within ethnic and nationality groups make designing language programs and training and recruiting language teachers and counselors complex. Although most Latino children in the United States speak Spanish, some speak Portuguese; others use tongues indigenous to regional areas of Latin America. Foreign-born children from Africa report speaking more than 50 different languages, and about 70 different languages are spoken by immigrant children who classify themselves as Asians.

---

1 We have estimated these numbers for the entire U.S. population based on calculations of the data from the PUMS 5% of the 2000 census.

TABLE 3.1   Major Languages Spoken at Home Among U.S. Children 5–18 Years Old by Race-Ethnicity and Hispanic Origin, 2000

	Total (2,694,073)	Non-Hispanic White (1,776,174)	Hispanic (403,633)	Black (365,857)	Asian (112,044)
Language	English	English	Spanish	English	English
(N)	(2,227,340)	(1,682,680)	(278,108)	(344,780)	(46,713)
%	82.7	94.74	68.9	94.2	41.7
Language	Spanish	Spanish	English	Spanish	Chinese
(N)	(322,070)	(33,361)	(123,938)	(8,732)	(12,302)
%	12.0	1.9	30.7	2.4	11.0
Language	Chinese	German	Portuguese	French Haitian Creole	Vietnamese
(N)	(12,566)	(8,640)	(188)	(7,754)	(9,496)
%	0.47	0.48	0.05	2.1	8.5
Language	French	French		Kru	Korean
(N)	(11,675)	(8,398)		(1,003)	(7,302)
%	0.43	0.47		0.27	6.5
Language	Vietnamese	Russian		Amharic	Tagalog
(N)	(9,698)	(5,615)		(539)	(6,044)
%	0.36	0.32		0.15	5.4
Languages	German	Arabic		Cushite	Miao
(N)	(9,119)	(4,853)		(451)	(3,237)
%	0.34	0.27		0.12	3.3
Total %	96.3	99.45	99.65	97.4	76.4

SOURCE: Data from PUMS 5% of the 2000 Census (U.S. Bureau of the Census, 2003a), compiled by authors.

1 99.6% of Hispanic children speak either Spanish or English at home.
The remaining .4% speak many other languages: Russian, Polish, Chinese, Korean, Vietnamese, Tagalog, Japanese, Hawaiian, Arabic, and Navajo were among those reported to be spoken at home. However, less than 0.02% of Hispanic children speak each of these languages.

2 Percentages do not total to 100 because of rounding for subgroups.

Among the 70 languages, 25 are spoken by at least 1,000 Asian immigrant children, and 11 languages are spoken by at least 10,000 Asian immigrant children. Chinese immigrant children alone speak 20 languages—for example, Thai, Malay, and Vietnamese—although Chinese is the most common language, spoken by over 90% of Chinese foreign-born children. The linguistic situation becomes more complicated when considering different versions of languages. For example, a quarter million Chinese-speaking children reportedly speak eight different dialects. Thus, speakers of Mandarin or Cantonese, the two most common dialects among Chinese Americans, cannot easily communicate with each other through oral conversation.

School districts need to know the number of languages spoken, and the proportions of the school-age population who speak each of the languages, to allocate financial and human resources and make appropriate long- and short-term plans for language and other services. School districts also need to know the heritage languages spoken among the adult community to allocate language resources that aid communication between schools and newcomer ELL students, as well as to support the local community's efforts to maintain heritage languages for their children. Furthermore, familiarity with local language resources and dialects used in the community can assist schools both in deciding which foreign language classes to offer to students and in-service teachers and in evaluating supplementary linguistic resources (i.e., native speakers of a particular foreign language among students and local residents) for their classes.

Heritage-Language Attrition and Retention

Immigrants have not been the only people in the United States to lose their native languages. Indigenous peoples in North America and elsewhere have lost or are losing their heritage languages. Language attrition and retention has become a worldwide challenge, and the significance of maintaining heritage languages while acquiring a new language was long ignored by researchers. Recent research on bilingualism has shown that it fosters creativity and provides certain cognitive advantages: flexibility and greater abilities in abstract thinking and concept formation (Genesee & Nicoladis, 1995; Northwest Regional Educational Laboratory, 2001). Historically, a monocultural bias predominated in language research, and bilingualism was viewed as a "language handicap." Children who spoke a heritage language were labeled with "more limited vocabularies, deficient articulation, and more grammatical errors" than monolingual English-speaking children. However, ethnographic research has revealed that immigrant children who completed the transformation from heritage monolingualism to English monolingualism in a very short of period of time often faced emotional, psychological, and social problems. The rapid transition weakens ties to the children's original language and culture and may cause identity confusion and ambivalence toward heritage cultures, resulting in academic and socialization problems in school. When children are deprived of the language they, their families, and their community use most effectively, they lose the ability to participate fully in their families and communities, and their sense of social alienation increases (Lindholm-Leary, 2001).

Researchers (Crawford, 2000; Tuan, 1998; Tse, 2001) have further argued that the debates on monolingual versus bilingual education are not only academic but also political. While U.S. policymakers urge foreign-language education for monolingual English-speaking children, it makes no sense to deprive bilingual speakers of their heritage languages. Requiring language-minority students to give up their heritage languages and culture to become Americans neglects the untapped resources and language skills present in an ever-growing language-minority and immigrant population. Regretfully, foreign languages may even become stigmatized after contact with English because of the perceived lower status of the people who speak them. Meanwhile, endeavors for native-language retention among immigrant children and their families have been ignored, and the detrimental effects of native-language attrition have been invisible. Many factors contribute to heritage language loss or retention: political, social, economic, educational, cultural, linguistic, and personal, such as interlanguage marriages. To examine patterns of recent language assimilation here, we focus our analysis on the language transition across generations for races-ethnicities with large populations.

Heritage-Language and English Monolingual Speakers—The Intergenerational Transition

In this section, we first discuss the intergenerational patterns for how children become monolingual English speakers, as well as the trends among bilingual speakers. We then consider what affects children's language transition, focusing on immigrant children in comparison with all other children. Different ethnic and nationality groups achieve English proficiency and maintain heritage languages at different paces and to a different degree, and these variations are discussed in Chapters 5–8.

The 2000 census asked the following questions about language: "Is this person speaking a language other than English at home?" and "What language does that person speak?" The data generated from responses to these questions are limited because, being self-reported, they do not indicate how well the person spoke the heritage language. However, these questions are still useful indicators of language transition for the entire U.S. population, as well as for various population segments.

Table 3.2 shows that, in 2000 among U.S. children aged 5–18, 82.7% spoke only English at home and 17.3% spoke language(s) other than English at home. The percentage of children who spoke only English markedly increased with each generation. Although about 12% of school-age children in the first generation who came to the Unites States at age 6 or older speak only English at home, about 18% of 1.5-generation children who came to the United States at age 5 or younger speak only English at home, a 50% increase. Furthermore, the percentage (35.3%) of second-generation children who spoke only English doubled that of the 1.5 generation. It appears that the massive language shift from bilingual to English monolingual for U.S. children happens between the second and third generation: the percentage of third-generation children who spoke only English almost tripled that of the second generation, with 95% of U.S. third-generation, school-age children speaking only English at home. This cross-generation language shift indicates a speedy linguistic assimilation into English monolingualism within two generations. Likewise, it suggests a rapid diminishing of use of heritage languages. A persistent, though moderate, gender difference is also evident: females were more likely than males to switch to English-only among the first and 1.5 generations; in the second and later generations, they also were more likely than males to hold onto the heritage language longer.

TABLE 3.2   Percentages of U.S. Children 5–18 Years Old by Race and Ethnic Origins, Immigration Status, and Self-Reported English Proficiency and Language(s) Other Than English Spoken at Home, 2000

	All Children	Immigrant 1st Generation	Immigrant 1.5 Generation	Child of Immigrant	Native
	(2,694,073)	(58,376)	(67,416)	(365,206)	(2,203,075)
All Children					
Speaking English Only					
Both Sexes	82.7	11.8	17.9	35.3	94.4
Male	83.1	11.5	17.0	36.2	94.8
Female	82.2	12.0	18.9	34.3	94.0
Speak a Language Other Than English at Home					
Speak No English					
Both Sexes	.28	3.4	3.2	.7	.04
Male	.29	3.7	3.4	.7	.04
Female	.27	3.0	3.0	.7	.04
Do Not Speak English Very Well					
Both Sexes	5.6	40.1	30.5	18.9	1.7
Male	5.6	41.3	31.1	19.1	1.6
Female	5.6	38.9	29.6	18.6	1.8

(Continued)

TABLE 3.2 (Continued)

Speak English Very Well					
Both Sexes	11.5	44.7	48.4	45.1	3.9
Male	11.0	43.5	48.4	44.0	3.6
Female	11.9	46.0	48.5	46.3	4.2

All Non-Hispanic White Children					
(N)	(11,776,174)	(10,745)	(10,812)	(89,619)	(1,664,998)

Speaking Only English					
Both Sexes	94.7	18.7	29.3	68.5	97.1
Male	95.0	18.5	28.4	69.3	97.3
Female	94.4	18.9	30.2	67.6	96.8

Speak a Language Other Than English at Home

Speak No English					
Both Sexes	0.04	0.7	1.3	0.2	0.02
Male	0.05	0.7	1.5	0.2	0.03
Female	0.04	0.8	1.2	0.1	0.02

Do Not Speak English Very Well					
Both Sexes	1.5	27.6	18.2	6.2	1.0
Male	1.4	29.3	18.8	6.2	0.9
Female	1.6	25.7	17.5	6.1	1.1

Speak English Very Well					
Both Sexes	3.7	53.0	51.2	25.2	1.9
Male	3.5	51.2	51.4	24.3	1.7
Female	4.0	54.7	51.0	26.2	2.1

All Hispanic Children					
(N)	(403,633)	(28,756)	(36,601)	(182,790)	(155,486)

Speaking Only English					
Both Sexes	30.7	3.9	5.9	12.2	63.3
Male	31.3	4.0	5.8	12.9	64.4
Female	30.1	3.7	6.1	11.5	62.1

Speak a Language Other Than English at Home

Speak No English

Both Sexes	1.5	6.2	4.8	1.3	.3
Male	1.6	6.7	5.1	1.2	.25
Female	1.5	5.5	4.6	1.4	.25

Do Not Speak English Very Well

Both Sexes	23.2	47.4	37.7	27.7	10.0
Male	23.6	47.7	38.0	28.2	10.2
Female	22.8	47.1	37.5	27.2	9.9

Speak English Very Well

Both Sexes	44.5	42.5	51.5	58.8	26.5
Male	43.5	41.5	51.2	57.8	25.2
Female	45.6	43.6	51.9	59.9	27.8

All Black Children

(N)	(365,857)	(4,677)	(3,933)	(26,046)	(331,201)

Speaking Only English

Both Sexes	94.2	47.5	56.5	74.6	96.9
Male	94.7	47.4	57.8	75.5	97.3
Female	93.8	47.6	55.1	73.6	96.5

Speak a Language Other Than English at Home

Speak No English

Both Sexes	0.03	0.3	1.3	0.07	0.01
Male	0.03	0.2	1.0	0.08	0.01
Female	0.04	0.4	1.6	0.05	0.01

Do Not Speak English Very Well

Both Sexes	1.8	20.1	15.5	5.5	1.1
Male	1.7	21.1	15.1	5.4	0.9
Female	2.0	19.0	15.9	5.6	1.3

(Continued)

TABLE 3.2   (Continued)

Speak English Very Well					
Both Sexes	3.9	32.2	26.8	19.9	2.0
Male	3.6	31.4	26.1	19.1	1.8
Female	4.2	33.0	27.4	20.7	2.2
All Asian Children					
(N)	(112,044)	(13,733)	(15,674)	(63,883)	(18,754)
Speaking Only English					
Both Sexes	41.7	10.2	27.7	37.4	90.9
Male	41.9	9.6	25.2	38.7	91.4
Female	41.4	10.8	30.2	36.1	90.5
Speak a Language Other Than English at Home					
Speak No English					
Both Sexes	0.4	0.7	1.1	0.24	0.01
Male	0.4	0.8	1.1	0.25	0.01
Female	0.4	0.6	1.0	0.24	0.01
Do Not Speak English Very Well					
Both Sexes	19.1	41.8	26.1	17.5	2.2
Male	19.8	43.8	28.2	17.8	2.2
Female	18.3	39.5	24.0	17.1	2.1
Speak English Very Well					
Both Sexes	38.9	47.4	45.1	44.9	6.9
Male	37.8	45.8	45.5	43.3	6.4
Female	39.9	49.1	44.8	46.5	7.4

SOURCE: Data from PUMS 5% of the 2000 Census (U.S. Bureau of the Census, 2003a), compiled by authors.

1 Foreign-born children who immigrated to the U.S. at age 5 or younger are classified as 1.5 generation and those who immigrated to U.S. after age 5 are classified as 1st generation.

2 Percentages do not total 100 because of rounding for generation subgroups.

Intergenerational language transition varies widely, but consistently, across race-ethnicity. Figure 3.1 suggests that Asian children may have the fastest language shift among all children: 90% of first-generation Asian immigrant children spoke their heritage language at home, but less than 40% in the second generation still spoke those languages. Moreover, only 9% of Asian children in the third generation still spoke their heritage languages. The percentage changes are remarkable even at the 1.5 generation. Asian immigrant children who came to the United States at age five or younger were three times more likely to be monolingual English speakers than Asian children who came to the United States at an older age. Hispanic children also lost their heritage language rapidly. Although only 3% of first-generation Hispanic children spoke only English at home, third-generation Hispanic children were 21 times as likely to speak only English at home. The major language transition from bilingual to monolingual English happens during the transition from the second generation (12.2%) to the third generation (63.3%) for Hispanic children. For non-Hispanic White children, the major language shift happens between the first and second generations; for Black children, the language shift happens at a relatively even pace across each generation. The generation patterns across gender, as discussed in the previous paragraph, were consistent across the racial-ethnic groups

We offer several explanations for these trends. First, the proportions of children from non-English-speaking countries vary across groups. Hispanic immigrant children in the first generation were the least likely to speak only English at home (3.9%). Black immigrant children, in contrast, were the most likely to speak only English at home (48%) because a much higher proportion of Black immigrants came from countries such as Jamaica and Trinidad and Tobago, where English is the official language (see Chapter 6). The rates of first-generation immigrant children who were

FIGURE 3.1 Percentage of U.S. Children (5–18) Who Spoke English Only by Race, Hispanic Origin, and Generation, 2000

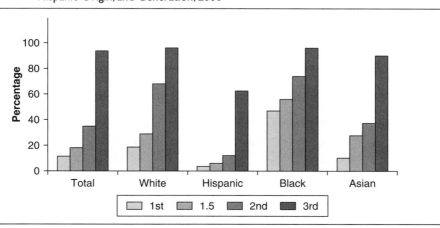

SOURCE: Data from PUMS 5% of the 2000 Census (U.S. Bureau of the Census, 2003a), compiled by authors.

monolingual English speakers were 10% for Asian children and about 19% for non-Hispanic White children. The high percentage of English-speaking non-Hispanic White children is attributable to the proportion of these children who came from English-speaking countries such as the United Kingdom, Canada, Australia, and New Zealand. Likewise, a considerable number of Asian children came from places where English was one of the official governmental languages, such as the Philippines, India, Hong Kong, and Singapore.

Another collection of sociodemographic and sociocultural factors may also affect heritage language maintenance or loss. In a study using census data from the year 2000, Rong (2005a) found that English-only families were more likely than heritage-language families to have a higher income, but income made no significant difference on a child's ability to speak a native tongue among children whose family language is not English. Age also had no relationship to native-tongue speaking, as children of various age groups are equally likely to speak a non-English language if their families do so, given that such other factors as age of arrival and length of U.S. residency are constant. An ethnographic study also revealed the relationship between birth order in a family and the likelihood of speaking heritage languages among the siblings (Rong & Jo, 2004). If both parents speak English, firstborn children were more likely than their younger siblings to maintain heritage-language proficiency longer, because firstborn children usually communicate more with parents, and thus have more opportunities to practice the heritage languages. The other children may communicate more among their siblings, who tend to speak English as their main or only language. Finally, the younger children are at entry to the United States and the longer they have resided in the country, the less likely they are to speak their native tongues, although the decline in heritage language use varies from group to group, depending on the language environment at school and home and in the community. What we see here, then, are languages interacting with and influencing each other, which we pursue in the next section.

Second-Language Adaptation—English Acquisition Among Heritage-Language Speakers

Learning English is crucial for immigrant students' success in U.S. schools and the workforce. With few exceptions, newcomers unable to speak English face enormous obstacles. Learning English is a basic step toward participating in the life of the larger community, getting an education, finding a job, obtaining health care or social services, and applying for citizenship. Language is one of the principal initial barrier confronting recent immigrants, from the least educated farm workers to the most educated professionals.

Learning a second language is a process known as linguistic adaptation. This refers to a situation wherein the child must speak two languages simultaneously at some point after immigration, and thereafter switches back and forth between languages. Although the ideal situation is to become bilingual in English and the heritage language, the most likely scenario is that the child becomes monolingual in English. This adaptation process requires many linguistic, psychological, and social skills, especially for those whose languages are quite different from English—such as Chinese, Vietnamese, Arabic, and many African languages. Mastery of the new language is not simply a matter of learning a language in the classroom, especially if acquisition of the new language is seen as the first step in losing the native tongue. The achievement of mastery over the language of a receiving society may be a profound psychological and sociological event to immigrant children and their families. It may even be seen as the first step in rejecting the original homeland and may consequently be resisted, consciously or unconsciously, by the immigrants themselves or, in the case of children, by their parents (cf. Rodriguez, 1982). A very practical educational issue is also involved. Pain and frustration occur within immigrant families because of the loss of effective communication between native-speaker parents and English-only-speaking children. Children need parental guidance and direction during their growth, including while they are learning the new language in their adopted country. Immigrant children, who acculturate into a society unfamiliar and alien at best, hostile and rejecting at worst, may need more help and comfort from their parents than native-born children. Conversations on intimate topics, such as friendship, dating, and marriage, are difficult enough without attempting them across language barriers. These realities present a dilemma to parents and children when pursuing English proficiency means a rapid loss of the ability to communicate in their heritage language.

We have one indicator of how quickly and well children develop proficiency in speaking English from the U.S. Bureau of the Census inquiry about a person's ability to speak English in the 2000 census. People who filled out the census long-form questionnaire were asked to evaluate themselves and others in the household for oral English usage with the following categories:

- Very well: no difficulty in speaking English;
- Well: minor to moderate problems;
- Not well: seriously limited; or
- Not at all: spoke no English at all.

Several researchers compared this self-reported oral English proficiency with samples from people who were interviewed, either over the phone or face-to-face, in English; they concluded that only people who reported speaking English "very well" had actually developed English proficiency (U.S. Bureau of the Census, 2003d). Therefore, speaking English "very well" has been used to signify oral English proficiency, and the other three stages (speaking English "well," "not well," and "not at all") were combined to indicate a lack of oral English proficiency. This question, like the two questions about heritage languages we discuss in the previous section, is certainly not an ideal scientific metric to accurately evaluate children's proficiency in English. Furthermore, oral English proficiency is different from the level of English proficiency required for school achievement. Collier (1995) describes the typical stages of second-language acquisition. Children may experience an initial "silent period" of one to three months, then begin to speak in short phrases. After a year, children begin to use conversational skills. The basic interpersonal communication skills of the first three stages may take 5–7 years. After this period, students may enter the cognitive academic language-proficiency stage wherein they are capable of using complex sentence structures to express creative and critical thinking. Although the census question cannot reveal these complex stages of proficiency, it has been asked in previous censuses and thus provides a consistent indicator over time of oral English proficiency in the U.S. population.

Oral English Proficiency

According to data from the 2000 census, among the 2.5 million foreign-born children residing in the U.S., 15.7% (375,400) reported speaking only English. Among children who spoke their heritage language at home, 3.3% (82,842) reported speaking no English, 35% (879,000) reported speaking limited English, and 47% (1,174,500) reported speaking English very well. Altogether, just under 1 million children—38.3% of all foreign-born children—had some difficulties speaking English. However, some foreign-born children, especially immigrant children in middle and high school, reported speaking English very well yet still may have had severe problems in reading and writing English that were undetected by teachers. Learning subject matter at these grade levels requires a much higher level of English mastery than simply speaking it.

Table 3.2 shows that more than 3 million children who reported speaking a language other than English at home were not proficient in English. The categories included in this group are children who speak "no English at all," and children who speak English but do not speak English "very well" (including children who speak English "not well" and who speak English "well"). More than 151,000 children reported speaking no English at all, including 121,000 Hispanic children, who comprised over 80% of all children who reported speaking no English. Across the cohorts of children who reported speaking no English were 3.4% of first-generation children, 3.2% of 1.5-generation, less than 1% for the second generation, and less than 0.1% for the third generation. The number of children reported as not speaking English very well also declines markedly across generations: 40% for the first generation, 31% for the 1.5 generation, 19% for the second generation, and less than 2% for the third generation. Although each generation has fewer and fewer children with problems in English proficiency, fewer and fewer children appear to be bilingual, as indicated by children who both speak a language other than English at home and speak English well. Although the 1.5-generation children were most likely to be bilingual (almost one in two), the proportions drop to less than 4% of children in the third generation. A clear gender pattern, consistent with the findings of Bleakley and Chin (2004), is also evident: female children were less likely to report speaking no English in the immigrating generation, and they were more likely to be bilingual across the generations.

Table 3.2 also reveals racial-ethnic differences in language transition across generations. The percentage of children who reported speaking no English was low for White, Black, and Asian immigrant children, and the percentage further declined with each generation. For all generations, a higher proportion of Hispanic children than other children reported speaking no English; however, Hispanic children also reported a higher percentage of bilingual speakers among all children for the 1.5, second, and third generations. In the third generation, 26.5% of Hispanic children were likely to be bilingual, a rate almost six times higher than the national average and much higher than in the third generation of either Black or White children. In gender difference, female children were generally less likely to report speaking no English, and they were more likely to be bilingual across race-ethnicity and generation groups.

Because the census data did not include how well the children spoke their heritage language, we summarize data gathered by Portes and Hao (1998), using purposefully developed instruments and local samples to examine the rates of bilingualism among 5,000 second-generation 8th- and 9th-grade students of 77 nationalities in southern California and south Florida in the 1990s. In contrast to the census questions, children in Portes and Hao's study were asked about their English and heritage-language proficiency more comprehensively, including their self-perceived proficiency in oral, reading, and written forms. The findings reveal that, although the majority of second-generation children had developed excellent English proficiency, less than half of them had kept some ability in their heritage language. Furthermore, about three-quarters of the children studied preferred using English, and only about a quarter of the children were functionally bilingual. Although the English preference rates are very similar across ethnic groups, Hispanic children were most likely to maintain their heritage language (61%) and develop bilingual fluency (39%), and Asian children were least likely to maintain their heritage language (20%) and develop bilingual fluency (7%). Second-generation Asian children also had the lowest percentage who reported knowing English well (90%) or very well (68%).

What Affects Immigrant Children's Second-Language Adaptation?

Why do some children—and some adults—learn English faster, better, and more easily than others? Unsurprisingly, children who grow up in families where English is the only spoken language learn English more easily than children raised in homes where a language other than English is spoken, but the latter circumstances characterize most immigrant homes. A less obvious influence on English acquisition is exposure to English before immigration. English has become the worldwide language of business, science, and technology as well as youth cultures. With the exception of very young children, many immigrants arrive in the United States with an existing linguistic repertoire. The linguistic attributes of newcomers are the product of language-specific selection processes (Stevens, 1994). First, other things being equal, potential immigrants born and raised in countries where English is a dominant or official language have a large advantage over potential immigrants born and raised in non-English-language countries. A considerable proportion of the immigrants legally admitted to the United States during the 1970s and 1980s had some exposure to English before immigrating. About a quarter of the immigrants legally admitted during the 1990s and 2000s were from English-language countries, or countries where English was one of the official languages. Second, people who did not come from English-language countries believed that exposure to English through education, training, and social and cultural life in home countries was important to the rapidity and ease with which they could adjust to an English-language-dominated environment. Although the linguistic characteristics of immigrants on arrival in the United States contribute to their children's acquisition of English, data supporting this contention are generally unavailable.

Scholars (e.g., Bleakley & Chin, 2004; Heath, 1986; Jiobu, 1988; Rumbaut, 2005) have argued that many demographic factors affect English acquisition, especially length of time in the United States and age on arrival. Other variables such as characteristics of children and their families' socioeconomic conditions, living arrangements, and degree of linguistic isolation are also influential. In this section, we examine the effect of each of these factors on English acquisition among immigrant children who speak a heritage language at home. We also discuss the aggregated effects of two or more factors on English acquisition in these children. Neighborhood language diversity and English environment, and the availability and quality of ESL or bilingual education programs, are also relevant, and undoubtedly a child's acquisition of English results from the interaction of all these effects; however, we have no data to examine these interactions directly.

Exposure to English

Over time and with increased exposure to second-language input, individuals' levels of proficiency in a second language increase. Figure 3.2 shows the percentage distributions of immigrants' self-reported proficiency in speaking English in 2000, in relation to the length of their residency in the United States. These data show that oral English proficiency increased the more time they had lived in the United States. This general

FIGURE 3.2 Percentage of Heritage-Language Speaking Children (5–18) Who Reported Speaking English Very Well by Years of U.S. Residency and Age of Arrival, 2000

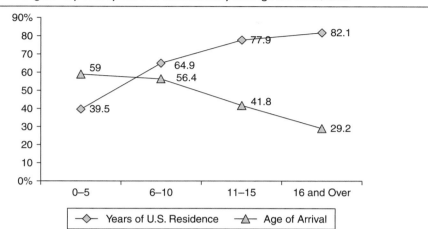

SOURCE: Data from PUMS 5% of the 2000 Census (U.S. Bureau of the Census, 2003a), compiled by authors.

finding—and the interpretation that this relationship reflects English language acquisition as it occurs in the United States—is common (Jasso & Rosenzweig, 1990). Length of residence in the United States is probably the best single indicator of exposure to English language input. Age of arrival is another influence on children's English acquisition. The decline of English proficiency illustrated in Figure 3.2 reveals that children who arrive in the United States at an older age may have more difficulty in linguistic adaptation.

Table 3.3 shows that immigrant children's proficiency in English in 2000 had improved over a period of 15 years of U.S. residency. Among all children who spoke a language other than English at home, 40% of those who had been in the country for five or fewer years reported speaking English very well, while double that proportion of children who had been in the United States ten years or longer reported that they spoke English very well. After 15 or more years' of U.S. residency, 82% of immigrant children had developed English proficiency and also maintained their heritage language. However, the data provided by Figure 3.2 and Table 3.3 show that a marked change in linguistic adaptation occurs between years 6–10 of U.S. residence. After this period, the pace of language adjustment slowed down somewhat, and after a period of 10–15 years' residence, the rates for oral English proficiency improvement changed little. Conversely, the percentage of children who reported speaking no English declined with the length of residence; 7% of immigrant children reported speaking no English within their first five years' U.S. residency, but less than 0.5% of immigrant children reported the same after having lived in the United States for more than 15 years.

Table 3.3 also indicates the influence that the age of an immigrant on arrival in the United States has on linguistic adaptation. Among heritage-language-speaking (HLS) children who came to the United States at age 5 or

TABLE 3.3   Percentages of English Proficiency by Year of U.S. Residence and Age of Arrival for U.S. Foreign-Born Children 5–18 Years Old Who Speak a Language Other Than English at Home, 2000

	Total	0–5	6–10	11–15	16 and Older
	(106,845)	(51,614)	(36,495)	(16,683)	(2,053)
Years in U.S.					
Children Who Spoke a Language Other Than English at Home and Reported:					
Speaking No English	3.8%	7.1%	0.9%	0.7%	0.4%
Speaking English Not Very Well	41.2%	53.4%	34.1%	21.4%	17.5%
Speaking English Very Well	55%	39.5%	64.9%	77.9%	82.1%
	Total	0–5	6–10	11–15	16 and Older
	(106,845)	(55,344)	(33,155)	(16,264)	(2,082)
Age of Arrival					
Children Who Spoke a Language Other Than English at Home and Reported:					
Speaking No English	3.8%	3.9%	2.4%	5.4%	15.1%
Speaking English Not Very Well	41.2%	37.1%	41.3%	52.8%	55.0%
Speaking English Very Well	55%	59.0%	56.4%	41.8%	29.2%

SOURCE: Data from PUMS 5% of the 2000 Census (U.S. Bureau of the Census, 2003a), compiled by authors.

younger, 60% had developed English proficiency, compared to less than 42% of children who came to the United States when they were 11 or older. Age 10 appears to be a critical point; the English acquisition for children who came to the United States after that age was noticeably slower. This is consistent with other research on language learning. Many researchers believe that the ability to learn new languages declines with age. For example, Bleakley and Chin (2004) report that immigrants from non-English-speaking countries who arrive young—up to age 8 or 9—attain English language skills comparable to those of immigrants from English-speaking countries. For children who are older on arrival, however, English-language skills are markedly lower. Newport (2002) explains this by positing that younger children can construct instrumental variables for linguistic adaptation, whereas Lennerberg (1967) points out that linguistic adaptation is linked to physiological changes in the brain and to maturational changes just before puberty that may sharply reduce a child's ability to acquire second languages.

Interplay of Other Factors on English Proficiency

In addition to length of U.S. residency and age at arrival, many other factors in children's lives affect English acquisition. We examine the relationship of several factors from the 2000 census data with the linguistic adaptation of immigrant children.

Over 9.3 million children reported speaking language(s) other than English at home, including approximately 2.1 million foreign-born children. Table 3.4 suggests the adverse effects of children's physical and learning disabilities on their English proficiency. Although physical disabilities appear to have a noticeable effect on the oral English proficiency of all children speaking a heritage language at home, learning-related disabilities appear even stronger, especially among immigrant children: 55% of immigrant children who do not have learning-related disabilities reported oral English proficiency compared to only 37% of learning-disabled children.

Residential location also appears to affect children's linguistic adaptation. Children living in suburban areas were more likely to develop oral English proficiency than children living in other areas, with the lowest proficiency rates observed in immigrant children living in inner-city areas (52%). This connection between residential locations and oral English proficiency is consistent for all children; however, the proficiency differences

TABLE 3.4   Percent of U.S. Children 5–18 Years Old Who Reported Language(s) Other Than English Spoken at Home and Spoke English Very Well by Social, Economic, and Other Characteristics and Immigration Status, 2000

	All Children (466,733)	Immigrant Children (106,845)
Percent of Children Who Reported Physical Disabilities (One or Multiple Limitation(s) in Mobility, Personal Care, Hearing and Visual, etc.)		
Yes	62.1%	49.8%
No	66.3%	55.3%
Percent of Children Who Reported Learning-Related Disabilities (Difficulties in Remembering, etc.)		
Yes	57.1%	37.2%
No	66.3%	55.3%
Percent of Children Who Lived in Inner-City Area		
Inner City	63.4%	51.8%
Suburban	69.1%	59.1%
Other Areas	65.4%	53.8%

(Continued)

TABLE 3.4   (Continued)

Percent of Children Who Lived in Household by Poverty Level		
Under Poverty	57.5 %	44.3%
Poverty Index Between 101–500	67.8%	57.8%
At or Above 500 Poverty Level	76.2%	72.7%
Percent of Children Who Lived in Households Without Father		
Yes	68.7%	57.2%
No	65.5%	54.7%
Percent of Children Who Lived in Households With Two Parents		
Yes	65.7%	55.3%
No	67.1%	53.7%
Percent of Children Who Lived With Parent (Household Head) Having Less Than Four-Year Education		
Yes	53.5%	40.5%
No	67.0%	56.6%
Percent of Children Who Lived With Parent (Household Head) Having at Least a High School Diploma		
Yes	71.2%	56.2%
No	60.1%	47.2%
Percent of Children Who Lived With Parent (Household Head) Having at Least a Four-Year College Degree		
Yes	75.1%	69.0%
No	64.3%	51.6%
Percent of Children Who Lived in Linguistically Isolated Household		
Yes	34.7%	23.9%
No	76.2%	79.6%

SOURCE: Data from PUMS 5% of the 2000 Census (U.S. Bureau of the Census, 2003a), compiled by authors.

Note: Percentages are the proportion of children in each category who report English proficiency.

by residential location seem more distinctive for immigrant children than for other children.

Family income, family living arrangements, and parental education are other factors that may affect immigrant children's linguistic adaptation. Table 3.4 reveals substantial gaps in oral English proficiency among children from poor, middle-class, and affluent family backgrounds. HLS children, both immigrant children and all children, from families with higher incomes are more likely to have oral English proficiency than those from lower income families; however, the size of the gaps by family income are more striking for immigrant children, especially within the poverty segment. The size of the proficiency gap between affluent and poor immigrant families is 28.4%, however, the same gap among all children is only 18.7%. Moreover, among the nation's poorest children, although about 58% of all children who speak heritage languages at home reported oral English proficiency, the percentage for immigrant children was only 44%, 14% lower. These self-reported English proficiency gaps are not as great for children with higher family incomes. The proficiency gap between all children and immigrant children for those with moderate family incomes is 10%, and for children from the most affluent families, it is only about 3.5%. Approximately three-quarters of immigrant children from affluent family backgrounds reported proficiency in speaking English compared to less than half of poor immigrant children.

Nevertheless, among all foreign-born children who speak a language other than English at home, the relationship of family income to children's oral English proficiency is greater in the first 3–5 years after immigration, but this connection gradually diminishes as the length of U.S. residency increases. Using 1990 census data, we (Rong & Preissle, 1998) found that, for all children who immigrated to the United States between 1987 and 1990, those from higher-income families were 53% more likely than their counterparts with less affluent backgrounds to report oral English proficiency. The size of the gap gradually diminished the longer each cohort resided in the United States. Among the 1975–1979 cohort, children from higher-income families were only 16% more likely to report oral English proficiency than their less affluent counterparts. In contrast to family income, we found that family living arrangements have little connection to HLS children's English proficiency. The observable tiny differences actually favored both immigrant and all children who lived with their mother only.

Parental education, on the other hand, is strongly related to HLS children's English proficiency. As might be expected, immigrant and all children with more highly educated parents were more likely to report oral English proficiency than children with parents with less education. The trend is very clear in Table 3.4. We emphasize two points here. First, at each increasing level of parental education more children were reported to have English proficiency. However, the size of the differences across levels of parental education was different for all children than that for immigrant children. All children who speak a heritage language at home, including many native born children, appear to be especially advantaged when their parents have finished high school, but for immigrant children the stronger connection is with parents who have completed college. Second, the pattern related to parental education is very similar to that related to family income: The English proficiency differences between immigrant children and all children were larger for children whose parents had less education, but the difference is smaller when parents have postsecondary or higher levels of education.

Finally, Table 3.4 shows a striking, but predictable, gap in English-speaking proficiency between HLS children who live in linguistically isolated households and children who do not: the gap is 55.7% among immigrant children and 41.5% among all children. However, immigrant children who speak heritage languages in homes that are *not* linguistically isolated report somewhat higher English proficiency than do the broader group of all heritage-speaking children who do not live in linguistically isolated families.

Some of these patterns are illuminated by other language studies. Stevens (1994), for example, suggests that individuals with less education are disadvantaged in the acquisition of a complex cognitive skill such as proficiency in a second language. Data from other sources indicate that, among lesser-educated young adolescents who immigrated as school-age children, lack of literacy in their first language is an impediment to second-language learning. Other studies relate adults' and children's success in the acquisition of a second language to social, cultural, and institutional factors (Gonzalez, 2003). The Urban Institute (2006) has reported that poverty, legal status, and other measures of hardship appear to affect children's English proficiency. DiCerbo (2000) emphasizes the impact of poverty on children's language transition. Many ELL children and youth live in segregated neighborhoods and attend schools with other disadvantaged children, whether they are in rural areas or inner cities. Furthermore, schools with high concentrations of poor students tend to be substandard facilities. In addition, such schools may offer limited or no language support for very young children. Using inferential statistical analyses, Rong (2005a) found that some of these factors act together to have a large impact on immigrant children's English acquisition. For example, 100% of HLS speakers who came to the United States at age 16 or older, and lived in linguistically isolated households, reported limited oral English proficiency; a similar pattern characterizes children who lived in linguistically isolated households and had resided in the United States for less than five years. However, children who came to the United States at an older age (8–12) may have the same oral English proficiency as children who came to United States at a young age (0–5) if the length of residence and household linguistic status are held consistent. Rong also found that children's family socioeconomic backgrounds (inner-city location, poverty status, low parental education), in combination with the other factors, amplified the negative relationship to children's English acquisition.

Of course, factors other than those suggested by census data affect HLS children's English proficiency. For example, immigrant children schooled in linguistically-segregated schools may have more difficulty in learning English. According to SASS (the School and Staffing Survey) 1999–2000, 51% of ELL students attended schools where over 30% of their fellow students are also ELL students, but only 4% of non-ELL students go to such schools (National Center for Educational Statistics, 2005). All of these patterns change over time and across place, as we consider in the next two sections.

Demographic Changes Across Time

The rapidly expanding immigrant population and the languages they have brought with them, from 11% heritage-language speakers in the United States in 1980 to 18% in 2000, has aroused an anxiety about whether English would continue to be the integrating language. However, our findings, shown in Table 3.2, indicate a clear pattern of language assimilation over four generations. Children are rapidly learning English and losing their native languages simultaneously, and the fundamental shift toward English across the generations is unaffected by the high immigration level of the 1990s.

Table 3.5 compares data from the 1990 and 2000 censuses on the self-reported English proficiency rates of children aged 5–17 who reported speaking a language other than English at home. The percentage of children who spoke heritage languages at home increased 4.5% in a period of 10 years, and the percentage of children who spoke English with difficulty increased 1.3%. Nevertheless, the percentage of HLS children who reported speaking English very well increased 3.2%. This suggests that, despite the increase in immigration into the United States over the last few decades, immigrant children may be continuing to make a satisfactory transition to English.

TABLE 3.5   Language Spoken at Home and Self-Reported English-Speaking Ability for Persons 5–17 years, U.S., 1990 and 2000

	1990		2000	
	Number	%	Number	%
All speakers	45,342,488		53,096,003	
English only	39,019,514	86.1%	43,316,237	81.6%
Language Other Than English at Home	6,322,934	13.9%	9,799,766	18.4%
Speaks English				
Very Well	3.934,691	8.6%	6,286,648	11.8%
With Difficulties	2,388,243	5.3%	3,493,118	6.6%
Percent Who Report Speaking English Very Well Among Just Those Who Speak Language(s) Other Than English at Home		62.2%		64.2%

SOURCES: U.S. Bureau of the Census 1990 (CPHL- 96) (U.S. Bureau of the Census, 1993a) and 2000 Table 2, 2000 (PHC-T- 20) (U.S. Bureau of the Census, 2003d). Compiled by authors.

Alba and Nee (2003) argue that today's language assimilation patterns may be different from those of the early 20th century, but they do not appear to pose any threat to English as the common language. They also show how current bilingual realities of U.S. society are grounded in developments from the nation's past, especially in marginalized communities with a history of heritage languages. Crawford (2000) compares 2000 census data with census data from 110 years ago on the percentage of people who reported speaking no English. The percentage of all U.S. people who spoke only a heritage language in 1890 was higher than it was in 2000, 3.6% and 1.3% respectively, a pattern state by state as well as nationally. These data indicate the shift to English may be accelerating among recent immigrants. Martin and Midgley (2003) speculate that, because most recent immigrants settle in U.S. cities, they are more likely to be exposed to English than were workers on farms and in rural industries in previous centuries. These shifts in settlement occur across space as well as time.

Geographic Variations

Knowing the geographic dispersion patterns of school-age HLS children and understanding how these patterns have developed over time can be helpful in policy making and educational planning because these comparative data illustrate state and regional differences as well as the changes across two points of time, 1990 and 2000. In Chapter 2, we discuss the effect of the immigration movement on states over the last 25 years by putting them into three roughly defined categories: traditional gateway states, new gateway states, and other states. In this section, we further consider the characteristics of children who were heritage-language speakers in these three geographic areas. We compiled data from census 1990 and 2000 data and pulled out several states for each category to serve as examples to illustrate our points.

Table 3.6 shows that the U.S. HLS population of children aged 5–17 increased 55% between 1990 and 2000. Although the three traditional gateway states—California, Texas, and New York—still had more HLS children than the rest of the nation, their percentage increase was moderate because of the vast number of HLS children already resident in these states in 1990. However, the increase in the number of HLS students is striking in new gateway states because of the increase in newcomers in these states with very small immigrant populations in 1990. The number of HLS children doubled between 1990 and 2000 in North Carolina and increased by more than 150% for Georgia and Nebraska. Wyoming and West Virginia, classified as "other states," had no significant increases in HLS children between 1990 and 2000. Although Wyoming, a state with a very small population, had a 34% increase in HLS children from 1990 to 2000, West Virginia's overall population decline from 1999 to 2000 was accompanied by a similar decline in HLS children.

TABLE 3.6 Linguistic Characteristics of Children 5–17 Who Spoke a Language Other Than English at Home, 1990 and 2000

	Percentage Increase In Heritage-Language-Speaking-Population (1990–2000)	Spoke Heritage Language		Spoke English Very Well		Spoke Spanish		Percentage Lived in Linguistically Isolated Household	
		1990	2000	1990	2000	1990	2000	1990	2000
United States	55%	13.9%	18.4%	62%	64%	66%	70%	28%	27%
Traditional Gateway States									
California	53%	35%	42.6%	58%	61%	72%	76.1%	36%	31%
New York	32.5%	23.3%	26.9%	65%	67%	59%	58%	27%	27%
Texas	42%	28.2%	32.4%	60%	63%	92%	91%	28%	27%
New Gateway States									
Georgia	166%	4.5%	9.4%	65%	58%	48%	63%	18%	31%
North Carolina	116%	4.7%	8.2%	60%	57%	58%	70%	10%	30%
Nebraska	150%	3.6%	8.4%	70%	61%	50%	73%	11%	28%
Other States									
Wyoming	34%	3.9%	5.4%	72%	73%	62%	67%	13%	12%
West Virginia	-21%	2.7%	2.4%	69%	66%	42%	53%	5%	8%

SOURCES: Data compiled by the authors from the PUMS 5% of census data for 1990 and 2000 (U.S. Bureau of the Census, 1993b, 2003a).

Patterns among the traditional gateway states, the new gateway states, and other states varied. First, traditional gateway states continued to have a much higher percentage of HLS children than the country as a whole, while new gateway states had lower percentages despite substantial increases over time. Other states had less than a third of the national percentage. Second, trends among HLS children in English proficiency and in linguistically isolated households in new gateway states were the opposite of those for the nation and for traditional gateway states. For the nation as a whole between 1990 and 2000, a higher percentage of HLS children reported English proficiency and a lower percentage reported living in linguistically isolated households. Although the three traditional gateway states are consistent with the national trends, the new gateway states had a decrease in the percentage of HLS children who reported speaking English very well and an increase in the percentage of children who reported living in linguistically isolated households. Third, the proportion of Spanish speakers among HLS children increased nationally and also within most individual states, with the exception of New York and Texas.

Many factors explain the changes between 1990 and 2000 for the various types of states. The new gateway states had higher percentages of newcomers in their HLS population than did the traditional gateway states where the heritage-language speakers were spread out between the first and second generations. Heritage-language speakers who are newcomers need time to learn English and are more likely to live in linguistically isolated households. Furthermore, the traditional gateway states have established ethnic and immigrant communities with years of experience and solid infrastructures in education and social service systems for dealing with immigration issues, including linguistic adaptation. However, the new gateway states have many opportunities to make new policies and develop effective systems to work with HLS children. Despite their rapid increases in the HLS population, the proportions are still much smaller in the new gateway states than in the traditional gateway states. Although HLS students attend schools that are linguistically segregated and the level of linguistic segregation appears to have risen in the past 5 years, the level of linguistic segregation is lower in schools in new gateway states. Census data further indicate that in the 22 new gateway states where only 4% of students are ELL, 38% of them attend schools where more than 30% of the students are ELL. In the six traditional gateway states, where 13% of the students are ELL, the percentage is much higher—60% of ELL students are in schools where more then 30% of the students are ELL (U.S. Bureau of the Census, 2003c; U.S. Bureau of the Census, 1993a).

Summary

The language transition patterns we have presented here indicate that Spanish continues to be the most common heritage language spoken by K–12 students in the U.S., although more than 400 other languages are spoken. Although more children are speaking heritage languages than ever before, English-only is the dominant pattern among U.S. children. Limited English proficiency is most common among the foreign-born, especially among first-generation immigrants. The prevalence of limited oral English proficiency declines across generations and largely disappears by the third generation, though rates for the third generation vary considerably across groups. Hispanic children have the highest percentage of limited English proficiency in the third generation, but Hispanics continue to show a clear trend toward greater mastery of English with each passing generation.

Living in a linguistically isolated household, length of U.S. residency, and age of arrival are related to children's English proficiency. Other likely influences are disabilities, especially learning-related disabilities, socioeconomic status, living in inner cities, and membership in certain ethnic groups; also, males tend to be somewhat more disadvantaged than females in developing oral English proficiency. The interaction of these factors may further hinder immigrant children's chances to develop English proficiency.

Finally, we compared language data from 1990 and 2000 and found a higher percentage of HLS children who had oral English proficiency in 2000 than in 1990. The exceptions to this pattern occurred in new gateway states where newcomers dominate the increase in HLS populations. Having identified some of the patterns of language transition among immigrants, we now turn to recommendations for educational policymakers and other leaders in U.S. schools.

RECOMMENDATIONS

As we have noted previously, the increase in the heritage-language-speaking population in the midst of three decades of massive immigration has prompted fears that the position of English as the traditional U.S. language is threatened. Some educators voice related concerns that bilingual education may delay children's English acquisition and jeopardize the development of children's language abilities for life (Krashen, 1999; Rossell & Baker, 1996). However, we have found no systematic evidence for such claims in the established research scholarship. On the contrary, most scholars (e.g., Genesee, Paradis, & Crago, 2004) advocate policies and practices based on an additive bilingual model, rather than a subtractive, monolinguistic language education approach.

In Chapter 1, we discuss additive and subtractive approaches to the acculturation of immigrants to the United States; these perspectives permeate the debates on language transition. The additive bilingual model emphasizes a holistic process of language transition, including the consideration of second-language learning of English, heritage-language maintenance, and children's social, cultural, and psychological development. The subtractive language education model, on the other hand, is a deficit model that considers immigrant children's heritage languages as a roadblock to the development of their English proficiency. The goal of programs based on the subtractive model is the quick replacement of the heritage language with English. The inferiority of students' heritage languages is subtly or explicitly assumed. This approach has serious costs for immigrant children, their families, the schools, and the country. Some scholars (e.g., Nieto, 2000; Skutnabb-Kangas, 2000) charge this subtractive model as linguicism, a form of prejudice intended to devalue some people's languages and to create and maintain unequal divisions of power and resources among groups. As a result, immigrant and language minorities might be kept economically and politically subordinate (Valenzuela, 1999).

In contrast, the additive bilingual model of language transition is built on valuing the strengths students have in their native language and culture, drawing on the instrumental values of ethnic identity and the resources in the immigrant family and community. This broad approach allows students to use their transnational experience to achieve cross-cultural and multilinguistic understanding and skills. Proposed by Collier (1995), the additive bilingual model, focusing on the linguistic authenticity of school-age children, is based on four components: the interdependence of sociocultural processes with linguistic, academic, and cognitive development. Our five recommendations for aiding heritage-language speakers' effective language transition are based on four premises:

First, educators must understand the diversity in children's language situations and the many influences on heritage-language speakers' linguistic transition. We have discussed many of the factors suggested by the U.S. census surveys, but others remain; for example, the social and cultural capital children bring to language learning, and the effectiveness of the instruction delivered by educational institutions (Thomas & Collier, 1997).

Second, the second-language adaptation, the learning of English, is one of the links in HLS children's linguistic transition. The other two possibilities, first-language loss or maintenance, are inseparable parts of the same process. In both the short and long terms, policies and practices must consider all facets of linguistic transition to be supportive for children.

Third, language education policies and practices affect children's development in their lives outside the classroom. Any practice to aid children's language transition focusing only on the replacement of a heritage language with English and limited to classroom instruction is too narrowly defined and may negatively influence children's academic, social, and psychological development.

Fourth, language policies and practices should be developed from our understanding of the current situation, our knowledge of the past, and our projection for the future. Because ELL student numbers will only increase at current rates of immigration, all schools must set language education service as a permanent priority. Our past 150-year history has demonstrated that as soon as immigrants and their children learn English, they are replaced in the pool of ELL learners by new immigrants and their children.

Recommendation One: Understand Language Transition and Its Variations Among Heritage-Language Speakers

Many educators become frustrated because programs and curricula work effectively with some ELL children, but not with others. We have suggested some of what may cause these variations. However, developing academic English proficiency takes much longer than simply becoming fluent in U.S.-accented English. Because our own research shows that children vary in many ways and live in complex realities, we believe that no single prescription works effectively for all children. States and local school systems should be well informed about the characteristics of the ELL children they serve, and they should identify the available resources to design and tailor their programs to meet a wide diversity of students' needs, including students across grades and school levels and in a range of socioeconomic environments.

Oral English Proficiency and Academic English Proficiency Are Different

Oral English proficiency may be necessary, but is not sufficient for academic English proficiency. Guerrero (2004) reports that school personnel often fail to distinguish between "social" English, also known as basic interpersonal communication skills (BICS), and "academic" English, or cognitive academic language proficiency. Social English is an individual's ability to engage in informal conversation; academic English requires a more comprehensive and analytic level of understanding. These two kinds of communication in English also require somewhat different vocabularies. Researchers have found that some native-born ELL students may speak fluent, "unaccented" English, but still have difficulties in reading and writing English (Nappi, Harritt, Rong, Chang, Hayes, Jung, Jackson, & Clark, 1999). The popular idea that a motivated student can acquire a second language in a short time may be a misconception. Several scholars (e.g., Collier, 1987; Collier, 1995; Hawkins, 2004), examining child immigrants and language-minority students in many different regions of the United States, with varying characteristics and backgrounds, have found that developing oral communication skills in English as a second language requires two or three years. Acquiring proficiency in understanding instructional language, however, requires up to four to six years. Four to twelve years of second-language development are needed for the most advantaged students to reach deep academic proficiency and compete successfully with native speakers. This length of time, of course, varies according to students' abilities, motivations, readiness, and access to effective English instruction and other learning resources in English in the home, community, and school. In our own working experience with ELL children, immigrant children may fully develop their oral and written English proficiency after 10 or more years of U.S. residency, but they also may either lose their fluency in their native tongues or fail to develop fluency in their heritage language that matches their age-appropriate psychological maturation and level of social sophistication.

Because linguistic adaptation for academic proficiency in English takes years, researchers (e.g., DiCerbo, 2000) oppose the sudden withdrawal of the support of the home language. They argue that the use of the home language in bilingual classrooms enables the ELL child to avoid falling behind in school work and also provides a mutually reinforcing bond between the home and the school. This bond enables ELL learners to participate more effectively in school activities, providing them in turn with more opportunities to learn English.

Elementary and Secondary Newcomers Have Different Language Needs

Requirements for academic English proficiency differ from grade to grade. Functioning well in middle or high school requires high levels of academic English proficiency; students must use English to learn core subject matter and demonstrate their content knowledge at the grade level in question. Teenage newcomers who enter middle or high school shortly after immigrating to the United States require extensive language supports so that they can master English quickly and catch up their study of content areas. However, classroom assistance of this type may be rare in middle and high schools. Even when bilingual or ESL services are available, such supports may lack the quality or adequate duration to have any effect, or they may not be geared to helping these students learn the higher-level subject matter (Fuligni & Hardway, 2004). Especially in the new gateway states, the typical programs provided are ESL, and they are not bilingual in any sense.

When bilingual instruction is unavailable for ELL learners entering middle or secondary U.S. schools, alternatives have been suggested: (a) teach the second language through academic content; (b) focus on strategies to develop thinking skills and problem-solving abilities; and (c) provide continuous support for staff development, particularly for activation of students' prior knowledge, respect for students' home language and culture, cooperative learning, interactive and discovery-based learning, intense and meaningful cognitive-academic development, and ongoing assessment using multiple measures. To build rapport and model learning, teachers and support staff who work with ELL learners should learn some phrases and expressions in the languages that their students speak (Ovando & Collier, 1998; Villalva, 2006).

Although teenage newcomers may face the pressure to develop proficiency in English in little time, younger children have their own problems. In our previous study of immigrant education from the 1990 census data, we (Rong & Preissle, 1998) found that seven of ten 5-year-old newcomers had difficulties speaking English, and a third could not speak any English at all. Immigration during this critical period of language development can devastate children not only in their linguistic skills in a first language, but also in concept development, logical reasoning, and other cognitive abilities. Children who lack age-appropriate skills in their first language usually experience additional difficulties when trying to learn a second language. That may be the case for many young immigrant learners with limited English skills. Our findings also indicated that young children are more likely than older children to live in inner cities, in families with lower incomes, and in linguistically isolated households. However, because of language barriers, lack of information and networks, or long working hours, ELL students' parents may not know where and how to find help for their children. A much higher percentage of 5- to 7-year-old immigrant children have not attended school, compared to U.S.-born children of the same age group. Lack of oral English proficiency among these young children may account for their absence from school, but it further aggravates the English acquisition problem. Programs such as Head Start and Smart Start, designed to help children from disadvantaged backgrounds, must make every effort to recruit these children by reaching out to immigrant families and communities.

Recommendation Two: Recognize Variations in "Limited" English Speakers

In this section, we discuss three groups of students who may need special language supports: alinguistic learners, U.S.-born English speakers whose families use heritage languages, and newcomers from English-speaking countries. These students' problems have been either unrecognized, underestimated or ignored, or misunderstood by teachers and administrators.

Alinguistic Learners

Children who have lost the ability to use their heritage languages but never developed proficient English may be overlooked. Some young children may periodically be more or less alinguistic during their language transition: they may be losing their heritage language before they develop full English proficiency if they came to the United States at an earlier age, or if they were born in the United States into a linguistically isolated household. If this alinguistic period continues too long, recovery requires long-term and extensive language therapies. G. Li (2003, 2007) has reported several very serious alinguistic cases among Chinese immigrant children in Canada. Chinese-speaking parents and English-speaking teachers had assumed the children were communicating in the language they did not know. No one realized until too late that these children were not using any language appropriate to their age. To detect this problem, teachers and parents should be communicating. Recommendations for the appropriate treatment of these children require assessing the whole family's linguistic situation, including the family's language and socioeconomic backgrounds, the parents' English proficiency, and the parents' education.

Academic English Proficiency in Second-Generation Children

Many children who are born in the United States and speak fluent, U.S.-accented English lack adequate academic English proficiency to complete school tasks appropriate to their ages. These students fall into two categories (Alba, 2002). The first category includes children from the many immigrant families who have been unable to integrate economically and socially with mainstream society and who thus remain linguistically isolated, such as refugees, immigrants who work in ethnic enclaves, and undocumented immigrants. The second includes those who experience high levels of migration back and forth, and thus spend significant time in their parents' home countries. To help both groups of children, educators should evaluate their academic English proficiency and refer them to work with specialized teachers who can provide them with workable strategies for these circumstances.

English Difficulties Among Children From English-Speaking Countries

English spoken in other countries is not the same as U.S. English. Even fluent English-speaking immigrants from Britain, Australia, or Canada need to learn U.S. idioms, expressions, and accents. Linguicism has many forms. One form is tolerating only phonetic U.S. English in U.S. classrooms. Students who suffer most from this problem are immigrants from former British colonies, where English is the official language. For example, Black immigrant children from Africa or the Caribbean are often placed in ESL classes because teachers cannot understand their accents. The lack of teacher understanding coupled with peer teasing can make class participation isolating or humiliating for these immigrant students (Alidou, 2000) and others who speak English with accents. One immigrant student described his feelings about this:

> [It is] not that I do not know enough words to express my thoughts. I know I sounded awkward when I spoke with Melanie for the first time, but she should have tried to understand that this is not my native tongue. . . . She should not have laughed and said that my accent was hilarious. I decided there is no need to try again, I contented myself with the fact that nobody noticed my accent in the paper. (Popova, 1999, p. 82)

Recommendation Three: Support Efforts to Maintain Heritage Languages

Linguists and developmental psychologists have argued that the ability to speak a native tongue may help a child learn English better, and social workers and sociologists agree that open communication between children and parents benefits children in their schooling and later careers (e.g., Genesee & Nicoladis, 1995). However, fluent bilingual students remain the exception. Many schools consider heritage-language speaking to be a hindrance to children's improvement of their English skills, and very few U.S. schools encourage immigrants to retain their heritage language. This situation has been aggravated by the No Child Left Behind (NCLB) legislation of 2001.

Program Selection

Language policies shift with changing sociopolitical goals and movements; this results in different financial priorities across states and communities. According to Genesee, Paradis, and Crago (2004), language transition programs in the United States fall into five categories: bilingual-education programs, developmental-bilingual programs, two-way-immersion-bilingual programs, transitional-bilingual programs, and second-language (L2)-only or English-only programs (ESL). The first three are associated with the additive bilingual-education framework aimed to promote children's academic knowledge and cognitive skills along with the development of full bilingualism. The last two programs shift children into an English-only, monolinguistic direction.

Examining interactions among student background variables and instructional treatments and their influence on learning outcomes, researchers found that two-way bilingual education at the elementary-school level is the most promising program model for the long-term academic success of language-minority students. English speakers and language-minority students learn academically through each other's languages, language-minority and language-majority parents are involved in close home-school cooperation, and schools provide continuous support for staff development (Collier, 1995). Transitional bilingual programs are reasonably acceptable programs for secondary schools because few alternatives have been developed for the high school level. Nevertheless, ESL programs have been the predominate model for supporting ELL students' second-language adaptation in most new gateway states. The support and cooperation of immigrant communities require communication with parents about the goals, objectives, approaches, and outcomes of bilingual programs. Parents of ELL children must be informed about the type of language instruction their children are receiving and told that they have the right to refuse bilingual instruction for their children.

Influence of the No Child Left Behind Legislation

Allocating resources for programs that serve ELL students is a political and a financial decision. Requiring special services and specifically trained teachers for ELL programs has been a new financial demand of school systems in new gateway states and an increasingly heavy burden for school systems in traditional gateway states. Financial support from the federal government is available, but hardly sufficient. School programs can be funded by federal grants, such as Title II grants, a program under the NCLB Act of 2001. Title II provides formula grants of supplemental financial assistance to states and schools to ensure that children who are limited English speakers, including immigrant children and youth, attain English proficiency, develop high levels of academic achievement in English, and meet the same achievement standards as other children (Crawford, 2006). However, because the NCLB Act created a formula for subsidizing the instruction of English-language learners, allocations for states and school districts depend on their 5 to 17 year–old ELL population, as counted in the 2000 census and in some later surveys conducted by the U.S. Bureau of the Census. To obtain the funds they are entitled to receive, schools must track local changes in their immigrant populations.

NCLB has generated many controversies during its implementation and evaluation, especially concerning its influence on schools and children's lives. To ensure that ELL students perform well on standardized content area assessments, changes have been made in curricula for ELL students regardless of which programs—dual language, bilingual, or English immersion—they attended. NCLB proponents believe that, because ELL students are required to learn the same content and pass the same assessments as other students, NCLB could better integrate and align ELL students' classroom instruction with instruction provided to all students. Because NCLB holds schools accountable for ELL students' English proficiency, the law may alter language programs and produce an increased focus on rapid English acquisition. Critics of NCLB argue that the "one test fits all" practice is narrowing the curriculum only to subjects covered by standardized tests, especially in schools that have difficulty meeting their performance targets (e.g., Valenzuela, 2005). With English proficiency foremost among their goals, schools may come to rely less on dual-language-immersion programs that build students' English and native-language skills, instead adopting ESL transitional bilingual or English-immersion programs, even for younger ELL students.

School officials may be more inclined to immerse ELL students exclusively in English, regardless of an ELL student's readiness to learn exclusively in English or readiness to acquire subject matter at a particular grade level. Parents who want their children to continue receiving at least some instruction in a language other than English may find their options increasingly limited. This shift in language education may particularly affect ELL children from disadvantaged family backgrounds, because they lack supplementary resources for their linguistic transition. Our position on NCLB is consistent with what we have advocated in the other chapters. We believe that NCLB's decontexualization model is inadequate for already disadvantaged children. Children with more resources, however, are likely to have access to support for their heritage-language development.

Community Language Schools

The organizations that have traditionally shouldered responsibility for maintaining children's heritage languages are ethnic community language schools. They also provide an ethnic system of supplementary education (Zhou & Kim, 2006). Many ethnic groups have a history of over 100 years of operating such schools during weekends and summer breaks. For example, many Chinese have Saturday Chinese Language Schools, and Jewish communities offer Sunday Hebrew Schools. Rather than studying heritage languages in classes in regular school, students may be participating in after-school activities and extracurricular events that assist in the learning of the heritage language. Parents and other individuals in the community often organize and run these events. Depending on the needs of the community and the resources available, children may be taught their heritage language by a qualified language teacher or by community volunteers and parents. Ethnic language schools may not merely teach the parental native language, which sometimes may not interest children and youth; they may also provide a range of academic-related programs and recreational activities that supplement regular school curricula and, more important, serve as a place for children to interact with one another and do their homework. Ethnic language schools also create job opportunities for educated HLS adults and provide children and their parents with role models of successful adults in their ethnic community. Regular schools can rely on community language schools as community centers to work with parents on upcoming events in school districts, as well as distributing information on children's health and social welfare and/or changes in curriculum, programs, and schedules (Rong & Jo, 2004).

Because these community language schools maintain children's heritage languages and support general educational goals, they compensate for the lack of public funds and public facilities in many ethnic neighborhoods. School districts should find ways to work with community language schools to aid bilingual and dual-language efforts. State education departments can also collaborate with language schools to find and retain qualified teachers for ELL programs, encourage children to attend language schools regularly, award official foreign-language credit hours to children who fare well in the language schools, and retrain language schoolteachers for state licensure for bilingual or foreign language programs certified in many school districts. To maintain language resources (in addition to English) needed by the United States and support immigrant communities, government officials at all levels should consider providing funding for community language schools.

Finally, Portes and Rumbaut (2006) advocate mutual adaptations and accommodations across multiple ethnolinguistic groups in the workforce, in education, and around all communities. Schools need to encourage children to retain their mother tongues—if not by formal instruction, then in informal activities, such as cultural and social occasions. Teachers may ask immigrant children about the activities in their weekend language schools and praise children for this extra effort to maintain their heritage languages. Foreign-language speech competitions also encourage immigrant students to be bilingual. Unfortunately, competitions of this kind usually involve only European languages such as French and Spanish—rarely any Asian or Middle Eastern languages—partly because of availability of qualified teachers and partly because language politics affect educators and the general public, as well as heritage-language speakers themselves. The more prestigious and valued any culture or language is in the host country, the more accepted and supported immigrants feel when they practice their language.

Recommendation Four: Understand and Support Parents' English Acquisition

Educators may wonder why, having made the move to the United States, the majority of adult immigrants speak heritage languages at home. In the United States, the shift from a heritage language to English has usually occurred over three generations. Adult immigrants have commonly not learned English well. Most non-English-speakers who immigrate to the United States after they enter adulthood do not reach a high level of oral English proficiency and often retain heavy accents for the rest of their lives, though they may be highly accomplished in their careers. Two familiar examples are Henry Kissinger, Secretary of State in the 1970s, who immigrated when he was nearly 18 years old, and Arnold Schwarzenegger, film star and governor of California, who immigrated to the United States in his early 20s. Although language facility can always be improved, late language learners may never have the fluency of a native speaker. For this and other reasons, immigrant adults prefer to use their native tongues at home, especially if they have spouses who speak the same language. Their children may be transitionally bilingual; some using their parents' languages at home and English at school, but the majority lose their heritage language and becoming monolingual English speakers. This often causes complicated situations in parenting and other cross-generational communication. Although schools can do many things to support child-parent communication in immigrant families, at the least teachers should ask their students how they plan to communicate with their non-English-speaking parents if they decide to give up their native tongue completely. This is a question we have asked our own linguistic minority students many times. Sadly, we often see their regret many years later, when some of the children sit in university foreign-language classrooms to relearn their heritage language as young adults.

Most immigrants of all ages want to learn English. However, as we have emphasized, acquiring a new language is difficult for an adult, particularly for people who work long hours in linguistically isolated ethnic enclaves. Some 1.2 million adults were enrolled in state-administered English-as-a-Second-Language (ESL or English Literacy) programs during 2003–2004, but these classes frequently have long waiting lists. Because adult English proficiency helps children become fluent, schools should run or support family literacy programs in their own facilities or in community centers. Another interest schools may have in family literacy programs is their potential for identifying appropriate bilingual professionals or para-professionals to assist teachers in working with ELL students either in mainstream classrooms or in bilingual or ESL classes.

Funding for adult education is an issue. The federal government provides funding for states to support English-language learning by adults (NCELA, 2006), but it is complicated by NCLB requirements that mean states must set priorities for available monies. Although some adult immigrants can participate in family literacy programs in local schools with their children, these programs' focus is on children; many immigrant adults may have no access to such programs, and others may find that they do not meet their needs. For alternative sources of funding, schools may turn to private foundations or local businesses. Construction companies, for example, may fund adult literacy programs because they usually hire the largest cluster of recent immigrants.

Recommendation Five: Retrain Foreign Language Teachers

Because of the rapid increase in ELL students, many foreign language teachers in new gateway states have been diverted to bilingual education or teaching English as a second language. The assumption is that, if they can teach Spanish, for example, they can teach English to Spanish-speakers. Although some of the training and skills used in teaching a foreign language are applicable to teaching English, other factors differ. Instructional purposes, curricula, the sociodemographic profiles of students, and class environments and contexts make teaching English to Spanish-speakers different from teaching Spanish to U.S. monolingual English-speakers. Assigning Spanish teachers to work with ELL students may respond to urgent local needs and help cope with the shortage of bilingual and ESL teachers. However, to make this strategy effective, educational leaders must plan to significantly retrain the foreign language teachers as part of their professional development, while aggressively recruiting and training new bilingual and ESL teachers in preservice and in-service teacher-training programs.

CONCLUSION

Communities need to hear experts' voices in their language debates. Educators—including policymakers, educational administrators, and teachers—are usually active and responsible community citizens, willing to take stands on many language education issues and to support children in their linguistic transitions. Teachers should be a major force against the misconceptions and biases that have often influenced educational planning and policy development and played roles in educational theories and practices. To serve as examples of what we mean for educators to take stands, we conclude by emphasizing the following four issues: the English-only movement, neighborhood and school segregation, NCLB and ELL learners, and financing the programs that support ELL students.

In this and previous chapters, we have reviewed problems with the subtractive approach to the acculturation of immigrant children, but the English-only movement and its outcomes may also restrict dissemination of public health, transportation, and safety messages and have severe consequences not only for immigrants themselves but also for the community. The English-only argument is not something new, though across time it has been framed differently and served different interests. This politically charged position has enjoyed several surges throughout U.S. history, accompanying the peaks and troughs in immigration. We are not in a unique situation. Martin and Midgley (2006) report that, at the beginning of the 21st century—just as at the beginning of the 20th century—most immigrants did not speak English on arrival.

In various sections of the book thus far we have introduced data on racially and linguistically isolated neighborhoods and the possible consequences of isolation aspects of children's lives, including their second-language adaptation. Language learning does not occur in a vacuum; school, family, and community all play a part. As we have noted, ELL students have been more likely to be schooled with other ELL students, and language-minority students may be further segregated racially. Many urban schools with large ELL populations also have large Hispanic, Asian, and low-income student populations, because children in immigrant families often share these characteristics. To change children's linguistically isolated situations, state and local governments and citizens need to support funding and staffing for adult English programs. More important, the ongoing residential and school segregation by race, ethnicity, income, and language must be reviewed, scrutinized, and eventually reversed.

Finally, policies and practices for language education should—like other policies providing variable responses to a diverse student population—seek multiple ways in which to work. Educators must resist the one-size-fits-all proclivities in laws such as NCLB. The additive, whole-child second-language adaptation approach relies on ELL children's strengths, including their transnational and transcultural knowledge, linguistic abilities, and life experiences. Funding is crucial for the development of school curricula and teaching strategies to support a constructivist approach to children's language learning and provide youngsters with an empowering sense of how their lives can connect productively to the new world that they inhabit (Rong, 2006; Valenzuela, 2005).

4

Educational Attainment

The rapid expansion of the immigrant student population in U.S. schools has stimulated considerable research focusing on their educational attainment. Researchers are addressing questions such as these, about which we have as yet no conclusive findings.

- How do immigrant and nonimmigrant students differ in educational attainment?
- In what areas of educational attainment do they differ?
- How do the differences vary across race, ethnicity, and gender?
- What environmental factors, separately or jointly, are connected to the differences?

Looking at patterns of race and ethnicity in immigrant children as compared with the general population of children, in this chapter we use the PUMS 5% 2000 U.S. census data to examine patterns of general school enrollment and enrollment in public or private schools among children 5–18 years old. We then analyze the school dropout rates of youth between the ages of 16–18 by race and ethnicity across gender and immigrant generations, and we consider a variety of influences on dropping out. At the end of the chapter, we provide recommendations for improving the educational attainment of immigrant students in particular and all students overall.

EDUCATIONAL ATTAINMENT
OF U.S. IMMIGRANT CHILDREN

In 2000, foreign-born children generally had lower school enrollment rates than did nonimmigrant children. Table 4.1 shows the difference nationally between foreign-born children and children overall. Foreign-born children, both as a whole and within racial-ethnic groups, had lower school enrollment rates than all children in the same population segment. The gap for Hispanic children is larger than for White, Black, and Asian children. Among both all children and all immigrant children, the enrollment rates for Asian, non-Hispanic White, and Black children were higher than the national rates for all immigrants overall and for all children overall; the rates of enrollment for Hispanic children, both in the immigrant and the general child population, were lower than the national rates.

Private-school enrollment rates also reveal differences between immigrant and nonimmigrant youngsters. Private schooling often indicates variations in family background factors, such as family income and religious needs. Enrollment in private school may also suggest students' career directions toward mathematics and science, the arts, or the military, as

TABLE 4.1 Educational Characteristics of U.S. Children 5–18 Years Old by Race-Ethnicity and Immigration Status, 2000

	All Children (2694073)	Immigrant Children (125792)
% of Children (5–18) Enrolled in Schools in 2000		
All Children	96.3%	94.5%
Non-Hispanic White	96.5%	96.2%
Hispanic	95.4%	92.8%
Black	96.3%	95.6%
Asian	97.1%	96.8%
% of Children (5–18) Enrolled in Private Schools in 2000		
All Children	10.8%	6.0%
Non-Hispanic White	12.9%	12.3%
Hispanic	6.0%	3.0%
Black	6.0%	6.0%
Asian	11.9%	8.1%

SOURCE: Data from PUMS 5% of the 2000 Census (U.S. Bureau of the Census, 2003a), compiled by authors.

well as parents' academic and behavioral expectations of their children and their views of public and private education. Table 4.1 shows that nationally, immigrant children are less likely to enroll in private schools than are children from the general population. The difference in private school enrollment between foreign-born children and those in the general populations is minimal for White and Black children, but noticeable for Asian and Hispanic children. Non-Hispanic White children, both immigrants and those in the general population, are most likely to enroll in private schools, while Hispanic immigrant children are least likely to do so. In the next section of the chapter, we focus on dropouts because this is a major issue in educational attainment for immigrants and nonimmigrants alike.

School Dropouts

Lower school completion rates for several language-minority groups can be attributed to many personal and structural factors. Some people, of all ages—foreign-born and native—have never been in any school. However, the majority of people who are neither in school nor holding a high-school diploma have dropped out of school, mostly from high school. Although each state sets different legal ages at which youths may leave school, all states require school attendance until at least age 16. Dropping out of school is central to the educational attainment among youths in many ethnic and nationality groups, especially among Hispanic groups such as Mexican, Dominican, and Central American immigrant youth

We have used several census questions to probe the school dropout issue. For purposes of this discussion, a dropout is any person aged 16–18 who self-reportedly had not received a high school graduation diploma and was not in school when the census long-form survey was conducted. The majority of these persons were high school dropouts; a small fraction had never reached high school, and some had never even started middle school. These measures may also underestimate the actual dropout rates, because the data include only children who lived with parents and other guardians. In most states, young people can live independently after reaching age 18, and we speculate that young people not in school may be more likely to live by themselves.

Table 4.2 shows the school dropout rates by immigrant generation, race-ethnicity, and gender. In 2000, for all 16- to 18-year-olds who lived with parents or guardians, the dropout rate was about 6% overall, 6.3% for males, and 4.8% for females. Hispanic youth have the highest dropout rates, and Asian youth have the lowest dropout rates. Males had higher dropout rates than females across all racial-ethnic groups, though the dropout gender ratios were more pronounced for Hispanic and Black youth than for Asian and non-Hispanic White youth.

Across generations, among all youth, the dropout rates have a recursive pattern rather than a straight-line decline from the first to third generations.

TABLE 4.2   Percent of U.S. Children 16–18 Who Were Identified as School Dropouts* by Race-Ethnicity and Immigration Status

	All Children (521,741)	Immigrant 1st Generation (23,301)	Child of 1.5 Generation (10,261)	Native Immigrant (55,753)	(432,426)
All Children					
All	5.6%	9.9%	6.9%	4.9%	5.4%
Males	6.3%	11.5%	8.1%	5.4%	6.1%
Females	4.8%	8.1%	5.6%	4.3%	4.6%
Non-Hispanic White					
All	4.7%	4.9%	5.0%	3.4%	4.7%
Males	5.3%	6.1%	4.3%	3.6%	5.3%
Females	4.0%	3.5%	5.8%	3.1%	4.0%
Hispanic					
All	9.2%	15.7%	9.9%	7.0%	8.5%
Males	10.6%	18.1%	11.8%	8.0%	9.3%
Females	7.8%	12.9%	7.7%	5.9%	7.6%
Black					
All	6.9%	4.6%	4.0%	3.8%	7.2%
Males	7.9%	4.6%	4.5%	4.3%	8.2%
Females	5.9%	4.6%	3.4%	3.3%	6.2%
Asian					
All	3.0%	3.5%	3.3%	2.3%	3.7%
Males	3.1%	3.8%	3.8%	2.2%	3.7%
Females	2.9%	3.1%	2.8%	2.4%	3.7%

SOURCE: Data from the PUMS 5% of the 2000 Census (U.S. Bureau of the Census, 2003a), compiled by authors.

* Dropouts are persons who did not graduate from high school but were not enrolled in school in 2000.

The rates decline from the first generation to the second generation, and then they rise slightly in the third generation (see Figure 4.1). With a dropout rate of 4.9%, second-generation youth, the children of immigrants, are less likely to drop out than youth of other generations. This generational pattern is consistent for both males and females overall, though males had higher dropout rates than females in each generation, and the pattern operates across all racial-ethnic groups. However, in comparing the dropout rates for the third generation to those of the first generation, we find two different patterns: Black and Asian youth had higher dropout rates in the third generation than did their first- and 1.5-generation counterparts, but non-Hispanic White and Hispanic youth in the third generation had lower dropout rates than their first- and 1.5-generation counterparts. Gender seems to further complicate these differences (see Table 4.2). For example, White females, Black males and females, and Asian females of the first generation have lower dropout rates than their third-generation counterparts, but first-generation Hispanic males and females and first-generation non-Hispanic White males had much higher dropout rates than their third-generation counterparts. Nearly one in five first-generation Hispanic male youths had dropped out of school, a proportion that dropped to less than one in ten among their third-generation counterparts.

Dropout Rates by Selected Socioeconomic Characteristics

In addition to race and ethnicity, generation status, and gender, many other variables are relevant to school dropout rates. Table 4.3 shows the relationship between school dropouts among immigrant children and children in the general population and a variety of socioeconomic variables: residential locations, poverty level, family living arrangements, parental educational levels, household language status, household heads' U.S.

FIGURE 4.1 School Dropout Rates for U.S. Youth 16–18 by Race and Ethnicity and Immigration Status, 2000

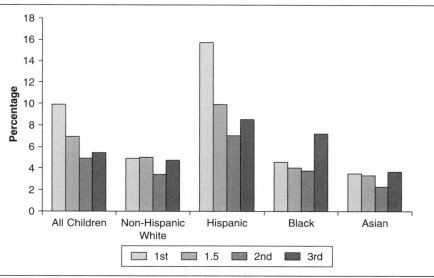

SOURCE: Data from the PUMS 5% of the 2000 Census (U.S. Bureau of the Census, 2003a), compiled by authors.

citizenship, and self-reported physical and learning-related disabilities among children.

Regardless of where they lived, immigrant youth had higher dropout rates than the general youth population. However, the difference in dropout rates between immigrant youth and youth overall is wider for those living in inner cities and other areas than for suburban youth. Immigrant and nonimmigrant youth who lived in suburban areas were least likely to drop out from school. The dropout rate for immigrant youth was highest for those living outside inner city and suburban locations in "other" and presumably more rural areas.

Poverty, of course, has a strong relationship to youth dropout rates. Regardless of immigration status, the dropout rates decline as family income increases. Immigrant youth had higher dropout rates than did the general youth population at each level of the poverty index, but the difference is much less noticeable among youth whose families were under the poverty line than youth whose families were at a higher income level. Family living arrangements are also related to youth dropout rates. Youth who resided in two-parent families and lived with a father were less likely than others to drop out of school. However, the relationships between these family living

TABLE 4.3   Percent of U.S. Children 16–18 Who Were School Dropouts by Socioeconomic and Other Characteristics and Immigration Status, 2000

	All Children (521,741)	Immigrant Children (33,562)
% of All Children Who Lived in Inner Cities		
Inner City	7.3%	9.4%
Suburban	4.3%	6.8%
Other Areas	5.8%	10.7%
% of All Children Who Lived in Household, by Poverty Level		
(The census poverty index ranges from 1 to 500, with people at 100 or lower defined as in poverty. People at 500 of the poverty index are more affluent than 75% of the U.S. population.)		
Under Poverty	11.4%	11.9%
Poverty Index Between 101–499	5.7%	8.9%
At or Above 500 Poverty Level	2.3%	3.8%
% of Children Who Lived in Households Without Father		
Yes	8.3%	9.9%
No	4.8%	8.8%

% of Children Who Lived in Households With Two Parents		
Yes	4.3%	7.9%
No	8.6%	12.8%
% of Children Who Lived With Parent or Household Head Having Fewer Than Four Years of Education		
Yes	13.0%	15.6%
No	5.4%	8.3%
% of Children Who Lived With Parent or Household Head Having at Least a High School Diploma		
Yes	3.8%	4.1%
No	12.8%	14.2%
% of Children Who Lived With Parent or Household Head Having at Least a Four-Year College Degree		
Yes	1.7%	2.4%
No	6.7%	10.7%
% of Children Who Reported Physical Disabilities (One or Multiple Limitation[s] in Mobility, Personal Care, Hearing and/or Vision, etc.)		
Yes	8.7%	10.9%
No	5.3%	8.8%
% of Children Who Reported Learning-Related Disabilities (Memory Difficulties, etc.)		
Yes	9.0%	11.6%
No	5.4%	9.0%
% of Children Who Lived With Parent(s) or Household Head(s) Who Are U.S. Citizens		
Yes	5.3%	8.8%
No	9.4%	10.9%
% of Children Who Spoke a Language Other Than English at Home		
Yes	7.6%	9.6%
No	5.1%	5.4%
% of Children Who Lived in Linguistically Isolated Households		
Yes	17.0%	17.4%
No	5.3%	6.0%

SOURCE: Data from PUMS 5% of the 2000 Census (U.S. Bureau of the Census, 2003a), compiled by authors.

arrangements and youth dropout rates are less pronounced for immigrant youth than they are for the general youth population.

Parental education is clearly connected to youth dropout rates. The more education parents reported, the less likely their children were to have dropped out of school. Immigrant youths whose parents graduated from college were 4.5 times less likely to drop out of school than immigrant youth whose parents did not graduate from college, a ratio that is 1 to 4 for the general youth population.

Table 4.3 also indicates that youth with physical disabilities or learning disabilities were more likely to drop out of school than youth who had no such conditions. With or without these conditions, immigrant youth were more likely than nonimmigrants to be school dropouts. However, the difference in the dropout rate related to physical and learning disabilities was less marked for immigrant youth than for the general youth population.

Dropout Rates by Immigration-Related Characteristics

Table 4.3 also presents the relationships between each one of the three immigration-related variables and dropout rates. First, youth whose parents were U.S. citizens were less likely to be dropouts than those whose parents were not. Second, youth who spoke a language other than English at home were more likely to be dropouts, and, third, youth who lived in linguistically isolated households were more likely to drop out of school than others. Of these three conditions linguistic isolation has a stronger relationship to dropout rates than either of the other two

FIGURE 4.2 School Dropout Rates for U.S. Immigrant Children (16–18) by Years in U.S. and Age of Arrival, 2000

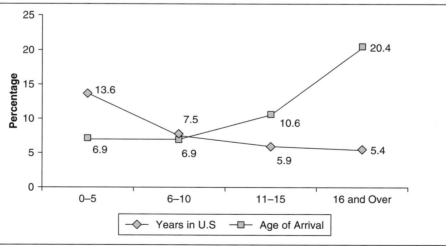

SOURCE: Data from PUMS 5% of the 2000 Census (U.S. Bureau of the Census, 2003a), compiled by authors.

TABLE 4.4 Dropout Rates by Immigration-Related Characteristics of
U.S. Foreign-Born Children 16–18 Years Old, 2000

	0–5	6–10	11–15	16 +
Years in U.S.	13.6%	7.5%	5.9%	5.4%
Age of Arrival	6.9%	6.9%	10.6%	20.4%
Self-Report	English-Only	No English	Did Not Speak Very Well	Spoke Very Well
English Proficiency	5.4%	52.3%	12.3%	5.4%

SOURCE: Data from PUMS 5% of the 2000 Census (U.S. Bureau of the Census, 2003a),
compiled by authors.

Figure 4.2 shows the relationships among years of residence in the
United States, age of arrival, and school dropout rates for immigrant youth.
The longer these youth live in the United States, the lower their dropout
rate. The dropout rate for 2000 was almost 14% among newcomers, but less
than 6% for immigrant youth who had lived in the United States for 11 or
more years. Five years' residence is the critical period for reducing these
dropout rates. Age of arrival is also connected to dropout rates. The dropout
rate for youth who had arrived in the United States at 16 or older is over
20%, but less than 8% among youth who had arrived before the age of 11.
Eleven is thus the crucial age. Gonzalez (2003) has also found that the older
the immigrants are at arrival, the lower their educational attainment is.

Finally, Table 4.4 indicates that youth who reported that they spoke no
English had a dropout rate of more than 50%. In contrast youth who spoke
only English and youth who spoke a language other than English, but also
spoke English very well, had similar low dropout rates.

Interacting Connections With School Dropout Rates

Having examined the connections between dropout rates of immigrant
youth and a variety of other factors, we consider in this section what may
be the compound effects of several of these factors when they occur together. First, we present the interrelationship among family income, linguistic status of youth, and dropout rates across race-ethnicity for
foreign-born youth. Second, comparing immigrant youth with native-born
youth, we discuss the interrelationship among family income, inner-city
residence, and school dropout rates across race-ethnicity.

FAMILY INCOME AND LINGUISTIC STATUS

In the previous section, we report that increased English proficiency and
higher family income are related to lower dropout rates, and that speaking

a heritage language is connected to higher dropout rates. These findings support a somewhat more traditional view of assimilation. However, when we examine family income and English proficiency simultaneously, to probe the relationships of heritage-language speaking with school dropout rates, the patterns of school dropout rates among various groups become complex. Table 4.5, based on 2000 census data, shows the general pattern of dropout rates for all 16- to 18-year-old foreign-born youth, from both low and high family income levels and across race-ethnicity and gender groups. For all foreign-born youth, the dropout rates were high among children who reported that they spoke no English, and the dropout rates for youth from higher-income families were a few points higher than the dropout rates for youth from low-income families. Among youth who reported that they did not speak English well, the dropout rates were significantly lower than they were among youth who spoke no English, and youth from high-income families had lower dropout rates than youth from low-income families. The pattern is the same for both males and females.

However, when we compare the dropout rates of youth who spoke only English with those of youth who reported being bilingual, specifically among youth from low-income families, we see a lower dropout rate for bilingual youth than for youth who spoke English only; but when we make the same comparison among youth from high-income families, we find a higher dropout rate among bilingual youth than in the English-only group. An interaction occurs here among gender, linguistic status, and family income. For female immigrant youth the dropout rates are lower for bilingual youth in both low- and high-income families. It is the bilingual males who account for higher dropout rates in high-income families. These two different dropout patterns, connected to gender and family income level, occur among White youth and Hispanic youth. The relationship between dropping out and being bilingual is especially strong for Hispanic male and female youth from low-income families: the dropout rates for males were half that of English-only males and for females two-thirds of the English-only females. For Asian and Black youth, being bilingual appears to lower the dropout rates only for males from low-income families. For the other subgroups, either these factors have no connection to dropping out or speaking English only appears to contribute to staying in high school until graduating. These patterns are consistent with our findings from the 1990 census (Rong & Preissle, 1998).

Family Income, Immigration Status, and Inner-City Residence

Having examined connections among family income, linguistic status, and school dropout rates, we turn to connections linking inner-city location, income, immigration status, and dropping out of school. Figure 4.3A, based on data from Table 4.6, shows that, among inner-city youth who lived in poverty, the native-born of the third generation and higher had higher dropout rates than immigrant youth. This pattern occurs in the total youth population and for all race-ethnic groups. Although the difference in

TABLE 4.5   School Dropouts by Race-Ethnicity, Family Income Level, and Linguistic Status Among Immigrant Youth Age 16–18, U.S., 2000 (in percentages)

			Male		Female	
	L	H	L	H	L	H
All Children						
No English	50.4	53.7	54.3	57.2	45.4	50
Lack Proficiency[a]	12.5	8.6	14.1	10.3	10.7	6.4
Bilingual[b]	7.4	2.6	8.2	3.4	6.6	1.2
English-Only[c]	12	1.8	12.2	1.4	11.9	2.3
Non-Hispanic White						
No English	55	X	50	X	X	X
Lack Proficiency	11	6	14	10	8	0
Bilingual	6	1.6	7	2.3	5	1
English-Only	8.8	1.8	11.4	2.0	6	1.5
Hispanic						
No English	51	53	54	55	46	50
Lack Proficiency	16	15	18	17	13	12
Bilingual	9	5.4	10	6.7	8	4
English-Only	23	6	20	5.2	25	7
Black						
No English	X	X	X	X	X	X
Lack Proficiency	12.2	0	11	0	14	0
Bilingual	5.7	3.6	4	0	7.4	6.4
English-Only	5.2	1.8	5.4	0	5	4
Asian						
No English	X	X	X	X	X	X
Lack Proficiency	5.2	4.8	5	4	5	5.6
Bilingual	4.2	2.1	5.2	2.7	3	1.5
English-Only	4.5	1.1	7	0.5	2	1.5

SOURCE: Data from PUMS 5% of the 2000 Census (U.S. Bureau of the Census, 2003a), compiled by authors. L and H indicate low and high income.

a Lack proficiency: Youth who reported speaking a language other than English and cannot speak English "very well." This category includes youth who reported speaking English "not well" and "not very well."

b Bilingual: Youth reported speaking a language other than English and speaking English "very well."

c English only: Youth who reported speaking no language other than English.

d X indicates the number in the cell is too small for a valid statistical estimate.

TABLE 4.6 School Dropout Rates Among 16–18 Year Old U.S. Children Living in Inner-City Areas by Race-Ethnicity, Immigrant Status, and Poverty Level, 2000

	At or Below Poverty Level		More Affluent Than 75% of the Population	
	Immigrant	Natives	Immigrant	Natives
All Children	11.0%	12.2%	3.9%	2.8%
Non-Hispanic White	7.2%	11.0%	2.7%	2.3%
Hispanic	13.3%	14.1%	8.7%	5.2%
Black	6.7%	12.0%	4.4%	3.5%
Asian	6.2%	22.7%	2.4%	4.3%

SOURCE: Data from PUMS 5% of the 2000 Census (U.S. Bureau of the Census, 2003a), compiled by authors.

dropout rates is smallest for Hispanics, both immigrant and native youth in this group had higher dropouts than most others.

The difference is greatest among Asian youth. Asian immigrant youth had the lowest dropout rates among youth in all racial-ethnic groups with a family background of poverty, but Asian youth in the third generation and higher with family backgrounds of poverty had the highest dropout rates. This anomaly is due to the very small population of Asian youth between the ages of 16–18 who lived in poverty in the inner city, by the highly dichotomized socioeconomic conditions we specified, and by educational attainment among various Asian nationality groups, which we discuss in Chapter 5. The patterns revealed in Figure 4.3A suggest that immigrant youth are effective in keeping themselves in high school until graduation,

FIGURE 4.3A School Dropout Rates for U.S. Inner City Youth (16–18) Who Lived in Poverty by Race and Ethnicity and Immigration Status, 2000

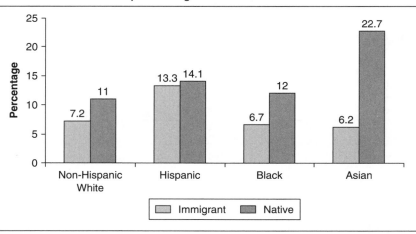

SOURCE: Data from PUMS 5% of the 2000 Census (U.S. Bureau of the Census, 2003a), compiled by authors.

FIGURE 4.3B School Dropout Rates for U.S. Inner City Youth (16–18) Who Lived in Affluent
Households by Race and Ethnicity and Immigration Status, 2000

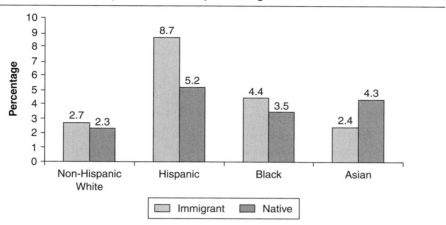

SOURCE: Data from PUMS 5% of the 2000 Census (U.S. Bureau of the Census, 2003a),
  compiled by authors.

despite the devastating effects of family poverty, poor neighborhoods, and
substandard schools.

Figure 4.3B shows the obverse of the pattern represented in Figure 4.3A.
Among inner-city youth from affluent family backgrounds, immigrant
youths had higher dropout rates than native youths among the non-
Hispanic White, Hispanic, and Black populations, and the difference is
greater among Hispanic youth than it is for the other groups. For Asian
youth, immigrants had lower dropout rates than native youth. Clearly, immigrant and native-born youth from affluent, inner-city families were less
likely to drop out of school than youth who lived in poverty, regardless of
their race-ethnicity. The explanation may be simple: though all these youth
lived in inner cities, the poor and the affluent usually do not live in the same
parts of inner cities, and youth from affluent families are also much more
likely to go to private schools than to substandard public schools.

Summary

In 2000, immigrant children were less likely than children in the general population to be enrolled in school; they were also less likely to be enrolled in private schools and more likely to drop out of school. These
patterns are connected to race-ethnicity. In the 5–18 age group, Hispanic
children had the lowest school enrollment rates, whether or not they were
immigrants. Black and Hispanic children had the lowest rates of enrollment in private schools, whether or not they were immigrants. Hispanic
youth also had the highest dropout rates among all children. However, the
school dropout rate across immigrant generations is curvilinear for all
racial and ethnic groups. Children of immigrants have the lowest dropout

rates across all race-gender groups. Dropout rates for the first generation and the third generation are inconsistent across racial-ethnic and gender groups. With a few exceptions, females had lower dropout rates than males across immigrant generations and racial-ethnic categories.

Inner-city residency, poverty, family living arrangements, parental education, and physical and learning disabilities had an apparent effect on dropout rates, but immigrant youth did not appear to be as much affected by these circumstances as their counterparts in the general population. Children's English proficiency, length of U.S. residency, and age of arrival were also related to dropout rates, but the connections varied across groups. Immigrant youth appeared better able than native-born youth to pursue their schooling, despite facing the combined adverse conditions of poverty, inner-city residency, linguistic isolation, and uncertain citizenship status. Finally, poor immigrant children who were bilingual seemed to have an educational advantage over even English-only-speakers.

These are overall national patterns, and they vary for each nationality origin group within a race-ethnicity. A high proportion of immigrant students from certain nations arrive in the United States with serious deficiencies in their formal education because of economic desperation, political turmoil, and war in their home countries. These deficiencies in education may be aggravated by the immigration process, poor inner-city school systems in the United States, and the difficult and complicated situation that newcomers face in a strange country. Although such distress has always been common among immigrants, most school districts are unprepared to respond to these newcomers, who tend to concentrate in urban areas and are likely to be poor.

ISSUES AND CONTROVERSIES

People may assume that immigrants do not do as well as native-born students because of the difficulties they encounter while immigrating and settling in the new country. Immigrant parents generally do have less income and education than the general population, but researchers (e.g., Verdonk, 1982) have discussed other disadvantages that immigrant children may have.

1. Most immigrant students lack the English proficiency required for classroom learning in U.S. schools, because English is neither their primary language nor effectively used at home.

2. Immigrant children may lack adequate support from their families; their parents may not speak English well, or may not be aware of or understand the U.S. educational system. Contact between immigrant parents and schools may be negligible.

3. Immigrant parents' ideas, norms, and beliefs about schooling and raising children may conflict with those espoused in schools.

4. Many immigrants and their families suffer from uncertain legal status. The anxiety this produces in families may affect children's health and development.

5. A gap occurs between institutional integration—access to governmental institutions—and social integration—access to interpersonal contacts. Because of this gap, discrimination that is forbidden by law nevertheless occurs in everyday life.

6. The majority of students who are recent immigrants are members of racial-ethnic minorities who have historically had lower educational attainment than White students, for many social, economic, and political reasons.

This characterization, however, has been increasingly scrutinized by researchers and educational practitioners. Many people believe these ideas may represent the experiences of only some immigrants, because recent achievement data and classroom performance suggest more complicated realities. Many teachers who have worked with immigrant students are optimistic. McDonnell and Hill (1993) report that teachers who have worked with immigrant children believed that recently immigrated students were better motivated and "brighter" than their native-born or more established immigrant students. Other researchers have also found that immigrant students bring with them expectations from their schooling experiences in their homelands—including doing homework, respecting teachers and other school staff, and valuing the opportunity to have a free education (Alba & Nee, 1998; Grant & Rong, 1999).

This should not be surprising, because educational historians have documented that a disproportionate share of the best educated and most successful adults, as well as of the children who perform best in school, are immigrants or the children of immigrants. For example, German children did well in 19th-century schools, and Jewish children excelled in early 20th-century education (Ravitch, 1974), though this has received little attention from the public (see Glazer, 1977). In recent years, young Cubans have completed more years of education on average than non-Hispanic Whites (U.S. Bureau of the Census, 1983), and the academic accomplishment of Asian-American children has attracted attention from researchers, news media, and the public (Hirschman & Wong, 1986; Suzuki, 1977; Wei, 1986). Immigrant minorities have also done well in many other parts of the world, with Greeks, Yugoslavs, and Italians in Australia being a few notable examples (Taft & Cahill, 1981), and the many language minority immigrants in Canada providing other instances (Anisef, 1975).

Furthermore, recent scholarship emphasizes that a large proportion of the immigrant population has had higher educational attainment than the general population. In the first three waves of immigration to the United

States, the education of immigrants often lagged behind that of natives. Using census data from 1820 to 1980, Rong (1988) shows that, for a century, foreign-born Whites who came to the United States had far less education than native Whites, and their foreign-born children did not do as well as native-born White children in U.S. schools. She also reports that the gap in enrollment rates between foreign-born White children and native-born White children has narrowed over the years: the ratio of 2:3 in 1890 had reduced to almost no difference in 1970. Moreover, the children of immigrants—the second generation—did better in educational enrollment and completion of primary and high school than did either immigrants or later generations.

Other studies have further found that, though second-generation students do better educationally than either immigrant or nonimmigrant students, immigrant youths who have arrived at a young age may perform similarly to second-generation students (e.g., Chiswick & DebBurman, 2004; Kao & Tienda, 1995; Rong & Brown, 2001; Rong & Grant, 1992). More recent work has even suggested that students with increasingly less time in the United States are doing well. With data collected from locations where immigrants live in high concentrations, researchers have found that newcomers reported higher grade-point averages than students whose families had lived in the U.S. longer (Portes & Rumbaut, 2001; Rumbaut & Portes, 2001).

Consequently, we offer four counterpoints to the six presuppositions that we list at the start of this section. These explain why immigrant children may do better educationally than nonimmigrant children.

1. Many recent immigrants were professionals and were well educated in their home countries. They brought human capital with them to the United States, and they directly entered professional and management occupations. Recent immigration policy has favored certain professionals, and immigrant children may benefit from growing up in a family with parents who are professionals.

2. Talk about immigrants' "edge," or their presumed motivation, also suggests an explanation for educational success. Given their willingness to move to an unfamiliar place for a new start, immigrants, on the whole, have higher educational and occupational aspirations than indigenous groups and are reportedly more determined than nonimmigrants of comparable class backgrounds to overcome difficulties and achieve upward social mobility. Their children may adapt their families' traditions and values and work hard in school.

3. Immigrant children are more likely than nonimmigrants to come from intact families, and their parents are likely to believe that education can enhance their children's opportunities to compete for jobs. Many immigrants have close connections with their ethnic communities, which reinforce positive messages sent to children

and affirm parental authority. High expectations, assumptions about the value of schooling, and parental and community control appear to support the immigrant child's decision to persist in school despite disadvantaged family economic conditions, poor neighborhoods, or low English proficiency.

4. In studying the influence of minority status on educational attainment, Ogbu (1978, 1987) divided minorities into two groups, calling them voluntary and involuntary. Voluntary minority groups are those who migrate willingly from one environment to another; this group includes most recent immigrants, including most Asian, African, Caribbean, Middle Eastern, and Latino immigrants. Most people from voluntary groups consider education and schooling to provide a route to a better life; they press their children to perform well, and their children may outperform the native-born in many societies. Although immigrant minorities experience racial discrimination and economic disadvantages, they emphasize the improvements in their lives as compared to their peers in the homeland, and they assume the negative experiences are temporary. Ogbu contrasts these responses with those of involuntary minority groups, African-Americans, Native Americans, and Hispanics in areas annexed by the United States, for whom caste-like barriers have precluded upward mobility. Voluntary and involuntary minorities both experience cultural differences from mainstream U.S. society, but to succeed, involuntary minority members must also overcome centuries of exclusion.

Variations in the Educational Attainment of Immigrant Children

Immigration in the 1990s brought the most diverse population ever to the United States, a population that included a variety of experiences and skills as well as diverse cultural backgrounds. This immigrant population is also the most polarized in respect to the labor demand of the U.S. economy: many White, Black, and Asian immigrants arrived with education and high-level job skills and quickly became scientists, engineers, professors, lab technicians, and entrepreneurs. However, other immigrants, especially many Mexicans, took jobs at minimum wage (or less), encountering numerous housing, health care, employment, and legal problems related to their immigration status, all of which may contribute to barriers to their successful integration into the U.S. mainstream. Many have limited English skills or may be preliterate in their own languages. For example, in 2000, nearly 80% of Mexican immigrant parents were not high school graduates, and one of seven had less than four years of education. Still other immigrants, such as refugees from Cambodia and Laos, might have suffered psychologically and physically in labor camps and jails before leaving their home countries. These divergent backgrounds are reflected in patterns of settlement in the United States and may affect children's identity formation, linguistic transition, and education attainment in schools. This diversity requires flexibility and support from state and local policymakers to help newcomers become self-sufficient learners in schools.

The data in this chapter and in Chapters 5–8 show that the levels of English proficiency and the amount of education immigrant students may have in the United States, as compared to the general student population, vary widely, depending on nation of origin, age and gender, socioeconomic status, and year of entry and length of residence. However, as our findings have revealed, race-ethnicity matters more than immigration status and many other demographic factors in explaining educational attainment.

We have used school dropout rates to measure the educational attainment of children K–12 to probe the many factors contributing to children's educational achievement. We believe the causes of dropping out of school among immigrant youth are complicated, but not mysterious. Our findings reveal that many immigrant students, especially those who arrived most recently and those who arrived in the United States as teenagers, have difficulty in adjusting in U.S. schools, especially immigrant youth who are from a family background with one or multiple disadvantages. These findings are consistent with those of other researchers (e.g., Cahan & Davis, 2001). Most immigrants take several years to gain a working knowledge of English, and the secondary-school curriculum demands both language competence and substantial previous content knowledge. To survive in high school peer cultures, foreign-born teens also need to adjust to nonacademic features of U.S. high schools. Students who have made progress in their home-country schools can usually take regular mathematics courses within one year of immigrating, because mathematics relies less than other subjects on English facility—and because the mathematics curricula in many foreign countries are more demanding than those in the United States. Nevertheless, students whose education has been disrupted by immigration often take much longer to catch up in secondary school. Before they have a chance to catch up, they are already older than their classmates. Few teenage immigrants who enter U.S. schools with insufficient academic preparation ever make the transition to full-time English-language instruction, and many leave school without a diploma, several years behind in grade-level attainment.

Confounding these problems is the need most immigrant children from low-income families have to work (McDonnell & Hill, 1993). Young women who are 13 or 14 years old may not be expected to earn money outside their homes, but they may be responsible for maintaining the household and caring for younger siblings and cousins while their parents work several jobs. Young men of similar age may be expected by their families to work full time. Many immigrant males start to work before they reach the age of 16. Mexican and Central American teenagers are often too mature and carry too many adult burdens to participate in typical secondary-school programs. They may have had lives that forced them to adopt adult perspectives prematurely and permanently.

We can also ask how different patterns of relationships between dropout rates and linguistic status, across various ethnic groups and family income levels, can be explained. Our findings show the benefits of bilingualism, especially for Latino children from low-income families, the population segment most likely to drop out of school. Gibson (1988) has argued for the positive effects of biculturalism and bilingualism on language-minority children's schooling. Rong and Brown (2001) have argued that the negative effects of rapid Americanization among Black immigrant children may lead these children to adapt the inner-city adversarial anti-school youth popular culture, and therefore drop out of school. Similarly, the education and career motivation of 1.5- or second-generation children may support the dreams of their parents, but that dream may also fade away when these Americanized teens encounter racial discrimination and xenophobia in schools and larger society. They may be immersed in youth popular culture and may adapt an anti-achievement ethos, resulting in a decline in their school performance.

However, some scholars have argued that, to fill the intergroup and intragroup achievement gaps among racial minority youth, educators should consider reforming schools to support disadvantaged teens, rather than focusing on changing the perceptions of the youths themselves. Ainsworth-Carnell and Downey (1998) used the first follow-up of the National Education Longitudinal Study to test four key components of Ogbu's theory, which we discuss in the preceding section, and failed to validate his ideas. Their findings have shown that certain children living in inner-city areas are able to do well, despite adverse conditions and the children's own beliefs. A key difference between children who did well in schools and those who did not is the availability and accessibility of community-based resources, such as after-school tutoring and other educationally-oriented programs that serve children (Zhou, 2003). Other scholars (e.g., Tyson, Darity, & Castellino, 2005) argue that school structures, rather than cultural differences, may help explain the anti-achievement ethos among marginalized U.S. youth. These researchers believe that institutional structures may shape how culture is enacted in school in response to a burden of high achievement among Black students, as well as whether it manifests itself; they also argue that students in all racial-ethnic groups confront similar dilemmas about high academic achievement and tend to use similar strategies for downplaying achievement. Patterns of social inequality, reproduced and affirmed in tracking, may well exacerbate the well-documented anti-achievement ethos among U.S. youth. They have concluded that radical systemic changes, rather than reorganization of people's cultural beliefs, provide the solution to the low educational achievement among marginalized groups in schools.

The findings in this chapter that reveal differences in school dropout rates by gender are consistent with an established pattern: U.S. female students generally outperform male students, regardless of their immigration status (Grant & Rong, 1999; Grant & Rong, 2002). Nevertheless, some Latino girls may be expected to leave school to help their mothers, and pregnant girls may be expected to leave school to raise their babies. Among Southeast Asians, traditions advocate early marriages, early employment of young men, and early childbirth in these young families. However, for all racial-ethnic groups, immigrant families have to go through dramatic changes and make enormous efforts to adjust when they start their new lives in the United States. New lifestyles are mixed with the traditions they brought with them from their homelands. To explain the gender gap, some scholars (e.g., N. Lopez, 2003; Pedraza, 1991; Portes & Rumbaut, 1996) believe that immigrant communities in the United States do not necessarily replicate their native cultures, but rather combine traditional norms and practices with novel responses to the unique structural conditions that they encounter. Thus, they speculate that immigration might enhance women's achievement by freeing them from patriarchal norms in their countries of origin.

RECOMMENDATIONS

In this chapter, we have presented information on students' educational attainment, using the PUMS 5% of the 2000 census data, and interpreted that information from material in the literature on immigration and education. In this last section, we make five recommendations based on what we have discussed. To help students sustain and raise their educational attainment and achievement, we must not only consider immigrant children's characteristics, their families, and their neighborhoods in relation to their educational attainment, but also account for power, representation, and school control, as well as the social, racial, and gender stratification of the U.S. society.

A common misunderstanding is that the educational difficulties of immigrant children are the result of their initial adjustment to the host society. With the exception of helping children learning English, educators need to depend only on lengthier duration in United States to make the other problems go away. However, as noted by Beiser (1995), although migration and resettlement likely do affect a child's development, a number of factors—including post-migration stressors and lack of personal, family, and community resources—may generate long-term problems (health, psychological, legal, etc.) Furthermore, educational policies can significantly affect children's initial and continuing adjustment: The academic and human climate of the child's school, the tracking system and ELL student placement, teachers' perceptions and students' self-concepts, academic outreach efforts, and peer influence have been found to be among the factors affecting the educational and career aspirations of immigrant students (Kim, Rendon,

& Valadez, 1998). Therefore, we believe recommendations for promoting immigrant children's education should be formulated broadly.

Recommendation One: Recognize How Demographic Changes Have Transformed Schools

Educators should clearly acknowledge the classroom reality in the United States and its demographic future. To treat all students equally, educators must acknowledge immigrants' vast diversity in attributes such as national origin, language, social class, race-ethnicity, and religion; they must recognize and respect the wide range of identities and cultural competencies of these youngsters and value each child's culture. Educators also should understand what this diversity means for instruction, curricula, school environment, and student culture. This knowledge and understanding will enable educators to work effectively with parents and communities to identify and support the various needs among immigrant students. Logan and Deane (2003) caution that the United States is moving from a nation of a majority, with a few minority groups, to a nation of many minorities.

Educators should be alerted to the polarizations in socioeconomic backgrounds and educational attainment within a race and ethnic group. For example, the large gaps between East Asian and Southeast Asian students, as well as within the Asian nationality groups, are dramatic. Substantial gaps also occur among immigrant students from South America, Central America, and Mexico. Educators also need to attend to the differences between Black immigrants and U.S. Black students in inner cities.

Educators should further understand the implications of various immigration-related education issues for students at different grade levels and with various lengths of U.S. residence. For example, immigrant students tend to do better in school at levels through middle school; by adolescence, they may become disillusioned, and their attitudes toward teachers and scholastic achievement may turn negative (Galster, Metzger, & Waite, 1999). Others have observed that, although children of immigrants may start out with better health and higher educational aspirations, these strengths can dissipate over time. As adolescents, the longer children of immigrants have lived in the United States, the more likely they are to report involvement in risky behaviors (Hernandez & Charley, 1998).

Recommendation Two: Adapt Curriculum and Instruction to Immigrant Youth

Our second recommendation is to plan instruction responsive to the heterogeneity inherent in every classroom. Educators know that the mythological "general" or "average" child does not exist and that all learners exhibit a variety of needs and strengths. Teachers need to know more about instructional differentiation, informal diagnosis, and assessment through observation, as well as positive reinforcement, behavior support plans, and community building (Goodwin, Genishi, Asher, & Woo, 2005). These changes should include altering course offerings and adjusting and developing teaching materials to make them more suitable for immigrant students. It must also include modification of conventional instructional strategies and acquisition of the skills needed to work with children who speak little English.

Successful schools are those that provide variable curricula to address various immigrant students' needs. Curriculum specialists in school districts must assure that curricula not only include, but also accurately reflect, the history and achievements of the multicultural citizenry of the immigrant population. Teachers in schools with a significant number of immigrant students need to select teaching materials that contain role models from a wide range of nationalities. School libraries should also provide children's books relevant to pre- and post-immigration experiences of immigrant adults and children.

Teachers who work with immigrant children, especially newcomers, should change their lesson design and teaching strategies, as well as note-taking, testing, and homework assignments. Compared with native readers, a higher percentage of immigrant children are slow English readers. Because many schools in other countries—for example, schools in African and Caribbean countries—have different assessment systems, classroom disciplinary structures, and classroom cultures (Alidou, 2000; Zehr, 2001), schools should seek multiple forms of instruction and other approaches in working with immigrant students. Teachers should be provided in-service programs that consider background issues affecting immigrant students, such as absence policies, discipline issues, and parental involvement. They should be prepared to provide instruction appropriate for students from diverse backgrounds, rather than relying on how they themselves were taught.

Schools and teachers should also draw on immigrant parents as resources. Immigrant parents are ideal guest speakers and expert informants for curriculum and program development and cultural instruction. When parents feel welcomed by schools and become comfortable in the school environment, they can contribute to their children's schools in multiple ways, such as becoming translators, event organizers, advocates, and volunteers. They can also operate at a wider level, becoming communicators and mediators between schools and communities.

In summary, schools should take an additive approach to incorporate immigrant students and their families' strengths, including their transnational and transcultural knowledge, linguistic resources, and life experiences, into the development of school curricula and teaching strategies. This will contribute to developing curricula and strategies that will better help children's learning in a constructivist approach, while also providing children with an empowering sense of how their lives can connect productively to the world that they inhabit (Rong, 2006; Valenzuela, 2005).

Recommendation Three: Improve Each School and Its Environment

A welcome and supportive school environment is crucial for immigrant students. To show students that teachers are culturally attentive and eager to work with immigrant students, teachers should first learn how to pronounce the students' names correctly, as many immigrant students from Asia, Africa, and Central and South America may carry family names or given names with which most Americans are unfamiliar. We have found in our own work with international students that people appreciate efforts to learn and practice their names; they are patient teachers of how to say their names appropriately. Teachers also need to be aware of, and remember, the students' countries of origin and their religions. Alidou (2000) reminds educators that parents feel more welcomed by teachers and schools when they notice these efforts.

Because the majority of immigrants are non-White and are enrolled in racially diverse schools, improving schools' ethnic-racial climates is imperative. Some Black and Latino immigrant students report a mutual distrust between them and their teachers and other school staff, and Asian immigrant students report feeling misunderstood and discriminated against by fellow students (e.g., Olsen, 1997). Researchers (e.g., Albertini, 2004; Ruck & Wortley, 2002) have also reported that immigrant minority students were more likely to be suspended or involved with the school's policing authorities and were most likely to perceive teacher treatment as being discriminatory. These perceptions were especially strong for Black students. School counselors thus should train classroom teachers to communicate better with students and to effectively address the psychological stress suffered by immigrant students trying to integrate in an environment foreign to them. An inviting, friendly, and fair school environment not only keeps students in school longer, but also supports their academic efforts.

All school personnel should be trained to maintain a culturally supportive environment, so that immigrant students can attain personal and academic success. School administrators and school counselors can be appointed to advocacy roles to give them a platform from which they can present information to the appropriate school district resource-granting bodies to obtain additional resources to support school cultural climate change. These resources should be used to implement school-counseling programs and provide other supports so that ethnic minority adolescents can experience academic success (Mitchell, 2005).

Conchas (2006) says that high-achieving minority students tend to have some degree of institutional support by virtue of belonging to advanced school programs. Variance of institutional support can, to a certain extent, determine how minority students perform in school. Racial stereotypes hamper students' opportunity structures, depriving them of the institutional support that could improve their academic trajectories (Conchas, 2006). Mexican students have comprised the group most marginalized and most pessimistic about their opportunities. Conchas has identified three factors accounting for success in the urban schools studied: successful schools (1) were racially well integrated, (2) fostered a sense of community and teamwork, and (3) provided valuable educational and career opportunities (see also Portes, 2005).

Recommendation Four: Build Networks With Families and Communities

Effective educators work well with families and communities. Rong and Brown (2002) emphasize that the history of education of immigrant children is a history of alienation, subordination, and negligence. Immigrants and their children have been invisible in the decision-making about immigration-related educational issues (See also Borman & Baber, 1998; Nieto, 1995). Schools usually see immigrants as passive learners, or as the "served," and rarely approach the families and communities as valuable partners who can play significant roles in deciding what may be best for the children's schooling. School leaders should be aware of the imbalance in power, representation, and control that have plagued minority participation in educational decision-making in the United States. We believe schools can help immigrant families in multiple ways; to work with them as partners, school personnel should understand immigrant parents and their communities.

Starting a life in a new country means that families must acquire large amounts of new information and establish local connections to help in getting around. Schools can provide relevant information to immigrant families to ease this process. Schools should be aware of the ethnic communities within their districts and should inform the newcomers' families about existing social networks, such as an association of individuals from a particular country, or a neighborhood immigrant resource center. Connections like these can introduce immigrants to the range of available opportunities. Schools also need to inform students and their parents about how U.S. society differs from their native countries and how to cope with U.S. institutions, including schools (i.e., rules and regulations, assessment systems and how they relate to retention, grade promotion, and graduation, etc.), colleges, occupational opportunities and employment networks, and varied social situations closely related to their lives.

The ability to work with immigrant parents starts in developing an awareness of, and understanding about, their concerns and expectations. The continuing tendency of immigrant minority families to settle in poor, inner-city neighborhoods means that their children are more likely to attend poorly performing, under-funded, and highly segregated inner-city schools. Under these circumstances, the segmented assimilation framework we introduced in Chapter 1 asserts that maintaining the culture of origin can have a protective effect for immigrant children. Communities may be able to reinforce the achievement-related behavioral norms that parents try to teach their children, thus helping adolescents to avoid the pitfalls of the adversarial anti-school youth popular culture. Teachers should understand that maintaining ethnic identity represents an immigrant community's effort to protect its children from the destructive cultural effects of inner cities' poor minority neighborhoods.

However, children and parents may see things differently. For example, Waters (1999) finds that in the United States, children of West Indian immigrants tend to identify more strongly along racial lines than do their parents and exhibit a significantly higher level of identification with U.S. Blacks—often in contrast to their parents' attempts to distance themselves from this group. According to Waters, even first-generation children are likely to distance themselves from their parents' cultural ethos. When children acculturate faster than their parents, it is called dissonant acculturation. According to Portes and Rumbaut (2001), this type of acculturation leads to parent-child conflict and a breakdown in communication between the generations. The generational identity gap diminishes parents' ability to guide and support their children, and dissonant acculturation may be a major risk factor for downward assimilation among the second generation. Because family and community have such strong instrumental values for children's education, schools should work with state and local governments to direct resources and efforts toward strengthening neighborhood social structures and organizations that help immigrant families keep their authority to monitor their children's behavior, sending a clear and unified message to children that education matters.

However, educators should understand that not all immigrant families want to be connected to ethnic communities. DeWind and Kasinitz (1997) raise the possibility that immigrants' avoidance of incorporation into the U.S. mainstream may have costs as well as benefits. Strong ties within the community may burden immigrants with excessive obligations to relatives and other co-ethnics. These disadvantages could potentially outweigh the benefits of ethnic associations, posited by the segmented assimilation theory.

Recommendation Five: Educate Educators to Work With Immigrants

The professional development of pre- and in-service school personnel is critical. Filling vacancies by recruiting people who are minorities and immigrants, as well as people with bilingual competencies and intercultural communication skills, is also essential. This ensures that schools have an adequate number of teachers and administrators with personal experiences to engender empathy and understanding of the issues in educating immigrant children. The training of pre- and inservice teachers must be changed to accommodate the demographic shifts in the classroom and meet immigrant students' needs adequately.

First, teacher preparatory programs and in-service programs must broaden teachers' knowledge and experiences about diversity in immigration and among immigrants. Goodwin et al. (2005) emphasizes that these youngsters not only bring many different skills, strengths, and needs to the classroom, but also represent unique histories, cultures, stories, values, languages, and beliefs. By understanding the complexity of the immigrant experience, educators will gain an increased sensitivity to the circumstances of immigrant students in their schools and classrooms.

Many educational ethnographic studies (Phelan, Davidson, & Yu, 1998) reveal a relationship between immigrant children's self-identities and their educational efforts and career aspirations. Teachers need to be aware of various identities and to understand the different states of identity development. Heritage language is part of an immigrant child's identity, and it can be a resource as well, especially for inner-city youth who otherwise lack resources. Our findings reveal that maintaining their heritage language helps immigrant children in a low-economic stratum to stay in high school and eventually graduate.

In working with ELL students, teachers and counselors can learn Spanish or certain Asian languages at an introductory level, and teacher preparation programs can reconsider adding minimal foreign language requirements. To ensure their participation in the education of linguistically diverse students, teachers should develop basic understandings of the tools, materials, and techniques appropriate for second-language learning (Gonzalez & Darling-Hammond, 1997). Teachers also need to be able to use these strategies to create a language-rich classroom environment and atmosphere of community-based learning. They need to learn how to access resources and agencies to inform their work with ELL learners and ease students' transitions into an unfamiliar cultural and linguistic environment (Lucas, 1997).

Finally, we consider the assessment of NCLB policy and its implementation to understand how this policy may affect immigrant students' educational attainment. The demographics of U.S. elementary and secondary schools are changing rapidly as a result of record-high immigration. These demographic shifts are occurring alongside implementation of the No Child Left Behind Act, the landmark 2001 federal law that holds schools accountable for the academic performance of limited-English-speaking children and other groups that include many children of immigrants.

NCLB, a controversial policy from its very beginning, generates both praise and strong objection to this day. Many scholars (e.g., Valenzuela, 2005; Velasco, 2005) have argued that NCLB relies on a decontexualization model that discounts the severity of the adverse effects of poverty and high-poverty neighborhood residency on many aspects of children's lives. These effects, such as their physical condition, family structure, linguistically isolated household conditions, and the like, directly or indirectly affect immigrant children's language transition and schooling. These scholars also believe that NCLB ignores the variations in school quality and the complex realities facing students in schools. Enormous inequalities, both initial and persistent, are embodied in the gaps in school resources throughout the education system. As a result, the reform strategies for implementing NCLB work against the stated goals of the law, and poor inner-city children are further behind in the current educational system than they were before the implementation of NCLB. There are a few reports indicating that NCLB may be responsible for higher dropout rates (Noguera, 2005; Swanson, 2004). However, this policy's effects on immigrant students' schooling requires extensive examination based on national and local educational data.

To explore some of what teachers, educational leaders, and policymakers need to know to make a difference in the education of immigrant children, we turn now to a set of chapters on newcomers from different parts of the world. In Chapters 5–8, we discuss the immigration-related educational issues of youngsters from Asia, Africa and the African Diaspora in the Caribbean, Latin America, and the Middle East. We also further explore educational attainment and language transition among immigrant children from individual countries in these regions and conclude each chapter with recommendations specific to this area.

5

Immigrant Children From Asia

Asian immigration to the United States has expanded dramatically in the last two decades. Although Asian immigration to the United States has a history of more than 160 years, over 70% of Asian-Americans are recent immigrants who have arrived since the 1965 Immigration Act was passed. The number of immigrants from Asian countries has risen rapidly since then, and the Asian-American population has doubled in each of the last three decades: 1.7 million in the 1970s, 3 million in the 1980s, 6.8 million in the 1990s, 12.3 million in 2000, and 14 million in 2005. The U.S. Asian population is projected to be 17 million in 2010 and 34 million in 2050, accounting for 5% and then 8% of the U.S. population. The Asian presence in this country was once symbolized by a Chinatown in a few major cities; now as many as eight metropolitan areas in the United States have large Asian populations, from about a half million Asian-Americans in Chicago to over 1.25 million Asian-Americans in Los Angeles/Long Beach in California. Although Asians have often been viewed uniformly as a single "model minority," a vast diversity exists among various Asian nationality groups and within each nationality.

Despite their "model minority" image, Asian-Americans have had a very long history in the United States of exclusion, alienation, and marginalization. Asian-Americans have suffered severe persecution and discrimination, yet many Asian nationality groups have maintained a hold on their own cultures that are noticeably different from U.S. mainstream culture, and on the integrity of their viable, solid communities for more than a century in the United States (Sung, 1987; Zhou, 1995). Asian-Americans were known under one umbrella as "the Orientals" in an earlier era; "the Model Minority" in a later time; and the great binary race, "between the model minority and the delinquents," recently (S. Lee, 2001). Widespread public interest in Asian-Americans is due to a curiosity about their "exotic cultures," comparison of their socioeconomic statuses with those of other racial minorities, or the contrast of the great divisions among Asian-Americans. Other Americans may be unaware of the racial nature of the historical and current actions against Asian-Americans or may interpret the anti-Asian phenomenon in the mass media, work places, and other aspects of social life differently because of the deeply rooted "model-minority" stereotype. According to Asian studies scholars (e.g., S. Lee, 1996), this stereotype was neither welcomed by other minority groups nor necessarily appreciated by Asian-Americans themselves because it obscures differences among Asian-Americans and also tends to turn minority groups against one another, especially in the case of stories of successful Asians being used to undermine the struggles of disadvantaged minority groups.

This chapter is divided into five parts. First, in the section, Asian-Americans and Asian Immigrants in the United States, we address questions such as these: Who are they? Why did they come and how did they come? How have they been received and how have they progressed in the United States? To answer these questions, we sketch the immigration history of Asian-Americans in general and the variations among major Asian nationality groups, followed by an immigration-related sociodemographic briefing. In the second section, Asian-American School-Age Children, based on U.S. 2000 census data with supplementary data from other sources, we present information on children, their families and surroundings, and their educational attainment. This is followed by a summary of key points in the third section, a fourth section highlighting theoretical explanations of the findings as well as the bearing of the findings on related theories, and recommendations for policies and practice in the fifth section. The format we use in this chapter is repeated in the remaining chapters on immigrants from other parts of the world.

ASIAN-AMERICANS AND ASIAN IMMIGRANTS IN THE UNITED STATES

Asian-Americans represent a variety of cultural heritages and immigration experiences. Apart from the obvious cultural differences that reflect their origins from many Asian nations, Asian-Americans of different ethnic groups immigrated to the United States under various circumstances and immigration laws. Without a common language spoken among most Asians, retention of native tongues may be more difficult for Asians than for Hispanics. Asian immigrants speak more than 50 languages, not including dialects:

Chinese, for example, can mean Chinese, Mandarin, Cantonese, Hakka, and such. Nevertheless, some factors, such as culture, religion, written characters, philosophy, and family and personal values, are shared among many, if not all, Asian groups:

- The same Chinese characters have been retained in Japanese and Korean calligraphy.
- Confucian thought on education, family values, and the relationship between authority and the individual have been honored in East, Southeast, and South Asia for many centuries.
- Buddhism and its versions have also been adopted among people in almost every country on the Asian continent.

Hence, the rich tapestry of Asian cultures tends to be overlooked in the United States, but the term "Asian" is still used to signify this greatly diverse array of people. The information presented herein was compiled from materials published by Daniels (2002), Nakanishi & Nishida (1995), Ng (1995), Takaki (1998), Weinberg (1997), and Wu (2002).

A HISTORICAL SKETCH

In this section, we review the history of Asian-American immigration to the United States and the influence of immigration laws and policies on the Asian immigration experience. Our review shows that the making of immigration law usually involves political, social, and economic battles. How federal and state governments accommodate the immigration movement is inextricably linked to broader societal attitudes about immigration and toward particular groups of immigrants. Unfortunately, the review of these laws and policies reveal clear traces of Eurocentricity, internal colonization, and the labor exploitation of newcomers.

The Asian-American population consists of a large percentage of recent immigrants, as well as a number of Asian immigrant descendants who have lived in the United States for many generations; Asian immigration history goes back about 250 years. Historically, many Asian-Americans were perceived as members of the two most populous groups—Chinese or Japanese. However, Filipino Americans' immigrant experiences, for example, tell a somewhat different story, partly because Filipinos became colonial subjects of the United States in 1898 during the Spanish-American war.

As early as 1763, Filipinos established the small settlement of Saint Malo, in the bayous of today's Louisiana, after fleeing mistreatment aboard Spanish ships. Chinese sailors arrived in Hawaii in the later 18th century, where many settled, and a smaller proportion of Chinese, Korean, and Japanese laborers were brought to Hawaii during the 19th century to work on sugar plantations. Later, Filipinos were also brought in there as laborers. Though some Chinese laborers were present in Hawaii before 1835 (Takaki,

1998), a larger number of Chinese and Japanese began immigrating to the mainland United States in the mid-19th century. This may explain why many Asian history scholars have traced Asian immigration to the United States back to the mid-19th century, rather than three-quarters of a century earlier. The majority of these immigrants to the continental United States were sojourners from China, attempting to temporarily escape the economic turmoil in their hometowns (Weinberg, 1997). The labor demand from the California mining industry and the construction of the Transcontinental Railroad drew a large number of Chinese immigrants to California and other parts of the U.S. mainland. As the possibility of returning home with a nest egg diminished for the contract laborers, they began to settle and work in labor-intensive industries such as farming and laundering (Takaki, 1998). A surge in Asian immigration in the late 19th century caused some natives to fear the growing number of Asians in the U.S. labor market. Several anti-Asian laws were adopted, with the Chinese as the main target.

At the time, U.S. immigration policies were Eurocentric; although they were viewed as unfriendly toward all newcomers, they were particularly hostile toward Asians (Daniels, 2002). Many of the laws can be viewed as strategic exclusions of Asians (as non-White peoples) designed to legitimize the long-term exploitation of Asian laborers in this country and the formulation of Asians as an inferior species of humans. These laws and policies have been frequently contested, sometimes successfully, sometimes not, by both Asian-Americans and non-Asian-American advocacy groups. A typical example is the Naturalization Law of 1790 (also called the Free White Person Restriction) that specified citizenship eligibility only to Whites; it remained in effect until 1952 (Takaki, 1998). This law and its later version in 1870—which granted Black people, but not other non-White people, the possibility of citizenship—excluded all Asians from naturalization and denied them the rights and benefits that come with citizenship. Under this law and its later amendments, Asians could not own property or marry outside their groups, but especially not with Whites. Their children had to attend racially segregated schools or receive no schooling at all. The law greatly limited the growth of the Asian immigrant population as well as their opportunities and entitlements and, therefore, made Asian-Americans an invisible and marginalized minority in U.S society for a very long time.

In addition to the Naturalization Law of 1790, other discriminatory immigration laws were passed in the early years. The Chinese Exclusion Act of 1882 and the 1917 Immigration Law were enacted to prohibit Chinese and Asian Indian immigration, and the 1924 Oriental Exclusion Act prohibited immigrants from almost all Asian countries except the Philippines. The 1924 Immigration Act set quotas for immigration that favored Northern and Western European immigrants and were intended to exclude "undesirable" immigrants, such as Asians.

Immigration policies such as these render immigrants, especially racial minorities, highly likely to be used as scapegoats in times of political crisis and economic downturns when nativist feelings are high (Ravitch, 1974; Tyack, 1974). At the same time that poorer Asian immigrants were demeaned as "societal burdens" and "welfare-addicted," well-to-do Asian immigrants were resented as "job takers " and "crossovers." Hardworking Asian immigrants in the West Coast states earned themselves the nickname "Yellow Peril," a term projecting a false threat to natives' jobs, values, and lifestyles. One of the most unjustified policies for Asian-Americans in U.S. history was the War World II internment of about 120,000 West-Coast Japanese-Americans. Most of them were retained in the camps until the end of the war; meanwhile, their adolescent sons were fighting Germany and Japan for the United States. Since that time, Japanese-Americans have filed lawsuits against the U.S. government for this internment. President Reagan finally signed the Civil Liberties Act of 1988, officially apologizing for Japanese-American internment and providing reparations of $20,000 to each living victim. The lesson learned from this historical incident, as put by Tateishi and Yoshino (2000), is that these camps "will forever stand as reminders that this nation failed in this most sacred duty to protect its citizens against prejudice, greed, and political expediency" (p. 2), and that the United States should especially protect the most vulnerable segment of its society, the immigrant minority peoples.

The McCarran-Walter Act of 1952 was the first major step away from over 150 years of Eurocentric U.S. immigration policies. However, although the McCarran-Walter Act repealed the Naturalization Act of 1790, it retained the quota system that effectively banned nearly all immigration from Asia. For example, the annual quota of Chinese immigrants at that time was only 50 people. Not until 1965, with the passing of the Hart-Cellar Act (Johnson, Farrell, & Guinn, 1997, p. 1057), was the quota system altered to include equal immigration quotas for all countries and a preference for family reunification. It opened the borders to immigration from Asia for the first time in nearly half a century, significantly increased the number of Asian immigrants, and changed the nationality composition of this population.

Looking back over the history of Asian immigration during and after World War II, we posit that a large number of Asians who came to the United States were political refugees. In the wake of World War II, immigration preferences favored family reunification. This may have helped attract highly skilled workers to meet U.S. workforce deficiencies. One instance related to World War II was the Luce-Celler Act of 1946, which helped immigrants from India and the Philippines. The end of the Korean and Vietnamese Wars and the so-called "Secret Wars" in Southeast Asia have brought many Asians to the United States, as people from Korea, Vietnam, Laos, and Cambodia arrived in several waves of refugees, an influx that continues today.

Although various Asian-Americans groups have been linked in the minds of many Americans, each group has its own heritage culture and language, and their history and immigration experiences are quite different from one another. The history of each Asian ethnic group has been written by many scholars (e.g., Kitano & Daniels, 2005), and here we make only a few key points about each of the six largest nationality groups in the U.S. Asian-American population. Then we move on to discuss the sociodemographics of Asian immigrants.

The three largest groups of Asian immigrants are the Chinese, Japanese, and Filipinos. Several distinct differences characterize the immigration experiences of these peoples. Early Chinese immigrants to the mainland United States, coming from a country that in the late 19th century had a fragile economy and weak government and working mostly as manual laborers, were the target of much hostile treatment from federal, state, and local governments in the United States, particular in the West Coast states. As summarized by Daniels (2002),

> What makes the Chinese experience unique in American ethnic history was not what they did but what was done to them. What was done to them includes both discrimination and extralegal violence and a whole series of discriminatory ordinances and statutes from the municipal to the federal level. (p. 245)

This experience may partially explain the bifurcated nature of the Chinese-American community that persists today, a community that, despite great achievement, still contains segments with considerable poverty and isolation.

Within the United States, however, at several points in history (e.g., the Gentlemen's Agreement of 1908 with the Japanese government), Japanese-Americans were viewed and treated differently from other Asians because of Japan's identity as an imperialist power and its strong economy in the late 19th and early 20th centuries. The Japanese represented the largest Asian population presence in the United States prior to World War II. They grew continuously from that large population base until, in 1970, the nearly 600,000 Japanese Americans in the United States made them the largest Asian subgroup. Because of their large numbers and lengthy immigration history, Japanese-Americans, among all Asian-American nationalities, have the highest rate of native-born citizenship and the most powerful political representation in federal, state, and local governments and legislatures. They are among the most widely recognized Asian-American subgroups with very high percentages of college graduates and individuals in professional and management jobs. Though many keep some of their unique cultural values and customs, Japanese-Americans have been successfully assimilated into U.S. institutions.

Filipinos were not affected by the quota system, as they were considered to be U.S. nationals because of the colonial nature of the relationship between the United States and the Philippines in the late 19th and early 20th centuries. Thus, despite being the second-largest Asian-American group in the United States with a lengthy immigration history,

Filipino-Americans have been labeled the "invisible" Asians, because of their "easy" integration due to their ability to speak English and their status as U.S. nationals. However, this label also points to a lack of political power and representation at the municipal or state level. This is partly due to the lack of visibility of Filipino-American role models in the wider community and media. Intermarriage rates between Filipinos and members of other Asian nationalities and racial-ethnic groups have been high.

In spite of a prior history of immigration, Korean immigration to the United States was virtually nil in the early 20th century. A large number of Korean immigrants—as many as 150,000—came to the United States after the end of the Korean War in 1953. This increased as a result of the passage of the Immigration and Nationality Act of 1965, at which time Koreans became the fourth-largest Asian group in the United States. Koreans are among the most educated and highest paid of all the Asian immigrant groups in the United States. Many run their own businesses such as restaurants, dry cleaning shops, and other small retail businesses.

Asian Indians may adjust to U.S. schools more easily than many other immigrant groups because they have fewer language barriers—English is widely spoken in India among the professional classes—and more education credentials. They also come from an ethnically and religiously diverse, democratic society. Asian Indians are now among the fastest growing ethnic groups in the United States, second only to Mexican-Americans. Indian-American adults are more highly represented in high-tech industries than any other ethnic group in the United States. They have the highest educational qualifications and the highest median income of any national-origin group.

Mass immigration of Vietnamese, Hmong, and Laotians to the United States began after 1975, after the end of the Vietnamese war (although large numbers of Cambodian refugees were not able to immigrate to the United States until 1979). The first-wave Vietnamese immigrants were generally better educated and had more skills than those who came in 1978 and later years. The Vietnamese are in many ways different from other Southeast Asians. Hmong immigrants lacked formal education because many had been farmers in the hills of Laos and had little or no access to schools. Although they remain one of the poorest Asian ethnic groups in the United States, many second-generation children have performed well in school compared to other low-income ethnic groups. In many of the large cities where Hmong-Americans live and work, tensions have developed between them and neighboring ethnic groups. Hmong people have often been targets of discrimination; their destitute arrival in the United States stereotyped them as welfare dependents at the same time that their willingness to work made them targets as competitors for manual-labor jobs.

A Sociodemographic Briefing

The term "Asian-American" may lead to the misconception that this is a homogeneous group. It is actually an umbrella label applying to a variety of peoples who originate from countries in Asia but who are of different heritages, and have different views, values, languages and dialects, cultural and religious practices, lifestyles, and physical appearances. Any profile of Asian-Americans should acknowledge the heterogeneity of their sociodemographic backgrounds, their educational and occupational statuses, and their family structures (Logan, 2001; Reeves & Bennett, 2004; U.S. Bureau of the Census, 2007a). However, the term "Asian," as used in the 2000 census, refers to individuals originating from any of the people of the Far East, Southeast Asia, or the Indian subcontinent. It is not limited to nationalities but includes ethnic groups as well, such as Hmong, who lived along the Laotian and Vietnamese border. The Asian-American population includes people who claimed Asian identity alone or Asian identity in combination (bi- or multiracial, including Asian). In addition, it also includes those who originate from nations with different social, economic, and political systems such as China, Taiwan, and Hong Kong.

The 2000 census counted 12.3 million Asian-Americans, approximately a 70% increase over the 1990 census count. Eleven Asian groups composed at least 1% of the total Asian population. The six largest groups were Chinese (2.7 million: 22%), Filipino (2.4 million: 19%), Asian Indian (1.9 million: 15.5%), Korean (1.2 million: 10%), Vietnamese (1.2 million: 10%), and Japanese (1.2 million: 9.4%). Cambodians (212,000), Hmong (185,000), Laotians (197,000), Pakistanis (209,000), and Thais (150,000), together with Asians from other countries, account for less than 13% of the Asian-American population. Asian Indians are the fastest growing group—more than doubling in the past decade. Asian Indians constituted the fifth-largest subgroup in 1990, but are now the third-largest. The Japanese have the longest history in the United States, but their growth in recent years has been modest.

Sixty-nine percent of Asian-Americans were born in foreign countries, a proportion that has declined slightly since 1990, when it was 71%. Vietnamese, Koreans, Pakistanis, and Thais constitute the highest proportion of foreign-born (about 75%), while the Japanese constitute the lowest proportion of foreign-born (40%). Seventy-six percent of the Asian-American foreign-born population entered the United States between 1980 and 2000, and 43% entered between 1990 and 2000. Over 85% of Cambodians, Pakistanis, and Hmong came to the United States in the past 20 years. The Hmong, with their large numbers of recent immigrants, constitute the youngest group of Asian-Americans, with a median age of 16.3 years.

A greater proportion of Asian households were maintained by married couples than in the nation as a whole (62% vs. 53%), except for the Japanese, who had the largest percentage of non-family households (41%), a figure higher than the total U.S. non-family household rate (32.5%). The average household size for Asian-Americans was 3.1 persons, compared to the national average of 2.6 persons. All Asian-American nationality groups had a larger mean family size than the national average except Japanese families (2.3 persons). Among Asian groups, the Hmong had the largest family size with 6.1 persons (down from 6.8 in 1990) and also the highest percentage (78%) of families maintained by married couples.

In 2000, over 80% of all Asians 25 years old and over had at least a high school education; the national rate was approximately the same. Education is highly valued in Asian communities, although the level of education attained by different groups varies widely. The proportion of individuals completing high school or more was 91% for Japanese, compared with 40% for Hmong. At the college level, 44% of Asians had graduated with at least a bachelor's degree by 2000, compared to 24% of the total U.S. population. Asian Indians had the highest levels of education (64%), and Laotians and Hmong had the lowest (about 8%). Two other Asian nationality groups had lower percentages of individuals graduating from college than the national rates: Cambodians (9%) and Vietnamese (19%).

Asian families had higher median family incomes ($59,324) in 1999 than all U.S. families ($50,046), mainly because Asian families had more members in the workforce and higher levels of education. Four Asian-American groups had higher median family incomes than the total Asian median income, including Asian-Indians and Japanese, each of whom had median family incomes above $70,000. The other Asian groups had median family incomes lower than the median income for Asian-Americans as a whole. For example, the Hmong median family income ($32,384) was less than half that of the Japanese and Asian-Indians. About 12.6% of Asian families were living in poverty in 1999, a rate slightly higher than the 12.4% of all U.S. families. Hmong and Cambodian families had the highest family poverty rates, 38% and 29% respectively, but these had significantly declined from 62% and 42% in 1989. The poverty rates for Vietnamese families was 16%, reduced from 26% in 1989. The lowest poverty rates were recorded for Filipinos (6.3%), Japanese (9.7%), and Asian-Indian (9.8%) families. Asian-Americans were more likely than the total population to have jobs in management, professional, or related occupations (45% vs. 34%), but the percentages within subgroups varies from 60% of Asian-Indian workers to 13% of Laotian workers. Over half of the Asian population lived in the West in 2000, and approximately two-thirds of Asians lived in just six states—California, New York, Texas, Hawaii, New Jersey, and Illinois. The Asian-American population is heavily urbanized, with nearly three-quarters of Asian-Americans living in metropolitan areas with populations greater than 2.5 million.

Asian-Americans also have an array of religions, including Hinduism, Islam, Christianity, Taoism, Shintoism, Buddhism, and Confucianism. Confucianism has had a long history and broad impact in many Asian countries, especially East Asian countries. However, many see Confucianism as a sociocultural philosophy configuring the relationships among individual, family, and society, rather than as a religion. Christianity is common among Asian immigrants. For example, Korean-American immigrants historically have had a very strong Protestant heritage. About 75% of Koreans living in the United States are Protestants, and the majority of Filipino immigrants are Roman Catholics.

ASIAN IMMIGRANT SCHOOL-AGE CHILDREN

The population of Asian-American children aged 5–18 was about 1.5 million in 1990, 2.5 million in 2000, and around 3 million in 2005. Figures 5.1A and B present the nine Asian-American nationalities with the largest proportion of school-age children. For example, Chinese Asian-Americans include the most school-age children, at 22% of the population, followed by Filipinos (19%), Koreans (12%), Asian Indians (12%), and Vietnamese (11%). The composition for immigrant Asians is similar to that of the total Asian-American population, but Japanese have a smaller share of the Asian immigrant children population. Both Koreans and Asian Indians have a relatively large proportion of school-age children compared to the total Asian-American population of children, indicating the relative recentness of immigration from these two countries compared to other Asian countries.

Generational Makeup

Table 5.1 shows very different patterns of generational composition between Asian-American and all American children, as well as between different nationality groups within the Asian-American population. For example, although less than 20% of the nation's school-age children were either foreign-born or children of foreign-born parent(s), almost 90% of Asian children were either foreign-born or children of foreign-born parents. The majority of Asian children were second-generation (62%). However, the

FIGURE 5.1A   U.S. Asian Children (5–18) by Nationality, 2000

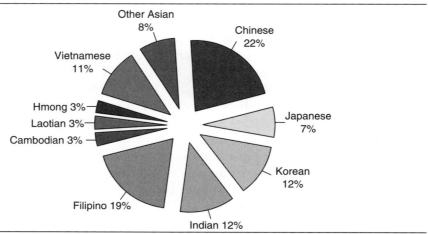

SOURCE: Data from PUMS 5% of the 2000 Census (U.S. Bureau of the Census, 2003a), compiled by authors.

proportion of foreign-born Asian children (18%) is larger than the proportion of third-generation Asian children, that is, U.S.-born Asian children with U.S.-born parents (10%).

When we compare the patterns of generational makeup across the various Asian-American subgroups, we observe several distinctive features.

Asian children as a whole are a multigenerational group, with a considerable percentage of U.S.-born (second and third generation), but still

FIGURE 5.1B   U.S. Asian Immigrant Children (5–18) by Nationality, 2000

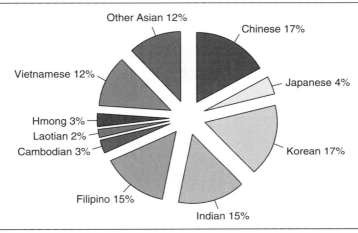

SOURCE: Data from PUMS 5% of the 2000 Census (U.S. Bureau of the Census, 2003a), compiled by authors.

TABLE 5.1   U.S. Asian Children 5–18 Years Old by Ethnicity, National Origin, and Immigration Status, 2000

	All Children	Immigrant Children		Children of Immigrant	Native Children
		1st Generation	1.5 Generation		
All Children	100	2.2%	2.5%	13.6%	81.8%
(N)	(2,694,073)	(58,376)	(67,416)	(365,206)	(2,203,075)
All Asian Children	100	13.3%	15.1%	61.5%	10.1%
	(84,974)	(11,302)	(12,831)	(52,259)	(8,582)
Chinese	100	12.9%	11.6%	66.1%	9.4%
	(18,270)	(2,357)	(2,125)	(12,076)	(1,712)
Japanese	100	7.3%	7.6%	28.0%	57.1%
	(5,889)	(429)	(449)	(1,647)	(3,364)
Korean	100	16.2%	26.1%	53.3%	4.6%
	(10,543)	(1,703)	(2,746)	(5,614)	(480)

(Continued)

TABLE 5.1   (Continued)

Asian Indian	100	16.0%	18.0%	64.1%	1.9%
	(10,398)	(1,664)	(1,874)	(6,660)	(200)
Filipino	100	11.7%	11.2%	65.0%	12.1%
	(16,424)	(1,918)	(1,845)	(10,668)	(1,993)
Cambodian	100	4.4%	20.0%	74.7%	0.9%
	(2,835)	(124)	(567)	(2,119)	(25)
Laotian	100	5.2%	15.7%	76.6%	2.5%
	(2,195)	(115)	(345)	(1,681)	(54)
Hmong	100	8.2%	20.5%	70.9%	0.4%
	(2,620)	(215)	(536)	(1,858)	(11)
Vietnamese	100	19.2%	13.7%	65.4%	1.7%
	(9,014)	(1,731)	(1,238)	(5,895)	(150)

SOURCE: Data from PUMS 5% of the 2000 Census (U.S. Bureau of the Census, 2003a), compiled by authors.

1 Foreign-born children who arrive in the United States at age 5 or younger are classified as the 1.5 generation; those who immigrated to the United States after age 5 are classified as 1st generation.

2 Percentages may not total to 100 because of rounding percentages of subgroups.

3 The total number of all Asian nationality groups is not equivalent to the number for all Asian children because other Asian nationalities such as Thai and Pakistani are not included in this table.

including a significant number of recent immigrants. However, these patterns for all Asian children are not constant across all of the nationality subgroups. Chinese and Filipino children mirror this pattern because Chinese and Filipinos have a long history of immigration to the United States and have continued to immigrate in large numbers to this country over the past three decades. The Japanese population is skewed toward third-generation children (57%), with less than 15% of the population being immigrants. These statistics reflect the long-standing Japanese presence in this country, as well as their low rate of recent immigration. Furthermore, many foreign-born Japanese children or the U.S.-born children of Japanese parents were on temporary visas in 2000, residing in the United States for education or business, and therefore not actual immigrants.

Contrary to the Japanese pattern, several other Asian nationality populations are skewed toward the immigrant generation. Koreans, Asian Indians, Hmong, and Vietnamese all have less than 5% of their population representing the third generation but over 30%—or as high as 40%, in the case of Koreans—in the immigrant generation. The different generational makeup across the nationality groups clearly indicates that these latter groups have a more recent immigration history with the United States and have relatively younger immigrant-ethnic communities within the country.

The length of immigration history and the establishment of multigenerational ethnic communities have significant implications for social policies, language education, local politics, and collaborations among schools, families, and communities, which we elaborate on more later in this chapter.

THE CHARACTERISTICS OF FAMILIES

In this section, we consider the attributes of children's families. This includes their economic conditions, their living arrangements, and parental education, language use, and citizenship status.

Socioeconomic Backgrounds of Families

Asian-Americans overall are more likely than the general population to live in the inner city; however, first generation Asian immigrants are not more likely than all U.S. immigrants to live in inner-city neighborhoods. Table 5.2 reveals that all Asian children were about 68% more likely to live in inner-city neighborhoods than all U.S. children, and that Asian immigrant children were slightly less likely than all immigrants to live in inner-city neighborhoods. Japanese, regardless their immigrant status, were the least likely inner-city residents within the Asian population. Korean, Asian Indian, and Filipino immigrant children were also less likely to

TABLE 5.2   Characteristics of Families and Living Environments of U.S. Asian Children 5–18 Years Old by Ethnicity, National Origin, and Immigration Status, 2000

	All Children (112,044)	Immigrant Children (29,407)
% of Children Who Lived in Inner Cities		
All Children	13.1%	26.0%
All Asian Children	21.9%	24.0%
Chinese	26.4%	29.1%
Japanese	11.0%	11.9%
Korean	17.2%	16.1%
Asian Indian	17.3%	21.8%
Filipino	16.5%	18.3%
Cambodian	48.6%	50.2%
Laotian	30.3%	35.9%
Hmong	51.2%	57.8%
Vietnamese	21.4%	25.1%

(Continued)

TABLE 5.2   (Continued)

Poverty Rates (% of Children Who Lived in Household in Poverty)		
All Children	14.8%	27.1%
All Asian Children	13.2%	18.3%
Chinese	11.9%	18.0%
Japanese	4.9%	9.7%
Korean	10.6%	14.2%
Asian Indian	8.0%	13.3%
Filipino	5.1%	5.6%
Cambodian	41.4%	46.5%
Laotian	31.3%	40.2%
Hmong	44.1%	59.1%
Vietnamese	21.4%	28.2%
% of Children Who Lived in Household With Total Family Income at or Higher Than 75th Percentile		
All Children	18.4% 10.7%	
All Asian Children	26.9%	19.8%
Chinese	34.1%	23.1%
Japanese	42.9%	49.9%
Korean	27.6%	27.9%
Asian Indian	38.7%	24.9%
Filipino	24.0%	16.6%
Cambodian	4.7%	3.2%
Laotian	4.2%	1.3%
Hmong	1.3%	1.2%
Vietnamese	13.3%	4.3%
% of Children Who Lived in Households With Two Parents		
All Children	72.8%	80.4%
All Asian Children	85.5%	86.3%
Chinese	87.9%	84.9%
Japanese	84.3%	92.5%
Korean	87.0%	87.7%

Asian Indian	92.8%	92.3%
Filipino	82.5%	82.7%
Cambodian	70.2%	73.8%
Laotian	80.2%	83.3%
Hmong	89.8%	88.2%
Vietnamese	81.7%	84.4%

% of Children Who Lived in Households Without Fathers

All Children	21.5%	13.3%
All Asian Children	10.4%	10.0%
Chinese	8.7%	11.0%
Japanese	11.4%	6.3%
Korean	9.5%	9.4%
Asian Indian	5.0%	5.6%
Filipino	12.1%	11.7%
Cambodian	23.4%	21.6%
Laotian	12.9%	11.3%
Hmong	6.9%	9.3%
Vietnamese	13.1%	11.2%

% of Children Who Lived With Parent or Household Head Having Fewer Than Four Years of Education

All Children	1.5%	8.9%
All Asian Children	5.6%	7.2%
Chinese	4.3%	5.2%
Japanese	0.2%	0.6%
Korean	0.5%	0.6%
Asian Indian	0.8%	1.3%
Filipino	0.4%	0.7%
Cambodian	35.0%	45.3%
Laotian	27.2%	42.4%
Hmong	42.4%	62.5%
Vietnamese	7.6%	9.0%

(Continued)

TABLE 5.2   (Continued)

% of Children Who Lived With Parent or Household Head Having at Least a High School Diploma		
All Children	80.8%	53.7%
All Asian Children	81.2%	77.6%
Chinese	79.3%	75.4%
Japanese	96.9%	98.5%
Korean	95.3%	96.0%
Asian Indian	90.7%	86.3%
Filipino	91.9%	91.4%
Cambodian	37.6%	28.1%
Laotian	45.0%	30.4%
Hmong	41.5%	21.8%
Vietnamese	62.0%	51.9%
% of Children Who Lived With Parent or Household Head Having at Least a Four-Year College Degree		
All Children	23.0%	22.7%
All Asian Children	43.1%	44.0%
Chinese	51.0%	49.4%
Japanese	55.1%	79.7%
Korean	40.8%	56.2%
Asian Indian	67.1%	59.3%
Filipino	41.6%	49.7%
Cambodian	5.8%	4.2%
Laotian	5.6%	3.3%
Hmong	5.2%	1.7%
Vietnamese	17.2%	7.4%

SOURCE: Data from PUMS 5% of the 2000 Census (U.S. Bureau of the Census, 2003a), compiled by authors.

live in inner-city neighborhoods than other Asians. Although the Vietnamese, total and immigrant, have similar proportions living in inner city neighborhoods as the general Asian pattern, the Hmong and Cambodians have inner-city resident rates that double the national rates with more than half of the immigrant children from these two groups living in inner-city neighborhoods in 2000.

Table 5.2 shows how the poverty rates vary among the Asian nationality groups. Although Asian families had lower poverty rates than all U.S. families (13.2% vs. 14.8%) and Asian immigrant families had lower poverty rates than all U.S. immigrant families (17.3% vs. 27.1%), the disparity in poverty rates among the Asian groups is disturbing: Chinese, Korean, Asian Indian, and Filipino families all have lower poverty rates than the national average, Japanese families have one of the lowest poverty rates in the United States (9.7% for immigrant and 4.9% for all), but the poverty rates for Cambodian, Laotian, and Hmong families are double or even triple the poverty rates for all U.S. children as well as all immigrant children. Hmong families had one of the highest poverty rates in the nation.

The proportion of affluent Asian families in the group reflects the same division: Asian children, immigrant or not, were more likely to live in households belonging to the more affluent segment of the population than U.S. children on average (26.9% vs. 18.4% for all children and 19.8% vs. 10.7% for immigrant children). Furthermore, most East Asian immigrant groups had a higher proportion of population (19.8%) in the affluent category than did all U.S children (18.4%), although they were less likely to be affluent compared to Asian people of all generations as a whole. The only exceptions were foreign-born Japanese children—who tended to be more affluent than all Japanese—as did foreign-born Korean children.

However, the discrepancies within the Asian population are much larger than the gaps between Asians and the rest of the U.S. population. Almost 50% of foreign-born Japanese families are affluent, and the proportions of affluent Chinese, Korean, and Asian Indian immigrants are more than double the national average for immigrants. On the other hand, the East Asian groups and Southeast Asian groups differ markedly. The percentages of Cambodian, Laotian, and Hmong children who are from affluent families are extremely low: 1% for both Hmong and Laotians.

Family Living Arrangements

Family living arrangements were very similar across the nationality groups. Asian children were more likely than U.S. children as a whole to live in two-parent households and more likely than U.S. children as a whole to live with a father. Table 5.2 illustrates the same pattern for Asian immigrant children. This general pattern is consistent for all Asian nationalities, except for Cambodian children. That most Asian-American children follow this pattern is remarkable, considering their high poverty rates and concentration in inner-city neighborhoods. For example, although 58% of Hmong children lived in inner-city neighborhoods and 59% were in poverty, more than 80% of them lived with two parents, and less than 10% lived without a father. Educators who work with Hmong children should see these advantages in their family structure and try to use this unique strength to help children overcome their other limitations. With a few exceptions, immigrant Asian children were more likely than all Asian children as a whole to live in two-parent households and live with a father.

Parental Educational Attainment

As we discussed in Chapter 2, we organize parental educational attainment in three levels because attainment at various levels suggests different issues. Nationally, less than 2% of U.S. children were from families where parent(s) had less than a four-year education; however, the percentage for U.S. immigrant children, at 9%, is four times higher than the national average for all children. Asian children on average are more likely to come from families with parents who did not have four years of education (5.6%), but Asian immigrant children are less likely than other immigrant children to have the least-educated parents (7.2%). Parents from India, the Philippines, and all East-Asian countries except China had lower percentages with the least education than the national average (1.5%); however, the percentage with the least education among Hmong, Laotian, and Cambodian parents was many times higher than the national average. Hmong immigrants have the highest percentage of parents in the nation who had less than four years' education (62.5%).

The patterns for high school graduation rates among Asian-Americans are the same as the nationality patterns for achievement at the lowest level of education. Parents originating from India, the Philippines, and all East-Asian countries except China had higher high school graduation rates than the U.S. average. Furthermore, the immigrant parents had high school graduation rates comparable to, or higher than, all people within the same nationality group. Parents from Southeast Asia had much lower high school graduation rates than both the U.S. average and the Asian average. The only difference between Asian and other U.S. parents at the least education level and high school graduation level is this: Although the Asian-American adult population had a higher proportion with the least education than the national average, their high school graduation rate was the same as the national average. When the comparison moves to the higher level of education—four-year college completion—Asian parents are much better educated than all U.S. parents.

Asian-American parents (43.1%) as well as Asian immigrant parents (44%) were almost twice as likely to have a degree from a four-year college as all U.S. parents (23%) and all U.S. immigrant parents (22.7%). Parents from India, the Philippines, and all East Asian countries have a much higher percentage of college graduates than the national average, with no clear pattern relative to immigration. At 80%, immigrant Japanese parents had the highest rate of college graduation among all Asian nationality groups, regardless of immigration status. The second- and third-highest rates were among Asian Indians (67.1% for all Indian and 59.3% for immigrant Indian parents). Parents from other Southeast Asian countries had a much lower percentage of college graduates compared to the national average and the average rates for Asian adults as a whole.

In summary, no consistent patterns occur in educational attainment across the nationality groups for all three educational levels. We suggest several explanations for these variations. Low education rates can be expected among parents from Asian countries that historically had higher illiteracy rates than the U.S. average (such as China and all Southeast Asian regions).

Also, many Hmong adults were never educated in any written language in their own tribes before they came to the United States. Moreover, many immigrant adults, especially the ones who came to the United States past high school age, might not have had the opportunity to get a more formal education in the United States because of employment in enclaves, very low income, a lack of proficiency in English, an inability to register for continuing education due to legal status, and such. However, at the high end of the educational ladder, the college-graduation rates for Asian immigrants are double the national rates; half to more than half the immigrant parents from the countries that provided a large number of economic immigrants have at least a college degree (India, the Philippines, and all East Asian countries). These new phenomena since the 1990s can be explained by U.S. immigration policy and supply-and-demand theories. Although the majority of Latinos came to the United States to fill jobs in agricultural, construction, and service industries, technically skilled Asian immigrants have been recruited to this country in response to demands from high-tech industries and universities, as well as from service industries. In contrast, most early-wave immigrants from Southeast Asia were political refugees, and, more recently, most have come for family reunification. Compared with economic immigrants, some political refugees had less education and inadequate preparation for immigration, such as lower English proficiency and lack of information about their destination country. They also experienced a more difficult psychological adjustment because of trauma during the wars and chaotic conditions that characterized their escaping journeys.

Household Language Situation and U.S. Citizenship Status

Our study of the language situations of Asian families results in two observations.

First, children from countries where English is or was the official language (or one of the official languages), such as India and the Philippines,

TABLE 5.3 Immigration-Related Characteristics of U.S. Households for Asian Children 5–18 Years Old by Ethnicity, National Origin, and Immigration Status, 2000

	All Children (112,044)	Immigrant Children (29,407)
% of Children Who Spoke a Language Other Than English at Home		
All Children	17.3%	84.9%
All Asian Children	63.7%	79.4%
Chinese	74.7%	89.9%
Japanese	30.9%	93.1%
Korean	64.7%	56.0%

(Continued)

TABLE 5.3   (Continued)

Asian Indian	66.2%	77.3%
Filipino	34.1%	71.3%
Cambodian	86.5%	92.2%
Laotian	88.2%	95.7%
Hmong	96.2%	97.6%
Vietnamese	88.4%	96.3%
% of Children Who Lived in Linguistically Isolated Households		
All Children	4.5%	34.4%
All Asian Children	21.2%	30.5%
Chinese	28.6%	40.4%
Japanese	11.8%	58.9%
Korean	26.9%	28.8%
Asian Indian	9.1%	12.8%
Filipino	7.4%	12.4%
Cambodian	25.9%	20.1%
Laotian	26.2%	28.9%
Hmong	34.0%	44.5%
Vietnamese	39.0%	54.8%
% Household Heads Who Are U.S. Citizens		
All Children	91.6%	31.5%
All Asian Children	68.3%	41.2%
Chinese	71.8%	33.8%
Japanese	76.8%	8.8%
Korean	63.4%	52.2%
Asian Indian	58.6%	31.6%
Filipino	80.4%	57.7%
Cambodian	47.4%	39.4%
Laotian	54.5%	39.4%
Hmong	45.0%	21.3%
Vietnamese	68.3%	43.1%

SOURCE: Data from PUMS 5% of the 2000 Census (U.S. Bureau of the Census, 2003a), compiled by authors.

included a lower percentage of foreign-born children who spoke a heritage language, and a lower percentage of children living in linguistically isolated households, than children from other nationalities.

Second, children from nationality groups with longer and multigenerational immigration histories in the United States had a lower proportion of heritage-language speakers and of linguistically isolated households in the total population.

The difference in heritage-language speaking in 2000 between the total population of all generations of Asian-Americans and the Asian immigrant population was large. For example, the Japanese-American population is highly skewed to the third generation, and the percentage of heritage-language-speakers for all Japanese children in the United States was only 31%—the lowest among all Asian nationalities—though more than 93% of foreign-born Japanese children spoke their heritage language (see Table 5.3). Also, less than 12% of all Japanese children lived in linguistically isolated households, compared to 59% of foreign-born Japanese children. Chinese children displayed similar, but less striking, patterns. On the contrary, among children from the nationality groups with a high concentration of foreign-born or first-generation, such as Cambodian and Laotian, the gaps in percentage of heritage-language speakers between the total population of all generations and the immigrant population were small.

Asian immigrant parents, as a whole, reported a higher percentage of U.S. citizenship than all immigrant parents; however, the rates and the ratios between the total population of all generations and immigrants vary across nationality groups. About three-quarters of all Asian parents and two-fifths of Asian immigrant parents reported U.S. citizenship in 2000. Filipino, Japanese, and Chinese are the three Asian nationalities with the highest citizenship rates (80%, 77%, and 72%); however, the citizenship rates for the immigrant population were higher among Filipino, Korean, and all Southeast Asian nationalities, except the Hmong.

THE CHARACTERISTICS OF ASIAN CHILDREN

We turn now to attributes of the children themselves. In this section we examine children's disabilities, length of residence in the United States and age at arrival, and their oral English proficiency.

Disabilities

The total population of U.S children, including all generations, had lower rates of physical disabilities and higher rates of learning-related disabilities than the population of Asian immigrant children. Table 5.4 indicates this general pattern. Comparing Asian-American children with all U.S. children, nationally, 3% of U.S. children and 5.1% of Asian immigrant children were reported as having one or more physical disabilities, and 4.4% of U.S. children and 2.2% of immigrant children were as reported

TABLE 5.4   Other Characteristics of U.S. Asian Children 5–18 Years Old by Ethnicity, National Origin, and Immigration Status, 2000

	All Children (112,044)[1]	Immigrant Children (29,407)
% of Children Who Reported Physical Disabilities (One or Multiple Limitations in Mobility, Personal Care, Hearing and Visual, etc)		
All Children	3.0%	5.1%
All Asian Children	2.8%	4.2%
Chinese	2.2%	3.4%
Japanese	1.9%	1.9%
Korean	2.3%	2.6%
Asian Indian	2.9%	4.0%
Filipino	2.8%	4.4%
Cambodian	4.9%	8.3%
Laotian	4.2%	7.6%
Hmong	4.9%	7.1%
Vietnamese	3.9%	6.8%
% of Children Who Reported Learning-Related Disabilities (Difficulties in Remembering, etc.)		
All Children	4.4%	2.2%
All Asian Children	1.8%	2.0%
Chinese	1.4%	1.2%
Japanese	2.5%	1.7%
Korean	2.1%	2.8%
Asian Indian	1.2%	1.3%
Filipino	1.8%	1.5%
Cambodian	2.3%	2.8%
Laotian	2.1%	3.0%
Hmong	3.3%	4.3%
Vietnamese	2.0%	2.8%

SOURCE: Data from PUMS 5% of the 2000 Census (U.S. Bureau of the Census, 2003a), compiled by authors.

1 The numbers refer to Asian children only.

having learning-related disabilities. Asian children as a whole reported slightly lower rates of physical disabilities (2.8% for all Asian children and 4.2% for Asian immigrant children) and much lower rates of learning-related disabilities (1.8% and 2% respectively) than all U.S. children and U.S. immigrant children.

Physical disabilities are differentially reported among the Asian nationality groups. While children with Southeast Asian origins had higher rates than the national rate, the children of the other Asian nationalities had lower rates than the national rate. For learning-related disabilities, while each of the Asian nationality groups of all generations had lower rates than U.S. children as a whole, Hmong, Laotian, Cambodian, Vietnamese, and Korean immigrant children had higher rates than U.S. immigrant children overall. The general pattern that immigrant children were reported to have fewer physical disabilities than the total population of all generations occurred among all Asian immigrant nationalities except Japanese children, whose rates were the same for both all Japanese children and Japanese immigrant children. However, the proportion of immigrant children with fewer learning-related disabilities varied among the Asian nationalities. Hmong, Laotian, Cambodian, Vietnamese, and Korean immigrant children had higher rates of learning-related disabilities than the total population of children within the same national origin.

Length of Residence and Age of Arrival

In 2000, over two-fifths of Asian immigrant children of school age in the United States had been in the country less than five years. Seventy-seven percent of them had come to the United States after 1990 (see Table 5.5). Japanese children had the largest proportion of immigrants who had

TABLE 5.5 Immigration-Related Characteristics of U.S. Foreign-Born Asian Children 5–18 Years Old by Ethnicity and Nationality, 2000

	0–5	6–10	11–15	16 and Above
Years in U.S.				
All Children	47.3%	34.0%	16.5%	2.3%
All Asian Children	42.5%	34.4%	19.1%	4.0%
Chinese	49.9%	33.4%	14.5%	2.2%
Japanese	74.3%	17.1%	7.1%	1.6%
Korean	40.4%	25.2%	27.1%	7.3%
Asian Indian	51.8%	30.5%	15.2%	2.5%
Filipino	39.8%	40.3%	17.9%	1.8%
Cambodian	11.4%	16.6%	48.1%	23.9%

(Continued)

TABLE 5.5   (Continued)

Laotian	12.8%	32.2%	49.4%	5.7%
Hmong	15.2%	49.7%	34.0%	1.2%
Vietnamese	34.7%	53.1%	9.6%	2.7%
Age of Arrival				
All Children	53.4%	30.1%	14.5%	1.9%
All Asian Children	53.2%	30.2%	15.0%	1.6%
Chinese	47.4%	33.1%	17.4%	2.7%
Japanese	51.1%	32.2%	15.4%	1.3%
Korean	61.7%	22.4%	14.6%	1.4%
Asian Indian	53.0%	29.4%	15.7%	2.0%
Filipino	49.0%	33.8%	15.6%	1.7%
Cambodian	82.1%	12.2%	5.5%	0.3%
Laotian	75.0%	19.8%	3.9%	1.3%
Hmong	71.4%	22.9%	5.6%	0.1%
Vietnamese	41.7%	40.6%	16.2%	1.5%

SOURCE: Data from PUMS 5% of the 2000 Census (U.S. Bureau of the Census, 2003a), compiled by authors.

Note: Percentages do not total to 100 due to the rounding of percentages for subgroups.

come to the United States since 1995 (74%), followed by Indian (52%) and Chinese (50%) immigrant children. The majority of Cambodian, Laotian, and Hmong immigrant children had been in this country for over five years, and a larger proportion of them (48% of Cambodian, 49% of Laotian, and 34% of Hmong) had been here more than ten years.

The age-distribution patterns at the time of arrival of immigrant children is the same for Asian immigrant children and all U.S. immigrant children, with more than half of both groups having arrived in this country at age five or younger, but one of six having arrived in this country at 10 years or older. Most Asian nationality groups follow this pattern, with one exception: a larger percentage of Cambodian (82%), Laotian (75%), and Hmong (71.4%) immigrant children arrived at five or younger, as compared to the general age-distribution pattern.

Oral English Proficiency

Table 5.6 presents the self-reported English proficiency rates among children speaking languages other than English at home. Among all generations of HLS children, 66% reported speaking English very well, compared to 55% of immigrant children. A higher percentage of Asian immigrant

TABLE 5.6   Self-Reported English Proficiency for Asian Children
Who Spoke a Language Other Than English at Home

	All Children			Immigrant Children		
		Not Very			Not Very	
	No English	Well	Very Well	No English	Well	Very Well
All Children	1.6%	32.3%	66.1%	3.8%	41.2%	55.0%
All Asian Children	0.6%	32.7%	66.6%	6.3%	39.1%	54.6%
Chinese	0.5%	32.9%	66.6%	1.1%	43.8%	55.1%
Japanese	2.9%	40.2%	56.9%	5.8%	57.9%	36.4%
Korean	0.6%	31.4%	68.0%	1.2%	46.3%	52.5%
Asian Indian	0.2%	19.0%	80.8%	0.4%	22.5%	77.1%
Filipino	0.2%	24.8%	75.0%	0.2%	29.1%	70.8%
Cambodian	0.5%	35.6%	63.9%	0.8%	30.1%	69.1%
Laotian	0.6%	34.1%	65.3%	0.7%	38.2%	61.1%
Hmong	0.9%	50.9%	48.2%	0.6%	62.1%	37.4%
Vietnamese	0.6%	42.1%	57.3%	0.7%	57.8%	41.5%

SOURCE: Data from PUMS 5% of the 2000 Census (U.S. Bureau of the Census, 2003a),
    compiled by authors.

Note: Percentages do not total to 100 due to the rounding of percentages for subgroups.

children reported speaking no English than all U.S. HLS children (6.3% vs.
3.8%), but similar percentages in these two groups reported speaking English very well (54.6% vs. 55%). However, the highest percentage who reported speaking English very well were children from English-speaking
countries (India and the Philippines) or who had lengthy U.S. residency,
such as those who had come to the United States at a young age (Cambodian and Laotian children mainly). The lower English proficiency rates
among Japanese children may be attributed to the high proportion of newcomers in their immigrant population, and the lower English proficiency
rates among Hmong children may be explained by their lower socioeconomic status and high frequency of linguistic isolation in the United States.

When we consider length of residency, age of arrival, heritage-language
speaking, and oral English proficiency simultaneously, it is not easy to determine which nationality groups in the immigrating generation were more
linguistically assimilated than the others. Although the Southeast Asian immigrant children (except Hmong) tended to have lengthier U.S. residencies,
to have arrived in the United States at a younger age, and to speak better
English, they also had a very high percentage who spoke heritage languages at home. Asian Indian and Filipino children had the highest percentage who spoke English very well and spoke English only, but they also had
a fairly large portion of newcomers: 52% of Indian children and 40% of Filipino children had resided in the United States less than five years.

Education of Children

Using available data from the 2000 census, we compiled three educational indices. These three indices are general enrollment rates for ages 5–18, enrollment rates in private schools for ages 5–18, and school dropout rates for ages 16–18.

General Enrollment

Table 5.7 shows that Asian-American children, as a whole, were more likely to be enrolled in school than U.S. children (97.4% vs. 96.2%); Asian immigrant children were also more likely to be enrolled in school than all U.S. immigrant children (96.8% vs. 94.5%); and the enrollment gap between all Asian children and Asian immigrant children (97.4% vs. 96.8%) for 2000 was smaller than that between U.S. children as a whole and all U.S. immigrant children (96.3% vs. 94.5%). Almost all Asian nationality groups, as a whole and in the immigrant generation, had higher or equal enrollment rates compared to the national rates, except Cambodian and Laotian children. At 98.2%, Hmong's immigrant children had the highest school enrollment rates among all Asian nationality groups despite their low socioeconomic status and lower English proficiency.

TABLE 5.7   Educational Characteristics of U.S. Asian Children 5–18 Years Old by Ethnicity, National Origin, and Immigration Status, 2000

	All Children (112,044)	Immigrant Children (29,407)
% of Children (5–18) Enrolled in Schools in 2000		
All Children	96.3%	94.5%
All Asian Children	97.4%	96.8%
Chinese	98.0%	97.1%
Japanese	97.6%	97.8%
Korean	98.0%	97.9%
Asian Indian	97.9%	97.6%
Filipino	96.9%	96.0%
Cambodian	95.7%	92.8%
Laotian	94.9%	94.4%
Hmong	96.8%	98.2%
Vietnamese	96.8%	96.7%

% of Children 5–18 Enrolled in Private Schools in 2000		
All Children	10.8%	6.0%
All Asian Children	12.2%	8.1%
Chinese	12.7%	7.7%
Japanese	16.9%	17.9%
Korean	10.9%	11.2%
Asian Indian	14.7%	8.2%
Filipino	16.5%	10.1%
Cambodian	2.3%	2.3%
Laotian	1.6%	0.2%
Hmong	1.2%	1.2%
Vietnamese	7.7%	3.8%
% of Children 16–18 Years Old Who Were School Dropouts (Persons Who Did Not Graduate From High School But Were Not Enrolled in School in 2000) by Race-Ethnicity and Immigration Status		
All Children	5.6%	9.0%
All Asian Children	3.0%	3.4%
Chinese	2.0%	2.5%
Japanese	1.9%	1.5%
Korean	2.1%	2.3%
Asian Indian	1.7%	2.6%
Filipino	2.4%	3.3%
Cambodian	5.9%	7.0%
Laotian	8.5%	8.6%
Hmong	4.0%	2.8%
Vietnamese	3.4%	3.8%

SOURCE: Data from PUMS 5% of the 2000 Census (U.S. Bureau of the Census, 2003a), compiled by authors.

Enrollment in Private Schools

Asian children were more likely to enroll in private schools than U.S. children as a whole (12.2% vs. 10.8%), and Asian immigrant children were also more likely to enroll in private schools than all U.S. immigrant children (8.1% vs. 6.0%). For example, at 17.9%, immigrant Japanese children had the highest private school enrollment rates, almost three times the national rates for all U.S. immigrant children; Japanese American children as a whole also had higher private school enrollment rates than all U.S. children. Children from Southeast Asian countries had much lower percentages of enrollments in private schools than the national rates and the rates for all Asian children—especially Laotian and Hmong children, who had the lowest private school enrollment rates among these groups.

The high private school enrollment rates for individual nationality groups may be due to a combination of factors. For example, some Japanese children went to Japanese schools in the United States—and received instruction in all subjects in Japanese—because many of these children's parents were employed in Japanese companies or international companies in the United States, and their children were expected to return to school in Japan in the near future, when the families returned home. High socioeconomic status of the family is also a factor, making enrollment in private school affordable. The high private school enrollment rates (16.5%) among Filipino children can be explained partly by their Catholic backgrounds.

High School Dropouts

Nationally, 5.6% of children aged 16–18 did not receive high school diplomas and were not enrolled in school in 2000. This percentage is 60% higher among immigrant children (9%). Asian children show a much lower dropout rate than the national rate, and the difference between all Asian children and Asian immigrant children is moderate (3.0% vs. 3.4%). For several nationality groups, including the Japanese and Hmong, immigrant children actually had lower school dropout rates than all children within the individual nationality group. For example, Hmong immigrant children had a dropout rate of 2.8%, compared to 4% for all Hmong children. Dropout rates were lowest among Japanese immigrant children and all Indian children (1.7%), but highest among Laotian children (8.5% for all Laotian children and 8.6% for Laotian immigrant children). None of the Asian immigrant nationality groups had higher dropout rates than the rate for all U.S. immigrant children; however, the dropout rates for Cambodian (5.9%) and Laotian children (8.5%) were higher than the national rates for all U.S. children (5.6%).

Effects of the Factors Combined

How does language transition affect the level of children's educational achievement? How do the effects differ across groups?

Again, we used school dropout rates as a measure to study the effects of assimilation on educational achievement. Based on 1990 census data (Rong & Preissle, 1998), no clear pattern emerges on how the length of U.S. residence affects the dropout rates among Asian immigrant children of various groups. Southeast Asian 17-year-olds are the only group with a pattern similar to Mexican immigrant children. Twelve percent of 17-year-old Southeast Asian children who came to the United States between 1987 and 1990 had dropped out of school; the percentage fell to 8% for the 1982–1984 cohort, and further fell to 2% for the 1975–1979 cohort. The dropout rates for 18-year-olds seem to follow the same trend except for the 1987–1990 cohort. Of all Asian groups, Southeast Asian youths are the only ones with this trend—a decline in dropping out with increased length of U.S. residence. In many cases, youths in the current cohort are less likely to drop out from school than those from the earlier cohort.

Finally, how do the combined effects of length of U.S. residence, linguistic adaptation, and family income affect Asian children's dropout rates? We (Rong & Preissle, 1998) divided immigrant children by three linguistic statuses: youth who spoke an Asian language but lacked English proficiency; youth who spoke an Asian language but also spoke English very well; and youth who were monolingual English speakers. Our data indicate a general pattern: Asian youth who lacked English proficiency, regardless of level of family income, had the highest dropout rates. However, among youth from high-income families, the dropout rates for youth who were monolingual English speakers were lower than the dropout rates of bilingual speakers for most of the Asian groups. Among youth from low-income families, no clear pattern distinguishes the effects of English monolingualism or bilingualism on dropout rates. Youth from low-income families who were bilingual do not necessarily drop out of school at higher rates than monolingual English speakers, except for Filipino children—0% vs. 9% in favor of monolingual English speakers. Southeast Asians show a pattern similar to Mexicans: monolingual English speakers were more likely to drop out of school than bilingual speakers—11% of monolingual English speakers, versus 6% of bilingual speakers. Asians generally had very low dropout rates, and few Asian dropouts fell into the category of the least educated (less than four years of schooling). Dropouts from low-income families in the Southeast Asian group were more frequently monolingual English speakers (6%) than bilingual speakers, with or without English proficiency.

SUMMARY OF DEMOGRAPHICS FOR ASIAN CHILDREN

Asian children, as a whole, have the most schooling, the highest grade point averages, the lowest dropout rates, and an overrepresentation in the gifted programs in almost all states across the United States (U.S. Department of Education, 1993a, 1993b, 2006a, 2006b). Even when controlling for socioeconomic differences, Asian children's performance patterns persist. Previous research with cross-racial and ethnic group comparisons (based on the Current Population Survey, U.S. Bureau of the Census, 1986, 1989) shows that Asian students generally have done better than either Black or Hispanic students in school and equally well or slightly better than non-Hispanic White students in years of school completed, percentage of high school graduates, percentage of college graduates, and most other educational measures (Grant & Rong, 1999; Rong & Grant, 1992). This fits evidence we have discussed already that immigrant minorities persist in school longer and, once initial language handicaps are overcome, achieve a greater degree of academic success than non-immigrant involuntary racial minorities (Gibson, 1988; Ogbu, 1987). Although Asian-Americans currently constitute only 4.5% of students in U.S. schools, their level of educational achievement is instructive to study.

The marked differences between Asian immigrant children and other immigrant children are multiple:

- Asian children are more likely to have highly educated parents who work in professional and management occupations.
- Asian children are more likely to live in two-parent families and do well in their education.
- However, contrary to the generally held perception, the high achievement and more favorable socioeconomic status of Asian-American students as a group is not shared by all Asian-American students, who are indeed a diverse and heterogeneous group in many aspects.

Census data show clear divisions among the Asian nationality groups. While East Asian, Indian, and Filipino children are more likely to come from higher socioeconomic status families, Southeast Asian children tend to come from families with more disadvantaged backgrounds. Poverty rates and parental education vary even among the more successful groups, such as the Chinese and Japanese, as well as between Filipinos and Indians. Furthermore, although Asian children in general may be more likely than others to live in affluent families, Hmong families had the highest poverty rates in the nation, though their poverty rates declined significantly between 1989 and 1999. The differences in socioeconomic status among the various Asian-American nationalities may be partially explained by differences in the following areas: reasons for immigration (economic immigrants vs. political refuges); types of visa (visa for high-tech occupation vs. visa for family reunification); history of immigration to the United States (long-term immigration history, back to the early 19th century—with multigenerational communities—vs. immigration since 1975, with two-generation communities); and the duration of parental residence in the United States.

As we discuss in Chapters 2–4, disadvantages in socioeconomic status influence the characteristics of Southeast Asian children, who showed generally higher physical and learning-related disability rates and lower English proficiency rates. The combination of these multiple disadvantages has hindered Laotian, Cambodian, and, to some extent, Vietnamese children in their educational achievements. However, despite these unfavorable conditions, about 90% of Hmong children lived with two parents, and immigrant Hmong children showed high school enrollment rates and low dropout rates.

Our findings on Asian-Americans contradict the common image of Southeast Asian immigrants (cf. Caplan, Choy, & Whitmore, 1991; Trueba, Jacobs, & Kirton, 1990). Because of their low socioeconomic status and their difficulties before and during immigration, Southeast Asian immigrant children have been predicted to experience problems in educational achievement. What we have found, however, is that these children actually did better than children in most other groups at similar socioeconomic levels (e.g., Central American children) and even better than some groups at higher socioeconomic levels (e.g., some Black and Hispanic groups). Southeast Asian children have lagged behind other Asian children, partly because of their particular situations; nevertheless, the differences in educational attainment for Asian children aged 5–18 do not reflect the bipolar patterns found in their family socioeconomic statuses and parental educational attainments.

DISCUSSION

The majority of Asian-American children are both minority group members and immigrants, and researchers anticipate youths with this dual status may be less successful in U.S. schools because they face the barriers of racism and xenophobia and the challenges of linguistic adaptation and cultural adjustment to U.S. institutions and society (Suzuki, 1977). Therefore, the "success" of some Asian groups and the deep socioeconomic divisions within Asian-Americans raise questions about why some Asian groups do so well but others do not, and why most Asian students do well compared to many other racial minority students. We believe that no single explanation fully accounts for the patterns evident from the 2000 census data or adequately addresses the question of why there are inter- and intra-group variations in educational achievement. We have adapted a more comprehensive framework for these questions by, first, briefly describing a few relevant theories developed before 1990 and, then, discussing three relatively current and influential theories: cultural match, relative functionalism, and cultural ecology theories, with a critique on model-minority stereotype. We also briefly consider the postulated explanations involving immigration-related demographic characteristics and historical timing.

Review of the Literature

Lee and Rong (1988) review several early explanations for Asian-Americans' success, such as "model minorities" (Kitano, 1976) or "middle men" (Bonacich, 1973). In general, these ideas assert that Asian-Americans have benefited from selective immigration, relatively favorable entry conditions, and favorable "niches" in the host economy (Lieberson, 1980). Their success has been attributed to their relevant cultural and social attributes and key demographic characteristics such as high intelligence, cultural fitness, and high visibility as petite bourgeoisie and professionals.

Conchas (2006) summarized three more current theoretical perspectives for Asian-American successes: cultural fit, functionalism, and cultural ecology. These theories can guide our understanding of educational achievement by Asian-American students in U.S. schools.

Cultural Match

Cultural match or fit, the theory that immigrant incorporation is facilitated by similarities between the host and the home societies, suggests that Asian culture promotes education. Scholars assert that Asians possess traits highly regarded by the dominant White group: a propensity for hard work, self-motivation, a respectful nature, and appreciation for the delay of gratification for future success (Conchas, 2006). The higher academic expectations of Asian parents generally, compared to U.S. parents, may be attributed to their cultural beliefs about how effort results in educational success. The high educational achievement of East Asian children may be explained by their deeply rooted tradition of valuing education and parental authority associated with Confucianism (Ma, 2007). However, Confucianism does not explain the variations in achievement among Asian nationality groups—or even within Chinese-Americans—and the very high educational achievement among Asian Indian students.

Functionalism

Conchas (2006) points out that functionalist theory, which emphasizes how changes in one part of a system result in changes throughout the system, suggests that the high educational achievement of Asians is strongly influenced by specific opportunity structures for Asian immigrants that are associated with social mobility; high educational achievement cannot be attributed solely to cultural factors without consideration of these socioeconomic structures. Asians possessed the high tech and science-mathematics skills that the U.S. economy sought. These attracted Asian immigrants and influenced Asian immigrant parents to encourage their children to pursue them. Sue and Okazaki (1990), however, compared two contrasting hypotheses involving hereditary differences in intelligence between Asians and Whites and Asian cultural values that promote educational endeavors. Their findings cast serious doubt over the validity of the genetic hypothesis and suggest an alternative hypothesis concerning cultural values. They and other scholars (Goyette & Xie, 1999; Okutsu, 1989) believe that, while cultural values may play a role in success, Asian-Americans' obsession with education is fundamentally an induced coping mechanism to assist survival in an environmentally hostile society.

Because of their historic exclusion and marginal status in U.S. society, Asian-Americans of all ethnic groups may view education as a functional avenue to overcome discrimination and other barriers, and attain higher social and economic status, when other means of social mobility are blocked. The high expectations of parents may also be consistent with the induced reaction to the social-occupational barriers they perceive. Asian parents may view education as an effective channel of upward mobility for their children, and thus place a high instrumental value on educational achievement. J. Li (2001), writing about Asian-American's experiences in Canada, claims that parents' understanding of Canadian society, and their perception that visible minorities are disadvantaged, has prompted them to form a minority ideology and to advise their children to pursue not only more education but also specifically science-related careers. However, functionalism does not specify how different opportunity structures develop for various Asian groups, presumably due to their different immigration histories and experiences, and also cannot explain why groups with similar opportunity structures might also achieve differently.

Cultural Ecology

As described in Chapter 4, Ogbu (1978, 1987) developed what he later came to call a cultural ecology theory to explain differential school achievement among minority groups in societies around the world. He drew from the idea of interacting natural, physical, cultural, and social environments that mutually influence one another. He wanted to explain the relationships among the unique contexts of incorporation of various groups in the United States, minority status, perceptions of limited opportunity structures, and academic achievement. East Asians and Asian Indians, for example, are considered to be "voluntary minorities" who came to this country mostly to improve their economic conditions. Southeast Asian (Vietnamese, Hmong, etc.) and other political refugees are considered to be semi-voluntary minorities because they did not prepare for immigration, were unable to bring personal belongings and family property, and planned to go back to their home countries when the political conditions changed. East Asian students tend to do well in school because they foresee upward mobility and compare their situations favorably with their peers back in their homeland; political refuges may not focus on achieving success in the host country because they continue to track changes in their home countries, which they still consider as their final destinations. Cultural ecology theory not only tries to explain the different achievement patterns between Asian students and other domestic and immigrant minority groups, such as Blacks and Mexicans, but also tries to shed light on the divisions among Asian students. However, the cultural-ecological framework does not satisfactorily explain the differences among the various groups of voluntary economic immigrants, as well as the success of some political refugee groups, such as Cubans. Furthermore, as Conchas (2006) cautions, it may unintentionally reinforce the "model-minority" stereotype.

In the 1960s, the idea of being considered a model minority sounded like a compliment to Asian-Americans, compared to the racial inferiority labels imposed on this group before that time period. However, critical race theorists (e.g., Pang & Cheng, 1998) have suggested that the model-minority reflects only a fraction of the truth. They highlight the negative effects of this stereotype and the assumptions underlying it that foster racism and intergroup hostility.

First, it creates a monolithic image of a large population, thereby dismissing the wide range of Asian-American experiences by erasing ethnic cultural, social-class, gender, language, sexual, generational, achievement, and other differences among Asian-Americans. For example, this stereotype ignores the poverty and illiteracy in Asian-American communities.

Second, the stereotype not only overlooks the racism that Asian-Americans experience, but also discounts the charges of racial injustice made by African-Americans and other minorities (Daniels, 2002). The model-minority stereotype creates another layer in the dichotomization of U.S. society into Whites and Blacks. It reestablishes the U.S. racial hierarchies and relations of power that have been challenged by in-surges of other large populations such as Asians and Latinos who do not fit well into the structuring of society into Whites and Blacks (S. Lee, 2005). Arguably, with the model-minority stereotype, dominant groups create a cultural hegemony that divides racial minorities and sets them against one another to reinforce the status quo. This phenomenon is most glaring in our educational system (Conchas, 2006).

Other Explanations

Two additional explanations have been offered for the differential school achievement of various groups in U.S. society: demographics and historical timing.

Demographic Explanations

Many immigration-related demographic factors may contribute to students' educational achievements. For example, researchers report that length of U.S. residence and recency of immigration have an impact on immigrant success. For the majority of immigrants, those who comprise the 1.5 generation or who have lived here for a long time differ in many respects from those who recently immigrated: in linguistic transition, social and psychological adjustment, progress in school, and such (Kao & Tienda, 1995; Rong & Grant, 1992). Economic disadvantages may also be attributed to being largely first-generation immigrants. Southeast Asians, for example, generally have come to the United States in the past 20 years, whereas two-thirds of Japanese families have been in this country for several generations. Unlike East Asians and Filipinos, who have a history of immigration to the United States that extends over 100 years and more than five generations, 95% of Southeast Asians are foreign-born and therefore do not have the multi-generational ethnic communities, ethnic industries, and employment networks of longer-term and better established U.S. residents (cf. Smith-Hefner, 1990, 1993; Takahashi, 1998).

Another highly recognized demographic factor is the effect of children's immigration generation within a nationality group. Some studies show that Asian-American students of the first and second generations had better academic performance at each grade level, and faster rates of improvement across the years, than those of the third and later generations (Grant & Rong, 1999; Rong & Grant, 1992). Mathematics and science were the two subject areas that most distinguished the first two generations from later generations. Even after controlling for the effects of major background characteristics, the observed generational differences in academic performance and its growth were significant (Zhang, 2003).

Studies also report different attitudes toward school and schooling among different generations. Kaufman (2004) reports that Chinese immigrant students were motivated to work hard and valued demanding teachers, difficult curricula, and discipline more than their second-generation Chinese peers; the second-generation students talked of wanting more entertaining, knowledgeable teachers; they seemed either unwilling or unable to work as hard for academic success as the first generation. These findings indicate that differences in students' perceptions of their own effort and success in school may depend on the social environment framed by the immigration generation in which students find themselves, as well as the culturally-driven actions available within those environments.

Historical Timing

Using critical social-historical analysis of Asians' experiences in America, some scholars assert that the success of some Asian-American groups has been a function of historical timing: a more favorable sociopolitical environment in the United States since the civil rights movement, and new immigration laws. Transnational theories add to these the rise of the Asian-Pacific Rim and the business and political relationships between Asian countries and the United States (Alba & Nee, 2003; Rong, 2005b). Lee and Rong's (1988) analysis of Asians' experiences in the United States show that Asian-Americans have not always done well because of the historical structural restrictions embodied in immigration-related laws, policies, and other social restraints. As we have noted previously in the chapter, on arriving in large numbers in the United States in the middle of the 19th century, the Chinese were viewed by many native-born Americans as being intellectually inferior; they were also considered incapable of participating in western-style democratic social life. Thus, the laws and policies of the day banned them from educational and business opportunities and prevented them from being integrated into mainstream society. No large-scale progress in these areas was made for a long time, at least until the 1970s.

The success of Asian-Americans during the era of the emergent Pacific Rim—primarily the 1980s—can also be partially explained by a match between the experiences and skills of Asian immigrants, on the one hand, and business needs and opportunity structures on the other (cf. E. Kim, 1993).

As U.S. markets have become increasingly dependent on international trade with Asian countries, foreign investment, imported engineers and scientists, expanding investment from Japan, China, India, and other Asian countries, and the influx of Asian professionals and business people have met these changing needs. Jo (2004) explores the changing representations of Asians in the history of the United States and delineates the underlying power relationships in the racial discourse of the United States in their international context. She argues that the representation of Asians, especially the model-minority construct, has been influenced by the domestic and global economical and political milieu.

We have shown so far that all theories have merit, but no one theory can account fully for the differences between Asian students and other students, much less for the achievement variations among different Asian nationality groups. The discrepancies in Asian children's schooling outcomes may be best explained through a comprehensive framework integrating various theories in multiple domains and at various levels. Our recommendations for what policymakers and educational leaders can do to improve the education of Asian immigrants in U.S. schools draw to some extent on this comprehensive theoretical framework.

RECOMMENDATIONS

Asian educational issues have received little attention among U.S. policymakers, because youth in this group are assumed to be doing well compared with other minority groups. However, census data from 1990 and 2000 show considerable variations in rates of disability, school enrollment, high school completion, and dropout rates among Asian youth. Asian immigrant youth are also hampered, to different extents, by their lack of English proficiency and other personal and family characteristics. Attention to these variations is crucial. Many Asian-American scholars (see Hsia, 1988; Peng & Wright, 1994; Wei, 1986) stress that ignoring these youngsters' urgent needs because other members of the same ethnic group are doing relatively well in U.S. schools is not a sound policy. Furthermore, many Asian children are doing well in school, but this does not mean that U.S. schools are doing well by Asian children with their specific issues, or that Asian parents are satisfied with the schools their children attend. In addition to concerns about the quality of education schools provide and the discipline problems in many middle and high schools, parents have other issues.

Unfortunately, many Asian immigrant youth from non-English-speaking and low socioeconomic backgrounds have been retained in school and have dropped out because their language and other needs were not met. Moreover, Asian students' academic success does not always extend into the social aspects of schooling. In particular, an unintended consequence of their success has been possible racial isolation, social alienation, and psychological depression (Choi, 2001).

Therefore, educators need to be aware of and understand four discrepancies between Asian realities and their "model minority" image:

- First, as demonstrated by our data analyses, Asian-Americans are heterogeneous. Despite many successful cases, Asian children are from family backgrounds varying in educational achievement, language resources, occupation, and income.
- Second, psychological and sociological studies have revealed many problems in Asian immigrant children's emotional development, identity reconstruction, and intergenerational communication.
- Third, racial prejudice against Asian-Americans plays itself out in a different form: many have experienced sufficient success in education to be viewed as ethnic crossovers, and they may face a future of overeducation and underemployment.
- Fourth, Asian-American students in inner-city schools have been more likely than other students to be physically and verbally harassed by peers because of the resentment from other students when teachers show a preference for Asian students (e.g., Kiang & Kaplan, 1994; Rosenbloom & Way, 2004).

Educators need to recognize the undesirable consequences of the "model-minority" stereotype. One such consequence is that, although many Asian-American students are highly successful, large numbers of them are in need of assistance, support, and encouragement from parents, teachers, counselors, and institutions (H. Kim, 1997) in their linguistic and cultural adaptation. Nevertheless, Asian-Americans from disadvantaged backgrounds tend to be bypassed for supportive services and programs available for children with special needs. Focusing on the latter two points, we make the following four recommendations.

Recommendation One: Recognize the Distinctions Among "Being Well," "Doing Well," and "Feeling Good"

Bankston and Zhou (2002) argue that most Asian-American adults might be well educated, middle class, and residentially integrated into mainstream communities, although some Asian ethnic enclaves exist in New York City, San Francisco, and several other large cities. However, abundant literature suggests that the high levels of Asian-Americans' educational attainment do not always result in other kinds of success (e.g., Barringer, Takeuchi, & Xenos, 1990). In examining data from the National Longitudinal Study of Adolescent Health, Bankston and Zhou found that Asian youth do show the lowest levels of reported self-esteem of the major racial-ethnic groups, but also the highest grade-point averages. This finding complicates the frequently mentioned suggestion that the academic achievement of minority students may be hindered by low self-esteem in a White-dominated society.

Examining school-related psychological concerns, Way and Chen (2000) suggest that Asian children, including those from higher socioeconomic backgrounds, face depression and insecurity. Researchers also report difficulties among Asian students in making friends outside their race or ethnicity, difficulties inconsistent with their good academic performance. Educators should pay attention to social relationships in schools: Asian-American students' interactions with their peers, their feelings of safety, and their ability to build friendships with students outside of their own racial and ethnic group (Kasinitz, Mollenkopf, & Waters, 2002; Rosenbloom & Way, 2004).

Immigration itself can result in numerous psychological problems. Asian immigrants unfamiliar with the U.S. legislative and legal processes, who lack social and political connections, may find themselves powerless to influence the making and implementation of school policies (Portes & Rumbaut, 1996). Although the Asian population has rapidly increased in the United States in the last three decades, in many states and regions—and especially in the new gateway states—Asian-Americans are still a first-generation immigrant population, a small percentage of the population, and likely vulnerable to being ignored and discriminated against. The psychological issues among Asian children are discrete, but not random or accidental. Teachers and school counselors should be aware of the isolation and frustration of the Asian newcomer students in their great efforts to overcome language barriers and make adjustments to U.S. educational institutions. For the second generation, most children of Asian immigrants hold firm to the ideology of assimilation and aspire to achieving parity with the society's dominant group. However, they are still keenly aware of their nonwhite racial status and are likely to internalize the disadvantages associated with it. This paradox can cause extreme stress under what may appear to be calm and silent Asian "masks" (Tuan, 1998; Yeh, 2004; Zhou & Sao, 2005).

Regrettably, Asian children's psychological problems have usually been under-identified by schools and not treated in a timely manner because of the nondisturbing nature of their problems. Asian parents may not actively seek professional help in schools, psychological clinics, or hospitals, because of misconceptions about the value and necessity of services of this kind (Uba, 1994, 2002). They often lack information about assistance programs; some may underestimate the severe consequence of these psychological problems; they may also have reservations about psychological treatment because of certain cultural traditions.

Immigrant children are under extreme pressure to rapidly integrate into peer culture in school and mainstream U.S. culture, and it is evident that Asian children have moved quickly toward Americanization. Monocultural ideology and monolinguistic practice in bicultural families and communities can cause intergenerational conflict as well as marginalization. Asian children struggle with these two opposite stereotypes: "permanent foreigner" (Tuan, 1998) and "Banana," a derogatory nickname for U.S.-born Asian children. They are also striving to gain balance while switching back and forth between two worlds, one of which is usually not understood in schools. Although all immigrant groups from non-English-language countries have shown a tendency toward bilingualism, census data reveal that Asian groups have weaker ties to their native languages than do Hispanic children. True, unlike Hispanic-Americans, Asian-Americans have not been bound by language, and the cultural symbol of their Asian identity is not represented by native tongues, although native languages may be the cultural symbol for each nationality. Some Asian groups who come from countries where English is an official language, such as Filipinos and Asian Indians, show a trend toward English monolingualism. Rong (1997) reports that, among second-generation Asians, over 95% reported speaking English very well, and the proportion of children who reported speaking a language other than English dropped to less than 20%. Among the third generation, all reported speaking English very well, and the percentage of children who reported speaking a language other than English at home decreased to less than 5%. Rong's study is consistent with studies done by other scholars (e.g., Portes & Hao, 1998, 2002). Although researchers report great efforts made within Asian-American communities to retain their languages and cultural heritages, this may be a difficult aspiration. Educators need to understand that many of these students have to use home and school as a dual frame of reference to negotiate expectations at both institutions (Teranishi, 2004). Schools not only need to encourage children to maintain their bilingualism but also need to provide resources, such as having dual-language programs, supporting community language schools (see Chapter 3), and involving the community to become part of the school's cultural life. Teachers and school psychologists also have to recognize the psychological problems resulting from being caught between the two worlds and provide children adequate consolation.

Educators believe that parents' expectations motivate their children to pursue high goals with hard work, enhancing self-efficacy and nurturing good study habits. Asian parents' high expectations, in fact, have often been praised as the crux of their children's high achievement. However, not many educators understand that Asian parents are uneasy under the double pressures of the model-minority stereotype and the marginalization of the social and racial environment (Louie, 2001, 2004). On the one hand, the internalization of the model-minority stereotype may cause parents to be unwilling to accommodate alternatives, resulting in counterproductive anxiety in their children (Kuhn, 2006; J. Li, 2001, 2003). On the other hand, the induced response to the perceived social and racial disadvantages may make Asian parents urge their children to enter science and high-tech related careers, as well as other careers with high earning potential, to optimize the opportunities for success in their children's futures. Although the majority of these children share similar expectations with their parents, some children experience intense difficulty in reconciling the vast differences presented in the dual process of self-fulfillment and family obligation, and this can undermine the evolving relationship between parental expectations and children's school achievement (J. Li, 2004). For those Asian children who desire not to enter college directly after high school graduation and Asian children who want to choose fields other than high-tech and high-earning fields—fields such as the arts, music, social work, and teaching (e.g., Rosenbloom & Way, 2004)—teachers and school counselors should not only find ways to support these students, but also need to work with their parents.

Recommendation Two: Identify and Work Effectively With Disadvantaged Asian Children

Assimilation, such as rapid Americanization, may have different consequences for children from affluent professional families and children from disadvantaged backgrounds. Before we address the issues of disadvantaged Asian children, we consider the relationship between cultural assimilation and structural assimilation, as well as the different consequences from either or both of them.

Some Asian immigrants, such as the recent highly trained and well paid Indians, Japanese, and Chinese immigrant professionals, seem to be well-assimilated structurally but not always culturally. They have kept close ties with kin in their home countries through digital technologies and frequent international air travel. They celebrate traditional festivals and drink tea and wines in an "exotic" way with their U.S. colleagues. They speak their mother tongues publicly without apology and send their children to community language schools to maintain their home languages, cultures, and values. The finalists of the prestigious Westinghouse Award (now the Intel Science Talent Award), National Spelling Bee, and some other science-related awards over the last 20 years have included many of the sons and daughters of these Asian professionals (e.g., Siemens Foundation, 2007). In contrast, other Asian immigrant youth who have resided in the United States long enough to become monolingual English speakers may have fully assimilated into the U.S. popular cultures but are still unable to join the middle class; this pattern has been too common among some Chinese who have resided in this country for generations, as well as many Southeast Asian newcomers.

One of the major untold stories of the model-minority stereotype—apart from the division of the socioeconomic status among Asian-Americans—is the tendency for division within any particular Asian-American nationality group. For example, our findings show that within-group differences are very pronounced among Chinese immigrants. Chinese children from family backgrounds of poverty and pre-literacy in ghetto areas have been invisible (on Korean inner-city children, see Lew, 2006), and the segment within the Southeast Asian population that has been doing well has not received much attention from the media. These within-group divisions may reflect different historical waves of immigration and different segments of a pre-migration class hierarchical structure. Because of the impact of the model-minority stereotype, the nation's schools have been particularly unprepared for educating Southeast Asian students. Hmong, Lao, Cambodian, and Vietnamese students face a number of challenges in language, linguistic discrimination, poverty, and cultural clashes within and between family and school. These children and their parents should be informed of, and invited to, many services and special programs for disadvantaged minority children.

For example, Asian children at lower socioeconomic levels are more likely to live in linguistically isolated households and report more problems in English proficiency. Unlike Asian-American children from professional families, these families may also lack resources to aid their children's linguistic transition. Programs for ELL students should recruit these students aggressively and provide a variety of means for their language adaptation. For example, to help this group, the Center for Applied Linguistics (CAL) reprinted Vietnamese school textbooks in English, so that teachers could learn more about what their new students had studied. However, sometimes no previous study had occurred. In the mid-1980s, teacher groups consulted by CAL reported difficulties with an increasing number of refugee children who had virtually no education because they had been in transit as refugees for as long as 10 years (McDonnell & Hill, 1993). Teenagers from Laos and Cambodia were particularly at risk in the schools on this account. The same condition is currently being reported for many new arrivals from Central America, where youngsters have often bypassed educational systems altogether (Portes & Rumbaut, 1996).

Recommendation Three: Develop and Implement Culturally Responsive Curriculum and Instruction

Parental encouragement to succeed, workable school policies, teachers' efforts, and a supportive school social environment facilitate children's school adjustment (Bhattacharya, 2000). Asian parents and students alike want to modify the current school curricula to reflect a more multicultural approach. Asian children from non-Western cultures who are asked to study only European values and history may perceive their own cultural heritage as unimportant or inferior; even history textbooks and cultural activities with Asian history included tend to focus on Chinese and Japanese history and tradition but neglect the other Asian groups. Many Asian youth complain that they live in the projected image of the host country with no Asian "character models" or "media models" in popular culture (Sung, 1987). Secondary schools should develop courses on the history of many Asian countries, not only China and Japan (Chan, 2007). Schools also need to develop Asian-American minority studies, including the histories and experiences of various groups of Asian-Americans who have immigrated to the United States, to increase students' awareness of the successes as well as the problems and difficulties Asian-Americans face today (Lee & Kumashiro, 2005).

Recommendation Four: Recruit and Retain Asian-American Teachers

Recruitment of Asian-American teachers is crucial to improving the quality of education that Asian-American children receive. For example, only 1% of the nation's elementary and secondary schoolteachers were Asian in 1990, but Asian students accounted for more than 3% of the U.S. elementary and secondary student population (Goodwin, Genishi, Asher, & Woo, 2005; Rong & Preissle, 1997). Asian students now account for more than 4.5% of U.S. pre-collegiate students, but Asian teachers still comprise less than 2% of the U.S. teaching force. Asian youth may need teachers who can serve as language and cultural brokers for the 80% of them who are first and second generation and may have difficulties with linguistic transition and cultural adjustment. They may also suffer from racial discrimination and economic barriers with no understanding of what is happening to them, because they may have no prior experience with these difficulties or with the underside of the model minority stereotype. In discussing outreach efforts, Lew (2006) found that the most important reason cited for immigrant parent involvement with school activities was bilingual outreach efforts by school staff and encouragement from other parents who spoke their native languages. Asian teachers may also help the school and all teachers to understand the rationales for and the effective strategies in working with Asian immigrant children and their families.

CONCLUSION

Because of the rapid growth of each of the large Asian-American groups, diversity is not only increasing in the two most dissimilar divisions (the well-to-do group and the struggling group), but also within each of the nationality groups spread in very different parts of the United States. Socioeconomic indictors for Asian-Americans in the latter half of the 20th century show that certain segments of some ethnic groups have made considerable strides, while the other groups still face uphill battles. Educators must realize that even those who are on the upper ends of the socioeconomic scale still face issues such as the glass ceiling, unequal returns on their education, blatant discrimination, hate crimes, and racial conflicts between the various racial and ethnic groups inside and outside schools. Asians will be acculturated into U.S. society in different ways and at different rates, reflecting these differences in each group's experiences (Logan, 2001). However, Nakanishi (1995) believes that the continuous and rapid growth of the Asian-American population has coincided with the growing political maturity and influence of Asian-Americans in the United States. Kitano (2001) observes that the 20th century saw progress for Asian-Americans, and they have reason to look forward to the 21st century with optimism.

6

Black Immigrant Children From the Caribbean and Africa

As the African-American experience moves into the 21st century, the fourth wave of immigration to the United States has brought new dynamics into the Black American population—a rapid increase in both the number of immigrants who are Blacks and their share of the Black American population. Because the Black population has comprised a very small fraction of the post-1900 immigrants compared to other racial and ethnic groups in the United States, most immigration studies have focused attention on increases in Hispanic and Asian populations over the last three decades. The U.S. Black population was not significantly affected by the first three waves of immigration, and the majority of the U.S. Black population in the 1950s was descended from slaves brought forcibly to Caribbean and mainland areas before the middle of the 19th century. However, Black immigration from Caribbean countries has grown noticeably since the 1970s, and the number of Black immigrants from African countries has risen sharply since the mid-1990s. Although only one of eight Black Americans was an immigrant or child of an immigrant in 2005, with the current trend in immigration, educators must be prepared to meet the educational needs of these children. Immigrant Black children from the Caribbean and Africa have somewhat different needs from those both of the domestic Black population and of other immigrant minority children.

Although Black immigrants may currently constitute a small percentage of students in United States schools, their dual status, as Black and immigrant, interests sociological researchers. Some scholars anticipated these children would be less successful in U.S. schools because of facing the triple barriers of racism, classism, and xenophobia (including linguicism); other scholars have regarded them as a "Black success story" in a racially segregated society (Bryant, 2007; Butcher, 1994; Farley & Walter, 1989; Model, 1991). The more recent research reveals significant intragroup differences in Afro-Caribbean populations, challenging the blanket notion of a "Black success story" among Caribbean immigrants (Kalmijn, 1996).

BLACK AMERICANS AND BLACK IMMIGRANTS IN THE UNITED STATES

We define Black immigrants as people who first identified themselves as non-Hispanic in a census question and then identified themselves as Black in a census question on race classification. These two steps exclude Spanish-speaking Black immigrants who come from countries such as Cuba and the Dominican Republic from the Black immigrant population we are studying in this chapter. We identify Black children's nationalities based on their self-claimed Afro-ancestry and place of birth.

The term "Caribbean Black" as used here refers to "Caribbean Black Americans with recent immigration history"; "African Black" refers to "African Black Americans with recent immigration history"; and "American Blacks" refers to "Americans of African origin, but with no recent immigration history." We also use the term "African-Americans" to refer to the whole Black population living in the United States.

A Historical Sketch

The information presented herein was compiled from materials published by Gilmore (2000), Higman (1997), Knight (1997), Roberts (2005), Rong and Fitchett (2008), and Sunshine and Warner (1998a). The Black presence in North America has more than 400 years of history, and it has been a heterogeneous group from its very beginning. Different groups of Blacks came to the United States from different nations and continents, in different eras, for different purposes, by different means, and with different migration patterns.

Among the flood of immigrants to North America, one group came unwillingly. About half a million African Blacks were brought to North America as slaves between 1619 and 1808, when slave trade into the United States became illegal. Because of the racial and Eurocentric nature of U.S. immigration and naturalization laws before 1965, most of the Black population in the United States in the 1950s was descended from the slaves brought from

Africa, often by way of the Caribbean. The Black immigrant population has expanded since the 1965 immigration reform; the more significant increase occurred in the last two decades of the 20th century (Kasinitz, 1992). However, the most impressive population growth so far happened at the beginning of this century. In 1960 125,000 foreign-born Black people were living in the United States (accounting for less than 1% of the Black population), 815,000 in the 1980s (accounting for 3% of the Black population), but about 2.7 million Black immigrants in 2005, a 2160% increase in a period of less than half a century. The foreign-born population now accounts for 8% of the entire Black population, and another 4% are second generation. About one in eight Blacks in the United States is an immigrant or a child of an immigrant. The U.S. Census Bureau has projected a further increase in the foreign-born Black population and their offspring. Current Black immigrants in the United States are composed of two major subpopulations: Afro-Caribbeans and people with recent sub-Saharan African ancestry.

African Black Immigrants

Compared with Caribbean Black immigration to the United States, significantly fewer Africans were able to move to the United States before 1990, due to the long distance between the African and Northern American continents and to historically unfavorable U.S. immigration policies, which restrained Black emigration from the African continent. Among the current 1.2 million immigrants from multiple African nations in 2005, Nigerians (166,000) are the single largest African immigrant group in the United States, significantly outnumbering immigrant groups such as Ethiopians (103,000), Ghanaians (83,000), Kenyans (67,000), and Liberians (58,000). Most African immigrants choose to live in large cities, such as New York, Washington, D.C., and Boston. Unlike Jamaicans or Haitians, who have established large communities in urban areas such as New York City and Miami, no large ethnic community for Black immigrants from a single African nation is currently found in the United States

The large-scale emigration of Black people from African countries is a very recent phenomenon. Between 2000 and 2005, the African immigrant population in the United States increased more than 40%. For example, there were 114,000 Nigerians in the United States in 2000, but 166,000 in 2005. Other African nationalities also experienced similar or higher rates of increase. More Blacks have migrated to the United States from Africa between 1990 and 2003 than in the two preceding centuries combined. As a result, for the first time in U.S. history, more Blacks are arriving in the United States from Africa than during the slave trade (Roberts, 2005). Although these numbers still represent a small fraction of the foreign-born U.S. population, this African influx could gradually become a substantial share of newcomers in years to come.

The increased flow of Africans over the last 10 years has been fostered by two components of the Immigration Act of 1990: the introduction of the diversity visa program and an increase in employment visas (Lobo, 2001). These two changes account for the increased inflow of skilled Africans to the United States and provide a swift path of entry for African immigrants who cannot qualify for a visa through close family ties with a U.S. resident. This increase in diversity and employment visas accounted for over 80% of the growth in African immigrants to the United States (Lobo, 2001). The increase is also tied to the more restrictive immigration policies and the economic recession in Western Europe, significantly shifting African migration flows from former colonial nations to the United States (Diamba, 1999). Furthermore, many Africans come to the United States not only for educational and economic opportunities, but also to escape from the political and economic turmoil in places like Somalia, Sudan, and Ethiopia. As a result, since 2000, about 20,000 African refugees have arrived annually in the United States (Arthur, 2000; Ehrlich, 2003).

Because of its diversity, long history of civilization, and site of human origins, the African continent is home to thousands of different ethnicities and language groups. However, two major official languages, English and French, used in African nations were the languages of the former colonial rulers of many African countries. Most African immigrants in the United States have come from English-speaking countries such as Nigeria, Ethiopia, and Ghana. However, African immigrants may speak indigenous African languages as well. For example, Nigerian immigrants may speak languages from the Niger-Congo language family, while Ethiopian immigrants may speak languages of the Nilo-Saharan language family. Both language families consist of more than a hundred African indigenous languages. It is, therefore, not unusual that some African immigrants can speak several African indigenous languages.

Caribbean Black Immigrants

Most Americans know about Caribbean countries from tourist experiences. We briefly review the history of Caribbean nations to show how complex historical factors have shaped the vast diversity among the Caribbean nations and the immigrants in the United States from this region. However, these nations have many commonalities, including struggling for freedom and national independence through the last two or three centuries.

The first inhabitants of the Caribbean were indigenous people from South and Central America who moved into Caribbean areas over 1,000 years ago. Then, European adventurers and gold-seekers landed in these islands in the late 15th century, and this resulted in a near-destruction of the native populations. The colonial powers organized a slave trade that brought 6 million Africans to the Caribbean region in the 18th and 19th centuries; these Africans became the basis for contemporary Caribbean societies. Therefore, African influences have largely shaped the development of Caribbean languages, religions, and cultures. Much of the story of the Caribbean, then, is one of a shared legacy of the historical experience of endurance, struggle, and independence (Sunshine & Warner, 1998b).

Caribbean Blacks' immigration history to North America has been long and slow. Caribbean Blacks began immigrating in small numbers to North America during the colonial era. The first period of Caribbean immigration to the United States in significant numbers was 1900–1930. More than 40,000 Blacks from Jamaica, Trinidad and Tobago, and other British Caribbean colonies moved to New York City during this period, forming small communities in places such as Boston and Philadelphia. The largest wave of emigration from the Caribbean—which continues today—began in 1965, when Britain restricted immigration from its former colonies in Africa, and the Hart-Celler Immigration Reform Act changed U.S. immigration policy and opened the door for an immigration surge. At present, Jamaicans represent the largest group in the Afro-Caribbean population in the United States.

Most Jamaican immigrants have been English speakers because English has been the official language there. Although immigrants generally take the most menial jobs, many Caribbean immigrants possess relatively high educational levels, so prior to their emigration they were physicians, nurses, college professors, writers, artists, and other highly trained professionals qualified to work in high-tech industries. Furthermore, urban Jamaicans have some exposure to U.S. culture through the popular presence of U.S. media (television, films, Internet, etc.). All these factors contribute to the relatively smooth incorporation of Jamaicans into U.S. society and its labor force.

However, the immigration experiences of Haitians are quite different. Haitian emigrants leave their country for the United States from a desire to improve family economic conditions or a fear of political persecution. Haitian immigration to the United States has occurred in several waves, each being associated with repressive conditions in Haiti (Stepick, 1998). The first wave began in 1957, when the immigrants were generally members of the well-educated political and economic elite. The second wave of immigrants, coming from the late 1960s through the early 1980s, were skilled laborers from the Haitian middle class. The next wave of immigrants became known as the Haitian "boat people": mostly lower-working-class people who experienced firsthand U.S. racial discrimination before they even arrived on U.S. soil. The prevailing stereotype of Haitian immigrants, unfortunately, became that of impoverished and ignorant "boat people," trying to escape unbearable conditions at home by attempting to cross national borders with little or no documentation. Through the 1980s, the U.S. authorities had welcomed Cuban boat people as refugees escaping Communism—but a high percentage of Haitians, fleeing a dictatorial government and attempting to reach the shores of Florida, were routinely sent back (DeWind, 1990). This has led to many civil rights protests about the unfair treatment they have received, in contrast to the asylum granted to Caribbean refugees from other countries.

For these and other reasons, Haitians have been viewed by many as having "quadric-disadvantaged status"—being Black, foreign and Francophonic, poor, and refugees. Their position in the U.S. racial-ethnic spectrum is ambiguous and, at times, isolating. The White majority perceives them simply as "Black." Yet within the larger Black community, Haitians are separated from African-Americans, and from other Black immigrants, by their language. Thus, their experience is often a lonely one, as Haitian youngsters taunted with the label "Franchise" can attest. At times, however, it can seem an advantage: knowledge of French—or at least Creole—enables Haitians, if they so desire, to distance themselves from the African-American population.

Besides the Jamaican and Haitian differences, the diversity in language and culture, political identity, and other social historical traits is immense within the Caribbean area (Sunshine & Warner, 1998b). First among these has been the variety of languages spoken. In addition to Creole, Black immigrants from Caribbean areas speak at least four European languages—English, Spanish, French, and Dutch—deriving from the occupied history by the four European colonial powers (Spain, England, France, and the Netherlands). The region has remained somewhat divided along these old colonial lines. Contacts and interactions across the linguistic barriers are relatively few. Another division is political status, due to each country's unique identity rooted in its history, language, and culture. In the last quarter-century, most of the Caribbean colonies have gained independence and become sovereign nations. Haiti was the first to acquire its independence in 1804, but other countries (Jamaica, 1962; Trinidad and Tobago, 1962) have gained their independence only in the last 50 years. These or other differences in political histories, and their relationships with the United States, may also explain the separate and clearly defined national identities, cultural-psychological characteristics, and various patterns of migration of the immigrants who have come from these island countries.

A second division among Caribbean immigrants is that of skin color and socioeconomic class, and efforts to mobilize united action among Caribbean immigrants have had to contend with these basic schisms. For example, as we have indicated previously, Haitian-Americans are divided by class as well as political differences. As new waves of immigrants have arrived, class differences have intensified. Not only were most of the early exiles from the Haitian elite well-educated and well-versed in both French and Creole, but also they were largely, although not entirely, light-skinned. The newer immigrants represent the Haitian majority with darker skin, less education, and fluency in only Creole. As a result, the established Haitian-American community initially shunned the newcomers.

In summary, the U.S. Black immigrant population came from two major regions: the Caribbean islands and the African continent. The differences between recent African immigrants and Caribbean immigrants are many. However, the diversity within Caribbean Black immigrants is also dramatic.

In addition to other influences we have discussed, the increase in the number of Black immigrants to the United States is due to the introduction of the 1965 Family Reunification and Refugee Law (Diamba, 1999). Black people in both the Caribbean and Africa have African origins, have experienced brutal European colonization in the past, and may have continually suffered postcolonial syndromes; however, the contexts of, causes for, and patterns of immigration from these two regions are different.

Until the post-World War II period, African territories, which were colonized mostly by European countries, did not have many formal and sustained contacts with the United States. The Republic of Liberia, the country established in the 19th century by former U.S. slaves, is a notable exception. In contrast, the United States' economic, political, and military involvement in the Caribbean region in the last two centuries indicates its close links to this area. Jamaica and Haiti—like the Spanish-speaking Caribbean nations such as Cuba and the Dominican Republic—have had the closest political and economic relations with the United States over many years, sending mostly non-Hispanic Black immigrants to the United States over a century-long period. U.S. involvement in the Caribbean is evidenced by all aforementioned countries except Jamaica being once occupied or supported by U.S. military forces.

Another difference between Caribbean and African immigrants may be the history of slavery. Most Caribbean Black immigrants have a family history of slaves who fought for their personal freedom as well as their countries' independence; by contrast, the majority of current Black immigrants from the African continent did not have a family history of being kidnapped and enslaved. The majority of Caribbean non-Hispanic Blacks (except for a considerable portion of Haitians) came to the United States for economic reasons; however, a large portion of Africans came to the United States to escape traumatic wars launched within and between African nations, resulting in genocides and ethnic cleansings of large numbers of African peoples.

A SOCIODEMOGRAPHIC BRIEFING

The information presented in this section was compiled from materials published from *Black Diversity in Metropolitan America* by Logan and Deane (2003) and *The American community—Blacks: 2004* (U.S. Bureau of the Census, 2007b).

The number of Black Americans with recent roots in sub-Saharan Africa nearly tripled during the 1990s, and Black immigrants with Caribbean origins have increased by over 60%. The census of 2000 shows that the number of Afro-Caribbeans in the United States was over 1.5 million, larger than some more visible ethnic groups such as Cubans and Koreans; in addition, over 600,000 people claim origins from the various African nationalities. In some metropolitan regions these "new" Black groups amount to 20% or more of the Black population. And, nationally, nearly 25% of the growth of the Black population between 1990 and 2000 was due to people from Africa and the Caribbean

More than half of these Black immigrants came to the United States in or after 1990. They include about 33% of foreign-born Blacks who entered the United States during the 1990s and another 18% in 2000 or later. Nearly 97% of foreign-born Blacks were Afro-Caribbean (67%) and African (30%). The 2005 American Community Survey data (U.S. Bureau of the Census, 2006) indicates that the majority of current Black immigrants came from Caribbean islands. Two Caribbean countries contributed the highest Black immigrant population: over 600,000 Jamaicans and 500,000 Haitians in a total non-Hispanic Black foreign-born population of 2.7 million for 2005.

In addition to these two largest Black immigrant groups, non-Hispanic Afro-Caribbean natives were mostly Barbadians, Grenadians, and Trinidadians and Tobagonians and those from Africa were mostly Ethiopians, Ghanaians, Kenyans, Nigerians, Somalilanders, and South Africans. Census data from 2000 indicate that non-Hispanic Caribbean Blacks are concentrated in a few states: about 50% live in New York and 20% in Florida, primarily Miami. Moreover, virtually all live in large cities. About one of three Black people living in New York City is foreign-born, and Caribbean Blacks constitute the largest immigrant group in New York City. Heavily concentrated on the East coast, six of ten Afro-Caribbeans live in metropolitan New York, Miami, or Fort Lauderdale; other metropolitan areas with large Afro-Caribbean populations are Boston, Nassau-Suffolk on Long Island, and Newark.

The African population, on the other hand, is much more geographically dispersed throughout the country. Only a quarter of Africans live in one of the largest metropolitan regions, and these metropolitan areas are geographically dispersed. The largest five metropolitan areas with the most Africans are Washington, D.C., New York City, Atlanta, Minneapolis-St. Paul, and Los Angeles-Long Beach. In all these places, the majority of Africans are from West Africa, especially Nigeria and Ghana. Often times, nationalities cluster within these cities. For instance, Washington, D.C., has large Ghanaian and Ethiopian communities; Minneapolis has large Somali and Ethiopian populations; and Houston's Africans are predominantly Nigerian.

The Black immigrant population differs from Asian and Hispanic immigrants because, for this group, the immigrants are socially and economically better off than native-born African-Americans who have no recent immigration history. Logan and Deane (2003) used census data on individuals from the 1990 5% Public Use Microdata Sample (PUMS 5% 1990) and the 2000 1% Public Use Microdata Sample (PUMS 1% 2000) to examine this pattern. The median household income of both Africans ($42,900) and Afro-Caribbeans ($43,650) in 2000 was higher than that of African-Americans ($33,790) and Hispanics ($38,500), but lower than non-Hispanic Whites ($53,000) and Asians ($62,000). The unemployment rates for Africans (7.3%) and Afro-Caribbeans (8.7%) and poverty rates for Africans (22.1%) and Afro-Caribbeans (18.8%) were lower than the unemployment rate and poverty rate for African-Americans (11.2% & 30.4%, respectively) and Hispanics (8.8% and 26%, respectively), but higher than the same rates for non-Hispanic Whites (4.0% and 11.2%, respectively) and Asians (4.6% and 13.9%, respectively). These patterns for 2000 are consistent with those from the 1990 census data. In addition, the average years of educational attainment of Africans (14.0 years) are higher than that for Afro-Caribbeans (12.6), African-Americans (12.4), Whites (12.5), and Asians (13.9). This suggests that Black Africans immigrate selectively to the United States based on their educational attainment and on employment visas connected to their occupations.

The neighborhood housing patterns among these three Black groups—American Blacks, Afro-Caribbeans, and Africans—are highly segregated from Whites. Compared to American Blacks and Afro-Caribbeans, Africans have the highest exposure to Whites (in 2000, just under half of the people in the neighborhood where an average African immigrant lived was White), and Afro-Caribbeans had the lowest exposure to Whites (under a third of the people in the neighborhood where an average Afro-Caribbean immigrant lived was White). Segregation of these three Black groups from one another is high (though declining from 1990), and these Black ethnic groups overlap only partially with each other in the neighborhoods where they live.

Intra-Black segregation is attributable partly to the different locations (state and metro areas) where immigrant Blacks and American Blacks resided in 2000. For example, the states that had the largest shares of the Black immigrant population—New York (28%), Minnesota (26%), Massachusetts (28%), Florida (19%), Washington (17%), and Connecticut (17%)—are states with low to moderate percentages of native-born Blacks. These states' Black population in 2000, as a percentage of the total state population, ranged from 3.3% for Washington to 15.8% for New York. States with a Black population of over 20% had the lowest percentages of foreign-born Blacks. For example, the population in Mississippi was 37% African-American, but less than one in 1000 was foreign-born (U.S. Bureau of the Census, 2007b).

Segregation among Black ethnic groups may also result from important socioeconomic differences among them. In the metropolitan areas where they live in largest numbers, Africans tend to live in neighborhoods with higher median income ($45,567) and education level (29.3% of residents with a college education) than Afro-Caribbeans ($41,328 median income and 20% of residents with a college education) and American Blacks ($35,679 median income and 17.5% residents with a college education). In these metro areas, Afro-Caribbeans tend to live in neighborhoods with a higher percentage of homeowners than either American Blacks or Africans.

In summary, the Black population with recent immigration history has numerous advantages compared to the American Black population. They had higher incomes and educational attainment and lower poverty rates and unemployment rates. Not only do they typically live in somewhat different neighborhoods, but also, in most metro areas, these neighborhoods have a higher socioeconomic and educational standing (Logan & Deane, 2003).

BLACK AMERICAN IMMIGRANT SCHOOL-AGE CHILDREN

The fourth wave immigration of recent years requires the U.S. educational system to make fundamental changes to meet the needs of immigrant students. In working with Black immigrant students in this context of the continuously expanding immigrant population of all races and ethnicities, educators must be aware of, and understand, the differences between Black immigrants and non-Black immigrants and the variations among Black immigrants themselves. The various nationality groups have multiple needs. We have addressed some of this diversity in our brief immigration history and sociodemographic profile of the adult populations, and we turn now to the children themselves.

As described in the opening pages of this chapter, to compile data for Black immigrant children, we used several data points from the 2000 census survey to determine who is considered a Black child. Based on research interests identified in existing literature, discussed thus far, and on the size of nationality groups in the generational cohorts, we selected three national-origin groups for closer examination.

We selected Jamaicans and Haitians because they were the two largest Black immigrant groups in 2000, and they differ in ways we have already considered. We selected the Nigerian group because it is the largest resident immigrant group among U.S. Africans, and data on Nigerian children permit appropriate comparisons with Caribbean immigrant children. We also present descriptive data about other African immigrants.

The population of Black American children aged 5–18 was about 7 million in 2000. Figure 6.1A indicates that less than 5% of all Black children were identified with Caribbean origins; the remaining children were overwhelmingly non-immigrant African Americans. Because Nigerian children comprised less than one half of 1% of the general Black child population in 2000, their proportion is too small to represent on Figure 6.1A. If it were shown, the proportion of all Black African children on this figure would be somewhat larger than the proportion of Afro-Caribbean children.

Figure 6.1B represents a different view of immigrant Black children by national origin. Among the 172,000 U.S. school-age Black immigrant children in 2000, about 31,400 are from Jamaica, 30,000 from Haiti, 12,400 from Nigerian, 7,000 from Somalia, 5,500 from Ethiopia, 5,000 from Ghana, 4,220 from Liberia, 4,060 from Kenya, and 3,000 from Sudan. Jamaican immigrant children (18%) comprised the largest national-origin group among Black immigrant children in 2000; Haitian immigrant children were the second largest group, 17% of all Black immigrant children. Nigerian children, representing 10% of all Black immigrant children, were the largest group of immigrant Africans. The population composition indicates the continuing immigrant influx from Caribbean countries in the last several decades, as well as the most recent immigration flow from the African continent.

Generational Makeup

Table 6.1 shows the very different generational structures between Black Americans and all American children, as well as with Afro-Caribbean and African groups. Although almost 20% of children in the general school-age population were either foreign-born or the child of foreign-born parents, less than 10% of Black children were either foreign-born or the child of foreign-born parents.

FIGURE 6.1A   U.S. Black Children (5–18) by National Origin, 2000

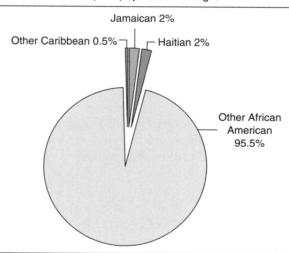

SOURCE: Data from PUMS 5% of the 2000 Census (U.S. Bureau of the Census, 2003a), compiled by authors.

FIGURE 6.1B   U.S. Black Immigrant Children (5–18) by National Origin, 2000

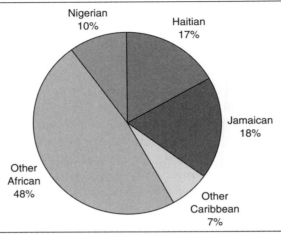

SOURCE: Data from PUMS 5% of the 2000 Census (U.S. Bureau of the Census, 2003a),
compiled by authors.

Comparing Jamaican, Haitian, and Nigerian children reveals several noticeable features. Although both Jamaican and Nigerian child populations include all generations of immigrants, a majority of the children were concentrated in the second generation, but the percentages of first-generation children (foreign-born) were much larger than those for the third generation. Haitian children show a two-generation population structure; a quarter of Haitian children were foreign-born in 2000, and almost three-quarters of them were children of foreign-born parents. Less than 3% of Haitian children were from families without recent immigration history. These differing generational structures reflect the many different Black groups currently immigrating to the United States and how they compare with the native-born Black population, as we have noted at the beginning of the chapter.

CHARACTERISTICS OF CHILDREN'S FAMILIES

In this section we consider the attributes of children's families. This includes their economic conditions, their living arrangements, and parental education, language use, and citizenship status.

Socioeconomic Backgrounds of Families

Table 6.2 shows that Black American children are more likely than the general child population to live in inner cities, and immigrant Black children are more likely than, or as likely as, all immigrant children to live in inner cities. Jamaican children, regardless of immigration status, were

TABLE 6.1 U.S. Black Children 5–18 Years Old by Ethnicity, National Origin, and Immigration Status, 2000

	All Children	Immigrant Children		Children of Immigrant	Native Children
		1st Generation	1.5 Generation		
All Children	100	2.2%	2.5%	13.6%	81.8%
(N)	(2,694,073)	(58,376)	(67,416)	(365,206)	(2,203,075)
All Black Children	100	1.3%	1.1%	7.1%	90.5%
(N)	(365,857)	(4,677)	(3,933)	(26,046)	(331,201)
Haitian	100	14.5%	11.2%	71.5%	2.8%
(N)	(5,548)	(806)	(623)	(3,966)	(153)
Jamaican	100	18.2%	13.9%	57.3%	10.6%
(N)	(4,888)	(888)	(680)	(2,802)	(518)
Nigerian	100	19.1%	16.7%	53.9%	10.4%
(N)	(1,727)	(330)	(288)	(930)	(179)
Other African Blacks	100	0.6%	0.6%	4.8%	94.0%
(N)	(350,869)	(2,207)	(1,971)	(16,839)	(329,852)

SOURCE: Data from PUMS 5% of the 2000 Census (U.S. Bureau of the Census, 2003a), compiled by authors.

1 Foreign-born children who arrive in the U.S. at 5 or younger age are classified as the 1.5 generation; those who immigrated to the U.S. after age 5 are classified as 1st generation.

2 Percentages may not total to 100 because of rounding percentages of subgroups.

3 The other African Black Children include children whose nationalities were not identified by their parents as well as those from other African nations such as Ethiopia, Ghana, Kenya, Liberia, Somalia, and South Africa. Data for these national-origin groups were not presented separately because of the insufficient number of these national-origin groups for cross-group descriptive statistical comparison.

most likely to live in inner cities, and Haitian children were least likely to live there.

We have four observations from the census poverty data for Black school-age children.

- First, Black children in the general population were more likely to live in poverty than all U.S. children, and Black immigrant children were less likely to live in poverty than all immigrant children.
- Second, as we have noted from other data, the poverty pattern for Black families is the opposite of the pattern for other race and

TABLE 6.2   Characteristics of Families and Living Environments of U.S. Black Children 5–18 Years Old by Ethnicity, National Origin, and Immigration Status, 2000

	All Children (365,857)	Immigrant Children (8,610)
% of Children Who Lived in Inner Cities		
All Children	13.1%	26.0%
All Black Children	30.9%	35.8%
Haitian	25.9%	25.1%
Jamaican	37.7%	40.1%
Nigerian	29.9%	29.5%
African Blacks Other Than Nigerian	30.9%	38.9%
Poverty Rates (% of Children Who Lived in Households in Poverty)		
All Children	14.8%	27.1%
All Black Children	30.6%	25.9%
Haitian	25.5%	30.7%
Jamaican	15.1%	16.5%
Nigerian	13.1%	15.2%
African Blacks Other Than Nigerian	31.0%	29.4%
% of Children Who Lived in Households With Total Family Income At or Higher Than 75th Percentile		
All Children	18.4%	10.7%
All Black Children	8.0%	8.2%
Haitian	6.2%	3.7%
Jamaican	13.1%	9.3%
Nigerian	20.6%	14.4%
African Blacks Other Than Nigerian	7.8%	8.3%
% of Children Who Lived in Households With Two Parents		
All Children	72.8%	80.4%
All Black Children	41.8%	61.2%
Haitian	59.8%	61.8%
Jamaican	52.4%	53.8%
Nigerian	73.4%	78.0%
African Blacks Other Than Nigerian	41.2%	61.1%

% of Children Who Lived in Households Without Father		
All Children	21.5%	13.3%
All Black Children	51.2%	30.6%
Haitian	31.0%	27.8%
Jamaican	40.3%	36.8%
Nigerian	20.8%	16.3%
African Blacks Other Than Nigerian	51.8%	31.4%
% of Children Who Lived With Parent or Household Head		
Having Fewer Than 4 Years of Education		
All Children	1.5%	8.9%
All Black Children	0.9%	3.7%
Haitian	4.4%	4.4%
Jamaican	0.8%	1.0%
Nigerian	0.4%	1.0%
African Blacks Other Than Nigerian	0.8%	4.9%
% of Children Who Lived With Parent or Household Head Having at Least a High School Diploma		
All Children	80.8%	53.7%
All Black Children	75.2%	68.7%
Haitian	59.4%	49.1%
Jamaican	75.0%	65.0%
Nigerian	95.2%	94.7%
African Blacks Other Than Nigerian	75.3%	72.6%
% of Children Who Lived With Parent or Household Head Having at Least a Four-Year College Degree		
All Children	23.0%	22.7%
All Black Children	11.5%	21.8%
Haitian	12.4%	7.9%
Jamaican	16.5%	9.5%
Nigerian	70.6%	67.2%
African Blacks Other Than Nigerian	11.1%	24.1%

SOURCE: Data from PUMS 5% of the 2000 Census (U.S. Bureau of the Census, 2003a), compiled by authors.

ethnic groups. In 2000 immigrant families generally had higher poverty rates than families in the general population, but immigrant Black children (26%) were less likely to live in poverty than the general Black child population (31%).

- Third, the size of the gaps in poverty rates between the general Black child population and the immigrant child population differs across Afro-Caribbean and African groups. For example, while the difference in poverty rate is less than 1.4 % for Jamaican children and about 2% for Nigerian children, it is more than 5% for Haitian children.
- Fourth, while Nigerian children had lower poverty rates than all U.S. children, and Jamaican children had the same poverty rates as all U.S. children, the poverty rate of Haitian children is almost double that of all U.S. children. Further, the variation in poverty rates was substantial across the three selected immigrant groups.

Black children were generally less likely to live in affluent households than other children. Immigrant Black children overall (8.2%) were as likely as the general Black child population (8.0%) to live in affluence, but for the three selected immigrant nationality groups, the gaps in affluence rates between immigrants and the general population favor the general population. For example, the affluence rate for Jamaican immigrant children was 9.3%, compared to 13% among the general population of children with Jamaican heritage. By contrast, Nigerian children (both general population and immigrant) had the highest affluence rates among all Black groups and showed a higher affluence rate than all U.S. children (both general population and immigrant), while the rate of affluence for Haitian children (general population and immigrant) is about a third of the national rates

Family Living Arrangements

Several noticeable features in family living arrangements are illustrated in the descriptive statistics in Table 6.2. First, Black children were less likely than U.S. children as a whole to live in two-parent households and more likely than U.S. children as a whole to live without a father. Similarly, Black immigrant children were also less likely than all immigrant children to live with two parents and significantly more likely than all immigrant children to lived in households without a father. Nigerian children as a whole are slightly more likely than all U.S. children to live with two parents and also slightly less likely than all U.S. children to live without a father. But Nigerian immigrant children were slightly less likely than all immigrant children to live with two parents and more likely than all immigrant children to live in a household without a father.

Second, immigrant Black children were more likely than all Black children to live with two parents (61% vs. 42%), and they were also less likely than all Black children to live without fathers (31% vs. 51%). Although all three nationality groups showed a similar family living arrangement pattern, the differences between the general population and immigrant population for Jamaicans and Haitians were smaller than for Nigerian children. Among the three nationality groups in the general and immigrant populations, Jamaican children had the lowest percentage of children who lived with two parents and the highest percentage of children in households without a father; Nigerian children had the highest percentage of children who lived with two parents and the lowest percentage of children in households without a father.

Parental Educational Attainment

As we first note in Chapter 2, because educational attainment at different levels suggests different issues with different causes, we present parental educational attainment in three levels. Nationally, 1.5% of U.S. children in 2000 were from families where parents had the least education (four years of education); however, the percentage for U.S. immigrant children, at 9%, is four times higher than the national average for all children. The educational attainment at the lowest level for Black parents follows the same pattern; the parents of Black children as a whole have lower rates of the least education (0.9%) than do parents for all Black immigrant groups (3.7%) and lower rates of the least education than parents for all children nationally (1.5%). Among Black children, differences between the general and immigrant populations in the least parental education favor the general population.

Jamaican and Nigerian children follow this same pattern in least education rates for parents, with smaller percentages of least educated parents in the general population than in the immigrant population. However, Haitian children in general had the highest percentages of parents who had not completed four years of education—a rate about three times the national rates—though the parents of Haitian immigrant children had a lower least-education rate than parents of all immigrant children. Parents of Haitian children as a whole and Haitian immigrant children have comparable rates of the least education.

Comparisons of parents' high school graduation rates indicate that immigrant parents (54%) were less likely to be high school graduates than all parents (81%), and this pattern holds for all Black children's parents as well as parents of children in the three nationality groups. The difference, though, in graduation rates between the parents of all Nigerian children and parents of Nigerian immigrant children is only about a half-percent. The differences in high school graduation rates between the parents of children in the general population and parents of immigrant children were around 10% for Jamaican and Haitian children. Parents of Black children as a whole had lower high school graduation rates (75%) than parents of all

U.S. children (81%), while parents of Black immigrant children (69%) had a much higher percentage of high school graduation than parents of all U.S. immigrant children (54%). However, parents of Nigerian children had substantially higher high school graduation rates (95%) than parents of all U.S. children, and the same rate for parents of Nigerian immigrant children is substantially higher than that of all U.S. parents of immigrant children. Parents of all Haitian children, as well as parents of Haitian immigrant children, had the lowest percentage of high school graduates among these three groups, 59% and 49% respectively.

Nationally, Black parents were less likely to be college graduates (11.5%) than all U.S. parents (23%), but parents of Black immigrant children (21.8%) were almost as likely as parents of all immigrant children (22.7%) to be college graduates. Immigrant Black parents had almost the same college graduation rates as all U.S. parents, and their college graduation rates were almost double those of parents of all Black children. However, this pattern of differences in college graduation rates between parents of Black children in the general population and parents of Black immigrant children does not occur in the three nationality groups, where the parents of the general population have higher percentages of college graduation than the parents of immigrant children. Among the two Afro-Caribbean groups and Nigerians, Haitian parents (all children and immigrant children) were least likely to have graduated from college, in contrast to Nigerian parents, who were most likely to be college graduates. With 71% college graduation rates for all Nigerian parents and 67% college graduation rates for Nigerian immigrant parents, Nigerian parents as a group had the highest college graduation rates of any parents of minority children except the parents of Japanese immigrant children, whose college graduation rate was 79% in 2000.

In summary, consistent patterns in educational attainment occur across the three nationality groups at all three educational levels. Although parents of children in the Black general population had lower rates than parents of all U.S. children in high school and college graduation, they did better than the parents of all U.S. children in having completed at least four years of educations. However, parents of Black immigrant children are generally better educated than average U.S. immigrant parents in having completed at least four years of education and high school, and these two groups have very similar rates of college graduation. However, the gaps between the immigrant Black child population and the general Black child population across the three nationality immigrant groups are more pronounced for Haitian and Jamaican parents than for Nigerian parents. Haitian children differed from the Jamaican children and Nigerian children in many socioeconomic variables: they were much more likely to live in poverty, and their parents were much less likely to be high school graduates or college graduates. Nigerian children were more likely to live in affluent families; about three-quarters of them had parents with college degrees.

The patterns we have delineated so far have several explanations. The high socioeconomic status and educational attainments of Nigerian families may be attributed to their pre-migration middle-class status and the types of immigrants they were (people in professional and management occupations who came to the United States to meet pressing technology and business needs). On the other hand, the distinctive differences between the two Afro-Caribbean groups may be due to language and cultural factors that affect the initial and continuing adaptation process: for example, most Haitians were Francophone Catholics, and most Jamaicans were Anglophone Protestants. At the beginning of the chapter we contrast the pre-immigration socioeconomic status of immigrants from these two Caribbean countries and their reception by U.S. authorities: a large percentage of Jamaican immigrants were from the middle- or lower-middle class and were trained professionals in their home country whereas a large portion of Haitians were from the poor classes. Nigerian immigrants may likewise differ from some of their African peers who suffered from the tumultuous conditions described previously in African nations such as Somalia. Pre-immigration differences among these groups contribute to post-immigration variations.

Households' Language Situation and U.S. Citizenship Status

In summarizing the language situations of Black families, Table 6.3 indicates that Black children in general were less likely to speak a language other than English at home than all U.S. children, and Black immigrant children were also less likely than all U.S. immigrant children to speak a heritage language at home. Almost all Jamaican children spoke English, regardless of their immigration status; two out of three Nigerian children, and over 50% of Nigerian immigrant children, came from families in which English was the primary language. However, less than one in four Haitian children—and only less than one in 20 Haitian immigrant children—used English at home; their primary languages, instead, were French and French Creole. For Black immigrant children for whom English was not the primary language, the most frequently spoken language was French Creole, followed by French, Amharic, Nigerian, and Spanish.

Black children (from both the general and immigrant child populations) were also less likely than U.S. children and U.S. immigrant children, in particular, to live in linguistically isolated households. Although less than 1% of Jamaican children and Jamaican immigrant children, and around 3% of African and African immigrant children, reported living in linguistically isolated households, the percentage of children of such households was higher for Haitian children: 22% for all Haitian children,

33% for Haitian immigrant children. These percentages are still lower than those for many ethnic immigrant groups in, for example, Asian and Hispanic populations.

Black children were more likely to live with parents who were U.S. citizens than all U.S. children, and Black immigrant parents also reported a higher percentage of U.S. citizenship than all immigrant parents. Not surprisingly, the percentage of U.S. citizenship among the parents of the three selected nationalities was lower than that for all U.S. children and for Black children as a whole because these three groups have a higher percentage of foreign-born members than occurs in the general Black population. However, the percentage of parents who were U.S. citizens was highest among Jamaican parents, immigrants and general population alike. The percentages of U.S. citizens among immigrant Haitians and Nigerians (40% and 29% respectively) were lower than for Jamaicans (51%) and also lower than the rate for parents for all Black immigrant children (43%). Many Jamaican immigrants came to the United States with immigrant visas, which makes becoming citizens easier and faster than other types of visas (Rogers, 2006).

THE CHARACTERISTICS OF BLACK IMMIGRANT CHILDREN

We now turn to attributes of the children themselves: children's disabilities, length of residence in the United States and age of arrival, and their oral English proficiency.

Disabilities

Three patterns are evident in Black children's overall health. First, Black children (both general population and immigrants) were more likely to be either physically disabled or learning disabled than all U.S. children. Second, the general Black child population had lower rates of physical disabilities and higher rates of learning-related disabilities than the population of Black immigrant children. Third, these variations in disability rates were not very pronounced across nationalities and immigration statuses. Table 6.4 shows that physical disabilities were highest among Haitian children at 4.5% and lowest among Nigerian children at 3.3%. Among immigrants, the physical disability rate was highest among Jamaican and Haitian children and lowest among Nigerian children. Learning-related disabilities were lowest also among Nigerian children and highest among Jamaican children for the general and immigrant populations of children. Nigerian children, regardless of immigration generation, had the lowest rates in physical and learning disabilities.

TABLE 6.3   Immigration-Related Characteristics of U.S. Households for Black Children 5–18 Years Old by Ethnicity, Nationality, and Immigration Status, 2000

	All Children (365,857)	Immigrant Children (8,610)
% of Children Who Spoke a Language Other Than English at Home		
All Children	17.3%	84.9%
All Black Children	5.8%	52.2%
Haitian	77.2%	94.0%
Jamaican	5.9%	7.0%
Nigerian	33.9%	54.1%
African Blacks Other Than Nigerian	4.3%	54.4%
% of Children Who Lived in Linguistically Isolated Households		
All Children	4.5%	34.4%
All Black Children	0.8%	14.3%
Haitian	21.7%	33.0%
Jamaican	0.5%	0.6%
Nigerian	2.8%	3.2%
African Blacks Other Than Nigerian	0.5%	14.7%
% Household Heads Who Are U.S. Citizens		
All Children	91.6%	31.5%
All Black Children	96.7%	42.8%
Haitian	58.3%	39.5%
Jamaican	66.6%	50.6%
Nigerian	58.4%	29.3%
African Blacks Other Than Nigerian	97.9%	42.9%

SOURCE: Data from PUMS 5% of the 2000 Census (U.S. Bureau of the Census, 2003a), compiled by authors.

Length of Residence and Age of Arrival

We turn our attention to only immigrant children in this section. Table 6.5 indicates similar patterns for Black immigrant children compared to all U.S. immigrant children in distribution of their length of residence; however, Black immigrants do tend to concentrate more in the immigrant cohort who had arrived in the United States within five or fewer years. In

TABLE 6.4   Other Characteristics of U.S. Black Children 5–18 Years Old by Ethnicity, National Origin, and Immigration Status, 2000

	All Children (365,857)	Immigrant Children (8,610)
% of Children Who Reported Physical Disabilities (one or multiple limitations in mobility, personal care, hearing and visual, etc.)		
All Children	3.0%	5.1%
All Black Children	4.5%	5.6%
Haitian	4.5%	5.9%
Jamaican	4.1%	5.9%
Nigerian	3.3%	3.6%
African Blacks other than Nigerian	4.5%	5.7%
% of Children Who Reported Learning-Related Disabilities (difficulties in remembering, etc.)		
All Children	4.4%	2.2%
All Black Children	5.0%	2.2%
Haitian	2.1%	2.0%
Jamaican	3.1%	2.2%
Nigerian	2.0%	1.6%
African Blacks other than Nigerian	5.1%	2.4%

SOURCE: Data from PUMS 5% of the 2000 Census (U.S. Bureau of the Census, 2003a), compiled by authors.

2000, 55% of school-age Black immigrant children in the United States had been in the country for less than five years, and about 85% of them had come to the United States within the past ten years. Nigeria was the country of origin with the largest proportion of newcomers (68%), followed by Haiti (51%), then by Jamaica (45%).

Black immigrant children are slightly older at arrival in the United States than are all U.S. immigrant children. Less than half of Black immigrant children arrived in this country at 5 or younger, more than 30% of them arrived between ages 6–10, and about one of five arrived in this country at 11 years or older. All three nationality groups follow this pattern. However, among these three groups, Haitian immigrant children had the highest percentage (22%) who had come to this country at 11 years or older, Jamaican immigrant children had the highest percentage (36%) of those who had arrived between the ages of 6–10, and Nigerian children had the highest percentage (46%) arriving at 5 or younger. However, the

TABLE 6.5 Immigration-Related Characteristics of U.S. Foreign-Born Black Children 5–18 Years Old by Ethnicity and Nationality, 2000

	0–5	6–10	11–15	16 and Above
Years in U.S.				
All Children	47.3%	34.0%	16.5%	2.3%
All Black Children	55.0%	29.1%	13.8%	2.0%
Haitian	51.2%	34.4%	12.3%	2.0%
Jamaican	44.7%	34.3%	18.1%	2.9%
Nigerian	67.5%	21.7%	9.2%	1.6%
African Blacks Other Than Nigerian	58.4%	26.5%	13.3%	1.8%
Age of Arrival				
All Children	53.4%	30.1%	14.5%	1.9%
All Black Children	45.8%	32.5%	19.3%	2.3%
Haitian	43.6%	32.3%	22.0%	2.1%
Jamaican	43.3%	36.3%	18.8%	1.6%
Nigerian	46.4%	30.7%	19.4%	3.2%
African Blacks Other Than Nigerian	47.2%	31.6%	18.7%	2.5%

SOURCE: Data from PUMS 5% of the 2000 Census (U.S. Bureau of the Census, 2003a), compiled by authors.

Note: Percentages do not total to 100 due to the rounding of percentages for subgroups.

differences in the distribution patterns for age of arrival across these three nationality groups are moderate.

Oral English Proficiency

Table 6.6 presents the self-reported English proficiency rates among Black children who reported speaking languages other than English at home. Among all Black heritage-language speakers, 68% reported speaking English very well, as compared to 61% of heritage-language speakers among Black immigrant children. Both percentages are higher than those for all U.S. heritage-language speakers (66%) and all U.S. immigrant heritage-language speakers (55%). Likewise, a lower percentage of Black immigrant children reported speaking no English than all U.S. immigrant HLS children (1.6% vs. 3.8%), and a lower percentage of all Black heritage-language speakers reported speaking no English than all U.S. heritage

TABLE 6.6   Self-reported English Proficiency Among Black Children

Who Spoke a Language Other Than English At Home

| | All Children | | | Immigrant Children | | |
| | | Not Very | | | Not Very | |
	No English	Well	Very Well	No English	Well Very	Well
All Children	1.6%	32.3%	66.1%	3.8%	41.2%	55.0%
All Black Children	0.5%	31.4%	68.0%	1.6%	37.1%	61.3%
(N)	(114)	(6,626)	(14,337)	(65)	(1,548)	(2,556)
Haitian	0.7%	26.2%	73.2%	1.9%	39.8%	58.3%
Jamaican	0.0%	25.3%	74.7%	0.0%	23.9%	76.2%
Nigerian	0.2%	22.9%	76.9%	0.3%	20.1%	79.6%
African Blacks Other Than Nigerian	0.5%	33.5%	66.0%	1.7%	39.5%	58.9%

SOURCE: Data from PUMS 5% of the 2000 Census (U.S. Bureau of the Census, 2003a), compiled by authors.

Note: Percentages do not total to 100 due to the rounding of percentages for subgroups.

speakers (0.5% vs. 1.6%). However, the variations in self-reported English proficiency for all three indicators (speaking no English, not speaking English very well, speaking English very well) are moderate for the general child population across the three nationality groups, but these variations are substantial for the immigrant child populations across the three nationality groups: 80% of Nigerian immigrant heritage-language speakers and 76% of Jamaican heritage-language speakers reported speaking English very well compared to 58% Haitian children. Because about two of five Haitian immigrant children did not speak English very well, this trend needs more attention from U.S. educators.

In summary, Jamaican immigrant children are the most linguistically assimilated nationality group, compared to Haitian and Nigerian immigrant children, taking into account their length of residency, age at arrival, heritage native language, and oral English proficiency simultaneously. Jamaican children have the lengthiest U.S. residence, are least likely to speak a language other than English and to live in linguistically isolated households, and are more likely to speak English only—and speak English very well—among the few who speak languages other than English. Haitian immigrant children comprised a considerable proportion of the newcomers who typically arrived in the United States at an older age, have the highest percentage of heritage-language speakers or live in linguistically isolated households, and tend to report speaking English less well. Nigerian immigrant children had the largest proportion of individuals who had arrived in the United States at age 5 or younger, and they were less likely to speak heritage languages or live in linguistically isolated households. Taking into account English acquisition for all children and for children who are heritage-language speakers (see Tables 6.3 and 6.6), Nigerian immigrant children were more likely than Haitian children to speak English very well.

EDUCATION OF CHILDREN

As we report for the other three racial-ethnic groups, we compiled data from the 2000 census to form three educational indices for all Black children (comparing the general population with the immigrant population) and Black children in three nationality groups. These three indices are general school enrollment rates for children aged 5–18, enrollment rates in private schools for children aged 5–18, and school dropout rates for youth aged 16–18.

General Enrollment

Black children in the general child population and immigrant population have slightly higher school enrollment rates compared to the national rates. Table 6.7 shows that Black children were more likely to enroll in school than U.S. children as a whole (96.7% vs. 96.3%). Black immigrant children were also more likely to enroll in school than all U.S. immigrant children (95.7% vs. 94.5%), and the enrollment gap between all Black children and Black immigrant children (96.7% vs. 95.7%) is smaller than the enrollment gap between all U.S. children and all U.S. immigrant children (96.3% 94.5%). The enrollment rates for all three Black nationality groups follow a similar pattern. Among these, Nigerian children (as a whole and in the immigrant generation) had the highest enrollment rates. The differences in enrollments between Jamaican children and Haitian children were minimal.

Enrollment in Private Schools

Table 6.6 indicates that Black children in the general population were less likely than all U.S. children to be enrolled in private schools, but Black immigrant children were just as likely as all immigrant children to be enrolled in private schools. However, the general population of Haitian and Jamaican children was as likely as all U.S. children to be enrolled in private schools, and Nigerian children were most likely to enroll in private schools. Nigerian immigrant children also were more likely than all U.S. immigrant children to enroll in private school, but Haitian and Jamaican

TABLE 6.7   Educational Characteristics of U.S. Black Children 5–18 Years Old by Ethnicity, National Origin, and Immigration Status

	All Children (365,857)	Immigrant Children (8,610)
% of Children (5–18) Enrolled in Schools in 2000		
All Children	96.3%	94.5%
All Black Children	96.7%	95.7%
Haitian	97.2%	95.5%
Jamaican	97.2%	95.7%
Nigerian	98.1%	97.2%
African Blacks Other Than Nigerian	96.3%	95.6%
% of Children 5–18 Enrolled in Private Schools in 2000		
All Children	10.8%	6.0%
All Black Children	6.0%	6.1%
Haitian	10.7%	3.7%
Jamaican	10.3%	4.8%
Nigerian	14.5%	11.0%
African Blacks Other Than Nigerian	5.8%	6.6%
% of Children 16–18 Years Old Who Were School Dropouts (Persons Who Did Not Graduate From High School But Were Not Enrolled in School in 2000) by Race-Ethnicity and Immigration Status		
All Children	5.6%	9.0%
All Black Children	6.9%	4.4%
Haitian	3.9%	5.0%
Jamaican	3.7%	5.0%
Nigerian	2.7%	1.2%
African Blacks Other Than Nigerian	7.1%	4.6%

SOURCE: Data from PUMS 5% of the 2000 Census (U.S. Bureau of the Census, 2003a), compiled by authors.

immigrant children were less likely than all U.S. immigrant children to do so. More children in the general population report enrolling in private schools than children in the immigrant population, and this pattern obtains for the three nationality groups. However, for all Black children, the difference in private school enrollment rates between Black children of all generations and Black immigrant children is minimal. These data suggest that Black children, immigrant or not, depend highly on public education.

High School Dropouts

Black children in general (6.9%) had higher school dropout rates than all U.S. children, while Black immigrant children (4.4%) had lower rates than all U.S. immigrant children. The national pattern of immigrant children having higher school dropout rates than children in the general populations is not applicable to Black children. However, children in all three nationality groups (for the general child population and immigrant children) had lower dropout rates than the national rates. Nigerian children had the lowest dropout rates among all the Black children examined here. With a school dropout rate of 1.2%, Nigerian immigrant children not only had the lowest dropout rates of all Black immigrant children, they—along with Israeli children—had the lowest dropout rates of all the national origin groups we examine in this book. However, Haitian and Jamaican immigrant children had higher school dropout rates than the general child population within their own national-origin group, but these dropout rates were low (approximately half the national dropout rate for immigrant children).

Analyzing retention and acceleration (children ahead of their age-appropriate grade) rates based on 1990 census data, Rong and Preissle (1998) report positively on Black immigrant children's educational progress in schools. In 1990 Black immigrant children were more likely to be ahead of others in grade levels. For example, at age 10, only 19% of native-born children and 26% of foreign-born children had finished 5 years of elementary school. However, among Black immigrant children, 30% of Jamaicans and Africans had completed elementary school. At age 14, 17% of native-born children and 21% of foreign-born children had finished 8 years of school in 1990, compared to 26% of Haitians, 23% of Jamaicans, and 31% of African immigrant children. At age 17, 11% of Haitian, 16% of Jamaican, and 17% of African immigrant children had graduated from high school, compared to 6% of native-born children and 8% of foreign-born children. The 17% high school completion rate among 17-year-old African Black youth was the highest for any group—including non-Hispanic Whites from English-speaking countries—in 1990.

Examining census data on educational attainment for youth aged 15–24 with a three-generation structure, Rong and Brown (2001) report that first- and second-generation Caribbean Black immigrant youths had higher educational attainment than Black children without immigration backgrounds. However, more recent studies have reported a downward trend corresponding to length of residency, in which newcomers attained higher grade point averages than students whose families had lived in the United States longer (Portes & Rumbaut, 2001; Rumbaut & Portes, 2001).

In higher education, a highly disproportionate percentage of Black students at elite universities are Africans, Afro-Caribbeans, or the children of African and Afro-Caribbean immigrants. *John Harvard's Journal* (2004) reported that over 50% of Black undergraduate students at Harvard University were first- or second-generation immigrant youths, though only a little over 10% of Black Americans are in these two generations. This pattern occurs at other universities such as Yale, Princeton, Columbia, Duke, the University of Pennsylvania, and the University of California, Berkeley.

SUMMARY OF DEMOGRAPHICS FOR BLACK AFRICAN CHILDREN

Black immigrant children were doing well in 2000; they were generally better off than the general Black child population. Compared with the Black native population, Black immigrant children as a whole were less likely to live in poverty and more likely to live in affluence, with two parents, and with parents who were college graduates. Black immigrant children were also as likely as native-born children to enroll in private schools and were 57% less likely than native-born Blacks to drop out from school.

Among the foreign-born population, the family income of Black immigrant children is lower only than that for the total of White immigrant children and some Asian groups; it is significantly higher than most Hispanic and Southeast Asian groups. Less poverty is found among Jamaican and Nigerian children than among all major Hispanic groups and Southeast Asians. Among Black immigrant children, Haitian children came from families with the lowest incomes and highest poverty levels, while Nigerian children came from families with the highest incomes and lowest poverty levels.

The three nationality groups we have examined in this chapter differ in socioeconomic status, language, culture, religion, and political and social systems in their home countries. Nigerian children and Jamaican children are more likely than Haitian children to live in households in better economic condition and with parents with more education. Among the three groups, Nigerians present distinctive characteristics. Nigerian children—immigrant or not—came from families in the best economic condition, with the best-educated parents, and these children, thus, did very well educationally. In the following section we offer in depth explanations for these differences.

DISCUSSION

The debates about why educational achievement gaps persist between Black students and Whites and Asians has continued in educational research, public policy discussions, and the popular media. Positions are taken on what should be blamed for the gaps and what needs to be done to improve the education of Black children in the United States. F. R. Lee (2002) observes that virtually every aspect of possible causes has been examined: inferior schools, lower teacher expectations, impoverished family background, poor neighborhoods, and a combination of some of these. With the rapid increase in Black immigrants from Caribbean and African countries over the last two decades, both the public and academic scholars have gradually focused on these groups and their records of success. Information on the differential educational and economic attainment between immigrants and native-born segments of the Black population has been integrated into the ongoing discussions and may suggest solutions to some of the problems.

How Black immigrant children have been assimilated into multiple stratification systems of race and social class in the United States has already challenged public stereotypes of U.S. Blacks. Black immigrants, like most immigrants, are characterized as being hardworking, self-reliant, and self-disciplined. Because many Black immigrant adults were college-educated and professionals prior to their immigration, children from immigrant families have been viewed as highly motivated for education and less likely to get into trouble of all kinds, due to sound parenting and resourceful communities (Crowder, 1999). In this section of the chapter, we first address relevant theoretical frameworks within the research literature and then apply the frameworks to explain inter- and intra-group differences. These frameworks, derived from segmented assimilation and critical race theories as well as more classical theories, facilitate understanding of the relationship among immigration, socioeconomic conditions, and education. They suggest a number of explanations for the observed differences in educational attainment between Black immigrants and U.S. Blacks and between African and Caribbean immigrants.

IMMIGRATION-RELATED SOCIODEMOGRAPHIC EXPLANATIONS

Children's educational attainment levels are closely related to their parents' education and occupations; children from wealthier and more stable family conditions do better than others (e.g., Bowles & Gintis, 1976; Jencks et al., 1972). As we have demonstrated in this chapter, Black immigrant children, in general, are more likely to live in households with better economic conditions and better-educated parents than non-immigrant Black children. They are also less likely to live in poverty, and more likely to live in affluent households that have two parents. However, their success may be related to other factors specifically related to immigration.

In addressing discrepancies between Black immigrants and nonimmigrants, some underscore the role of selectivity in emigration—where privileged class and educational background often contribute to who immigrates to the United States. This factor, in turn, positions these immigrants to more favorably compete in the U.S. economy (e.g., Pedraza, 1990). The high educational attainment of Nigerian children is a good example of this explanation. The supply-and-demand economic model suggests that many African and Caribbean immigrants were able to come to the United States because their education and expertise met the technology and management needs in U.S. business and higher education. Furthermore, peoples' conceptions of being "poor" in the countries from which most African and Caribbean immigrants come may be different from ideas held by people in the U.S. Black immigrants may assess their economic condition in the United States in comparison with the living conditions of their peers back home (Ogbu, 1991). The dual-frame migration ideology of most Caribbean immigrants may account for their optimism about social progress and their motivation to endure hardship and differential treatment due to the racial prejudice. Adult immigrants may incorporate this immigrant optimism into their parenting—even though many of them live in racially segregated neighborhoods and their children attend substandard inner-city schools.

Experiences in Different Social–Political Cultures

Several scholars (e.g., Vickerman, 1999; Waters, 1999) have argued that Black immigrants from English-speaking Jamaica come to the United States with historically-conditioned race identities and unique cultural frameworks, and these are challenged by the centrality of race and the specificity of Black racial constructions in the United States. These encounters result in a "Caribbean Ethnicity" among the Black immigrants: a hybrid identity blending race identities from Caribbean countries and from the United States. Dodoo (1997) explains this hybrid identity as the reason why Black Caribbean immigrants may have a justification for greater achievement motivation that many native-born urban U.S. Blacks lack. Race is usually minimized as a significant social factor in most English-speaking Caribbean societies—societies with a greater emphasis on merit as the basis for class formation and social mobility. Caribbean Blacks have, therefore, been socialized in the more favorable climate in their native countries. There, as a racial majority, they have had positive role models—from president of the country to schoolteachers—facilitating the development of confidence and leading to an orientation toward higher achievement. U.S. Blacks are disadvantaged compared to Caribbean Blacks because of their legacy of having endured harsh racism and post-slavery existence as a racial minority in the United States (see also Sowell, 1994). This framework suggests that Caribbean Blacks bring to the United States a different culture history and a strong desire to overcome not only the difficulties associated with their immigrant status, but also the hindrances due to race (see also Omi & Winant, 1994).

Ethnic Identity and Achievement, a Social-Psychological Explanation

For immigrants, becoming U.S. citizens is accompanied by a knowledge and perception of racism and of its effects and subtle nuances; Whites and members of U.S. minority groups may differ greatly in their perceptions and expectations of the world. In her ethnographic study of Caribbean Blacks, Waters (1991, 1994) reports that several identities are evident among these immigrant youths: an immigrant identity associated with nationality, such as Haitian and Jamaican; a pan-national identity, such as Caribbean or West Indian; a pan-racial identity, such as Black American; and an unhyphenated U.S. identity. Although foreign-born Black youths are more likely to volunteer a national identity, the length of U.S. residence of their families may shift their preference to a pan-national identity or a pan-ethnic identity. Fast-shifting identities among immigrant children often cause intergenerational conflicts between what children think they are and what their parents think they should be.

Owing to this native country–United States dual framework, Black immigrants tend to choose their nationality or pan-nationality, rather than race, in identifying themselves. The performance of their immigrant ethnicity takes many forms. Caribbean immigrants not only emphasize their accents, cultural traditions and ethos, and work ethics; they also show U.S. society that they have different views toward racial discrimination and alternative strategies to fight it, policies to correct historical mistakes, and Black immigrant optimism toward their future. Black immigrants also encounter prejudices additional to those faced by U.S. Blacks. They have had to cope with not only racial discrimination, but also linguicism and xenophobia. Furthermore, as newcomers, they may be less able to defend themselves and their families because of their more vulnerable legal status and inexperience with U.S. institutions. However, on the other hand, Black immigrants may believe that maintaining and emphasizing an immigrant identity—distinguishing themselves by nationalities—protects them from negative stereotypes and prevents their children from becoming involved with more popular, but less motivated, peer groups in school. Although identifying themselves as immigrants from other countries has not protected Black immigrants from experiencing racial discrimination in the United States, it may allow them to perceive it differently.

To a large extent, this immigrant identity unites ethnic communities; thus, the success of Black immigrants may also lie in the strength of their immigrant families and communities, which instill and embody unique human, cultural, and social capital in youth. The dual native country–United States framework represents a social-psychological resilience among Black immigrants, and strong community support helps them resist full assimilation and, consequently, provide better opportunities for their children. Black children living in the inner city often suffer from racial profiling and negative stereotypes attached to ghetto youths. Lacking effective ethnic resources and networks, many native inner-city Black children immerse themselves culturally, socially, and psychologically in the U.S. urban youth popular culture, with its strong anti-school and anti-mainstream elements (cf. Fordham, 1996). Portes and Zhou (1993) argue that the mode of incorporation of the first generation into U.S. society creates both different opportunities and variations in cultural-social capital in the form of ethnic jobs, networks, and values, which in turn create different pressures on the allegiances of children. Jamaicans' strong ethnic networks may generate social capital and networks of social ties from church, neighborhood, and voluntary organizations; these, then, may create avenues to job opportunities, as well as interwoven connections that reinforce parental authority and values.

These identity studies (e.g., Foner, 1987; Kasinitz, 1992; Kasinitz, Battle, & Miyares, 2001; Stafford, 1987; Waters, 1991, 1994; Woldemikael, 1989) help explain why Black students' educational attainment has varied from generation to generation. According to Waters (1994), because different identities are related to different perceptions and understandings of race relations and opportunities in the United States, they may also produce different results in youths' schooling. Urban youngsters who identify as ethnic Caribbean Blacks see more opportunities and rewards for their individual efforts and initiative, work longer hours, and watch less television. Urban youngsters who identify as Black Americans focus more on racial discrimination that limits opportunities for Blacks in the United States. They also are more likely to associate with oppositional cultures. Therefore, they have tended to do less well in school. However, difficulties in maintaining an immigrant identity result from pressure from society to eradicate immigrant cultures, especially ethnic variations within Black populations.

Waters (1999) reports on the factors influencing the type of identity youngsters develop. Youth are affected by the generational cohort they are a part of, the length of their U.S. residence, the social class background of their parents, whether they live in the inner city or the suburbs, their parents' social networks, the kind of schools they attend, and the structure and parental authority that characterizes their families. Second-generation youth, especially, move between differentiated identities not only in relation to their experiences of racialization in their specific residential location and in the United States in general, but also to the extent to which their lives are shaped within larger transnational social frameworks.

Bobb reports (2000) on the transnational social networks that West Indian immigrants create and use in building immigrant communities in the United States and in maintaining their ongoing linkages with home countries. She indicates that these networks form an important framework through which immigrant social acculturation and economic integration occur. They offer Black immigrants a level of insulation from racial constraints and help them resist the disempowering effects of racism and racial stratification that permeate U.S. society (see also Rong & Jo, 2002).

Some see the Black immigrant ethnic identity as a mixed blessing that seems to be working for some first-generation adults and children, but others oversimplify the Black immigrant ethnic-identity strategy as a game of psychological manipulation that reinforces views of "Good" Black vs. "Bad" Black. We agree with Foner (2001) and the other scholars we have cited in this section that immigration influences the politics of race and racial identity among, between, and within Black immigrant groups in the United States. Educators should see that the struggle for identity reconstruction and transformation among immigrant Black children is a complex process, and their ability to negotiate various aspects of native culture within the framework of mainstream society is a valuable asset that aids Black immigrants in their initial and continuing adjustment process.

Within- and Between-Group Differences

Studying African and Caribbean immigrant children's schooling means looking for shared themes and experiences while recognizing the important differences among the various immigrant groups from different countries. We have already described the differences in education and factors related to education between Black immigrants and U.S. Blacks, and we now apply the three theoretical frameworks we have just discussed to further consider differences between, and within, Black immigrant groups.

Compared with Caribbean immigrants, African immigrants have been invisible because of their recent immigration history and ignorance among many Americans about the various nationalities and cultures in African and Caribbean countries. Geographical closeness facilitates frequent contacts with peers in the homeland, generating sufficient cultural resources for Caribbean Black immigrants to maintain and revitalize their ethnic identity. Rong and Jo (2002) report how Jamaican immigrant parents kept their children bicultural through transnational and transcultural approaches, such as sojourner strategies of frequently sending children back to the home country. The difficulties for African immigrants in managing home visits over a much larger distance may prevent them from reconnecting with their cultural roots after they have initially immigrated to the United States. Also, no African immigrant community is available in the United States as large as, for example, the Jamaican community in New York or the Haitian community in Miami. The consequences of longer distances to the home country and absence of a large single-nation African community make it more difficult for low socioeconomic and refugee African immigrants to generate cultural, social, and psychological networks; their children may thus be more inclined to assimilate into the popular youth culture at a faster speed.

Finally, we have already noted that differences in socioeconomic status and educational attainment among Afro-Caribbean populations, such as Jamaican and Haitian immigrant children, can be partially explained by a variety of pre-immigration and post-immigration conditions, as discussed previously in the chapter. Researchers (e.g., Stepick, Stepick, Eugene, Teed, & Labissiere, 2001) summarize the differences between Haitians and Jamaicans and many other Caribbean immigrants as that, in general, Haitian immigrants encounter a much more hostile world. Unlike most Cuban immigrants and Southeast Asian refugees, Haitians have never been welcomed by the U.S. government. Unlike most Mexican immigrants, no economic niches await them. Unlike other Caribbean immigrants, Haitian immigrants neither speak English nor have cultural elements such as reggae music that are admired by the host society. Although their parents are well-off compared to Haitians in Haiti, adult Haitian immigrants in South Florida have exceptionally low levels of family income by U.S. standards. They are unprepared for the local labor market and have struggled greatly to integrate into it. Similarly, more recent Haitian immigrant parents have little experience with formal education, especially in English, and can provide little help for their children's studies. All of these factors conspire against Haitians, compared to other Caribbean immigrants.

Researchers, practitioners, and policymakers have observed differences within African immigrants as well (Alidou, 2000). In the past, African students, because of their limited number in schools and classrooms, adopted assimilation strategies to blend into the mainstream student population. Most of them were successful because they came originally from highly educated and upper-middle-class Anglophone families. Currently, however, cultural, economic, and educational diversity is increasing among new immigrants from Africa. Not all immigrants from Africa come to the United States to advance their educational and economic opportunities. As we have noted previously, because many are fleeing political instability and wars in their home countries, they arrive in the United States with no financial or social resources. In many cases, Africans in this situation are given refugees status and need access to more social services than immigrants who come for educational and employment opportunities. For example, the largest number of African immigrants is from Nigeria and Ethiopia (though the number for the latter is less than two-thirds of the former), suggesting two main reasons for immigration. Nigerians often leave their home countries to look for employment opportunities, while many Ethiopians are seeking political asylum in the United States (Arthur, 2000). Furthermore, a small percentage of African immigrants from Francophone countries are immigrants who come with informal or very limited formal education. According to the limited research literature on this topic (Zehr, 2001), students coming from this second group of immigrants seem to experience more problems adapting to and integrating into U.S. school and mainstream culture.

In summary, the explanations we have discussed seem to fit the segmented-assimilation theory we introduced in Chapter 1 and developed in Chapter 4, the idea that immigrant assimilation is partial and selective and that, for example, immigrants can integrate successfully into the business world while maintaining separate cultural worlds. Segmented assimilation emphasizes the structural context that furnishes the multiple and contradictory paths that various immigrant groups take and predicts complex outcomes from these variations (Portes & Rumbaut, 1996). Segmented-assimilation theorists have, however, been challenged for ignoring variations among ethnic-racial groups such as the U.S. Black population and overlooking the possibility that full assimilation of underprivileged Black immigrants can integrate them into the Black middle class, a rapidly expanding component among U.S. Blacks in the last two decades (Neckerman, Carter, & Lee, 1999; Pierre, 2004). We urge policymakers and educators to consider their own theories of how newcomers are incorporated into a host society. In the last section of the chapter we offer recommendations for how Black children from the Caribbean and Africa may be best supported by their U.S. schools and educational systems.

RECOMMENDATIONS

In this section, we offer four areas of recommendations to educational institutions with the framework of the additive approach, discussed previously, for supporting the socialization and identity transformation of Black immigrant students and helping them reach and maintain high achievement.

As we have emphasized throughout this text, an additive approach recognizes and builds on immigrants' cultures and languages as resources in their adaptation to a new society. Yosso (2005) articulates various forms of capital nurtured through cultural wealth, including aspirational, navigational, social, linguistic, familial, and resistant capital. These forms of capital draw on the knowledge students bring with them from their homes and communities into the classroom. The additive approach advocates mutual adaptations among schools, immigrant students, and their communities (see C. Suarez-Orozco, 2001b; Valenzuela, 1999) in creating a culturally supportive and caring environment for immigrant students.

Recommendation One: Adapt Curriculum and Instruction

The U.S. public is used to thinking of minority diversity in broad categories, such as Hispanic or Latino, Asian, Native American, and Black. The media representation of Black Americans regrettably focuses more on so-called Black problems than on the variations among these peoples in social classes, national origins, and attainment patterns. Because of the fourth wave of immigration, Black immigrants are becoming more visible in the

United States, as their presence and activity increasingly reshapes the social, cultural, and political landscape of this country.

Urban schools are becoming increasingly diverse, with populations including African and Afro-Caribbean immigrant children. Although most Americans understand that the society has diversified beyond the Black-White, minority-majority oversimplification of previous years, the assumption that Black students are all native-born is still prevalent in some places. To their credit, educators are recognizing the different issues and needs of immigrant and native Black student groups—one example is the discussion and debates on Black English Ebonics, the English dialect developed by Black Americans during their long-term segregation in the United States (Ogbu, 1999; Perry & Delpit, 1998).

However, educators should also challenge the new form of linguicism toward Black newcomers: discrimination against students with accents coming from former British colonies in Africa, such as Nigeria, Ghana, and South Africa. Some teachers question the acceptability of newcomer students using forms of English such as Creole in their classrooms, and other teachers consider Anglophone African immigrant children unprepared for mainstream classes because of their English accents. However, these students usually do not fit the limited-English-proficiency category, either. Crandall (1998) reports that some well-educated African students may be put either in grades below their age-appropriate level or in special-education classes. To combat this form of linguicism, educators must first request adequate language-proficiency assessments for new immigrant students and place them in appropriate language programs if their needs are validated.

Although most Black students in the United States share African ancestry, a variety of cultural histories, indigenous languages, and religions are found among African and Afro-Caribbean immigrant students, as we have documented in this chapter. Teachers in schools with a significant presence of Black immigrant students need to select role models from a wide range of nationalities and teach about them in class.

The lack of resources and information has often been an issue for teachers when they endeavor to teach about contemporary life in African nations and Caribbean countries. Alidou (2000) recommends several sources of information for teachers: collaborating with African study scholars who work in surrounding colleges and universities to develop units to teach about African countries; visiting African refugee camps located in urban areas that can be cultural resource centers; and recruiting volunteers from different African countries for community education. Teachers may also seek help from private international cultural centers that offer valuable information about world cultures and people; these are usually located in cities, among them New York and Houston.

Recommendation Two: Create a Caring and Culturally Supportive School Environment

Kasinitz, Mollenkopf, and Waters (2002) reveal that Black immigrants reported facing the highest levels of discrimination while shopping, interacting with police, looking for work, and even while working. Black immigrants from Caribbean countries reported the most segregation and being subjected to ridicule, mistrust, inappropriate work tasks, and even violence because of their looks, accents, and self-expressed immigrant ethnic identities (Ajibode, 2006). Many suffered from severe racial discrimination and lacked an understanding of how to defend themselves. Schools should create an environment that actively supports students' ethnic identity development and their expressions of heritage. Schools also need to inform students of their options when they are subjected to extreme racial prejudice. A school environment friendly to the languages and cultural heritages of African and Caribbean adolescents will decrease the stress of their initial cultural adjustment. We provide next two examples that schools can implement to improve the cultural environment for Black immigrant children.

Throughout this book we have cautioned against the prevalence of what has come to be called linguicism, or the prejudice favoring English-only usage and U.S.-accented-only English. The perception of many immigrants is that Americans want to hear U.S.-accented English, and they exhibit impatient, even unfriendly, attitudes when hearing other accents. Francophone newcomers from the Caribbean and Africa often experience prejudice because of their difficulties in speaking English, and Anglophone African and Jamaican students also experience prejudice because they speak "colonial English." Researchers (e.g., Alidou, 2000) report that many Black immigrant youth choose to isolate themselves socially, and maintain absolute silence in the classroom, to avoid being ridiculed and subjected to other humiliation. Schools should educate students and faculty alike to be culturally sensitive and encourage them to exert patience and extra attention when listening to the varieties of English usage.

To bridge cultural gaps between Black immigrant students and other students, schools can introduce African or Caribbean arts and music into the school youth culture. For example, Perry (1999) argues that expressive forms of Garifuna youth culture in the United States—in particular, music and dance—can be fashioned and re-worked within the contemporary sociocultural context of race and class. Through the performance of music and dance, he suggests, these youth can assert their racial membership in a transnational African or Black Diaspora, while simultaneously reinforcing their ethnic roots in a diasporic Garifuna peoplehood.

Recommendation Three: Work With Families and Communities

Many strategies used with Latino and Asian families and communities are also effective with Black immigrant families. Zhou (2003) stresses that children living in the inner city are vulnerable to various negative influences from their disadvantaged environment. Compared to suburban immigrant youth, these children often suffer from racial profiling and negative stereotypes and are likely to adopt a willful refusal of mainstream norms and values. Waters (1999) explains that, therefore, immigrant community identities have been developed as the means for inner-city Black immigrant youth to protect themselves from these possibilities.

Black immigrants have the highest metropolitan residence rates among all immigrant groups: over 85% of Black immigrant students live in metropolitan areas, about half of them residents of inner-city locations. The majority of their parents do not have K–12 schooling experience in U.S. schools, and so they may not understand the peer pressures in that cultural and social environment. Perceived by the wider society simply as "Black," Black immigrant students often socialize with American Black students, yet are aware of the differences in parental expectations between themselves and their African-American peers. They may identify with American Black youth when at school, but choose to emphasize their Caribbean heritage on other occasions. If school administrators, teachers, and counselors are aware of and understand these generational and cultural gaps, they will be able to help immigrant children navigate between various environments smoothly and competently.

Furthermore, schools can help bridge cultural gaps between Black immigrants and American Blacks, as well as among different ethnic and nationality groups, to make neighborhood-based resources available to all. Neighborhood enhancement can yield positive educational outcomes for diverse immigrant children (Zhou, 2003).

Recommendation Four: Enhance Pre- and Inservice Teacher Training

To develop effective intercultural communication with Black immigrant students, parents, and communities, Alidou (2000) believes that teachers must learn to recognize the cultural differences considered acceptable school behavior among African, Caribbean, and American Blacks. Teachers should show adequate understanding of immigrant students' behavior patterns and communication styles when they differ from those of White middle-class Americans; teachers should be sympathetic and persuasive when interpreting acceptable school behavior in the United States. Some of what U.S. educators consider misbehavior among Black newcomers might well be tolerated or even standard behavior in schools in Africa or the Caribbean. Alidou suggests that teachers should discuss these differences with parents and students in a positive manner before sending home notes critical of students' behavior. Teachers should initiate parent-teacher conferences to determine whether students are truly misbehaving, or if their behavior is culturally explainable elsewhere, and work out solutions together.

Furthermore, teachers and school counselors need to be trained to work with newcomers who have pronounced and unfamiliar English accents. Because of diverse sociohistorical and cultural backgrounds, both Black and White immigrants from Africa arrive in U.S. schools with different language proficiencies and different literacy skills. Unfortunately, English teachers—who should have learned the evolution of English around the world—often become frustrated when immigrant students' oral and written English differ from the U.S. version (Ovando & Collier, 1998). As we emphasize in our first recommendation, a common problem for immigrant students is that in many of their classrooms, U.S. English in its phonetic form is the only dialect tolerated. This intolerance of non-U.S. dialects delays students academically, particularly if English is their first language. To avoid this possibility, teachers should become familiar with various English dialects by listening to and watching international media.

School counselors should not presume that Black immigrant students are low achievers. Black students with high career goals have been perceived by some counselors as unrealistically fantasizing about their future goals, whereas White students have been seen as holding realistic expectations (Dworkin & Dworkin, 1999). Conversely, teachers and counselors should not assume the success stories of many African immigrants are universal, but see each African child case by case. As we have noted previously in this chapter, refugees are often not as well-educated as economic immigrants, and they are likely to have psychological problems because of the violent conflicts taking place in their home countries. In a study on the needs of Somali refugees in Minnesota, Ehrlich (2003) found that the refugees considered employment, housing, education, family, and a cultural support system to be major problems for them.

Historically, hostility and discrimination against Black people in the United States have been strong and pervasive. Conflicts of interest have also developed between African-Americans and Black immigrants—sometimes between long-time residents and fresh arrivals of the same ethnicity-race. U.S. Blacks usually coexist with immigrant minorities in urban areas. Many U.S. Blacks believe that their share of the social services budget has decreased because newly immigrated minority people require the same services. Leaders of African-American communities have found themselves at odds with immigrants over how scarce education dollars should be spent. Competition has developed for low-paying work and service jobs. Because of housing and occupational segregation, many Caribbean immigrants may have close contacts with the most vulnerable Black population, which tends to be poor, uneducated, and unemployed. Ironically, Black immigrants may adopt the mainstream's stereotypes of U.S. Blacks and perceive them as lazy, race-baiting, and disorganized (Vickerman, 1999; Waters, 1999).

Conversely, U.S. Blacks may express animosity toward the immigrants, labeling them as rude, arrogant, and ignorant of U.S. history and the racial hierarchy of contemporary society (Alba, 1990; McDaniel, 1995). Furthermore, recent Black immigrants who came to the U.S. voluntarily are qualified for affirmative action originally designed to help African Americans by eliminating historical discrimination and segregation in education and employment in the United States, a situation seeming patently unfair to many.

School may be one place for Black immigrants to develop a more objective, fairer understanding about Black Americans. Educators should understand the roots of the misunderstandings and help these youth build healthy and productive relationships with Black Americans during their ethnic and racial identity reconstruction process. For achieving this goal, Rong and Brown (2002) recommend that Black educators should help Black immigrant children close the gap between Black immigrants' expectations of the United States prior to their immigration and the current U.S. reality they have to face. Developing mutual understanding and empathy is crucial for building a broader, more inclusive African-American community that may provide social networks for all. Promoting these communal relationships may depend heavily on native-born U.S. Blacks whose families have been long-time residents in the United States. U.S. Blacks have struggled for more than 400 years to fight racism, and the majority of Black educators have been native-born Americans (Rong & Preissle, 1997). Black educators can serve as role models and cultural brokers for Black immigrant children. They can help Black immigrant children understand that the benefits enjoyed today by Blacks have resulted from the sacrifices made by all African-Americans, including immigrant Blacks, in their long struggle to obtain basic civil rights.

CONCLUSION

The massive influx of non-White immigrants significantly complicates traditional U.S. paradigms of race and ethnicity, and the study of recent Black immigrants and their children contributes to the dialogue on immigrant culture within the United States. Educators have known very little about the linguistic, cultural, nationality, ethnicity, and other diversities among the nation's Black immigrant students. To promote academic success for Black students, both immigrants and natives, our society and educators must acknowledge the importance of the presence of the immigrant segment in the Black population, as well as in the Asian and Latino population, including understanding the complexities in socioeconomic status and schooling patterns within the Black population, as well as their recent educational condition and achievement.

Ending this chapter, we pose more—and different—questions than those we address at the start. We wonder if, and how long, the achievement patterns of Black immigrants can be maintained through the 1.5 generation, as well as the second- and third-generation. These are often-asked questions (e.g., Portes & Rumbaut, 2001; Rogers, 2006):

- Will African and Afro-Caribbean experiences, often portrayed as the "successful Black stories," follow the classic assimilationist patterns of earlier European immigrants?
- Will they follow the "dissonant acculturation" and eventually join the "linked fate" of many inner city native-born U.S. Blacks? Or,
- Will they follow the segmented assimilation patterns of Asian or Latino immigrants: various ethnic groups from different origins, adapting different acculturation approaches and achieving different destinations?

To address these questions, we must also consider related macro-level issues (see also Butterfield, 2004; Jaynes, 2000):

- How has the increasing presence of African and Caribbean Black immigrants challenged United States conceptions of race and ethnicity?
- What role will racial prejudice play in these children's acculturation? Will racism make this process as difficult for these newcomers as it did for U.S. Blacks?
- Finally, will the dominant "Black-White paradigm" of racial politics in the United States be gradually dismantled, or will it continue to have a powerful influence on the dynamics of race and ethnicity in the country for decades to come?

Educators are certainly interested in knowing what all these mean for educating minority children, especially Black children. We hope that the material in this chapter contributes to the answers to some of these questions.

7

Immigrant Children From Latin America

Hispanics, or Latinos, are the largest and fastest growing ethnic group in the United States, and their rapid population growth has changed the racial and ethnic landscape in the country. Hispanic-Americans have represented the largest increasing proportion of the nation's labor force since 1970; in 2000, they became the largest minority population in the United States. The expansion of the Hispanic population has accelerated since the 1990s because of their high immigration rates, higher birthrates, and relative youth.

Two of three Hispanic-Americans are of Mexican origin. Although many Mexican-Americans' ancestors resided in the Southwest long before Anglo-Americans arrived in what is today's United States, 40% of Mexican-Americans—as well as a similar percentage of the U.S. Latino population—are foreign-born. Likewise, more than half of foreign-born Hispanics are recent immigrants who arrived in the United States since the 1990s. Figure 7.1 indicates that the Hispanic population has risen rapidly since 1970, with a 50% or higher growth rate in the last three decades. The numbers are 9.5 million in the 1970s, 14.6 million in the 1980s, 22 million in the 1990s, 35 million in 2000, and 42 million in 2005, accounting for about 14.5% of the total U.S. population. The U.S. Hispanic population is projected to be 105 million by 2050, accounting for 25% of the total U.S. population.

Educating Hispanic children is a pressing issue. The rapidly expanding Latino population in the United States, with a rapidly expanding share of the U.S. K–12 student population, has created enrollment pressures as well

FIGURE 7.1 The Increase of U.S. Minority Population by Race and Ethnicity 1970–2005

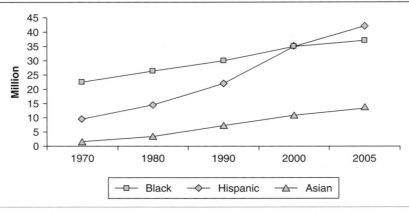

SOURCE: Data from PUMS 5% of the 2000 Census (U.S. Bureau of the Census, 2003a), compiled by authors.

as other challenges, such as quality education for all children, for the nation's schools. Figure 7.2 shows the percentage distribution, by age range, for non-Hispanic White, Hispanic, Black, and Asian populations. Thirty-five percent of the Hispanic population was under age 18 in 2000, compared to less than 23% of non-Hispanic White, 27% of Asian, and 32.5% of Black Americans. The percentage of children under 5 years old was particularly high for the Hispanic population, compared to young children of other racial-ethnic groups. Today, about a third of the children entering kindergarten in the nation's public schools come from Hispanic homes. Because of these population shifts, U.S. schools must respond promptly to Latino children's schooling access, their educational attainment, and their specific needs.

FIGURE 7.2 U.S. Population by Race and Ethnicity and Age, 2000

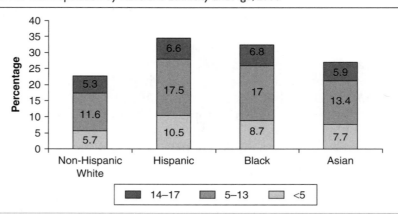

SOURCE: Data from PUMS 5% of the 2000 Census (U.S. Bureau of the Census, 2003a), compiled by authors.

As we have emphasized throughout this book, immigration, especially emigration from Mexico to the United States, is a contested political issue (Davis, 1990). Some communities in the United States have welcomed immigrants and their children and have appreciated the vitality and cultural diversity they bring to schools (e.g., Peshkin, 1991). Many Americans also see Latinos as an opportunity to reconnect to the rest of the Western Hemisphere southward, as well as an important human resource to the nation. In other locales, people see the increasing Hispanic presence as a potential threat to cultural unity, and they worry that the influx of immigrants depresses the job market for U.S. citizens. The large number of Latino arrivals may also arouse fears that youth from immigrant communities may drain already scarce school resources or compete with U.S.-born natives in job training and career development programs (Stewart, 1993).

In recent years, issues of increasing poverty rates among the immigrant population and concerns about the legal status of many newcomers, as reported in the mass media and repeated in politicians' rhetoric, make educating immigrant children a controversial, even polarizing, issue. Endless battles about the right to be educated and the right to be educated in both English and Spanish have ended in the courts. For example, in Chapter 1 we describe attempts to exclude children of undocumented immigrants from the public schools in Texas and Florida in the late 1970s and to limit education and health services provided to undocumented immigrants and their children with the 1994 passage in California of Proposition 187. These actions mainly target Mexican immigrant children and their families.

The debate extends well beyond educational access to the boundary of language and links to the ethnic socialization of Hispanic children and implementation of multiculturalism and pluralism in U.S. schools. In previous chapters we have indicated how English acquisition and maintaining home language have become controversial and the opposition to bilingual programs has often been combined with the movement for the establishment of English as the only official language. We elaborated in Chapter 3 the passage of Proposition 227 in California, in 1998, prohibiting bilingual teaching in public schools, as a typical example reflecting the language attitude of many Americans.

To make workable educational policies, we believe it is important to know how much people's opinions are based on their knowledge of the Hispanic-Americans and how much is built from misinformation, misunderstanding, and misconceptions. Viewing Latino-Americans as a homogeneous group may be a common misconception. Labels such as "Hispanic" or "Latino" are umbrella terms for large groups of persons who differ substantially among themselves (e.g., Waggoner, 1991). In this chapter we illustrate the inherent problems of lumping together Latino groups with various backgrounds and show how segmented economic and educational attainment patterns characterize these peoples.

HISPANIC-AMERICANS AND HISPANIC IMMIGRANTS IN THE UNITED STATES

Hispanic-Americans practice several religions, including Roman Catholicism, Protestantism, Judaism, and others. The major languages spoken by the U.S. Latino population are Spanish and U.S. English with smaller groups speaking Portuguese and a variety of indigenous languages including Mayan and Quechua. The major ancestries of Latino-Americans are European, African, and Native American, and a large portion of the Hispanic population is of mixed races. This diversity shows that the U.S. Hispanic population represents a merger of cultures, religions, and ethnicity-races. In this section, we show how the U.S. Hispanic population is fragmented by various histories and immigration experiences and divided by sociodemographic backgrounds.

As we note in the Introduction, the term Hispanic, as used in the 2000 census, refers to individuals originating from Latin American countries where Spanish is spoken; Hispanics may be of any race. Latino is a slightly broader term referring to peoples from Latin America, regardless of the language they speak. The terms Hispanic and Latino are used interchangeably in this book to mean people who self-identified by answering "Yes" to the 2000 census question, "Is this person Spanish/Hispanic/Latino?" We are aware that not everyone favors use of the terms Hispanic or Latino because they are artificially constructed categories including people of various races, cultures, and residency, across broad geographic areas. Many scholars also believe that these terms have been responsible for erasing the national identities and historical memory of various groups and their mixed-race backgrounds (Acuna, 2003).

However, we use the term Hispanic in this book to be consistent with the terms used in statistical data and reports published by U.S. government agencies, including the U.S. Bureau of the Census and the U.S. Department of Education. To simplify subsequent text and tables, we refer to Hispanic groups by country of origin—for example, Cuba, Mexico—although most so labeled are actually Cuban-American, Mexican-American, and so forth. We have not included Puerto Ricans in our analyses because Puerto Rico became a U.S. territory through annexation in 1898, and its residents were allowed to become U.S. citizens through the passage of the Johns Act in 1917. In census questionnaires, almost all (98%) Puerto Ricans classified themselves as native-born U.S. citizens.

A Historical Sketch

The information presented here was compiled from materials published by Acuna (2003), Carrasquillo (1991), Cordero-Guzman and Henken (2005), Daniels (2002), E. Garcia (2001), Gutierrez (2004), and Oboler and Gonzalez (2005).

Hispanics in the United States are both the largest group of new immigrants in the early 21st century and, together with Native Americans (who constitute the ancestors of many Hispanics), the oldest Americans. The influx of Hispanics into the United States has been a complex process. Different groups of Hispanics entered the country at different times, for different reasons (asylum, employment, reuniting the family, etc.), and with differential legal statuses on arrival (visitor, permanent resident, U.S. citizen, refugee, undocumented, etc.). They concentrated in varying degrees in different regions of the country (Southwest, Northeast, new gateway states, etc.) and in different locations (urban, suburban, and rural). As described by Cordero-Guzman and Henken (2005), these variations significantly affected immigrants' acceptance by U.S. society, the type and degree of assimilation, levels of civic and political participation, and levels of socio-economic mobility.

For instance, beyond the Spanish language, Cuban- and Mexican-Americans have little in common in their immigration history into the United States, though these two immigrant group share proximity to, and closely linked history with, the United States. The first large wave of Cuban immigrants, mainly White and professional, escaped a communist regime and settled in the United States as political refugees; Mexican-Americans entered the United States under completely different conditions. A large number of Mexicans "became U.S. citizens" in the 19th century through Mexico's defeat in the Mexican-American war and the annexation of the Mexican territories by the United States. A considerable number of Mexicans have recently entered the United States with or without permission; the latter has overshadowed the image of long-term legal Mexican immigrants. Cordero-Guzman and Henken (2005) remark that, not only do Latin Americans cross the border through immigration, but also, in the past, the border crossed them through annexation and conquest.

Mexican Immigration

The Mexican-American community is both old and new. The roots of many Mexicans in the United States are as old as those of Native Americans. Many Mexican-Americans are descendants of those who settled in the land that was either an independent republic or under Spanish or Mexican rule. The United States acquired southwestern territory by winning two wars, the Texas War of 1836 and the Mexican-American War, as well as by the Gadsden Purchase of 1853. In 1848, the United States took half of Mexico's land in the Treaty of Guadalupe-Hidalgo that ended the Mexican-American War. These events extended United States control over a wide territory (Texas, New Mexico, Colorado, Utah, Nevada, Arizona, and California) once owned by Mexico. The vast majority of Mexicans who were already living in these territories remained in the newly acquired land and became full U.S. citizens.

However, many Mexican-turned-U.S. citizens still lost their land in lawsuits before state and federal courts or as a result of legislation passed after the treaty. Furthermore, many Mexicans who had become U.S. citizens were sent to Mexico by the U.S. government through numerous mass deportations, during various time periods, stirred by economic recessions and political conflicts in the United States when nativism was high (Nevins, 2005). For example, during the great depression years of the 1930s, the United States government sponsored a repatriation program, under which as many as half a million Mexican-Americans—including large number of U.S. citizens of Mexican descent—were sent to Mexico on special trains chartered by federal and local governments (Daniels, 2002).

Mexican migration to the United States has gone through five historical phases since the ending of the Mexican-American War in 1848. The first noted immigration to the United States from Mexico occurred in the 1850s, during the Gold Rush. The second noticeable large-scale immigration from Mexico to the United States was prompted by the political turmoil caused by the Mexican Revolution of 1909–1910. The third phase of Mexican immigration was prompted by the Bracero Program (1942–1964) that admitted Mexican laborers on contract with the United States, creating a binational labor market with Mexico through a series of agreements. Almost 5 million Mexican temporary farm workers were admitted to the United States between 1942 and 1964 (Martin & Midgley, 1994). The Bracero program reached its peak in its final ten years, with an average of over 300,000 new contracts per year, before it was terminated by the U.S. government.

The fourth wave of Mexican immigration to the United States began after the passing of the Hart-Cellar Act in 1965 (Johnson et al., 1997), discussed in Chapter 1, which altered the discriminatory quota system based on "national origins" to include equal immigration quotas for all countries and a preference for family reunification. The most recent phase of Mexican immigration began in 1986, as a result of the passage of the Immigration Reform and Control Act (IRCA), in a time when the value of the Mexican currency (the peso) fell to half its value, driving the country into economic recession. Contrary to its initial intentions, also discussed in Chapter 1, this law—in combination with the effects of the North American Free Trade Agreement (NAFTA)—resulted in more Mexicans crossing the U.S. border. Much of the Mexican migratory influx then bypassed legal entry and resulted in the geographic dispersion across the United States of undocumented workers. Moreover, new work opportunities in poultry plants, slaughterhouses, and tobacco and other crop harvesting drew Mexican immigrants (regardless of their legal status) to states in the South and Midwest. This has transformed the Mexican-American population from a regional minority to a national presence (Acuna, 2003), whereas other groups, such as Cuban-Americans, remain regional or dispersed and smaller.

Cuban Immigration

The experiences of Cuban-American immigrants have been somehow different from the majority of immigrants from Latin America (Acuna, 2003; Daniels, 2002; Cordero-Guzman & Henken, 2005). Cuban immigration to the United States has a long history, dating from the 16th century. Before 1960 an estimated 100,000 Cubans were living in the United States. After Fidel Castro's Cuban revolution, political upheaval drove Cuban political refugees to the United States in larger numbers. From 1959 to 1963, approximately 220,000 people formed the first wave of Cuban refugees, most of them White, educated, and upper or middle class. The 1966 Cuban Adjustment Act granted Cubans political asylum and made them eligible for government-sponsored and subsidized programs (such as public assistance, Medicare, free English courses, scholarships, and low-interest college loans). This was called the "golden age" of the Cuban exodus, and no other system of refugee resettlement in the history of the United States was more generous and accommodating than the CRP (Cuban Refugees Program).

Cuban-Americans are far from homogeneous. The later refugees—340,000 escapees on the so-called "freedom flights" (U.S.-financed airlifts between 1965 and 1973) and 125,000 by emigration from the port of Mariel in 1980—included a large portion of working-class Cubans, as well as Cubans of mixed ethnicity-race (Acuna, 2003; Perez, 2001). U.S. immigration policy then became more stringent in the 1980s and 1990s. Before the 1980s, all refugees from Cuba were welcomed into the United States as political refugees. As a result of the 1995 revision, the so-called Wet Feet, Dry Feet Policy, of the Cuban Adjustment Act of 1966, only Cubans who reach U.S. soil—with feet on the ground—have been granted refugee status.

Dominican Immigration

The population of Dominican immigrants has increased rapidly and quietly in the United States since the 1960s; they were the fifth-largest group within the U.S. Latino population in 2004. They tend to settle in the Northeast: immigration records of Dominicans in the United States date from the late 1800s, and New York City has had a Dominican community since the 1930s. A considerable number of Dominicans lived in the United States before 1960. However, Dominican immigration accelerated in 1960s because of economic upheaval and political instability when the Dominican dictator Rafael Trujillo was assassinated and the United States subsequently sent a Marine invasion. The Dominican immigrant population has increased more than 14-fold in the last 30 years, from about 70,000 in 1970 to one million in 2004. Current estimates place the Dominican population in the United States, including undocumented immigrants, at about 1.5 million (Acuna, 2003). The Dominican population is a tri-ethnic-racial mixture of White, Black, and Taino Indian backgrounds.

Although they have been portrayed as less economically successful than Cuban immigrants, Dominicans have distinguished themselves as successful small-business owners within their ethnic communities, revitalizing neighborhoods and supporting small-scale enterprise (Bailey, 2001).

Central American Immigration

Compared with other U.S. Latino groups, Central Americans, as the newest arrivals, represent 7% of the U.S. Latino population, although this may be a significant undercount. They began coming to the United States as a result of the close political and economic links between the United States and the region, which were established in the late 19th and early 20th centuries. Central Americans include various types of immigrants: refugees, a large majority of them children sent alone by their parents; professionals in search of a better life in the United States; and mainly poor, undocumented individuals from urban and rural areas.

Because of their countries' ties with the United States, Panama and Honduras were the first Central American countries with a significant immigrant presence in the United States. However, fear and dissatisfaction with their homelands, provoked by increasing political violence and economic crisis, appear to represent the experience of recent Central American immigrants. The political destabilization of the region—the upheaval in Nicaragua and the civil wars in Guatemala and El Salvador—pushed people out, and they migrated north. Many Guatemalans, for example, are farmers from villages, driven off their land by the military in the 1980s escalation of the civil war. Most are of Mayan descent, and Spanish is their second language.

Nicaraguan immigration is the epitome of this kind of compelled emigration, when the geopolitical turmoil tore thousands of people from their homelands in the decades since the 1980s. The United States government funded counterrevolutionaries and imposed an economic embargo on Nicaragua after the 1979 overthrow of the Somoza dynasty and the establishment of the Sandinista regime. The Sandinistas were unable to stabilize the country, and about one-tenth of Nicaraguans left their country in the 1980s, some to the United States—the largest wave of documented Nicaraguan immigrants. The first wave of about 20,000 tended to be college-educated white-collar workers or business people, the majority of whom were political refugees; many settled in the Miami area. The later waves of Nicaraguan immigrants were more diverse (Acuna, 2003).

However, only a small portion of Central American refugees reach the United States. Most are refugees within their own countries, fleeing for safety from their original homes, or they have taken refuge in other Central American countries or Mexico. Mexico may have been the first country to offer Central American refugees asylum. For those who did arrive in the United States, their avowals of political persecution and petitions for legal residence tended to be consistently rejected at federal, state, and local levels. Because it soon became evident that the chance of political asylum was so low, many did not even apply, but have simply lived undocumented in the United States (Daniels, 2002).

South American Immigration

Although South Americans have been immigrating in small numbers to the United States since the days of the California Gold Rush, their numbers did not rise to significant levels until recently. This is likely due to the geographic distance of South America countries from the United States and the relative lack of direct U.S. involvement in their political and economic affairs (Espitia, 2004). The current influx of immigrants from South America is the result of major economic and civil strife during the last two decades, combined with increased urbanization, raised expectations, and the affordability of international air travel. Political and economic problems have especially plagued Colombia and Peru, where armed conflicts developed between the governments and an assortment of leftist guerrilla groups. Military dictatorships in Chile and Argentina also compelled many to emigrate.

South American immigrants to the United States since 1960 have been generally two types: working-class immigrants with low levels of education, searching for better jobs, higher incomes, and brighter futures for their children; and well-educated professionals, seeking to escape increased economic insecurity and the threat of violence and to make the most of their education and skills (Espitia, 2004). The South American professionals comprise a higher proportion of their immigration group than is found in any other U.S. Latino population.

We use Colombian immigrants to the United States to exemplify South American emigration. Before the 1980s, most South American immigrants were either political exiles or relatively wealthy individuals who tended to live apart from other Latino groups. Many middle-class Colombian merchants and others immigrated to the United States during the late 1950s and early 1960s, fleeing from their civil war (*La Violencia*). The growth of drug cartels that created instability during the late 1970s also drove many Columbians to migrate north. However, the later wave of immigrants, far more racially and economically diverse than its predecessor, gradually displaced professionals as the majority. The patterns of Peruvians and Ecuadorians entering the United States have been similar to that of Colombians, their moves triggered by political instability, corrupt governments, and economic upheavals.

Summarizing the history of Latino immigration, E. Garcia (2001) emphasizes that the great majority of these immigrants share a common language and to some extent a common culture. They also display a great diversity, coming from all social strata of Latin American nations and migrating for a number of quite different reasons and through different approaches. Some left to escape poverty or economic upheaval; others were fleeing wars or political persecution. Some came directly to the United States, while others arrived after harrowing escapes followed by years in refugee camps. However, most were attracted by the hope for a better way of life, including more desirable educational and economic opportunities for themselves and their children. Next, we illustrate the diversity in a discussion of the similarities and differences of Latino-Americans' social, economic, demographic, and educational backgrounds.

A Sociodemographic Briefing

The 2004 American Community Survey (U.S. Bureau of the Census, 2004) counted 40.5 million Hispanic-Americans—approximately a 16% increase over the 2000 census count (35 million) and an 85% increase over the 1990 census count (21 million). Ten subgroups in the Hispanic population in 2004 comprised a minimum of 0.6% of the total Hispanic population: Mexican (26 million, 64%), Cuban (1.4 million, 3.6%), Salvadorian (1.2 million, 3%), Dominican (1 million, 2.6%), Guatemalan (0.7 million, 1.7%), Columbian (0.7 million, 1.7%), Ecuadorian (0.45 million, 1.1%), Honduran (0.41 million, 1%), Peruvian (0.4 million, 1%), and Nicaraguan (0.25 million, 0.6%). Finally, about 20% of the Latino U.S. population is from elsewhere in Latin America. However, for this chapter we have compiled census data for the ten largest nationality subgroups.

In 2004, Hispanics had a median age of 27 years, about 9 years younger than the median age of the U.S. population (36.2 years); the Hispanic population had a larger proportion of young people and a smaller proportion of older people. More than one in three Hispanics were children (under 18 years), compared with one in five non-Hispanic Whites and one in four of the total U.S. population. About 5% of Hispanics were 65 and older, compared with about 15% of non-Hispanic Whites and 12% of all Americans. Measuring by median age, Mexicans are the youngest of U.S. Latinos (25 years old), and Cubans are the oldest (41).

Hispanic adults (7.5%) were generally less likely to be divorced than non-Hispanic Whites (10.7%) or the overall U.S. population (10.2%). However, Cubans (12.3%) and Dominicans (11.6%) had higher divorce rates than the national rates. Guatemalans, Hondurans, and Salvadorans had among the lowest proportions of divorced individuals, at about 5%. Generally, Mexican and Central American adults had lower divorce rates than South Americans, who in turn had lower divorce rates than Cubans and Dominicans.

Hispanic women aged 15 to 50 had higher birth rates (75 per 1,000) than non-Hispanic White women of the same age range (50 per 1,000). Guatemalan women and Mexican women had the highest fertility rates among Hispanic-origin groups. All Hispanic nationality groups except

South Americans had a higher percentage of unmarried women with a birth in 2003 than the national average. The average household size for Hispanic-Americans was 3.44 persons, compared to the national average of 2.6 persons, and all Hispanic-American nationality groups had a substantially larger mean family size than the national average, except for Cuban-Americans (2.7 persons).

The Hispanic population 25 and older generally had lower educational attainment than the U.S. population in 2004. They had a higher percentage of people with less than high school education than the national percentage (40.4% vs. 16.1%), a lower percentage with high school diplomas (60% vs. 84%), and a lower percentage with bachelor's degrees (12.7% vs. 27%). However, substantial variations occur among nationality groups. Salvadorans had the highest percentage of people with less than a high school education (59%) and the lowest percentage of people who had a high school diploma (41%) or a bachelor's degree (6%). People of South American ancestry had the most educational attainment among Hispanic groups, except for Ecuadorians. Colombian- and Peruvian-Americans had a lower percentage of people who did not finish high school and a higher percentage of people with a bachelor's degree than the U.S. general population.

Hispanic families had lower median family incomes ($35,929) in 2004 than all U.S. families ($44,684). South Americans had the highest median household incomes among all Hispanic nationality groups (Columbian, $41,566; Ecuadorian, $43,164; and Peruvian, $42,956); all other Hispanic nationality groups had a median income lower than $40,000. Among the lowest-income Hispanic households were Dominicans ($29,624) and Hondurans ($31,526). The median incomes for Mexican and Cuban households were $35,185 and $38,256, respectively.

About 22% of Latino families were living in poverty in 2004, a rate about 70% higher than the poverty rate of all U.S. families (13.1%). All Hispanic nationality groups had higher poverty rates than the national rate except for Colombians (10.6%). Dominican, Honduran, and Mexican families had the highest family poverty rates: 28%, 23.7%, and 23.6%, respectively. The lowest poverty rates reported for Hispanic nationality groups, except for South Americans, were for Salvadorans (15%) and Cubans (15.2%).

Of all ethnic-racial groups, Hispanic-Americans were less likely than the total U.S. population (34%) to have jobs in management, professional, or related occupations. However, the percentages within nationality groups varied, from 31% for Cuban-American workers to 10% for Guatemalan workers. Hispanic-Americans were more likely than the total U.S. population to have jobs in service (24% vs. 16%), construction (15.5% vs. 10%), and production, transportation, and material-moving occupations (18.5% vs. 13%). Central Americans and Dominicans were more prevalent in service occupations than the other Hispanic nationality groups. Mexican and Central Americans were more likely than other Hispanic nationality groups to have jobs in construction. Mexicans,

Dominicans, and Central Americans were more likely to be in production, transportation, and material-moving occupations than other Hispanic nationality groups.

About 61% of Hispanic-Americans were U.S.-born, 11% were foreign-born but naturalized U.S. citizens, and 28% foreign-born and not U.S. citizens. However, the percentage of foreign-born within different nationality groups varied greatly. While less than 40% of Mexicans in the United States were foreign-born, 61% of Dominicans, 71% of Guatemalans, and 72% of Peruvians were foreign-born. Cuba had the highest percentage of naturalized U.S. citizens (38%) among the foreign-born, due to their automatically granted legal refugee status once they reached U.S. land. By contrast, Guatemala had the highest percentage of non-U.S. citizens (56%) among the foreign-born, but all Central American-nationality groups had 50% or more foreign-born non-U.S. citizens.

Time of entry also varies. About one in five foreign-born Hispanics entered the United States in 2000 or later. More than one-third entered between 1990 and 1999, and 45% arrived in the United States before 1990. In comparison, 49% of all foreign-born Americans entered the United States prior to 1990. Among the Latino nationalities, Hondurans and Peruvians had the highest percentage of immigrants who entered the United States after 2000, at slightly over 24%. Cuba (12%) had the lowest percentage of recent immigrants who entered the United States after 2000, and also the highest proportion of the foreign-born entering the United States before 1990 (65%).

While Hispanics in considerable numbers resided in every state in 2004, most lived in just a handful of states. Nearly two-thirds of Hispanics—or more than 26 million—lived in California (30%), Texas (19%), Florida (8%), and New York (7%). Other states with relatively large numbers of Hispanics were Illinois, Arizona, New Jersey, Colorado, and New Mexico. These states accounted for another 15% of all Hispanics. Los Angeles County had the largest Hispanic population (4.7 million) in 2006, followed by Harris County, Texas, where Houston is located, and Miami-Dade County in Florida (1.5 million each). The state of New Mexico has the highest proportion of people of Hispanic origin (43%); the proportion of the populations of California and Texas with Hispanic origin exceeds 35% each. However, the states hosting the highest percentage of Hispanics in their foreign-born population were six southern states, from 51% in Arkansas to 60% in South Carolina.

LATINO-AMERICAN SCHOOL-AGE CHILDREN

Figure 7.3A shows the population figures for the ten largest nationalities of Latino-American children aged 5–18. With 86% of all Latino children, Mexicans are clearly the largest group of Latino-American school-age children, followed by Cubans (2.7%), Dominicans (2.6%), and Salvadorans (2%). Although the six other nationalities included in Figure 7.1 each have a considerable number of children (from about 35,000 Hondurans to 80,000 Colombians), each nationality counts for less than 1.5% of the total number of Latino children aged 5–18.

Figure 7.3B shows that the nationality distribution for immigrant Latino children is very similar to that for the overall Latino child population, although all Hispanic groups, except Mexicans and Cubans, have larger shares. About 77% of Latino immigrant children are of Mexican origin; the other Latin nationality groups with more than 2% of the Latino immigrant children population are Dominicans (4.2%), Colombians (2.9%), Salvadorans (2.8%), Cubans (2.7%), and Guatemalans (2.1%).

Generational Makeup

Table 7.1 shows very different patterns in the generational composition of Latino school-age children, compared to all U.S. children, as well as among different nationality groups within the Latino population. While less than 20% of the nation's school-age children were either foreign-born or children of foreign-born parent(s), almost 70% of Latino children were in these two categories. Over half of the Latino child population falls into the second generation (51%). However, the proportion of foreign-born Latino children (20%) is significantly smaller than the proportion of third-generation Latino children, that is, U.S.-born Latino children with native-born parents (29%).

FIGURE 7.3A   U.S. Hispanic Children (5–18) by Nationality, 2000

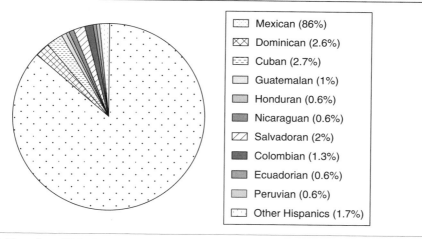

SOURCE: Data from PUMS 5% of the 2000 Census (U.S. Bureau of the Census, 2003a), compiled by authors.

FIGURE 7.3B   U.S. Hispanic Immigrant Children (5–18) by Nationality, 2000

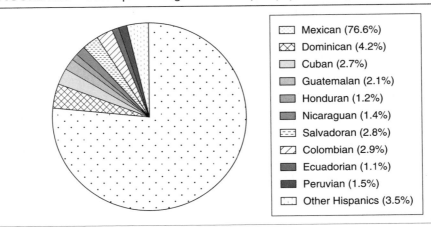

- Mexican (76.6%)
- Dominican (4.2%)
- Cuban (2.7%)
- Guatemalan (2.1%)
- Honduran (1.2%)
- Nicaraguan (1.4%)
- Salvadoran (2.8%)
- Colombian (2.9%)
- Ecuadorian (1.1%)
- Peruvian (1.5%)
- Other Hispanics (3.5%)

SOURCE: Data from PUMS 5% of the 2000 Census (U.S. Bureau of the Census, 2003a), compiled by authors.

Overall in 2000, one of five Hispanic children was foreign-born, one of two was a child with foreign-born parent(s), and one of three was a U.S.-born child with U.S.-born parents. However, these multigenerational patterns for all Latino children do not hold constantly across nationality groups. Mexican and Cuban children were more likely to be third generation (32% and 24%, respectively) than children in any other nationality group. They fit the general Latino pattern because they have had a long immigration history to the United States and, at the same time, have had continually large numbers of immigrants entering this country over the past three decades. However, immigrant children from Guatemalan, Honduran, Nicaraguan, Colombian, and Peruvian families were more likely to be foreign-born: each group had over 40% of its children born outside the United States.

The Characteristics of Families

In this section, we consider the attributes of children's families. This includes their economic conditions, their living arrangements, and parental education, language use, and citizenship status.

Socioeconomic Backgrounds of Families

Latino children are generally more likely than the overall U.S. child population to live in an inner-city location, but Latino immigrants are not more likely than all U.S. immigrants to live in inner-city locations. Table 7.2 shows Latino children as much more likely to live in an inner city than all U.S. children, yet Latino immigrant children were slightly less likely than immigrants overall to have inner-city residency. Cuban children, regardless of their immigrant status, were the least likely among the Latino

TABLE 7.1   U.S. Hispanic Children 5–18 Years Old by National Origins and Immigration Status, 2000

	All Children	Immigrant Children		Children of Immigrant	Native Children
		1st Generation	1.5 Generation		
All Children	100	2.2%	2.5%	13.6%	81.8%
(N)	(2,694,073)	(58,376)	(67,416)	(365,206)	(2,203,075)
All Hispanic Children	100	8.6%	11.1%	50.9%	29.4%
(N)	(292,923)	(25,290)	(32,439)	(149,025)	(86,169)
Mexican	100	7.3%	10.3%	50.1%	32.4%
(N)	(252,283)	(18,360)	(25,876)	(126,295)	(81,752)
Dominican	100	16.3%	15.2%	62.0%	6.5%
(N)	(7,676)	(1,253)	(1,167)	(4,755)	(501)
Cuban	100	11.9%	7.4%	57.3%	23.5%
(N)	(8,003)	(949)	(590)	(4,587)	(1,877)
Guatemalan	100	19.7%	21.3%	53.6%	5.4%
(N)	(2,942)	(579)	(627)	(1,578)	(158)
Honduran	100	23.2%	19.3%	49.2%	8.3%
(N)	(1,685)	(391)	(325)	(829)	(140)
Nicaraguan	100	14.8%	28.0%	50.8%	6.5%
(N)	(1,827)	(270)	(511)	(928)	(118)
Salvadoran	100	14.3%	13.3%	68.4%	4.1%
(N)	(5,772)	(825)	(765)	(3,945)	(237)
Other Central Americans	100	15.3%	15.0%	53.3%	16.4%
(N)	(1,989)	(303)	(298)	(1,061)	(327)
Colombian	100	22.3%	20.6%	48.8%	8.3%
(N)	(3,912)	(874)	(807)	(1,907)	(324)
Ecuadorian	100	18.5%	17.4%	55.7%	8.4%
(N)	(1,706)	(316)	(296)	(951)	(143)

(Continued)

TABLE 7.1   (Continued)

Peruvian	100	24.2%	21.7%	45.8%	8.4%
(N)	(1,889)	(457)	(409)	(865)	(158)
Other South Americans	100	23.9%	25.6%	38.9%	11.6%
(N)	(2,897)	(692)	(742)	(1,127)	(336)

SOURCE: Data from PUMS 5% of the 2000 Census (U.S. Bureau of the Census, 2003a), compiled by authors.

1 Foreign-born children who immigrated to U.S. at age 5 or younger are classified as 1.5 generation and who immigrated to U.S. after age 5 are classified as 1st generation.

2 Percentages do not total to 100 due to the rounding of percentages for subgroups.

population to live in the inner city, while Dominicans (around 61%) and Ecuadorians (above 40%) were the most likely.

Table 7.2 also shows the variation in poverty rates among Latino nationality groups. Latino families had much higher poverty rates than U.S. families in general (26.2% vs. 14.8%) and somewhat higher poverty rates than all U.S. immigrant families (33.9% vs. 27.1%). Among Latino groups, regardless of immigration status, only Cuban and Peruvian-American children had lower poverty rates than the national percentages. Dominican (34.4%), Honduran (29.8%), and Mexican (26.9%) families had the highest poverty rates among Latino groups. Both Peruvian families in general and Peruvian immigrant families in particular had the lowest poverty rates among Latino nationality groups (11.7% and 14.3%, respectively), and Dominican families had the highest rates (34.4% and 36.5%), though Mexican immigrant families had similar poverty rates (36.6%). However, Latino immigrant nationality groups other than Mexicans, Dominicans, and Hondurans all had poverty rates lower than the national rates for immigrants.

The proportion of Latino families in the affluent range (both general and immigrant Latino population) was two-thirds lower than either the proportion for all U.S. children or the proportion for all immigrant children. All Latino nationality groups, except Cubans (20.6%), had a lower-than-average percentage in the affluent segment of the U.S. population (18.4%); all Latino immigrant nationality groups except Colombians (14.9%) and Peruvians (10.7%) had lower rates of affluence compared to the national rates for immigrants (10.7%). However, Table 7.2 shows a marked difference between South Americans and other Latinos in family economic conditions. Except for children from Cuban families, Latino children from South America are generally better off economically than Latino children from other parts of Latin America. Mexican, Dominican, and Honduran children are more likely to live in families with difficult economic conditions than are Latino children from other nationality groups.

TABLE 7.2 Socioeconomic Characteristics of U.S. Hispanic Children 5–18 Years Old by Ethnicity, National Origin, and Immigration Status, 2000

	All Children (292,923)	Immigrant Children (65,357)
% of Children Who Lived in Inner Cities		
All Children	13.1%	26.0%
All Hispanic Children	22.2%	24.0%
Mexican	20.9%	22.3%
Dominican	61.0%	60.9%
Cuban	8.4%	4.2%
Guatemalan	34.7%	32.4%
Honduran	37.2%	32.5%
Nicaraguan	15.3%	14.1%
Salvadoran	34.5%	32.8%
Other Central Americans	26.2%	21.5%
Colombian	22.9%	20.3%
Ecuadorian	44.3%	44.6%
Peruvian	20.0%	18.9%
Other South Americans	18.5%	18.8%
Poverty Rates (% of Children Who Lived in Households Under Poverty Level)		
All Children	14.8%	27.1%
All Hispanic Children	26.2%	33.9%
Mexican	26.9%	36.6%
Dominican	34.4%	36.5%
Cuban	14.6%	25.5%
Guatemalan	24.1%	23.0%
Honduran	29.8%	31.0%
Nicaraguan	18.6%	23.2%
Salvadoran	22.9%	22.7%
Other Central Americans	18.1%	23.3%

(Continued)

TABLE 7.2   (Continued)

Colombian	17.4%	21.4%
Ecuadorian	19.2%	24.0%
Peruvian	11.7%	14.3%
Other South Americans	13.2%	17.1%
% of Children Who Lived in Households With Total Family Income at or Higher Than 75th Percentile		
All Children	18.4%	10.7%
All Hispanic Children	6.7%	3.6%
Mexican	5.9%	2.2%
Dominican	5.7%	3.9%
Cuban	20.6%	4.6%
Guatemalan	7.1%	8.0%
Honduran	8.3%	9.6%
Nicaraguan	7.8%	3.6%
Salvadoran	5.3%	4.8%
Other Central Americans	12.6%	8.8%
Colombian	14.9%	14.2%
Ecuadorian	8.8%	3.4%
Peruvian	13.7%	10.7%
Other South Americans	20.9%	17.1%
% of Children Who Lived in Households With Two Parents		
All Children	72.8%	80.4%
All Hispanic Children	73.4%	78.8%
Mexican	74.4%	81.9%
Dominican	49.8%	48.8%
Cuban	72.5%	77.5%
Guatemalan	70.6%	74.0%
Honduran	62.3%	63.0%
Nicaraguan	71.8%	71.8%
Salvadoran	70.9%	79.3%

Other Central Americans	68.3%	70.1%
Colombian	69.9%	72.4%
Ecuadorian	69.3%	70.4%
Peruvian	74.2%	71.6%
Other South Americans	77.3%	81.3%
% of Children Who Lived in Households Without Fathers		
All Children	21.5%	13.3%
All Hispanic Children	19.2%	13.3%
Mexican	18.3%	10.9%
Dominican	41.0%	38.4%
Cuban	21.2%	15.1%
Guatemalan	19.0%	15.4%
Honduran	27.2%	22.4%
Nicaraguan	19.9%	18.3%
Salvadoran	19.5%	19.2%
Other Central Americans	24.7%	21.0%
Colombian	21.9%	18.4%
Ecuadorian	22.8%	18.5%
Peruvian	17.5%	17.1%
Other South Americans	18.0%	14.3%
% of Children Who Lived With Parent or Household Head Having Less Than Four Years' Education		
All Children	1.5%	8.9%
All Hispanic Children	7.5%	12.3%
Mexican	8.1%	14.6%
Dominican	4.5%	7.0%
Cuban	1.2%	1.4%
Guatemalan	8.9%	10.9%
Honduran	4.8%	6.0%
Nicaraguan	2.5%	4.0%

(Continued)

TABLE 7.2 (Continued)

Salvadoran	9.7%	13.5%
Other Central Americans	2.1%	3.3%
Colombian	1.7%	1.4%
Ecuadorian	2.5%	3.1%
Peruvian	0.5%	0.8%
Other South Americans	0.6%	0.7%
% of Children Who Lived With Parent or Household Head Having at Least a High School Diploma		
All Children	80.8%	53.7%
All Hispanic Children	45.6%	30.3%
Mexican	42.8%	22.0%
Dominican	53.7%	45.5%
Cuban	75.7%	58.6%
Guatemalan	42.2%	40.6%
Honduran	51.8%	44.4%
Nicaraguan	64.9%	58.0%
Salvadoran	36.0%	31.5%
Other Central Americans	75.1%	65.7%
Colombian	76.5%	75.7%
Ecuadorian	66.9%	61.3%
Peruvian	87.8%	86.3%
Other South Americans	85.5%	82.4%
% of Children Who Lived With Parent or Household Head Having at Least a Four-Year College Degree		
All Children	23.0%	22.7%
All Hispanic Children	8.2%	7.7%
Mexican	6.4%	3.9%
Dominican	11.7%	11.0%
Cuban	26.1%	24.0%
Guatemalan	10.0%	12.9%

Honduran	11.9%	13.9%
Nicaraguan	16.7%	14.3%
Salvadoran	6.2%	6.2%
Other Central Americans	21.4%	19.1%
Colombian	27.3%	31.2%
Ecuadorian	18.3%	19.6%
Peruvian	32.3%	35.3%
Other South Americans	39.3%	39.8%

SOURCE: Data from PUMS 5% of the 2000 Census (U.S. Bureau of the Census, 2003a), compiled by authors.

Family Living Arrangements

Latino children were slightly more likely than all U.S. children to live in two-parent households (73.4% vs. 72.8%) and slightly less likely to live without a father (19.2% vs. 21.5%). Latino immigrant children were slightly less likely to live with two parents than were all U.S. immigrant children (78.8% vs. 80.4%), but the rates for living without a father (13.3%) were the same for both groups. The differences in these rates are not remarkably large among nationality groups, except that Dominican and Honduran children are less likely than either all U.S. children or all U.S. immigrant children to live with two parents and also more likely to live without a father.

Parental Educational Attainment

As we have for other analyses, we consider parental educational attainment at three levels (rates for less than four years of education, a high school diploma, and completion of a four-year college degree) because attainment at various levels raises different issues for children's schooling. Nationally, less than 2% of U.S. children were from families where parent(s) had the least education—less than four years—but the percentage for U.S. immigrant children's families, at 9%, is four times higher than the national average for all children. Latino children, on average, are more likely to come from families with parents who did not have four years of education (7.5%), and Latino immigrant children are more likely than other immigrant children to have parents who did not finish four years of school (12.3%). For all children, regardless of their immigration status, Salvadorans (9.7%), Guatemalans (8.9%), and Mexicans (8.1%) were the three nationalities reporting the highest rates of least educated parents. On the other hand, Peruvian (0.5%), Cuban (1.2%), and Colombian (1.7%) children were least likely to have parents with the least education. Among immigrant children,

Mexican (14.6%), Salvadoran (13.5%), and Guatemalan (10.9%) children were most likely to have parents who had not finished four years of school; Peruvian (0.8%), Colombian (1.4%), and Cuban (1.4%) children are least likely to have parents lacking a fourth grade education.

The nationality pattern for high school graduation rates is relatively similar to the one for this lowest education level. In general, Latino parents had much lower rates of high school graduation than all U.S. parents (45.6% vs. 80.8%). Latino immigrant parents also had much lower high school graduation rates than all U.S. immigrant parents (30.3% vs. 53.7%). Latino parents in all nationality groups, except Peruvian (87.8%), had lower high school graduation rates than the rates for all U.S. parents—though some of the nationality groups, such as Cuban and Colombian, had high school graduation rates close to the national rates. Salvadoran (36%), Guatemalan (42.2%), and Mexican (42.8%) parents had the lowest high school graduation rates among Latinos, regardless of their immigration status. Mexican (22%), Salvadoran (31.5%), and Guatemalan (40.6%) immigrant parents also had the lowest high school graduation rates among all Latino immigrant parents. Patterns for regional differences are similar to those for the lower attainment level: the rate of Latino parents from Cuba and South America graduating from high school was higher than that for Latino parents from Mexico, the Dominican Republic, and Central American countries.

Latino children were also less likely to have parents who were college graduates. About 8% of parents of all Latino children were college graduates, compared to 23% of parents of all U.S. children. About 7.7% of parents of Latino immigrant children were college graduates, compared to 22.7% of parents of all U.S. immigrant children. However, the variation among Hispanic parents with college degrees was striking: Peruvian (32.3%), Colombian (27.3%), and Cuban (26.1%) parents had higher rates of college graduation than the U.S. national rates, and the parents of immigrant children in those same three nationality groups had higher college graduation rates than the national rates among immigrants. Among parents of Mexican (6.4%) and Salvadoran (6.2%) children, college graduation rates were a third of the national rates. The rates for parents of immigrant children were also much lower than national ones: 3.9% for Mexican parents and 6.2% for Salvadoran parents, compared to 22.7% for all parents of U.S. immigrant children. Again—along with parents of Cuban children—parents of Latino children from South America were more likely to be college graduates, regardless of immigration status, than parents of other Latino children.

In summary, we see consistent attainment patterns at all three educational levels across nationality groups. The general trend is clear: Mexican, Salvadoran, and Guatemalan children tend to have parents who were less likely to complete four years of education or graduate from high school and college, regardless of their immigrant status. Cuban and South American children were more likely to have parents with more education.

Variations in Latino parents' education have several explanations. Mexico and some other countries in Central America have had historically higher illiteracy rates than the United States. For example, the illiteracy rate in Mexico in 2005 was 10%, about 20 times higher than the percentage of least educated adults in the United States (United Nations Development Programme Report, 2005). Furthermore, according to a current study of Mexican immigrants in New York City (Cortina & Gendreau, 2003), these migrants were more likely to come from the less affluent parts of Mexico City, from southern Mexican states with large indigenous communities, and from rural areas in less economically developed provinces of Mexico. The lower high school graduation rate may be explained by difficulties in operating and enforcing the nine-year compulsory education program in Mexico, and the lack of opportunities for Mexican rural immigrants to continue their education after they migrate to the United States. The lower college-graduation rates may be explained by the supply-and-demand forces in U.S. immigration policy: the majority of Mexicans came to the United States to fill jobs in agricultural, construction, and service industries—low-level jobs attractive to immigrants without college degrees. However, this is aggravated by the lack of adult-education programs for immigrant adults in the United States, especially for immigrants working in lower-end jobs. Not being able to complete high school and college keeps many Mexicans and other Latino immigrants in low-paying jobs and near or under poverty levels.

In contrast, many South American immigrants have been recruited to this country by high-tech industries and international trading companies, and some of them were entrepreneurs themselves. However, as we have noted previously, a considerable proportion of Latino immigrants from Central America (e.g., Guatemalans, Nicaraguans, Salvadorans) were political refugees who fled to the United States, with or without BCIS (Bureau of Citizenship and Immigration Services) permission. We have emphasized previously that, compared with immigrants moving for economic reasons and family reunification, political refugees are more likely to be inadequately prepared for immigration and to lack social networking for initial settlement, including finding proper jobs in the United States. They also have more difficulties adjusting to the new society, either because of a lack of English proficiency or because of psychological trauma suffered during the political turmoil or war that prompting their flight to the United States.

Household Language Situation and U.S. Citizenship Status

Two patterns emerge from examining the language situations of Latino families (see Table 7.3). First, Latino children, both immigrants and as a whole, were more likely in 2000 to speak a language other than English at home (73% and 95%) compared to all U.S. children and all U.S. immigrant children (17.3% and 85%) respectively. They were also more likely to live in linguistically isolated households (23.3% vs. 4.5%, and 43.5% vs. 34.4%). Although over 85% of Dominican, Salvadoran, Nicaraguan, and Guatemalan children (regardless of immigration status) spoke a language other than English at home, in six of the ten nationality groups (Mexicans, Dominicans, Cubans, Nicaraguans, Salvadorans, and Ecuadorians) over 95% of the immigrant children spoke a heritage language at home. Over 30% of Salvadoran, Guatemalan, and Dominican children, as a whole, lived in linguistically isolated households; over 55% of Cuban and about 46% of Mexican immigrant children lived in linguistically isolated households.

Second, although substantial variations occur across the nationality groups in the use of heritage languages, even more differences are apparent in the percentage of children who lived in linguistically isolated households in 2000. For example, while Dominican children as a whole were twice as likely as Cuban children to live in linguistically isolated households, Cuban immigrant children were twice as likely to live in them as Nicaraguan or Peruvian immigrant children. Strikingly, among all Latino children, Cuban children as a whole were least likely to live in linguistically isolated households, but Cuban immigrant children were most likely to live in linguistically isolated households among all Latino immigrant children. The substantial differences between the general and the immigrant populations of Cuban children may be attributed to the different waves of Cuban immigrants, discussed at the beginning of the chapter, who came to the United States in different social, political, and policy contexts, and to the neighborhood and schools hosting the newcomers with various levels of ethnic segregation. However, because Cuban immigrant children often settle in Cuban ethnic neighborhoods, the adults in their families may have less opportunity to learn English than those who reside in more heterogeneous communities.

In 2000 Latino parents as a whole reported a lower percentage of U.S. citizenship than all parents (57% vs. 92%, respectively), and Latino immigrant parents reported a lower percentage of U.S. citizenship than all U.S. immigrant parents (24% vs. 32%). The citizenship rates of Latino parents were lower than those of Asian and Black parents for both the general population and the immigrant population, but rates and ratios between the total (including all generations) and immigrants vary across the nationality groups. Cubans, Mexicans, and Colombians had the highest citizenship rates (70%, 58%, and 57%, respectively) among Latino nationalities for the total population; however, the citizenship rates for immigrant populations were higher among Hondurans, Colombians, and Peruvians. Cuban immigrant parents had the lowest percentage of U.S. citizens (16%) among all Latino immigrant nationality groups.

The higher percentage of Cuban immigrant children who lived in linguistically isolated households and the low percentage of parents of Cuban immigrant children who were U.S. citizens are partially due to length of

TABLE 7.3   Immigration-Related Characteristics of U.S. Households for Hispanic Children 5–18 Years Old by Ethnicity, National Origin, and Immigration Status, 2000

	All Children (2,694,073)	Immigrant Children (125,792)
% of Children Who Spoke a Language Other Than English at Home		
All Children	17.3%	84.9%
All Hispanic Children	72.7%	95.4%
Mexican	71.3%	96.5%
Dominican	91.0%	96.0%
Cuban	71.5%	97.1%
Guatemalan	85.0%	88.6%
Honduran	81.1%	87.6%
Nicaraguan	87.4%	96.0%
Salvadoran	90.8%	94.6%
Other Central Americans	65.5%	88.0%
Colombian	79.9%	84.1%
Ecuadorian	82.7%	95.3%
Peruvian	78.7%	88.3%
Other South Americans	74.4%	87.5%
% of Children Who Lived in Linguistically Isolated Households		
All Children	4.5%	34.4%
All Hispanic Children	23.3%	43.5%
Mexican	23.0%	45.7%
Dominican	30.3%	39.8%
Cuban	15.6%	55.4%
Guatemalan	35.3%	37.2%
Honduran	29.3%	35.2%
Nicaraguan	23.3%	27.3%
Salvadoran	33.9%	36.6%
Other Central Americans	14.0%	23.0%
Colombian	23.9%	33.5%

(Continued)

TABLE 7.3   (Continued)

Ecuadorian	23.0%	35.6%
Peruvian	20.2%	27.9%
Other South Americans	17.4%	27.8%
Household Heads Who Are U.S. Citizens		
All Children	91.6%	31.5%
All Hispanic Children	57.3%	23.7%
Mexican	58.0%	21.7%
Dominican	50.6%	32.1%
Cuban	69.8%	16.0%
Guatemalan	34.3%	29.1%
Honduran	49.7%	39.8%
Nicaraguan	40.0%	25.0%
Salvadoran	38.5%	28.1%
Other Central Americans	64.6%	40.3%
Colombian	56.8%	38.7%
Ecuadorian	52.1%	28.3%
Peruvian	54.4%	34.3%
Other South Americans	53.0%	30.1%

SOURCE: Data from PUMS 5% of the 2000 Census (U.S. Bureau of the Census, 2003a), compiled by authors.

residency: a relatively large portion of Cuban immigrants had been in the United States less than five years. We examine length of residency and other relevant data in next section.

The Characteristics of Latino Children

Now, we turn to attributes of the children themselves. In this section we examine children's disabilities, length of residence in the United States and age at arrival, and their oral English proficiency.

Disabilities

We make three observations about the relationship of Latino children's disabilities to their immigration status and nationality groups.

First, the overall child population (including all generations) had lower rates of physical disabilities but higher rates of learning-related disabilities than the immigrant children's population for the majority of the nationality groups. Data in Table 7.4 indicate this general pattern. Nationally, 3% of U.S. children and 5.1% of immigrant children reported one or multiple physical disabilities, whereas 4.4% of U.S. children and 2.2 % of immigrant children reported learning-related disabilities. Latino children, as a whole, reported higher rates in physical disabilities (4% for all children and 5.6% for immigrant children) and lower rates in learning-related disabilities (2.9% and 2.1%, respectively) than all U.S. children and all U.S. immigrant children.

Second, a clear division occurs among the Latino nationality groups in the prevalence of children's physical disabilities. While Cuban and Peruvian children (2.9%) had lower rates than the U.S. national ones, the children of the rest of Latino nationalities had higher rates than for the nation as a whole. For example, physical-disability rates for Dominicans, Nicaraguans, Hondurans, and Guatemalans were highest among Latino groups (5.4%, 5.2%, 4.9%, and 4.8%, respectively); these four nationality groups also report the highest rates of physical disabilities among immigrant children.

Third, although all of the Latino nationality groups in the general population had lower learning-related disability rates than U.S. children as a whole, various nationality groups visibly differed. Ecuadorians, Peruvians, and Salvadorans (2.1%, 2.3%, and 2.3%, respectively) had the lowest

TABLE 7.4   Other Characteristics of U.S. Hispanic Children 5–18 Years Old by Ethnicity, National Origin, and Immigration Status, 2000

	All Children	Immigrant Children
% of Children Who Reported Physical Disabilities **(One or Multiple Limitations in Mobility, Personal Care, Hearing and Vision, etc.)**		
All Children	3.0%	5.1%
All Hispanic Children	4.0%	5.6%
Mexican	4.0%	5.7%
Dominican	5.4%	7.2%
Cuban	2.9%	3.9%
Guatemalan	4.8%	6.2%
Honduran	4.9%	6.0%
Nicaraguan	5.2%	6.8%
Salvadoran	3.6%	5.0%

(Continued)

TABLE 7.4   (Continued)

Other Central Americans	3.1%	4.0%
Colombian	3.8%	4.5%
Ecuadorian	4.0%	5.7%
Peruvian	2.9%	3.8%
Other South Americans	3.0%	3.1%
% of Children Who Reported Learning-Related Disabilities (Difficulty With Memory, etc.)		
All Children	4.4%	2.2%
All Hispanic Children	2.9%	2.1%
Mexican	2.9%	2.0%
Dominican	3.6%	2.9%
Cuban	3.6%	1.7%
Guatemalan	2.4%	2.2%
Honduran	2.7%	2.9%
Nicaraguan	3.0%	1.9%
Salvadoran	2.3%	2.1%
Other Central Americans	3.5%	2.8%
Colombian	2.7%	2.3%
Ecuadorian	2.1%	2.3%
Peruvian	2.3%	2.1%
Other South Americans	3.1%	2.7%

SOURCE: Data from PUMS 5% of the 2000 Census (U.S. Bureau of the Census, 2003a), compiled by authors.

rates of learning disabilities, while Cubans and Dominicans had the highest (3.6% for each). Among immigrant children, while Dominican and Honduran immigrant children exhibited the highest learning disability rates (2.9%) among all Latino immigrant children, Cuban immigrant children had the lowest (1.7%). The learning-disability rates for Dominican and Honduran immigrant children were also higher than the national rates for all U.S. immigrant children.

Length of Residence and Age of Arrival

In 2000, almost half of Latino immigrant children of school age had lived in the United States for less than five years, and 80% of them had come to the United States after 1990 (see Table 7.5). This percentage distribution for length of residency is almost identical with national patterns for foreign-born children. Cuban children represented the largest proportion of newcomers (73%), followed by Honduran (56%), Colombian, and Ecuadorian children (55% each). More than 40% of Nicaraguan children had been in this country for 10 or more years, compared to less than 7% of Cuban immigrant children.

The age-distribution pattern, for when immigrant children first arrived in the United States, is identical for Latino immigrant children and for U.S. immigrant children as a whole. However, Nicaraguan and Mexican children (65% and 59%) were more likely than other Latino children to have arrived in the United States at age five or younger. Cuban, Honduran, Dominican, and Peruvian children were more likely to have come to the United States when they were older than five. Similarly, one in five Cuban, Honduran, Salvadoran, Colombian, and Ecuadorian children had come to the United States when they were 11 years old or older, the age to begin middle school.

TABLE 7.5   Immigration-Related Characteristics of U.S. Foreign-Born Hispanic Children 5–18 Years Old by Ethnicity and Nationality, 2000

	0–5	6–10	11–15	16 and Above
Years in U.S.				
All Foreign-Born Children	47.3%	34.0%	16.5%	2.3%
All Hispanic Children	45.4%	35.3%	17.3%	2.0%
Mexican	44.0%	36.4%	17.8%	1.9%
Dominican	39.3%	45.0%	13.7%	1.9%
Cuban	72.8%	20.9%	5.6%	0.7%
Guatemalan	44.8%	33.8%	18.2%	3.2%
Honduran	55.6%	27.8%	14.1%	2.5%
Nicaraguan	36.9%	21.4%	38.7%	3.1%
Salvadoran	46.3%	32.5%	18.3%	2.9%
Other Central Americans	47.3%	30.0%	19.5%	3.3%
Colombian	54.7%	26.7%	15.6%	3.0%
Ecuadorian	54.7%	28.6%	14.9%	1.8%
Peruvian	44.3%	38.3%	15.9%	1.4%
Other South Americans	55.2%	29.5%	13.7%	1.6%

(Continued)

TABLE 7.5 (Continued)

Age of Arrival				
All Foreign-Born Children	53.4%	30.1%	14.5%	1.9%
All Hispanic Children	56.2%	28.9%	13.1%	1.8%
Mexican	58.5%	27.9%	12.1%	1.6%
Dominican	48.2%	36.4%	13.8%	1.5%
Cuban	38.3%	38.1%	21.3%	2.3%
Guatemalan	52.0%	28.2%	16.6%	3.2%
Honduran	45.4%	31.3%	20.3%	3.1%
Nicaraguan	65.4%	22.7%	10.0%	1.9%
Salvadoran	48.1%	30.4%	17.9%	3.6%
Other Central Americans	49.6%	32.8%	14.9%	2.8%
Colombian	48.0%	30.0%	18.1%	3.9%
Ecuadorian	48.4%	29.4%	18.1%	4.1%
Peruvian	47.2%	35.0%	15.6%	2.2%
Other South Americans	51.8%	30.8%	15.6%	1.9%

SOURCE: Data from PUMS 5% of the 2000 Census (U.S. Bureau of the Census, 2003a), compiled by authors.

Note: Percentages do not total to 100 due to the rounding of percentages for subgroups.

Oral English Proficiency

Table 7.6 presents the findings for self-reported English proficiency among Latino children who reported speaking languages other than English at home. Among all HLS children (all generations), 66% reported speaking English very well compared to 55% of immigrant children. A higher percentage of Latino immigrant children reported speaking no English compared to all U.S. HLS immigrant children (5.7% vs. 3.8%), and a lower percentage reported speaking English very well (50% vs. 55%). While the highest percentage who reported speaking English very well were Peruvian and Nicaraguan immigrant children (70% and 64%, respectively), the lowest percentage of children who reported speaking English very well were Mexican, Honduran, Guatemalan, Cuban, and Salvadoran immigrant children (47%, 50%, 52%, 52.1%, and 52.5%, respectively).

Education of Children

Based on data available from the 2000 census, and as we did for Asian and Black children, we present three educational indices to represent Latino children's education. These three indices are the general enrollment rates for ages 5–18, enrollment rates in private schools for ages 5–18, and school dropout rates for ages 16–18.

General Enrollment

Table 7.7 shows that Latino children were somewhat less likely to be enrolled in school than all U.S. children (95.2% vs. 96.3%). Latino immigrant children were also less likely to enroll in school than all U.S. immigrant children (92.6% vs. 94.5%). The enrollment gap between all Hispanic children and Hispanic immigrant children (95.2% vs. 92.6%) is slightly larger than between all U.S. children and all U.S. immigrant children (96.3% vs. 94.5%). Almost all Latino nationality groups have enrollment rates lower than or equal to the national rates, except Cubans and Peruvians (96.5% and 96.6%). However, four of the ten immigrant nationality

TABLE 7.6 Self-Reported English Proficiency for Hispanic Children Who Spoke a Language Other Than English at Home by National Origins and Immigration Status, 2000

| | All Children | | | Immigrant Children | | |
	No English	Not Very Well	Very Well	No English	Not Very Well Very	Well
All Children	1.6%	32.3%	66.1%	3.8%	41.2%	55.0%
All Hispanic Children	2.2%	33.5%	64.3%	5.7%	44.2%	50.1%
Mexican	2.6%	36.3%	61.1%	6.2%	46.5%	47.3%
Dominican	1.5%	30.0%	68.5%	3.2%	39.7%	57.1%
Cuban	2.2%	22.0%	75.9%	6.9%	41.0%	52.1%
Guatemalan	3.6%	35.1%	61.3%	6.3%	41.8%	51.9%
Honduran	4.7%	35.1%	60.3%	8.3%	41.5%	50.2%
Nicaraguan	3.8%	24.1%	72.1%	7.7%	28.8%	63.5%
Salvadoran	2.9%	31.7%	65.3%	6.5%	41.0%	52.5%
Other Central Americans	1.0%	27.3%	71.7%	1.1%	32.1%	66.7%
Colombian	1.9%	26.0%	72.1%	3.5%	37.4%	59.2%
Ecuadorian	2.0%	27.1%	70.9%	4.3%	36.4%	59.4%
Peruvian	0.8%	23.1%	76.1%	1.2%	28.5%	70.3%
Other South Americans	1.6%	22.5%	76.0%	2.5%	28.1%	69.5%

SOURCE: Data from PUMS 5% of the 2000 Census (U.S. Bureau of the Census, 2003a), compiled by authors.
Note: Percentages do not total to 100 due to the rounding of percentages for subgroups.

groups—Cuban (95.6%), Peruvian (96%), Colombian (94.9%), and Dominican (94.6%) children—had higher enrollment than the national rates for all immigrant children. Salvadoran (90.1%), Nicaraguan (91.7%), Guatemalan (92.1%), and Mexican (92.2%) immigrant children had enrollment rates that were significantly lower than the rates for all immigrant children nationally.

Enrollment in Private Schools

Latino children in general were significantly less likely to enroll in private school than all U.S. children (5.4% vs. 10.8%), and Latino immigrant children were also less likely to enroll in private school than all U.S. immigrant children (2.7% vs. 6.0%). However, variations occur in the

TABLE 7.7   Educational Characteristics of U.S. Hispanic Children 5–18 Years Old by Ethnicity, National Origin, and Immigration Status, 2000

	All Children	Immigrant Children
% of Children (5–18) Enrolled in Schools in 2000		
All Children	96.3%	94.5%
All Hispanic Children	95.2%	92.6%
Mexican	95.1%	92.2%
Dominican	95.9%	94.6%
Cuban	96.5%	95.6%
Guatemalan	94.3%	92.1%
Honduran	93.8%	90.4%
Nicaraguan	94.3%	91.7%
Salvadoran	94.3%	90.1%
Other Central Americans	95.5%	93.7%
Colombian	95.9%	94.9%
Ecuadorian	95.9%	94.1%
Peruvian	96.6%	96.0%
Other South Americans	96.9%	96.9%
% of Children 5–18 Enrolled in Private Schools in 2000		
All Children	10.8%	6.0%
All Hispanic Children	5.4%	2.7%

Mexican	4.5	1.7%
Dominican	7.8%	3.3%
Cuban	17.6%	4.0%
Guatemalan	6.8%	6.4%
Honduran	6.3%	4.2%
Nicaraguan	9.3%	4.0%
Salvadoran	4.9%	3.2%
Other Central Americans	11.5%	6.0%
Colombian	11.9%	10.3%
Ecuadorian	12.0%	7.4%
Peruvian	13.1%	9.5%
Other South Americans	15.1%	11.4%
% of Children 16–18 Years Old Who Were School Dropouts (Persons Who Did Not Graduate From High School But Were Not Enrolled in School in 2000) by Ethnicity, National Origin, and Immigration Status		
All Children	5.6%	9.0%
All Hispanic Children	9.2%	13.9%
Mexican	9.9%	16.7%
Dominican	6.4%	7.6%
Cuban	5.4%	6.9%
Guatemalan	11.3%	13.2%
Honduran	15.2%	17.7%
Nicaraguan	7.8%	8.8%
Salvadoran	10.9%	15.4%
Other Central Americans	5.2%	7.8%
Colombian	4.3%	4.5%
Ecuadorian	6.5%	9.1%
Peruvian	4.1%	3.5%
Other South Americans	3.8%	3.7%

SOURCE: Data from PUMS 5% of the 2000 Census (U.S. Bureau of the Census, 2003a), compiled by authors.

private-school enrollment rates across Latino nationalities: while about 18% of Cuban children were enrolled in private school along with 13% of Peruvian children and 12% of Ecuadorian and Colombian children, Mexican and Salvadoran children had less than 5% private-school enrollment rates. Among immigrant nationality groups, Colombian (10.3%), Peruvian (9.5%), Ecuadorian (7.4%), and Guatemalan (6.4%) children had higher private-school enrollment rates than the national rates for immigrant children. Mexican (1.7%), Dominican (3.3%), and Salvadoran (3.2%) children had significantly lower private-school enrollment rates than the national rates for all immigrant children.

Many factors explain the variations in private school enrollment rates across nationality groups for Latino children—religion, accessibility of private schools (e.g., city or rural residency), and such—but economic conditions are the most likely influence. Cuban, Colombian, and Peruvian children were more likely to live in households with total family income at, or higher than, the 75th percentile of total U.S. children.

High School Dropouts

Latino teens aged 16–18 had much higher dropout rates than the national average, 9.2% vs. 5.6%, respectively; Latino immigrant teens also had higher dropout rates (13.9%) than those for all U.S. immigrant teens (9%). Honduran (15.2%), Guatemalan (11.3%), Salvadoran (10.9%), and Mexican children (9.9%) had dropout rates near or over 10%, much higher than the 5.6% national average. These four nationality groups among immigrant children also had higher dropout rates than national ones for immigrant children: about 18% of Honduran, 17% of Mexican, 15% of Salvadoran, and 13% of Guatemalan immigrant teens did not receive high school diplomas and were not in high school during the 2000 Census survey. However, Peruvian, Colombian, Cuban, and Dominican immigrant teens had lower dropout rates than the national dropout rates for all U.S. immigrant teens.

Combining Factors

How does language transition affect children's educational attainment? How do the effects differ across gender groups with different family economic backgrounds?

Again, we use school dropout rates as the measure to study the effects of language transition on educational attainment, because it is the severe dropout problem, as well as successful heritage-language retention, that separates Hispanics from many other groups. Along with increasing length of U.S. residence, four kinds of linguistic statuses have developed among immigrant Hispanic youth: youth who speak no English, youth who speak Spanish but do not fully develop English proficiency, youth who speak Spanish but also speak English very well, and youth who are monolingual English speakers. Taking family income into consideration (in poverty, at an income higher than 75% of the population, and between those extremes), we address the question of whether these four linguistic statuses are related to dropout rates.

We focus on Mexican youth aged 16–18 because they have the largest number in the PUMS 5% sample of the 2000 census, and the social and economic characteristics of immigrants from Mexico have not varied greatly over the years. Table 7.8 reveals that Mexican youth have a distinctive pattern for the relationship among language status, family income, and school dropout rate. Male youth generally have higher dropout rates than females. Those who reported speaking no English, regardless of the level of family income, have the highest dropout rates—60% to 70% for Hispanic male teens across all family income levels, vs. 50% to 57% for Hispanic female teens. The dropout rates for monolingual English youth, however, are more than twice those of bilingual speakers, except for male and female teens in high-income families (the number in these two categories is too small to report valid results). Interestingly, monolingual English youth have higher dropout rates than children who reported lacking English proficiency.

The findings from studying Mexican youth are not only consistent with the findings from studying Hispanic youth as a whole—as reported in Chapter 4—but also with the findings on Mexican youth we reported previously, using 1990 census data (Rong & Preissle, 1998). This information challenges claims that speaking a language other than English hampers Mexican youths' chances to graduate from high school. On the contrary, it indicates the importance of developing English proficiency, but also the potential danger of increasing dropout rates if youth give up their heritage language completely and become monolingual English speakers. Our findings from both the 1990 and 2000 census data clearly indicate that losing the ability to communicate in the heritage language can be hazardous to Mexican youth from low-economic family backgrounds.

SUMMARY OF DEMOGRAPHICS
FOR HISPANIC AND LATINO CHILDREN

Hispanic-Americans are diverse and heterogeneous in many respects; the census data show clear divisions among different Hispanic nationality groups. Although similarities have been found in the sociodemographic characteristics and educational attainment of Hispanic groups, important variations occur. The baseline data we report should be helpful for developing general educational and school policies and for planning class instruction and curriculum responsive to children's cultural and linguistic needs.

TABLE 7.8   School Dropouts by Family Income Level, and Linguistic Status Among Immigrant Mexican Youth Aged 16–18, U.S. 2000 (in percentages)

Gender	Male			Female		
Income Levels	L	M	H	L	M	H
No English	60%	60%	70%	50%	50%	57%
Lack Proficiency[1]	20%	23%	22%	15%	16%	17%
Bilingual[2]	10%	10%	9%	10%	7%	4%
English Only[3]	21%	24%	Note[4]	32%	18%	Note[d]

SOURCE: Data from PUMS 5% of the 2000 Census (U.S. Bureau of the Census, 2003a), compiled by authors.

1 Lack Proficiency: Youth who reported speaking a language other than English and cannot speak English "very well." This category includes youth who reported speaking English "not well" and "not very well."

2 Bilingual: Youth who reported speaking a language other than English and speaking English "very well."

3 English Only: Youth who reported speaking no language other than English.

4 Findings were not reported due to the small cell size (<15).

Socioeconomic divisions were noticeable in family poverty rates and parental education among Latino immigrants of different nationality groups. While only 24% of Hispanic immigrants lived in inner cities, the figure was 60% for Dominicans. The poverty rates for Mexican and Dominican immigrant families were three times the poverty rates of Peruvians (11%). Over 12% of all Hispanic immigrant parents had not completed four years of education; the percentages for Mexicans and Salvadorans were 15% and 14%, but 1% for Colombian and Peruvian parents. College-graduation rates likewise vary. Less than 8% of all Hispanic immigrant parents had a four-year college degree. However, the rates for Mexican parents was 4%, 6% for Salvadoran, 24% for Cuban, and for Colombian and Peruvian immigrant parents, the rates were 31% and 35%, respectively. The differences in socioeconomic status among the nationalities may be partially explained by the other differences discussed at the beginning of the chapter: reasons for immigration (economic immigrants vs. political refugees), residency status (legal or undocumented), types of visa (for high-tech occupations vs. family reunification), history of immigration to the United States (longer-term U.S. residency vs. recent immigration), and many other factors such as race and ethnicity, sojourner intention, and status. (Acuna, 2003; Cordero-Guzman & Henken, 2005; Daniels, 2002; Oboler & Gozalez, 2005).

We have discussed the advantages enjoyed by the earlier Cuban political refugees, many of whom have successfully settled in Miami and have established a solid community that has benefited later Cuban immigrants and many other Latino immigrants as well. On the other hand, thousands of Dominicans who migrated to the United States without documentation were apprehended by the United States Coast Guard, while others drowned during the turbulent journey across the Mona Channel. An overwhelming number of Dominican-Americans are young, poor, first-generation immigrants who came from rural areas. Many did not finish high school in their home country and did not learn English before they came to the United States. However, the signs are encouraging that Dominican-Americans are making progress. Second-generation Dominican-Americans are significantly more educated, as reflected by the higher percentage of them completing high school (Rong & Grant, 1995) and by their higher incomes and employment in professional or skilled occupations despite their background in poor families and inner-city locations.

Although previous studies typically combined Central Americans and South Americans into one category, our findings show the former group significantly differs from the latter group. Immigrant Central American children are more likely to have parents with fewer years of schooling and employment in menial jobs, to live in a linguistically isolated household, and to have English proficiency problems. Researchers (e.g., Chinchilla, Hamilton, & Loucky, 1993) have also explored the various problems they may have before, during, or after their immigration. As we emphasized at the beginning of the chapter, the majority of Central Americans who came to the United States in the 1980s fled war and deteriorating economic conditions. They entered the United States under unfavorable circumstances and harsh government policies, resulting in a high proportion of them remaining undocumented.

In their educational achievement, labor force participation rates, and median family income, Central Americans are quite dissimilar. Although in smaller numbers, Panamanians and Costa Ricans are the most accomplished among the Central Americans in the United States. Census figures indicate that Salvadorans are the largest group of Central American immigrants, accounting for 42% of the total, followed by Guatemalans and Nicaraguans, who make up 20% and 15% of Central American immigrants, respectively. However, Salvadorans were more likely than the other Central Americans to come to the United States after 1995; they also contained a higher percentage of immigrants who had not completed four years of schooling and had not completed high school.

In contrast to Central Americans, most South Americans came to the United States for professional and, to a lesser extent, political reasons. Many of them hold white collar, scientific, or executive positions. For example, Colombians tend to be middle class, professional, and urban. In recent years, however, a core of lower middle- and working-class South Americans has immigrated to the United States. Currently, about 500,000 South Americans, many of whom are new arrivals, live in New York State. Ecuador and Peru also have large concentrations of immigrants on the East Coast (Acuna, 2003).

DISCUSSION

Although the educational attainment gap between Hispanics and non-Hispanics is indisputable (see also Chapter 4), intra-group disparities among subpopulations of Hispanics are even more pronounced. What we have presented in this chapter suggests that the broad grouping of Hispanic-American masks important variations in children's educational attainment as well as the family backgrounds of groups from different national origins who make up this heterogeneous category. Although similarities occur among the Hispanic groups, children in some Latino groups do significantly less well than others. Mexican and Central American immigrant children (except Nicaraguan children) had lower enrollment rates and higher school dropout rates than immigrant children from other Hispanic nationality groups. Despite their relatively disadvantaged family backgrounds (inner-city residency, higher poverty rates, single-parent households, etc.), Dominican teenagers were more likely to stay in school and graduate with diplomas than teenagers from Mexico, Central American nations, and Ecuador.

How can these findings be explained? Most of the scholars we have cited agree that resources available to Latino children affect their levels of educational attainment. The combination of a large family and a small income can be devastating. To examine how Latino immigrants' educational resources are maintained, exhausted, or regenerated, as well as how the resources are transformed into educational and occupational attainments, scholars must consider the social context into which Latinos have been received and the schools that educate their children, To address these concerns, we focus our explanations for variations among Latinos on two interrelated theories—incorporation theory and segmented-assimilation theory.

Incorporation Theory

Incorporation theory is the idea that immigrant success depends on how people are viewed as well as by what they do. How the dominant group responds to immigrants varies with the ethnicity-race of the group. One of the major components of incorporation theory is internal colonialism. Scholars (e.g. Acuna, 1972; Pedraza, 1990; Tuan, 1995) have argued that racial minorities have suffered from internal colonization because of their racially-determined role in the system of production. Native Americans, Blacks, Puerto Ricans, and many Mexicans have been incorporated into U.S. society against their will through slavery, conquest, colonization, and annexation, and they have suffered from severe racial oppression, economic exploitation, and social marginalization. Trueba (1999) suggests that internal colonization theory can help us understand the educational circumstances of Hispanics in this country.

However, how Hispanic immigrants were received was also affected by the social-cultural characteristics of the immigrant groups, the time and location of U.S. entry, and the circumstances under which immigration occurred (Portes & Zhou 1993). For example, the differences in educational attainment among Mexican, Central American, and South American immigrant children may be significantly influenced by immigrants' social types. As we have noted, Mexican and Central American immigrants are likely to be labor migrants and refugees, on the one hand, while South Americans are likely to be entrepreneurial and skilled professionals, on the other hand. Additionally, each "wave" of immigrants from a specific country or region can differ from co-ethnics in other waves so as to affect U.S. settlement and attainment, such as the first-wave of Cuban political refugees before 1963 versus the later waves.

Nevertheless, patterns of Latino immigration to the United States are contradictory and intricate. For example, Mexicans are both economic immigrants and caste-like minorities. Their lower attainment may be attributed to multiple disadvantages: their lower socioeconomic status, the history of internal colonization, the undocumented status of many, and public hostility toward them and their children. Throughout this chapter we have compared the experiences of some groups of Latino immigrants with Cubans. Cuban-Americans, like Hungarians and other Eastern European immigrants, received more favorable treatment than other immigrants—instant residence permission, generous aid packages, and warmer welcomes. This stems from the historical period of the Cold War when these immigrants from the Eastern Block contested the superiority of the Soviet Union's political and economic systems.

As we have stressed repeatedly throughout the chapter, Central American immigrants to the United States have had different experiences. They often encountered an unfavorable and harsh reception, because their actions were perceived as being in conflict with U.S. foreign policy and military interests (Martin & Midgley, 1994; Martin & Widgren, 1996; Massey, 1993). Furthermore, studies on Central American youths suggest that having an undocumented status (Ferris, 1987; HMP & CSUCA, 1989) and experiencing life in war-torn countries prior to immigration (M. Suarez-Orozco, 1989) affect attainment in the United States. More than 500,000 Central Americans fled to the United States to escape civil war, and most of them became undocumented residents (Melville, 1985). Being minority, poor, and without legal status, many Central Americans may suffer refugee symptoms and have great difficulty in improving their children's education.

Incorporation theory is similar to what educational researchers have formulated as defensive identity (Suarez-Orozco & Suarez-Orozco, 1995) and resistant (Ogbu, 1994; Fordham, 1988) or oppositional, anti-school culture (Ogbu, 1987), introduced in Chapter 4 and elaborated in Chapter 5 as cultural ecology theory. These scholars explore the effects of psychosocial and emotional aspects of racialized, gendered, and classed identities on schooling and suggest that a society's multiple stratification system of race, gender, and social class has consequences for young people's education. Tuan (1995) argues that, to this day, caste-like minorities such as Blacks and Mexicans have continued to suffer from racism and to be affected by the bitter memory of their forbears' experience of oppression. Black and Mexican youths may respond to persistent racial discrimination and limited labor-market mobility by forming an attitude of ambivalence toward authority and school, resulting in various patterns of educational attainment.

Portes and Rumbaut (1996) specify the conditions under which immigrant minority youths might adopt anti-school cultures. The concentration of Hispanic immigrants in inner cities—where they are in close proximity to indigenous minorities with oppositional and resistant attitudes or to adults in ethnic communities who are not highly educated—provides them with easy entrance to the lowest stratum of U.S. society. Portes (1995) argues that, although the majority of them entered the United States "voluntarily," Mexican youths are more vulnerable to peer pressure than other Latino youths because the harsh history of the Mexican colonization has long-term negative psychological effects on these newcomers, as well as on residents of the receiving communities.

The problem with the structural emphasis in incorporation theory, however, lies in its tendency to ignore the power of collectives and slight the individual decisions made by migrants. This theory may overemphasize the vulnerability of being immigrant minority members and neglect their ethnic resources and social capital (Stanton-Salazar, 1997). For example, this theory cannot fully account for the Dominicans' experience: Dominican immigrant youths have suffered triple discrimination by virtue of race (Black), ethnicity (Hispanic), and immigrant status (Matthijs, 1996). However, the strong and enduring Dominican community in New York City sustains the newcomers to facilitate their initial adjustment (Alvarez, 1992; Pessar, 1995; Torres-Saillant & Hernandez, 1998). Therefore, their children are doing well in U.S. schools.

Segmented Assimilation and Additive Model

Incorporation theory has been recently elaborated by social scientists and educational researchers who advocate an additive approach to working with immigrant children (e.g., Gibson, 1998; Pedraza, 1990; Portes & Rumbaut, 1996; Sampson, Squires, & Zhou, 2001; Valenzuela, 1999; Zhou & Kim, 2006). As we suggest in Chapter 1 and elaborate in other chapters, the additive model conceptualizes assimilation as a more complex process that can involve selective assimilation and multiple stages of incorporation into U.S. society. Segmented assimilation is a more comprehensive theory that addresses the initial and continuing placement and access of various groups within the economic, political, and educational institutions of the society. However, segmented assimilation views individuals, family, and ethnic communities as agents and posits their social structures as both limiting and enabling.

The additive model is derived from segmented-assimilation theory and contrasts with the subtractive model based on the "melting pot" metaphor of forcing a homogeneous Americanization of everyone. The additive model suggests that some values and orientations of immigrant cultures, plus rapid and full cultural assimilation into the mainstream U.S. youth popular culture, including its distractions and cultural dissonance, might work against educational attainment. To prevent over-assimilation into anti-school cultures, the additive model maximizes the importance of parental and community influence over youth. In many immigrant groups, parents are adequately educated in their native countries, but nevertheless are blocked from high-status occupations in the United States. Under such circumstances, parents often invest heavily in the attainment of their offspring, whom they view as having better opportunities for educational attainment and social mobility. The combination of lofty parental aspirations, strong community control, and lack of incorporation of immigrant youth into popular U.S. youth culture can result in high educational attainment for children of immigrants.

An example of this is when children acquire English proficiency and mainstream culture without relinquishing their traditional ways or abandoning their native languages (Gibson, 1995). This supports our findings and explains why bilingual Mexican children—especially teens from low-income families—had lower school dropout rates than monolingual speakers; heritage-cultural capital may sustain children in school longer (see also Feliciano, 2001). This may also explain why Dominican children are doing well in school, despite the high poverty rates among their families and a population concentration in inner-city schools. A well-established Dominican ethnic community can help absorb newcomers and provide support for their initial and continued social, linguistic, and economic adjustment in the United States. Successful cases with the additive model have recently been reported among South and Central American immigrants (Orellana, 2001; M. Suarez-Orozco, 1989; Suarez-Orozco & Suarez-Orozco, 1995) and Cuban immigrant communities (Pedraza-Bailey, 1985).

Gender Differences in Attainment

Incorporation and segmented assimilation theories explain the gender differences in educational attainment we have reported in our findings. Earlier studies identified the gender differences that favored Latino males over females in school attainment (mostly based on the Mexican population) and attributed the problems to triple oppression by virtue of Mexican women's sex, low socioeconomic status, and the internal male dominance (*machismo*) common in Mexican-American culture (O'Connell, 1987; Vasquez, 1982). A cultural milieu that places high value on the family often reinforces the traditional roles of wife and mother at the expense of women's educational achievement and career aspirations.

However, more recent studies have revealed a gender-related attainment pattern among Hispanic immigrants paralleling that of U.S. White and Black women: female students did as well in K–12 schooling as male students in most areas of education (Grant & Rong, 1999; Grant & Rong, 2002). We have also reported lower dropout rates among Mexican female teenagers than among their male counterparts. According to incorporation theory, young male students may be viewed by U.S. school authorities as threatening and potential problems. Young females may be treated more sympathetically. If oppositional cultures diminish the educational attainment of some caste-like minority groups, such as Mexican and Dominican immigrants, among these groups women may be less likely than young men to join resistant cultures (see e.g., Gibson 1991; N. Lopez, 2002; Portes & Zhou, 1993; Rong, Brown, & Guo, 1996). Rodriguez (2002) also found that Nicaraguan and Cuban male students suffered in the company of involuntary minorities. Cuban and Nicaraguan girls, however, received community and parental supervision that may serve as a buffer to the incorporation of oppositional attitudes and their negative consequences on academic achievement.

From the viewpoint of segmented assimilation, Pedraza (1991) speculates that immigration may be advantageous for the education of women, especially for women from countries where men's education exceeds women's. The conditions of immigration or adaptations in immigrant communities might empower women and encourage them to persist in educational endeavors. Pedraza proposes that when men immigrate first and women follow—a pattern common in many ethnic groups—women who have lived independently may be less willing to resume traditional gender roles when they rejoin kin in the United States. Studies also suggest that girls tend to be more protected by families, spend more time in the home, and maintain their heritage language more often than boys do (e.g., N. Lopez, 2002; also see findings in Table 3.2). With stronger ties to the ethnic community, Hispanic women may be more able than men to maintaintheir immigrant identity while also achieving familiarity with U.S. schools and cultures (see, e.g., N. Lopez, 2002; Waters 1994). Finally, Hondagneu-Sotelo (2004) suggests cautiously that gender roles in various Latino subpopulations in the United States have gradually become more flexible—and perhaps even more egalitarian—over time.

In summary, incorporation theory explains the persistent lower attainment of caste-like minority groups and some political refugee groups who entered the United States during a time of unfavorable circumstances and harsh governmental policies. Incorporation theory also anticipates a lower educational attainment for caste-like minority males than females.

Segmented assimilation, however, anticipates a differential process: groups with fewer resources unable to generate social and cultural capital within the community may underperform educationally; women may take advantage of opportunities to improve their education, thereby breaking with traditional roles and patterns of dependence and asserting a newly-found freedom.

RECOMMENDATIONS

Variations in educational attainment across Latino nationality groups underscore the need to consider intra-ethnic differences within a broadly defined population. Findings in this chapter illustrate the problems of lumping Hispanic groups with various backgrounds and attainment together, indicating apparently segmented attainment patterns. On the basis of the information we have summarized, we also caution educators not to project stereotypes onto an entire Latino-American population using information from one or two groups. Thus, our first and foremost recommendation is to highlight the importance of separating the broadly-defined category of Hispanic into subgroups of different national origins. We need to make policy and practice guides to accommodate the various needs and implement them accordingly. The baseline data in this chapter should aid the development of theory, policy, and practice guides.

How does Latino immigration differ from other immigration? In addition to the prominent size of its immigrant population, Latin American immigrants are distinguishable from other immigrant groups in several distinct ways (see Acuna, 2003).

First, most Latin Americans in the United States live in close proximity to their homelands, and the relatively short distance between the United States and their countries of origin makes transnational migration (as visitor, sojourner, etc.) easy. Furthermore, to understand large-scale immigration from Latin American countries, we have to be aware of U.S. influences on home societies. Acuna (2003) argues that migration from Latin America has usually been the result of economic upheavals caused partly by the expansion of U.S. capital into the region and intensive recruitment of migrant labor by both private and state sectors in the United States. The systematic recruitment of immigrants from Latin America as a reserve labor force during times of labor scarcity in the United States during the 20th century has created a uniquely interdependent economic relationship between the United States and many countries in Latin America. These historical processes led, in turn, to the formation of complex social networks that continue to drive immigration long after original laws have changed and labor recruitment programs have been terminated.

Second, because of a long immigration history to the United States, many large, well-established co-ethnic Latino communities exist in the

United States. These Latino ethnic communities make assimilation more feasible for Latino newcomers than for other groups and also provide opportunities to preserve heritage languages and traditions.

We have made many general recommendations, as well as recommendations for specific ethnic-racial and nationality groups, in our previous chapters for how to work effectively with immigrant students. Many of those recommendations are applicable for working with Latino immigrant students. To avoid redundancy, we offer seven recommendations in this section, closely related to the unique characteristics of Latino immigrant students and the circumstances under which their immigration and acculturation occur. Because the recommendations focus more on the educational struggles of Latino immigrants, we caution readers to review them with discretion when considering strategies with students from a specific Latino nationality group.

Recommendation One: Consider Geographic Concentrations and Dispersions of Latinos

To make workable policies, educators must be aware of the concentration of Latino immigrant groups in their states and local schools. For example, Mexican immigrants are largely concentrated in the Southwest, where early generations lived before that territory became part of the United States. There are also large Mexican communities in the Midwest and New York. Cubans are concentrated in South Florida, particularly Miami. In 1990, over 80% of Dominicans in the continental United States lived in the New York and New Jersey region, with the overwhelming majority in New York City. This knowledge can provide educators with valuable information about the specific communities in their region.

However, the 2000 census indicates the clear trend of Latino immigrants to spread throughout the nation. Latino immigrants went to the new gateway states mainly for jobs, and transnational labor migration of this kind has allowed local industries in new gateway states—such as poultry, lumber, textiles, and construction—to maintain their globally competitive edge. Many of these new gateway states in the Midwest and South maintain themselves as low-wage, industry-accommodating states. As described by the Pew Hispanic Center (2005), the newcomers in new gateway states are more recent arrivals who tend to be poor, lack a high school diploma, not speak English or not speak it well, and be more likely to be undocumented than their counterparts in the traditional receiving areas and the United States as a whole. Many of them are working in so-called Mexican-type jobs: dangerous, difficult occupations with low wages, no health plans, and no unions (Gibson, 2002). All of these factors create challenges for designing programs to meet the needs of the newcomer students while also involving their parents.

Recommendation Two: Resist Anti-Latino Sentiments

With the rapid growth of the Latino population in the United States and the substantial transformation of the nation in ethnicity-race, the issue of immigration continues to polarize national discussions. Hispanic immigrants, especially Mexican-Americans, are likely to be the target of hate groups. Reports have been made on the increasing number of organized anti-Hispanic activities in southern states (Associated Press, 2005) and hostile attitudes and beliefs about Mexican immigrants in U.S. schools (e.g., Shannon & Escamilla, 1999). Schools must take actions to resist societal attempts to divide the teaching profession and fuel anti-immigrant sentiment among teachers and other school staff. Instead, educators, regardless of what they believe about U.S. immigration policies, should advocate equal educational opportunities for all children (Midobuche, 2001).

Teachers' attitudes toward students can be affected by what they believe, and students' perceptions of school climates (including discrimination) are strongly and consistently related to students' school performance. Studies on what affects students' schooling behaviors and achievement highlight the protective benefits of a friendly and supportive learning climate (Stone & Han, 2005). Therefore, U.S. educators not only need to sort out these issues for themselves in clear and unbiased ways, but also should use their classrooms as a vehicle to bring this information to students and the community. For example, Bryant (2004) reports that job outsourcing can create prejudice among angered native workers and result in their blaming their low wages and unemployment problems on Latino immigrant workers. Bryant believes that social studies education can play an important role in easing community tensions between Hispanic and non-Hispanic citizens by teaching students about the outsourcing of jobs while dispelling xenophobic myths and stereotypes. Social studies classes can also take the opportunity to discuss immigration-related issues such as this: "Do the taxes immigrants pay cover the cost of the public services they use, including schools, welfare, health care, and transportation systems?" Answers for this question will be complex, depending in part on how well both the short-term and long-term fiscal effects of immigrants can be measured. However, at minimum, educators can provide both sides of a heated and much-debated issue driven for decades by the anti-immigration agenda against low-waged and impoverished Latino immigrants (e.g., Harwood, 1986).

Recommendation Three: Understand the Effect of Social Class, the New Economy, and Segregated Neighborhoods on Latino Children's Life and Schooling

The history of immigration to the United States is full of legends of self-made individuals, but the stories of recent immigrants are more likely to reveal a polarization: the richer may do well, but the poorer struggle greatly. Researchers have reported that education and social status in home countries help some immigrants, such as those from Cuba, Hong Kong, Taiwan, and countries in South America, to carry their social connections, wealth, and human capital into the new world. When these people settle in middle-class neighborhoods, their children may enroll in schools that receive them enthusiastically and provide them with ESL and other needed services. Schools may see these middle-class immigrant students as enriching cultural diversity in their community and appreciate their parents with professional occupations as human resources for their PTA activities (Barringer, Gardner, & Levin, 1993; Gardner, Robey, & Smith, 1985). However, Latino working-class immigrants, especially Mexican, Dominican, and those from some Central American countries, have experienced labor exploitation, housing discrimination, linguicism (language racism), public health negligence, educational marginalization, and so forth (Villenas, 2002). Their socioeconomic disadvantages for the next generation are exacerbated by inequitable schooling and substandard educational facilities. The ethnicity-race of immigrants certainly plays critical roles in reproducing poverty in the host country.

First, social class is interdependent with ethnicity-race in the production of inequality. Societal racism can be the root of economic inequality, which, in turn, enhances ethnicity-race-linked exclusion, displacement in the labor market, and residential segregation. Sociologists have argued that where we live affects our proximity to good job opportunities, educational quality, and safety from crime, as well as the quality of our social networks (Jargowsky, 1997; Logan, Alba, & Zhang, 2002; Wilson, 1987). Studies cited in Chapter 2 as well as this chapter indicate the increasing ethnic, linguistic, and social class segregation of Latino immigrants.

Second, one of the other factors in poverty reproduction in the United States is the new economy. Because wages have stagnated in the past 30 years for those with only a high school or lower education level, poor and working-class Latino parents are more likely to work in multiple low-wage, service-sector jobs. Many may find themselves unable to understand and respond to the increasingly demanding, complex, and competitive educational system that their children attend (Day & Newburger, 2002). Moreover, some of them may realize that the resources required for successful learning are simply not available for their children in local schools.

In working with Latino students, schools must understand that educational inequalities begin at birth. Effective policies targeted toward Hispanic educational attainment need to address the economic circumstances of these students rather than focus primarily on language deficiencies or immigration status. Perez (2004) argues that the socioeconomic and health disparities between Latinos and others will not be diminished by Latinos themselves over time unless concrete steps are taken to design programs and policies relevant to the challenges faced by Latino families.

Beyond hierarchies of income, power, and status, recent research on class has also revealed how class is embedded in people's daily experiences, including social and academic life in the classroom and every part of schools (Ream, 2005). For example, not only do many Hispanic babies enter the world in poverty and without health care, but while these children are in schools, they are more likely to be placed in larger classes and taught by less experienced teachers. The academic curriculum in schools with a majority of Black and Latino students is often meager compared with the richer, more rigorous curriculum offered in White suburban schools (Viadero, 2003). In addition to support for working-class Latino children and families, educators' understanding about how social class shapes educational access, learning environment, aspiration, and achievement should be incorporated into educational policymaking, curriculum revision, and program design (Galen, 2007).

Recommendation Four: Work Effectively With Latino Children in Mixed and Undocumented Families

The anti-undocumented immigrant sentiments in the United States toward Latino immigrants, especially Mexican immigrants, are a mixture of misinformation, political rhetoric, and realities (Pew Hispanic Center, 2007). According to Passel (2006), over half of the 11 million undocumented immigrants in 2006 were Mexicans, while one in five was from other Latin American countries. However, not all "illegal" or undocumented immigrants are unauthorized border-crossers without permission from the U.S. government. People remain in the United States as "unauthorized" in many ways. For example, many people enter the United States legally but overstay their visas. Others flee to the United States with falsified passports (usually from a country other than their native countries) to get a U.S. visa for entry. However, Mexican immigrants have been targeted on the undocumented issue because of their large numbers, the political rhetoric of protecting the southern border, and nativist fears about an impending silent invasion of a darker and Spanish-speaking population (Acuna, 2003).

We have stressed before that about 5 million children (two-thirds of them U.S. citizens) live in families described as either mixed or nonmixed undocumented. These are the children of the most invisible workers in the lowest job-market stratum in the United States. The majority of them suffer inconceivable labor exploitation and are unprotected by U.S. laws governing workers' safety, health, and wages. They are also subject to arrest, retention, deportation, or time in jail.

Educators must understand the consequences when working with children in various situations. First, educators should realize the enormous difficulties in holding a mixed family together. When parents are facing deportation, their U.S.-born children usually have two choices: to be deported with their parents or to remain, staying with relatives or being taken into foster care to continue their education in the United States. Either choice has severe consequences. If families choose to split up, this may result in more single parent households and psychological and financial hardship for both adults and children. If parents bring their U.S. citizen children with them for deportation, these American children may have to start over in a country with a new language, different school system, and a questionable future.

The uncertain legal status of parents in mixed families limits family economic advancement and children's educational alternatives. Fernandez-Kelly and Curran (2001) report that it also undermines the capacity of parents to retain the authority to educate their children. Children from mixed families may grow up in environments characterized by a dearth of resources and in relative isolation from mainstream institutions. Researchers' observations of a division between legal and undocumented Nicaraguans underscore the significance of state policy as a facilitator or deterrent of children and adults' assimilation (Portes & Rumbaut, 1996). Some (e.g., Portes & Zhou, 1993) conclude that it is the context of reception that largely determines the kinds of adjustments newcomers may make. Unfortunately, continued stigmatization and exclusion have long-term negative psychological effects on undocumented immigrants and their family members, including children.

While working with Latino immigrant students, educators need to be aware of the arrangement of some families. On the one hand, many children may have split with their families and live in the United States by themselves with relatives and family friends: many children from Central and South America were sent to the United States without their parents in the 1970s and 1980s to escape military conflicts. On the other hand, people themselves cross borders, but leave their children behind with family members and may not able to reunite with their children for a long period of time because they cannot afford the risks or costs of returning home to retrieve their children. They face the difficult choice of allowing others to raise their children far away or hiring smugglers to bring them into the United States (Hondagneu-Sotelo & Avila, 2000; Romo, 2005).

Working with children from mixed or nonmixed undocumented immigrant families, educators need to be familiar with their right to a free public K–12 education as guaranteed by a 1982 Supreme Court ruling (*Plyler vs. Doe*) for all children residing in the United States, regardless of their immigration status. Educators should also be aware that undocumented students often suffer greater stress and worry than other immigrant children. People who work with children who may have undocumented parents or siblings should be particularly sensitive to their fears and insecurities and the issues surrounding their right to a free education in the United States. For example, schools should avoid actions that might imply to undocumented families that their right of access to education is in jeopardy: asking about a student's immigration status, for example, and requesting immigration-related documentation. Schools should provide services to each migrant student comparable to services offered to other students in the school district and ensure that migrant students are involved in the regular school programs offered to other students (CYFD of New Mexico State, 2007).

Recommendation Five: Improve Latino Youths' Opportunities for Higher Education

Dropping out of high school is a major educational issue for Mexican youth and some youths with Central American origins. College aspirations are reportedly related to students' persistence in high school and their efforts to get better grades and take advanced placement classes. Given the complex intertwining of K–12 schooling and higher education and the importance of graduating from high school and obtaining a college degree for future success in the labor market (Galen, 2007), we need to look beyond the scope of K–12 schooling and advocate higher education for Latino students. We also need to make their access to higher education a priority in later middle school and throughout their entire four years in high school (Lys, 2007).

For these reasons, providing public higher education to undocumented children should be a focus of discussions aimed at progressive legislation. As of 2006, ten states have enacted legislation to allow long-term unauthorized immigrant students to become eligible for in-state tuition if they meet certain requirements; federally this law is called the Development, Relief and Education for Alien Minors (or Dream) Act. California, Illinois, Kansas, Nebraska, New Mexico, New York, Oklahoma, Texas, Utah, and Washington—and the legislatures in fifteen other states—will try, or have already tried, to pass laws similar to the Dream Act (Belanger, 2001; Freedman, 2004).

According to U.S. Department of Education data (Tabs, 2003), Latino students not only enroll in college at lower rates, but also are less likely to complete postsecondary degrees once enrolled. Why are Latino students less likely to enroll in college than other students? This question has no simple answer. Scholars (e.g., E. Garcia, 2001) have argued that the lower U.S. Latino enrollment in college is a function, in part, of a history and structure of subordination. Opportunities for labor-market mobility may also affect patterns of educational attainment (35% of the U.S. adult population and 27% of all foreign-born U.S. immigrant adults were in management and professional occupations, but less than 13% of Latino immigrant adults were in management and professional occupations). Youths who have not seen prior generations of their ethnic group achieve economic and occupational mobility in U.S. society via education are less likely to maintain or increase educational attainment in later residential generations. The difficulty of college admission and the perceived limitations in future employment may send Latino immigrant students contradictory messages about the importance of graduating from high school and pursuing higher education.

As we have demonstrated in this chapter, a large portion of Latino students have been less prepared academically than other students. Schools should ensure that they provide appropriate academic planning to immigrant students. When school counselors advise Latino immigrant students who may have lowered aspirations for achievement, they should seek to determine why those aspirations have been lowered and work to provide students with a complete set of academic options—not only options leading to low-wage jobs. Additionally, school counselors should seek to increase family understanding of the educational system, as well as empower families to become involved in shaping their children's career planning experience. Because immigrant parents are often misinformed about the college admission process and their role in it, school counselors are obliged to support and inform these parents. This information would best be dispersed through parent informational meetings, scheduled at times and locations convenient to parents' work schedules.

Schools can also be involved in programs involving private foundations. Endeavors such as AVID (Advancement Via Individual Determination) has had success in helping Latino students get into college by identifying students of mid-range abilities in the eighth grade who demonstrate the potential to go on to college and enrolling them in college-preparatory classes, while also offering a system of social scaffolding to ensure their academic success (Guthrie & Guthrie, 2000).

Recommendation Six: Understand and Support Bilingualism

Although all immigrant groups have shown a tendency toward bilingualism, census data indicate that Hispanic children as a whole, more than any others, have the strongest ties to their native languages. As we have stressed in this chapter, in 2000 over 75% of all Hispanic children and more than 95% of Hispanic immigrant children reported speaking their heritage languages at home (from 84% of Colombians to 97% of Mexicans). Many political, historical, and practical factors account for the strong bilingualism among the U.S. Latino population.

First, most Hispanics have a common language that unites them and gives them a sense of community. This heritage language also helps the Latino population retain their cultural and political identity in the United States. If the majority of Asians are bound by race and Confucian values, and Caribbean black immigrants are bound largely by ethnicity-race and regional identity, then most Hispanics are bound by their ability to communicate in Spanish. Second, retention of the home language may also be perceived as a form of group resistance that fosters collective consciousness, ethnic solidarity, and values alternative to the dominant culture (Macias, 1993).

Why are U.S. Latinos able to maintain their heritage language? One of the practical reasons for Latinos' success in this matter is the continual and heavy flow of migrants and visitors from countries in Latin America to the United States. Expanding ethnic neighborhoods support many Hispanic enclaves, providing sufficient housing and job opportunities for people who speak Spanish only. The neighborhood dynamics also provide the children with regular contact with the Spanish language.

Educators need to reexamine traditional beliefs to consider what "rapid Americanization" actually does to newly immigrated children of various groups, especially its effect on their schooling. When educators design programs to address the initial adjustment of immigrant children, they also need to invent strategies to help these children draw strength from their home cultures, develop a positive sense of their ethnic-racial and immigrant identities, and nurture and maintain the native languages that can serve as resources. Carrasquillo (1991) suggests that second-language programs should play a key role in the education of Hispanic students. Therefore, every ESL program in this country must recognize the importance of the mother tongue.

Deprivation of immigrant children's ability to speak their heritage language is a form of discrimination; it comes from consistently underfunded schools where Mexican-Americans predominate and are punished for speaking Spanish, even at recess. Orellana (2001) and G. Lopez (2001) have documented that many Mexican-American students have been made to feel that they, their language, and their culture are unwelcome in schools. This has served only to reinforce cultural patterns that have led so many Mexican-Americans to drop out of high school. Bilingualism may have a specific meaning in Latino students' schooling, as we indicate in the findings in Chapter 4 and this chapter. Portes and Zady (2002) conducted a survey with a sample of over 5,000 second-generation students from 77 nationalities and 42 schools and found that, for the Spanish-speaking groups, the less they identified with their heritage culture and language, the lower their academic performance. Likewise, Lingxin and Bonstead-Bruns (1998) concluded in their study that—all else being equal—a higher heritage-language retention rate promotes academic achievement among Latino children.

Many educators believe that individual variations in necessity, ability, and motivation cause major differences in language adaptation. "Latino-Americans do not want to speak English" is a typical example of misconception and stereotype; in a recent Pew Hispanic Center survey (2005, 2006), by overwhelming margins, Latinos say it is very important that English be taught to children of immigrant families. Hispanics hold stronger views than either non-Hispanic Whites or Blacks (92% vs. 87% and 83%) about this matter. The reasons for the lack of English proficiency in some immigrant groups are complicated. An immigrant's opportunity to assimilate, either culturally or structurally, is limited by the combined effects of ethnicity, social class, and many other factors (for more, see Chapter 3). Sociolinguists maintain that the education of language minority students—including the learning of effective English—should be understood within this frame-work. For instance, Mexican immigrants from rural areas, with little educa-tion and few material possessions in their native countries, are more likely to stay at the bottom of the social or occupational strata in their new coun-try. They more commonly live in a racially or linguistically segregated neighborhood and are employed in an ethnically saturated job—a situation wherein disproportionate numbers of a given minority work in a given oc-cupation—that offers little socioeconomic advancement. Their children may receive inferior educations from schools not comparable to schools lo-cated in more affluent White neighborhoods. As a consequence, these immi-grants and their children may have less opportunity to learn English and to observe and integrate with middle-class U.S. culture.

For effectively working with Latino ELL students, qualified teachers are needed with the ability to motivate students to learn content areas through the second language. If all classroom teachers were required to be bilingual, all classrooms would be multilingual environments. It may be time to advo-cate that all educators learn a language other than English; the prioritized language could be Spanish. Many Schools of Education in the U.S have of-fered language courses for teachers, such as Spanish for Educators, that facil-itate the ability of future teachers and administrators to communicate with immigrant students and parents. However, more importantly, these courses also familiarize them with a cognitive process from which to understand sec-ond-language acquisition. Merchant (2000) claims that a lack of understand-ing about second-language acquisition results in teachers and administrators unintentionally perpetuating instructional practices and edu-cational policies ineffective in helping English-language learners achieve, ei-ther academically or socially.

Recommendation Seven: Consider the Impact of NCLB on Latino Immigrant Children's Schooling

While examining the implementation of the NCLB law for the schooling of Latino immigrant students and ELL speakers, researchers have expressed many concerns raised by the early results (Valenzuela, 2005; Velasco, 2005), including lower high school completion rates among Latinos (McNeil, 2005; Noguera, 2005). The results from more recent studies, however, are mixed and indicate a more complicated picture (Viadero, 2007).

The many concerns addressed in Chapter 4 apply to Latino immigrant children's education, so we do not repeat them here. In this section, how-ever we do discuss several concerns about NCLB unique to Latino immi-grant children's education. NCLB requires states to assess the "Adequate Yearly Progress" of each school annually. One way to demonstrate improvement in school-level test scores and dropout rates is to enroll higher-performing students and encourage academically-challenged students to head elsewhere. Ream (2005) reports that working-class Latinos may be particularly vulnerable to the "card shuffling" that results when school administrators push underperforming students out of their doors, often by using what have come to be called Opportunity Transfers, transfers from one school to another designed to ensure student and school safety and best provide for students.

Katz (1999) describes another obstacle to building positive teacher-and-Latino-student relationships caused by standardized testing. Some teachers may believe they must comply with school administrators' mandates to invest in students considered most likely to keep standardized test scores high. Therefore, they may display attitudes and implement practices perceived by students as discrimination, but which may be partially linked to structural conditions within the school—such as tracking and high teacher turnover—that preclude caring relationships with students.

Scholars have especially voiced concerns on poverty issues in urban schools and the NCLB law (e.g., Rong, 2006). Poverty is a growing challenge among children of immigrants—a development with far-reaching implications for the distribution of NCLB Title 1 formula grants. These grants are for instruction for the disadvantaged and are allocated to states and schools based on poverty levels. The poverty rates are especially high among the children of immigrants who are ELL (60%); these ELL students are highly concentrated in a few urban schools that are highly minority, predominantly low income, and disproportionately likely to fail federal standards.

Furthermore, immigrant Latino students in new gateway states—where the influx of Hispanics has been particularly dramatic—are likely to be hit harder by the NCLB than their counterparts in traditional gateway states. When public-school districts admit increasing numbers of Spanish-speaking students, the new residents are likely to encounter negative responses from longer-term U.S. residents. We have pointed out previously that new gateway states also lack an established ethnic community to absorb the new immigrants, bridge language and cultural barriers between newcomers and the schools, and intervene effectively on behalf of their children.

In addition to multiple standards and assessment approaches for accountability—rather than the current one-test-fits-all—our major recommendation here is to provide resources not only to poor urban schools but to their students as well. Education policy for disadvantaged families and communities should not be limited to conventional education alone. Socioeconomic policies that benefit lower-income families and communities should also be recognized as educational policies on behalf of immigrant children in these families and communities.

CONCLUSION

Any discussion of the educational attainment of Latino students must be embedded in a framework that takes into consideration a large number of factors extending well beyond ethnicity-race and immigrant status (Padilla & Gonzalez, 2001). Findings in this chapter indicate the importance of understanding the complex dynamics of the various Latino-American groups in the United States. Educators who work with Hispanic children should be aware of and understand that ethnicity-race, social class, gender, immigration history, and so forth shape experience and expectations differently across diverse groups. Therefore, successful programs must alter their approaches in line with new strategies that have proven effective by identifying the needs of students from various backgrounds.

U.S. schools must proactively address the specific educational needs of the large and still rapidly growing Latino population. In 2005, Hispanic students represented about 20% of public school enrollment, up from less than 12% in 1990. Latino students will account for 30% of U.S. public school students by 2025. Nevertheless, the current available data illustrate educational struggles and limited future options for the growing Latino student population. Ensuring the well-being of Latino children should be a national priority. In about ten years, 35% of Hispanics who are children today will be workers and taxpayers. Their educational preparation, labor, and productivity will be called on to keep the U.S. economy vibrant. Indeed, the stability and growth of the future U.S. economy greatly depend on maximizing educational and employment outcomes of Latino children (S. Perez, 2004). Ream (2005) believes we will deeply regret our lack of foresight if we are not able to provide the vision, planning, and resources required to deal effectively with Latino—and, more specifically, Mexican-American—children's underachievement.

8

Immigrant Children From the Middle East

Like immigrants from Europe, Asia, Latin America, and Africa and the African Diaspora, immigrants from the Middle East come from a region with great diversity—geographically, religiously, ethnically, linguistically, and otherwise. This diversity presents many challenges.

First, as the often-recognized crossroads of Africa, Asia, and Europe, the region's geographic boundaries have been debated. The narrowest geographic formulation of the Middle East runs from Egypt east, across the Arabian Peninsula through Iran and north through Turkey. The term "Middle East" is itself a western label for the area (Roudi-Fahimi & Kent, 2007). More recently, the Middle East has been viewed as including adjacent Muslim nations and, consequently, stretching west across North Africa through Morocco, south through the Sudan and Somalia, and east through Afghanistan and Pakistan. Because we discuss African and Asian immigrants in other chapters, we use the narrower definition of the Middle East for this discussion: Egypt, the Palestinian territories, Israel, Jordan, Lebanon, Syria, Turkey, Saudi Arabia, Yemen, Oman, the United Arab Emirates, Bahrain, Qatar, Kuwait, Iraq, and Iran.

Second, the Middle East is the acknowledged and celebrated home of five major world religions: Judaism, Christianity, Islam, Baha'ism, and Zoroastrianism. Pockets of indigenous religious practice also persist throughout the region alongside mainstream and sectarian versions of the five dominant religions (Lewis, 1998). Religiously, the Middle East is far more diverse than the predominantly Judeo-Christian Europe and western hemisphere, more like the religiously diverse continents of Asia and Africa.

Third, because of the hegemony of Islam since the 7th century, Arabic has become a dominant language, just as Spanish has been in Latin America and English has been in North America. Arabic is the official language in countries such as Egypt, Syria, Iraq, and those on the Arabian Peninsula. Christians, Jews, Baha'is, and Zoroastians, as well as Muslims, may claim Arabic as their native tongues. However, in the Middle East, other languages challenge that dominance. Persian and Azeri are the native tongues of many Iranians. Turkish is the common language in Turkey, but Kurdish and Armenian are also spoken. Assyrian (also known as Aramaic or Syriac) is spoken by some in the central area of the Middle East, and Hebrew is the official language of Israel (Kayyali, 2006; Lewis 1998).

Fourth, overlapping religious groups and intersecting language and geographic groups are Middle-Eastern ethnic groups whose histories and intermarriages have made them distinct (Lewis, 1998). These include Africans; Arabs; Armenians (from eastern Anatolia and the southern Caucasus); Assyrians and Chaldeans (Aramaic-speaking Christians, now mostly from northern Iraq); and Azeris (an ethnic group from northwestern Iran and the Republic of Azerbaijan whose members are usually Muslim, and whose backgrounds include Turkic, Iranian, and Caucasian elements). Others are Greeks; Jews; Berbers from northwest Africa who speak a common language, Arabic-speaking and Muslim Druze from Lebanon, Syria, and Jordan; Kurds (an ethnic group from neighboring parts of Iran, Iraq, Syria, and Turkey—mostly Muslim, but with a mix of other religions); Maronites (Arabic-speaking Catholics from Lebanon); Persians (from Iran); and Turks. In his overview of the peoples of the Middle East, Lewis (1998) highlights what he calls the multiple identities of individuals from this region, the various affiliations that any one person must balance: national, religious, linguistic, racial-ethnic, and such.

We add two additional dimensions of identity that affect the experience of Middle-Eastern immigrants to the United States: class and gender. As we note later on, the socioeconomic status of immigrants from this area of the world has varied considerably. Although many represent the rural poor from around the region, others in the post-1965 wave of immigration have been professionals (Kayyali, 2006; Schur, 2005). Likewise, although males dominated the initial wave of immigration from the region, later waves of immigrants have included women and girls. Females' experiences in the United States have varied, depending in part on the gender norms of their homeland communities. These norms vary considerably from one area of the Middle East to another, and gender expectations are hotly contested within countries, ethnic groups, and religious practices (Bilgé & Aswad, 1996; C. Nagel, 2005). The *hijab* (head scarf) expected of Muslim women, for example, may vary from something symbolic to the complete veiling of the head. Facets of identity, then, include gender and sex, class, ethnic-racial affiliation, religion, nationality, language, and other attributes as well.

In contrast to the preceding chapters, this chapter does not provide a demographic introduction to the population of Middle-Eastern immigrants to the United States. We have replaced that with a more general overview, drawing from a variety of sources, because the Census Bureau provides no publications representing Middle-Easterners as a group. The census does offer summaries of Americans of Arab descent (e.g., Brittingham & de la Cruz, 2005), but this omits Israelis and many other ethnic groups who have immigrated to the United States.

The multiple identities of immigrants and their children from the Middle East constitute a theme we reiterate in this chapter. We begin with a brief overview of the history of migration from the Middle East to the United States. Then, we provide an extensive discussion of the demographics of immigrant children from the Middle East, compared to immigrant children, all children, and native-born youngsters of Middle-Eastern origin. The final section of the chapter contains recommendations to educational policymakers and other educational leaders for accommodating these immigrants.

HISTORY OF MIDDLE-EASTERN MIGRATION TO THE UNITED STATES

If North Africa is considered part of the Middle East, then Arabic-speaking African slaves may have been among the first, albeit forced, Middle-Eastern immigrants to the Western Hemisphere in the 17th century (Aswad & Bilgé, 1996). Voluntary immigration from the Middle East to the United States is generally considered to have begun as a trickle in the second half of the 19th century, and the diversity of human beings found across the Middle East is represented in the identities of those who emigrated to the United States. Likewise represented among these immigrants are the range of motivations that brought others to the shores of the Americas: desire for religious and political freedom, hopes to better themselves and their children economically, escape from various forms of persecution, access to higher education and thus professional careers, and the opportunity to earn money to send to families at home.

In the period 1880–1922, 90% of those migrating from the Middle East were Arabic-speaking Christians, many from Lebanon, Syria, and Turkey, who sought economic opportunities (Aswad & Bilgé, 1996; Saliba, 2005), and a substantial proportion were economic sojourners—young men—who eventually returned home. Others, however, stayed on, and later brought their families to join them. These Christians were Eastern Orthodox and Eastern Catholics—such as the Maronites—and Coptics.

The turmoil in the early decades of the 20th century in the Ottoman Empire, centered in what is now modern Turkey, also brought many Armenian refugees to the United States. These peoples eventually settled throughout the United States; their offspring constitute a large proportion of U.S. citizens who trace their ancestry to the Middle East (Neff, 2005). However, 10% of these migrants were Muslims, most of them Sunni Muslims; these were the individuals responsible for establishing the first mosques in the United States, predominantly in the Midwest (Schur, 2005). With the coming of World War I and the passage of restrictive immigration laws in the 1920s, this first large wave of immigration came to a close. The second wave of immigration, roughly between the wars and into the 1960s, primarily consisted of the migration of families whose fathers and husbands had preceded them during the first wave (Kayyali, 2006).

The third wave of immigration from the Middle East began after World War II and the immigration reform laws of the 1960s. This group has been predominantly Muslim—Sunnis and Shiites—although smaller proportions of Christians, Baha'is, Jews, and others have also been represented. (Because the U.S. Census does not ask about religious affiliation, see Camarota, 2002, for how religion is estimated.) Other shifts in immigrants' identities from the earlier period are also noteworthy. Individuals in this recent wave reflect a wider range of socioeconomic and educational backgrounds and come from around the Middle-Eastern region rather than primarily from the northern area of Turkey, Lebanon, and Syria, as had the first wave. Although political shifts and violent events accounted for some emigration from the region in the early part of the 20th century, the current wave of Middle-Eastern immigration has been greatly affected by regional strife: Palestinian refugees from the various Israeli-Arabic conflicts; Lebanese uprooted by the civil wars of the 1970s and 1980s; the flight of many professional people following the Iranian Revolution of the 1970s; and Iraqis and others fleeing the Gulf wars (Aswad & Bilgé, 1996; Kayyali, 2006). The events of September 11, 2001, have further complicated and threatened the lives and well-being of many immigrants from the Middle East to the United States; we consider that in our recommendations section.

Migrants in the current wave of Middle-Eastern immigration have continued, however, to be concerned with economic matters. The largest Arab community in the United States is concentrated in the Detroit, Michigan, area where industries such as automobile manufacturing have attracted workers for the past 50 years (Abraham & Shryock, 2000). A pattern observed in some Muslim communities around the United States over this period is a change in religious practice. The secular orientation of many migrants who arrived at the beginning of the recent wave, together with the influence of U.S. religious observances, had led to an initial relaxing of some religious practices. In some parts of the United States, this has been followed by an increase in more traditional observances, as more devout individuals have arrived, bringing with them the expectations of their home community mosques (Haddid, 2005). As we emphasize in our recommendations section, immigrant children from the Middle East represent a range of diverse and multifaceted identities and are subject to changes over time as their communities change.

Next, we turn to demographic patterns from the 2000 Census relevant to these children. We consider their generational composition, the characteristics of their families, and differing attributes of the children themselves.

MIDDLE-EASTERN AMERICAN SCHOOL-AGE CHILDREN

To compile data for children from Middle-Eastern countries, we used the 2000 Census question about ancestry (see "Sources of Information," pp. 293–295) for children who were identified by their parents as having Middle-Eastern countries as their ancestral origins. We selected six nationality groups to present data on these youngsters based on the size of the group in the general population as well as in the immigrant population, and specific educational interests we had in comparing one group with the other nationality groups. For example, Iraqis were not one of the larger nationality groups among the general population of children claiming Middle-Eastern ancestry; however, Iraqi children were one of the largest groups among the immigrant Middle-Eastern child population. Furthermore, information about Iraqi children enables us to address several important issues about the education of Middle-Eastern children.

The population of children of Middle-Eastern origin aged 5–18 was about 400,000 in 2000. Figures 8.1A and B present the five Middle-Eastern American nationalities with the largest proportion of school-age children. For example, Iranian-Americans composed 17% of all Middle-Eastern American children, followed by Lebanese (16%), Egyptian and Israeli (7% each), and Syrian-Americans (6%). The makeup of immigrant Middle-Eastern children by nationality is different from the composition of the total Middle-Eastern American child population. Immigrant Iranian children comprised the largest group in 2000; Israeli, Iraqi, and Egyptian children were the next three largest groups, with 11%, 10%, and 9%, respectively. The difference between these two figures indicates the larger flow of immigrants from Israel and Iraq to the United States in the 1990s.

Generational Makeup

The generational makeup of Middle-Eastern school-age children is not only different from the generational structure of all U.S. children, but also varies across Middle-Eastern nationality groups, as Table 8.1 shows. Although less than one in five children in the general school-age population was either foreign-born or the child of foreign-born parent(s), about

FIGURE 8.1A   U.S. Children (5–18) Claiming Middle Eastern Ancestry, by National Origin, 2000

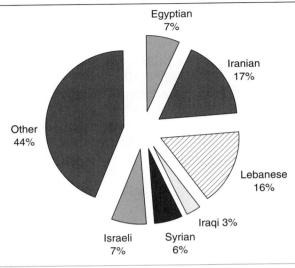

SOURCE: Data from PUMS 5% of the 2000 Census (U.S. Bureau of the Census, 2003a),
compiled by authors.

three-quarters of all Middle-Eastern children were either foreign-born or children of foreign-born parents. About half of all Middle-Eastern children were second-generation. The proportion of third-generation Middle-Eastern children (26%) is slightly larger than the percentage of foreign-born Middle-Eastern children (23.3%).

FIGURE 8.1B   U.S. Middle Eastern Immigrant Children (5–18) by National Origin, 2000

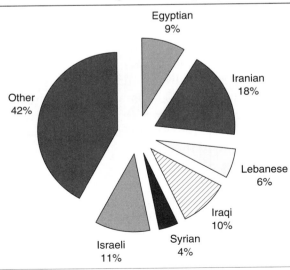

SOURCE: Data from PUMS 5% of the 2000 Census (U.S. Bureau of the Census, 2003a),
compiled by authors.

TABLE 8.1   U.S. Middle Eastern Children 5–18 Years Old by National Origin and Immigration Status, 2000

	All Children	Immigrant Children		Children of Immigrant	Native Children
		1st Generation	1.5 Generation		
All Children	100	2.2%	2.5%	13.6%	81.8%
(N)	(2,694,073)	(58,376)	(67,416)	(365,206)	(2,203,075)
All Middle-Eastern Children	100	10.4%	12.9%	50.9%	25.9%
(N)	(18,409)	(1,911)	(2,374)	(9,364)	(4,760)
Egyptian	100	13.7%	17.0%	61.7%	7.7%
(N)	(1,300)	(178)	(220)	(802)	(100)
Iranian	100	10.8%	14.7%	66.5%	8.2%
(N)	(3,074)	(330)	(450)	(2,042)	(252)
Lebanese	100	3.6%	4.8%	33.9%	57.7%
(N)	(3,019)	(107)	(145)	(1,024)	(1,743)
Iraqi	100	38.1%	33.2%	22.2%	6.5%
(N)	(572)	(218)	(190)	(127)	(37)
Syrian	100	7.9%	7.9%	34.6%	49.5%
(N)	(1,071)	(85)	(85)	(371)	(530)
Israeli	100	13.8%	23.4%	45.9%	16.9%
(N)	(1,315)	(182)	(307)	(604)	(222)
Other Middle-Eastern Children	100	10.1%	12.1%	54.5%	23.3%
(N)	(8,058)	(811)	(977)	(4,394)	(1,876)

SOURCE: Data from PUMS 5% of the 2000 Census (U.S. Bureau of the Census, 2003a), compiled by authors.

Note: Percentages do not total to 100 due to the rounding of percentages for subgroups.

Comparing the generational structures across various Middle-Eastern American children's nationality groups reveals several distinctive features. First, the group of Middle-Eastern children, as a whole, is multigenerational, with over 76% native-born (2nd and 3rd generation), but including a significant portion of immigrants. Second, the generational composition of Middle-Eastern children varies greatly across nationalities, with three distinct patterns: Egyptian, Lebanese, and Syrian children were highly skewed toward the native-born generations; Iraqi children were highly skewed toward the foreign-born generation; and Israeli children were spread across all generations. Although more than half of Lebanese children and almost half of Syrian children were third-generation, and about two of three Iranian and Egyptian children were second-generation, more than two of three Iraqi children had been born elsewhere, and about 40% of them came to the United States at age 6 or older. Therefore, we may expect most children of Lebanese or Syrian ancestry to largely reflect the attributes of the native generations of these groups, whereas the general Iraqi child population may be expected to reflect the attributes of Iraqi immigrant children. These differing generational patterns are evidence of the large number of immigrants from Lebanon and Syria in the 1960s, the heavy flow of immigrants from Iran and Egypt in the mid-1970s and 1980s, and a more current influx of Iraqi immigrants in the 1990s. Although more than 60% of children with Israeli ancestry were born in the United States, Israeli children show a continuous immigration to this country, with more than 37% of the children being foreign-born. As we have mentioned in previous chapters, the recency and length of immigration history greatly affect the establishment of multigenerational ethnic communities and influence community organizations, business establishments, language transition, and local political participation. Schools should be aware of the implications of the various generational structures across nationalities among the Middle-Eastern children with whom they are working and make adjustments in their school policies and practice models to accommodate the needs of recent immigrant children and long-term residential children, as well as the needs of children from different Middle-Eastern nations.

The Characteristics of Middle-Eastern Families in the United States

As we have stressed in previous chapters, the family unit is a central institution in many of the traditional cultures from which newcomers to the U.S. emigrate. Whereas in the United States and Western Europe the Enlightenment tradition has favored the individual as the basic unit of political and economic decision-making, in most other parts of the world, the family or the community may play that part. The family is important throughout the Middle East, but "Islam considers the family to be the basic unit of society" (Roudi-Fahimi & Kent, 2007, p. 11; see also Haddid, 2005, and D'Agostino, 2003, on the relationship between individuals and the Muslim community). In this section, we examine the demographics of family life among Middle-Eastern immigrants and their children.

Socioeconomic Backgrounds of Families

Table 8.2 shows that, although Middle-Eastern American children are *more* likely than the general child population to live in inner cities, immigrant Middle-Eastern children are *as* likely as all immigrant children to live

TABLE 8.2 Characteristics of Families and Living Environments of U.S. Middle Eastern Children 5–18 Years Old by National Origin and Immigration Status, 2000

	All Children (18,409)	Immigrant Children (4,285)
% of Children Who Lived in Inner Cities		
All Children	13.1%	26.0%
All Middle-Eastern Children	20.6%	26.5%
Egyptian	25.6%	29.9%
Iranian	19.6%	22.2%
Lebanese	13.9%	21.4%
Iraqi	24.8%	28.4%
Syrian	21.7%	43.5%
Israeli	10.7%	28.6%
Other Middle-Eastern Children	20.7%	25.8%
Poverty Rates (% of Children Who Lived in Households in Poverty)		
All Children	14.8%	27.1%
All Middle-Eastern Children	15.6%	30.4%
Egyptian	12.4%	21.1%
Iranian	9.8%	21.4%
Lebanese	10.1%	25.8%
Iraqi	43.7%	55.6%
Syrian	11.2%	28.2%
Israeli	16.2%	19.0%
Other Middle-Eastern Children	18.9%	34.5%
% of Children Who Lived in Households With Total Family Income At or Higher Than 75th Percentile		
All Children	18.4%	10.7%
All Middle Eastern Children	28.0%	15.3%

(Continued)

TABLE 8.2 (Continued)

Egyptian	27.7%	16.8%
Iranian	40.8%	21.2%
Lebanese	31.3%	15.9%
Iraqi	10.8%	4.4%
Syrian	29.0%	8.8%
Israeli	34.5%	35.0%
Other Middle-Eastern Children	21.9%	10.0%
% of Children Who Lived in Households With Two Parents		
All Children	72.8%	80.4%
All Middle-Eastern Children	85.2%	86.6%
Egyptian	87.7%	90.0%
Iranian	84.9%	83.2%
Lebanese	84.1%	76.6%
Iraqi	86.0%	87.0%
Syrian	86.1%	90.6%
Israeli	87.5%	91.6%
Other Middle Eastern Children	85.8%	86.9%
% of Children Who Lived in Households Without a Father		
All Children	21.5%	13.3%
All Middle-Eastern Children	11.0%	9.1%
Egyptian	8.5%	5.3%
Iranian	11.0%	12.7%
Lebanese	12.5%	15.9%
Iraqi	8.9%	7.6%
Syrian	9.6%	5.9%
Israeli	10.6%	6.5%
Other Middle-Eastern Children	11.2%	8.7%

% of Children Who Lived With Parent or Household Head Having Fewer Than 4 Years of Education		
All Children	1.5%	8.9%
All Middle-Eastern Children	1.7%	4.7%
Egyptian	0.6%	0.0%
Iranian	0.6%	2.1%
Lebanese	0.7%	3.2%
Iraqi	15.2%	20.9%
Syrian	0.9%	4.1%
Israeli	0.8%	1.8%
Other Middle-Eastern Children	2.0%	4.2%
% of Children Who Lived With Parent or Household Head Having at Least a High School Diploma		
All Children	80.8%	53.7%
All Middle-Eastern Children	86.7%	79.0%
Egyptian	95.9%	96.7%
Iranian	94.5%	86.5%
Lebanese	90.6%	75.0%
Iraqi	57.0%	47.8%
Syrian	86.1%	65.9%
Israeli	89.3%	88.6%
Other Middle-Eastern Children	82.5%	78.1%
% of Children Who Lived With Parent or Household Head Having at Least a Four-Year College Degree		
All U.S. Children	23.0%	22.7%
All Middle-Eastern Children	46.8%	41.5%
Egyptian	69.4%	74.1%
Iranian	65.0%	44.6%
Lebanese	44.3%	27.4%

(Continued)

TABLE 8.2   (Continued)

Iraqi	26.2%	18.9%
Syrian	43.7%	37.7%
Israeli	50.2%	51.1%
Other Middle-Eastern Children	38.5%	37.7%

SOURCE: Data from PUMS 5% of the 2000 Census (U.S. Bureau of the Census, 2003a), compiled by authors.

in inner cities. Immigrant children from Syria were most likely to live in inner cities, while Lebanese immigrant children were least likely to do so. The general population of Israeli-American children and Lebanese-American children were least likely to live in inner cities.

The data for poverty rates support two observations.

First, the poverty pattern for Middle-Eastern families follows the patterns for other immigrant groups: immigrant families generally had higher poverty rates than families of the general population. The gap in poverty rates between the general child population and the immigrant child population is consistent across all Middle-Eastern children's nationality groups. Although the difference in the poverty rates is smallest between Israeli immigrant families and all Israeli-American families, it is most pronounced between Syrian immigrant families and all Syrian-American families.

Second, in comparing the poverty rates of Middle-Eastern American families to all U.S. families, Middle-Eastern American families had slightly higher poverty rates than all U.S. families, and Middle-Eastern immigrant families also had slightly higher poverty rates than all U.S. immigrant families. Table 8.2 indicates that the disparities in poverty rates across the Middle-Eastern nationality groups were substantial. Although Iranian, Lebanese, Syrian, and Egyptian families all had lower poverty rates than the national average, Iraqi children had the highest poverty rates among all Middle-Eastern nationality groups—and the poverty rate, at 43.7%, was much higher than the national average of 14.8%. Iraqi immigrant families also had the highest poverty rates (55.6%) of all Middle-Eastern immigrant families, higher than the national rates for all immigrant families, likely reflecting what we have already observed to be the recent increase in migration from Iraq and the conditions that may have propelled that migration. These variations may also be tied to the general economic conditions in each nation from which individuals emigrated and to each country's gross domestic product, or GDP.

This economic disparity is similarly reflected in the proportion of Middle-Eastern families who were affluent across the nationality groups. First, Middle-Eastern children, immigrant and all children, were more likely to live in households belonging to the more affluent segment of the population than U.S. children on average: 28% vs. 18.4% for all children, and 15.3% vs. 10.7% for immigrant children. The proportion of affluent families among all Middle-Eastern nationality groups was higher than among families in the general population, except for Iraqis; the proportion of affluent families among almost all Middle-Eastern immigrant groups was higher than the proportion of affluent families in the total U.S. immigrant population, with the exceptions of Iraqi and Syrian immigrants. Children from Iranian families were more likely to be affluent than all other Middle-Eastern American children, while immigrant Israeli children were more likely to be affluent than all other immigrant Middle-Eastern children. These patterns may be a result of those accepted as immigrants from Iran—professionals and other highly educated individuals fleeing the Iranian Revolution—and from Israel, the ease of travel between Israel and the United States being an exception for Middle Easterners.

Family Living Arrangements

Several noticeable features about family living arrangements are evident in Table 8.2. First, similar to the national pattern reported in Chapter 2, immigrant Middle-Eastern children were somewhat more likely than all Middle-Eastern children to live with two parents and less likely than all Middle-Eastern children to live without fathers, though the differences for each category were small. Second, all Middle-Eastern groups showed a similar family living arrangement across nationality groups. Middle-Eastern children were more likely than U.S. children, as a whole, to live in two-parent households, and more likely than U.S. children, as a whole, to live with a father. This general pattern is consistent for all Middle-Eastern immigrant groups except immigrant Lebanese. With 77% of children living in two-parent families and 16% of children living without fathers, Lebanese immigrant children had the lowest percentage of children who lived with two parents and the highest percentage children who lived without fathers among all the Middle-Eastern immigrant groups. We speculate that these findings may be related to the Lebanese Civil War of the 1970s and 1980s and to unique migration patterns during the 1990s. Nevertheless, family ties, as we have already suggested, are a strength of Middle-Eastern American communities, and they provide resources for children's education. This is especially the case for Iraqi children; although they are the most likely to live in poverty, members of the Iraqi community still hold their families together. Educators who work with Middle-Eastern children should be aware of the strength of family coherence and depend on it as a valuable resource for supporting these children in their linguistic adaptation and cultural adjustment.

Parental Educational Attainment

Consistent with our practice in previous chapters, we present parental educational attainment according to three levels, because attainment at various levels suggests different issues. Nationally, 1.5% of U.S. children in

2000 were from families where parents had the least education (less than four years); however, the percentage for U.S. immigrant children, at 9%, is four times higher than the national average for all children. This national pattern holds also for Middle-Eastern children, although the difference is smaller. Middle-Eastern American children, on average, are slightly more likely than other children (1.7%) to come from families with parents who did not have four years of education, but the percentage of Middle-Eastern immigrant children whose parents had less than four years of education (4.7%) is about half of that for all U.S. immigrant parents. Middle-Eastern American parents from all nationality groups except Iraqi reported a *lower* percentage in the least-education category; Middle-Eastern immigrant parents except for Iraqis also reported a lower percentage in the least-education segment than all immigrants. Iraqi children, at 15%, were more likely than other Middle-Eastern children to have parents with the least education, and immigrant Iraqi children, at 21%, were more likely than all other immigrant Middle-Eastern children to have parents with the least education. Both Egyptian children as a whole and Egyptian immigrant children had the lowest percentage of parents in the least educated category.

In 2000, immigrant parents from all groups in the United States were less likely to be high school graduates than were natives, and this pattern holds for all Middle-Eastern nationality groups, except Egyptians, whose immigrant parents had a slightly higher percentage rate of high school graduation than all Egyptian-American parents. Moreover, Middle-Eastern parents were more likely than all U.S. parents to be high school graduates, and Middle-Eastern immigrant parents were also more likely than all U.S. immigrant parents to be high school graduates. Nationally, 81% of all children and 54% of all immigrant children had parents who had graduated from high school, while 87% of Middle-Eastern children and 79% of Middle-Eastern immigrant children had parents who were high school graduates. Egyptians had the highest percentage of high school graduates, and Iraqi parents the lowest among Middle-Eastern immigrant children and all Middle-Eastern American children. The parents' high school graduation rates varied more across nationality groups among Middle-Eastern immigrant children than among all Middle-Eastern American children, if we consider the Iraqi group as an exception.

Nationally in 2000, immigrant parents had the same college graduation rates as all U.S. parents, but Middle-Eastern immigrant parents were less likely to be college graduates than all Middle-Eastern parents. Middle-Eastern parents were more likely to be college graduates than all U.S. parents. Middle-Eastern-American parents, as well as Middle-Eastern immigrant parents (41.5%), were twice or almost twice as likely to have a degree from a four-year college as other U.S. parents and other U.S. immigrant parents. We speculate that availability of higher education in the United States may attract students from Middle-Eastern countries, some of whom then remain to pursue permanent residency and citizenship (see Sharabi, 2005). Parents from all Middle-Eastern nationality groups except

Iraqis had higher college-graduation rates than rates for all U.S. parents. Egyptian-American, Iranian-American, and Israeli-American parents all reported much higher percentages of college graduation than the national rate for native-born Americans, but great variations occur across nationality groups among the immigrant Middle-Eastern population. At 74%, immigrant Egyptian parents had the highest rates of college graduation among all Middle-Eastern nationality groups, immigrant or general population. The second- and third-highest rates of college graduation were among Israeli and Iranian immigrant parents. Iraqi immigrant parents had the lowest percentage of college graduates, as did the total Iraqi parents for all generations. Again, we speculate that these education rates may be related to how recently and under what conditions they emigrated from Iraq.

In summary, we have observed consistent patterns in educational attainment, across national groups, at all three educational levels.

- First, Middle-Eastern parents are generally better educated than average U.S. parents, with higher rates of both high school and college graduation. Middle-Eastern immigrant parents are also generally better educated than all U.S. immigrant parents at these two levels.

- Second, Middle-Eastern immigrant parents are less well educated than the general Middle-Eastern American parent population. However, the gaps in parental education between the immigrant Middle-Eastern child population and the general Middle-Eastern child population, across nationality groups, are not as pronounced as those within the Latino, Asian, and African populations.

- Third, the patterns for Iraqi children were visibly distinct from those of other Middle-Eastern children for many socioeconomic variables: their parents were more likely to be least educated and were much less likely to be high school graduates. However, at the highest level of education, the general Iraqi parent population had higher rates of college graduates than all U.S. parents. Nevertheless, the college graduation rates were lower for Iraqi immigrant parents than for all U.S. immigrant parents.

We offer several explanations for the patterns we have delineated so far. The generally high socioeconomic status and educational attainment of Middle-Eastern families may be attributed to their pre-migration middle-class status and the types of people who have immigrated. These include people in high-technology and management positions who meet designated areas of U.S. employment need, as well as a large number of entrepreneurs. One of our own students of Middle-Eastern origin emphasized the priority of education in his family and the higher status his family members accorded to education over wealth.

Educators, however, may need to focus attention on specific aspects of education for Iraqi children. Compared with economic immigrants and some political refugees from Iran and other Middle-Eastern countries, migrants from Iraq have left a less economically developed country. Iraqi immigrants might have less pre-migration education because of the very unstable political and economic situation in this country in the 1980s and 1990s, resulting from Iraq's wars with Iran, Kuwait, and the United States. Refugees who suffer from trauma during wars and political chaos are unable to make the same preparations for immigration as other migrants: they cannot anticipate their journeys by studying English, putting their financial resources together, or building networks in the United States. Iraqi adults might also have difficulty finding employment in the United States because of societal hostilities and suspicion of them, resulting from the United States-Iraq wars. Also, because of Iraq's recent history of wars and other political and military conflicts with several neighboring Middle-Eastern countries, Iraqi immigrants might also encounter difficulties in building themselves into the pan-Middle-Eastern and Arabic social and business networks. We find some of these same challenges for Iraqis when we turn to other aspects of the migration status of Middle-Eastern immigrants.

Household Language Situation and U.S. Citizenship Status

Table 8.3 reveals two important points about the language situations of Middle-Eastern families. First, in 2000, Middle-Eastern children were more likely to speak a language other than English at home than all U.S. children, and Middle-Eastern immigrant children were also more likely than all U.S. immigrant children to speak a heritage language at home. Second, less variation was reported about heritage-language speaking and household linguistic isolation among various nationality groups in the immigrant population than in the whole Middle-Eastern child population. The nationality groups that had a longer migration history to the United States, unsurprisingly, had the lowest proportion of heritage-language speakers and household linguistic isolation. The large variations across Middle-Eastern nationality groups might reflect, among other factors, the generational makeup of these groups. The nationality groups with a longer history of migration to the United States and composed of earlier immigrant cohorts—such as Lebanese and Syrian groups—had the lowest percentages of heritage-language speaking and living in a linguistically isolated household. The nationality groups with more recent histories of U.S. migration and composed of later immigrant cohorts—such as Iranians, Egyptians, and Israelis—had a moderate level of heritage-language speaking and living in linguistically isolated households. The Iraqi group is highly skewed toward the immigration generation and has the most recent experience of migration to the United States; in this group, 84% of children were reported to speak a heritage language and 33% were reported to live in linguistically isolated households. Among Middle-Eastern immigrants, the variation in the percentage of children who spoke a heritage language is small—from 86% for Lebanese children to 98% for Iraqi children—but the variation in the percentage of children reported to be living in linguistically isolated households was relatively large: 18% for

Lebanese children, 26% for Egyptian children, and 44% for Iraqi children. We speculate that, in homes reporting no linguistic isolation, adults may have arrived in the United States with competence in English.

Middle-Eastern-American children were less likely to live with parents who were U.S. citizens than all U.S. children; however, Middle-Eastern immigrant parents, as a whole, reported a higher percentage of U.S. citizenship than all immigrant parents. The rates for citizenship and the citizenship ratio between the total population and the immigrant population vary greatly across national groups. Over three-quarters of all Middle-Eastern parents, and about two-fifths of Middle-Eastern immigrant parents, reported U.S. citizenship in 2000. The percentages are very similar to those of Asian-Americans. Lebanese and Syrian parents reported the highest citizenship rates; Iraqi parents reported the lowest citizenship rates. Among Middle-Eastern immigrant parents, Lebanese and Iranian parents had the highest citizenship rates; Iraqi parents reported the lowest citizenship rates.

The living conditions and household attributes of children of immigrants and others of Middle-Eastern ancestry vary widely, undoubtedly affected by the history and circumstances of migration across national groups. In the next section of the chapter, we turn to the children themselves—and what census and other data indicate—to capture a national profile for Middle-Eastern immigrant youngsters.

TABLE 8.3   Immigration-Related Characteristics of U.S. Households for Middle Eastern Children 5–18 Years Old by National Origin and Immigration Status, 2000

	All Children (18,409)	Immigrant Children (4,295)
% of Children Who Spoke a Language Other Than English at Home		
All Children	17.3%	84.9%
All Middle-Eastern Children	57.7%	92.4%
Egyptian	66.8%	91.0%
Iranian	68.0%	95.3%
Lebanese	30.0%	86.1%
Iraqi	83.6%	97.6%
Syrian	39.0%	94.7%
Israeli	64.5%	89.8%
Other Middle-Eastern Children	62.2%	92.0%

(Continued)

TABLE 8.3   (Continued)

% of Children Who Lived in Linguistically Isolated Households		
All Children	4.5%	34.4%
All Middle-Eastern Children	10.5%	25.3%
Egyptian	13.1%	26.1%
Iranian	9.6%	21.9%
Lebanese	3.5%	17.5%
Iraqi	32.9%	44.1%
Syrian	7.1%	21.5%
Israeli	12.6%	23.1%
Other Middle-Eastern Children	11.5%	24.1%
% Household Heads Who Are U.S. Citizens		
All Children	91.6%	31.5%
All Middle-Eastern Children	77.5%	39.6%
Egyptian	72.6%	39.2%
Iranian	72.6%	42.3%
Lebanese	91.7%	51.2%
Iraqi	41.8%	22.6%
Syrian	84.8%	39.4%
Israeli	67.0%	36.2%
Other Middle-Eastern Children	78.2%	41.6%

SOURCE: Data from PUMS 5% of the 2000 Census (U.S. Bureau of the Census, 2003a), compiled by authors.

The Characteristics of Middle-Eastern Children

Experiences that children have in school are greatly affected by the characteristics youth take to school with them. As we have noted in previous chapters, identified disabilities, length of residence in the community, and language proficiency are three attributes that the 2000 census reported for various immigrant groups and their children.

Disabilities

We observe three patterns in summarizing the findings here.

- Middle-Eastern children, in both the general population and among immigrants, were less likely to be either physically disabled or learning disabled than U.S. children.
- The general Middle-Eastern child population had lower rates of physical disabilities and higher rates of learning-related disabilities than the population of Middle-Eastern immigrant children. These two patterns were similar to those reported for Asian children.
- The variation in disability rates across nationality groups, among Middle-Eastern immigrant children as well as among all Middle-Eastern children, was limited.

Table 8.4 shows that the rates of physical disabilities were highest among Egyptian children at 3.6%, and lowest among Israeli children at 1.4%. Among immigrants, the physical disability rate was highest among Iranian children and lowest among Israeli children. Learning-related disabilities were lowest among Israeli children and highest among Syrian children. Among the immigrant children, Israeli, Syrian, and Iranian children had the lowest learning disability rates at 0.6%, and the other groups had higher rates at 1.0% or 1.2%.

Length of Residence and Age of Arrival

In this subsection of the chapter on characteristics of Middle-Eastern youth in the United States, we focus only on Middle-Eastern foreign-born immigrant children. Table 8.5 indicates identical patterns for Middle-Eastern immigrant children, as a group, compared to all U.S. immigrant children in the distribution of the length of residence. In 2000, about half of the school-aged Middle-Eastern immigrant children in the United States had been in the country for less than five years, and over 80% of them had come to the United States after 1990. Iraqis had the largest proportion of newcomers (59%), followed by Egyptians (57%). Almost half of the Lebanese and Israeli immigrant children who were in the United States in 2000 had arrived in this country after 1995.

The distribution pattern for age of arrival in 2000 for all Middle-Eastern immigrant children is also identical with that of all U.S. immigrant children. Most Middle-Eastern immigrant children came to the United States at young ages. More than half of them arrived in this country at five or younger; about 30% of them arrived between the ages of 6–10; and about one of six arrived in this country at 11 years or older. All nationality groups follow this pattern. However, within the Middle-Eastern nationality groups, Israeli immigrant children had the highest percentage of individuals (63%) who had come to the United States at age five or younger. Iraqi immigrant children had the highest percentage of those who came to this country at an older age. That being said, the differences across these nationality groups are moderate.

TABLE 8.4   Characteristics of U.S. Middle Eastern Children 5–18 Years Old by National Origin and Immigration Status, 2000

	All Children (18,409)	Immigrant Children (4,285)
% of Children Who Reported Physical Disabilities (One or Multiple Limitations in Mobility, Personal Care, Hearing and Vision, etc.)		
All U.S. Children	3.0%	5.1%
All Middle-Eastern Children	2.6%	4.2%
Egyptian	3.6%	4.8%
Iranian	2.8%	5.4%
Lebanese	1.7%	5.2%
Iraqi	3.2%	3.9%
Syrian	2.4%	4.7%
Israeli	1.4%	1.2%
Other Middle-Eastern Children	2.8%	4.3%
% of Children Who Reported Learning-Related Disabilities (Difficulties With Memory, etc.)		
All U.S. Children	4.4%	2.2%
All Middle-Eastern Children	2.2%	1.2%
Egyptian	1.9%	1.0%
Iranian	1.6%	0.6%
Lebanese	2.4%	1.2%
Iraqi	2.3%	1.2%
Syrian	3.1%	0.6%
Israeli	1.4%	0.6%
Other Middle-Eastern Children	2.4%	1.7%

SOURCE: Data from PUMS 5% of the 2000 Census (U.S. Bureau of the Census, 2003a), compiled by authors.

Oral English Proficiency

Table 8.6 presents the self-reported English proficiency rates among Middle-Eastern children who spoke languages other than English at home; in this subsection of the chapter, we return to considering immigrant Middle-Eastern children, all children whose parents report Middle-Eastern

TABLE 8.5 Immigration-Related Characteristics of U.S. Foreign-Born Middle-Eastern Children 5–18 Years Old by National Origin, 2000

	0–5	6–10	11–15	16 and Above
Years in U.S.				
All Foreign-born Children	47.3%	34.0%	16.5%	2.3%
All Middle-Eastern Children	46.2%	33.0%	18.7%	2.0%
Egyptian	56.8%	26.4%	15.1%	1.8%
Iranian	38.3%	26.0%	31.7%	4.0%
Lebanese	49.2%	23.0%	23.8%	4.0%
Iraqi	59.3%	37.3%	2.5%	1.0%
Syrian	36.5%	43.5%	19.4%	0.6%
Israeli	48.1%	27.2%	22.9%	1.8%
Other Middle-Eastern Children	44.3%	38.6%	15.7%	1.4%
Age at Arrival				
All Foreign-born Children	53.4%	30.1%	14.5%	1.9%
All Middle-Eastern Children	55.4%	29.3%	13.7%	1.6%
Egyptian	55.3%	27.1%	16.1%	1.5%
Iranian	57.7%	25.1%	15.3%	1.9%
Lebanese	57.5%	25.0%	15.1%	2.4%
Iraqi	46.6%	34.1%	18.1%	1.2%
Syrian	50.0%	31.2%	16.5%	2.4%
Israeli	62.8%	26.0%	10.8%	0.4%
Other Middle-Eastern Children	54.6%	31.8%	11.8%	1.7%

SOURCE: Data from PUMS 5% of the 2000 Census (U.S. Bureau of the Census, 2003a), compiled by authors.
Note: Percentages do not total to 100 due to the rounding of percentages for subgroups.

ancestry, and other U.S. children speaking languages other than English at home. Among all Middle-Eastern HLS children of all generations, 78% were reported as speaking English very well, as compared to 71% of immigrant children. Both percentages are higher than the percentages for both all U.S. heritage-language speakers and all U.S. immigrant heritage-language speakers. A lower percentage of Middle-Eastern immigrant children were reported to speak no English than all U.S. immigrant HLS children (1.0% vs. 3.8%), and a lower percentage of all Middle-Eastern children reported speaking no English than all U.S. heritage-language speakers (0.7% vs. 1.6%). However, the variations in self-reported English proficiency in all three indicators (speaking no English, not speaking English very well, or speaking English very well) are moderate across the nationality groups, except for Iraqi immigrant children: 57% were reported as speaking English very well, compared to percentages for the other groups, which were all over 70%. Again, we speculate that this may be due to the how recently they emigrated from Iraq and the tumultuous circumstances that may have prompted that migration.

In summary, Lebanese and Syrian immigrant children can be viewed as the most linguistically assimilated nationality groups, compared to other immigrant Middle-Eastern children, when considering length of residency, age of arrival, heritage-language speaking, and oral English proficiency simultaneously. Children in these two nationality groups tend to have the longest U.S. residence, are likely to speak a heritage language at home, and are most likely to speak English very well among the heritage-language speakers. Iraqi immigrant children were reported to have the largest proportion of newcomers, a larger proportion of youngsters who arrived in the United States at an older age, the highest percentage of heritage-language speakers, and larger proportions of individuals speaking English less well.

TABLE 8.6 Self-Reported English Proficiency for Middle-Eastern Children Compared to All Other U.S. Children Who Spoke a Language Other Than English at Home

| | All Children | | | Immigrant Children | | |
| | | Not Very | | | Not Very | |
	No English	Well	Very Well	No English	Well Very	Well
All Children	1.6%	32.3%	66.1%	3.8%	41.2%	55.0%
All Middle-Eastern Children	0.7%	21.7%	77.7%	1.0%	27.8%	71.2%
Egyptian	0.7%	23.2%	76.2%	1.4%	27.9%	70.7%
Iranian	0.3%	19.2%	80.5%	0.4%	24.8%	74.8%
Lebanese	0.6%	19.8%	79.6%	0.9%	21.7%	77.4%
Iraqi	1.3%	37.7%	61.1%	1.0%	42.2%	56.8%
Syrian	0.0%	18.9%	81.1%	0.0%	24.8%	75.2%
Israeli	1.7%	22.5%	75.8%	0.9%	27.8%	71.3%
Other Middle-Eastern Children	0.7%	21.3%	78.0%	1.3%	26.8%	71.9%

SOURCE: Data from PUMS 5% of the 2000 Census (U.S. Bureau of the Census, 2003a), compiled by authors.

Note: Percentages do not total to 100 due to the rounding of percentages for subgroups.

Education of Middle-Eastern American and Middle-Eastern Immigrant Children

As we have reported for other groups in previous chapters, based on the available educational information from the 2000 Census, we compiled data to form three educational indices. These three indices are general enrollment rates for children aged 5–18, enrollment rates in private schools for children aged 5–18, and school dropout rates for youth aged 16–18. We discuss next the patterns we found for Middle-Eastern American children and Middle-Eastern immigrant children.

General Enrollment

All Middle-Eastern nationality groups, both in the general child population and among immigrant children, have higher or equal school enrollment rates compared to the national rates. Table 8.7 shows that Middle-Eastern children were more likely to be enrolled in school than U.S. children as a whole, Middle-Eastern immigrant children were also more likely to be enrolled in school than all U.S. immigrant children, and the enrollment gap between all Middle-Eastern children and Middle-Eastern immigrant children appears somewhat smaller than the enrollment difference between all U.S. children and all U.S. immigrant children. In 2000, Israeli children—as a whole and in the immigrant generation—had the highest school enrollment rates, compared to other Middle-Eastern nationality groups. The enrollment for Iraqi children as a whole is slightly higher than the national rates; the enrollment rate for Iraqi immigrant children is also higher than the rate for U.S. immigrant children.

Enrollment in Private Schools

Middle-Eastern children in the general population and among immigrant children were twice as likely as all U.S. children and U.S. immigrant children to be enrolled in private schools. Table 8.7 indicates that, at 36.8%, Israeli children had the highest private school enrollment rates—more than three times the national rates—and, at 29.9%, Israeli immigrant children had the highest private school enrollment rates among all Middle-Eastern immigrant children—more than four times the national rates. Syrian children had the second-highest private school enrollment rates for all children and immigrant children. Iraqi children, both all children and immigrant children, had the lowest private school enrollment rates among all nationality groups. These findings can be explained by several intertwined factors—such as families' abilities to finance private school tuition and their religious and linguistic priorities, or the extent to which migration was motivated by religious reasons and facilitated by ready access to visas—but we believe the patterns would be illuminated by further research.

High School Dropouts

Iraqi-American children had a much higher dropout rate than the national rate, and Iraqi immigrant children had a slightly higher dropout rate than U.S. immigrant children generally. However, all other Middle-Eastern nationality groups, in both the general child population and the immigrant

TABLE 8.7   Educational Characteristics of U.S. Middle Eastern Children 5–18 Years Old by National Origin and Immigration Status, 2000

	All Children (18,409)	Immigrant Children (4,295)
% of Children (5–18) Enrolled in Schools		
All Children	96.3%	94.5%
All Middle-Eastern Children	97.2%	96.6%
Egyptian	96.9%	95.5%
Iranian	97.5%	96.7%
Lebanese	97.2%	96.0%
Iraqi	96.5%	96.8%
Syrian	96.8%	95.9%
Israeli	98.6%	98.6%
Other Middle-Eastern Children	97.0%	96.3%
% of Children (5–18) Enrolled in Private Schools		
All Children	10.8%	6.0%
All Middle-Eastern Children	19.2%	12.1%
Egyptian	16.8%	8.0%
Iranian	16.9%	8.2%
Lebanese	22.6%	18.3%
Iraqi	5.4%	1.7%
Syrian	29.1%	28.2%
Israeli	36.8%	29.9%
Other Middle-Eastern Children	15.6%	9.7%

% of Children 16–18 Years Old Who Were School Dropouts* by National Origin and Immigration Status		
All Children	5.6%	9.0%
All Middle Eastern Children	3.3%	3.8%
Egyptian	2.0%	3.5%
Iranian	2.7%	2.9%
Lebanese	3.5%	8.2%
Iraqi	11.9%	11.7%
Syrian	3.9%	1.8%
Israeli	1.9%	0.9%
Other Middle-Eastern Children	3.2%	3.3%

SOURCE: Data from PUMS 5% of the 2000 Census (U.S. Bureau of the Census, 2003a), compiled by authors.

*Dropouts are those who did not graduate from high school but were not enrolled in school in 2000.

child population, had lower dropout rates than the national rates (5.6% for all U.S children and 9% for U.S. immigrant children). Israeli children had the lowest dropout rates among all Middle-Eastern children, including Middle-Eastern immigrant children. Interestingly, although Middle-Eastern immigrant children had slightly higher dropout rates than all Middle-Eastern children (3.8% vs. 3.3%), in several nationality groups such as Israelis, Syrians, and Iraqis, immigrant children actually had lower dropout rates than the dropout rates for the general Middle-Eastern child population.

SUMMARY OF DEMOGRAPHICS FOR MIDDLE-EASTERN CHILDREN

Middle-Eastern immigrant children share many commonalities with other immigrant children, especially in their differences from the general child population. Compared to the general child population of Middle-Eastern ancestry, Middle-Eastern immigrant children were more likely to live in inner cities and in poverty rather than affluence, have parents with less education, be physically disabled, and be members of linguistically isolated households. However, compared to the general Middle-Eastern child population, Middle-Eastern immigrant children were also less likely to have learning-related disabilities and more likely to live in two-parent families and speak a heritage language at home. Nevertheless, Middle-Eastern immigrant children do differ from other immigrant children. For example, compared to children whose ancestry is from other parts of the world, the differences in school enrollment and high school dropout rates were minimal between the general Middle-Eastern child population and the Middle-Eastern immigrant child population.

We also identify three other differences between Middle-Eastern immigrant children and other immigrant children crucial to understanding their experiences with education. First, Middle-Eastern children were more likely than others to have highly educated parents working in professional and management occupations. Second, as we have emphasized elsewhere, the six Middle-Eastern groups we have discussed here are diverse in language, culture, religion, and political and social systems. Given these diversities, we find the similarities in demographic patterns remarkable. The differences in socioeconomic status among the various Middle-Eastern nationalities may be partially explained by differences in pre-immigration socioeconomic status, different reasons for immigration (e.g., economic immigrants vs. political refugees), variations in types of visas acquired (e.g., visas for high-technology occupations vs. family reunification), and differences in the educational level of the parents and the duration of parental residence in the United States. Third, although visible cross-nationality variations are evident in many social, economic, and educational domains within the Middle-Eastern immigrant child population, the variations are generally less pronounced than those variations within the Asian and Hispanic child populations. The only group set apart from the other groups was Iraqi children. However, considering what these families and children have gone through since the early 1990s, we hope U.S. social and educational institutions can help them overcome their hardships and thereby catch up with the other Middle-Eastern children.

We turn next to our recommendations for what educational policymakers and practitioners should know and do to strengthen the education and schooling of Middle-Eastern immigrant children.

RECOMMENDATIONS

As we have emphasized throughout this chapter, immigrant children from the Middle East comprise a diverse group of youngsters from different nations, ethnic and racial groups, religious practices, linguistic traditions, and socioeconomic backgrounds. Complicating this diversity is a lack of research literature on Middle-Eastern immigrant children and their education, especially compared to the wealth of material on Asian and Latino youth. The events of September 11, 2001, have regrettably only intensified negative experiences of Middle-Eastern youth (for an example from the popular press, see Boal, 2001) and solidified the stereotype in the United States that all Middle-Easterners except Israelis practice Islam and enjoy wealth from oil revenues. This stereotype can be challenged in a number of ways, drawing from both research and reports of successful practice.

Recommendation One: Challenge Stereotypes

Policymakers, educational leaders, and teachers should recognize that, although Middle-Eastern immigrants were predominantly Christian prior to the 1960s and have been predominantly Muslim since then, migrants from this area represent the range of religious groups that we have discussed previously. Both the children and their communities must be examined from one locale to the next, around the United States, for their affiliations and identities. In her study of second-generation Iranian undergraduates, for example, Shavarini (2004) shows a common zeal for education among these youngsters whose parents left different communities in Iran: Muslim, Jewish, Baha'i, and Armenian. Similarly, cultural practices and expectations for gender behavior—another area vulnerable to stereotypes—vary considerably across the Middle-Eastern region and within countries, according to such factors as socioeconomic class. Throughout this chapter, we have emphasized the events that have resulted in difficult cultural environments for Middle-Eastern children in U.S. schools:

- U.S. allegiance over the years to Israel,
- tensions between the United States and the Muslim world over the Israeli-Palestinian conflicts (especially the Israeli-Hezbollah conflicts),
- the wars between the United States and Iraq, and
- the attacks on the United States from Al-Qaeda.

We ourselves have heard reports of Sikh youth being attacked, for example, merely because the attackers mistakenly associated Sikh turbans with Islam.

Fortunately, resources are available to help teachers and administrators assist Middle-Eastern, Arabic, and Muslim children in dealing with discrimination and hostility directed toward them in schools and communities. Special curricula on Muslims have been developed, such as the material offered by Teachers College, Columbia University (Kenan, 2005). Recommended policies and practices for schools with Middle-Eastern students are readily available (e.g., Roderick, 2001; Schwartz, 1999), and a small but growing literature addresses such issues as adolescent mental health (Timimi, 1995) and sexuality (Orgocka, 2004) among Middle-Eastern youth.

Next, we briefly identify a number of areas that U.S. educational leaders should be ready to address.

Recommendation Two: Acknowledge Children's Religious Diversity

Middle-Eastern immigrants vary not only by religious affiliation, but also by (a) whether they consider themselves more or less secular or (b) more or less religious, and (c) by the group or sect within religions to which they may belong. Generally, those immigrants from urban areas who are most educated and most likely to arrive in the United States with professional credentials are more likely to be most secular, but exceptions also occur to this pattern. Again, rather than assuming either a religious view or a secular orientation, policymakers and educational leaders must inquire about the perspectives of the communities represented in their areas.

The separation of church and state assumed by most U.S. educators can be a challenge to both school personnel and immigrant youth. First, public schools throughout the United States continue to be affected by Judeo-Christian practices directly and indirectly (McClellan, 1999). Christian communities have in recent decades asserted their freedom to communicate beliefs and expectations openly, and even where this may not be common, adults and youth in schools are expected to know the tenets of Christian and Jewish faiths in ways that have not been expected for the tenets of Islam, Baha'ism, and other world religions. The school calendar itself may be organized around the Christian holidays of Christmas and Easter, thus providing fewer conflicts for students and teachers adhering to Christian holiday practice than for those observing other religious calendars.

Youth who practice Islam can face special challenges in secular U.S. public schools (Haynes, 1998):

- First, by adolescence, many Muslims observe prayer patterns requiring time and a protected space within the school day.
- Second, modesty is highly valued for both boys and girls, and optional clothing for physical education and alternatives to public showering can reduce youngsters' anxiety while at school. Likewise, teachers and school staff should be informed about, and sensitive to, expectations for limited interaction across gender among many Muslim youth.
- Finally, most immigrants from around the world arrive in the United States with dietary practices and food prohibitions that should be respected. Meat alternatives to pork, and vegetarian alternatives to meat, are two important policies all public school lunchrooms should follow to provide a hospitable environment for all youngsters.

Educators and policymakers should especially be aware of what the separation of church and state means and does not mean. Teaching about religions has been encouraged by the U.S. courts, and individuals' freedom to practice their religions is protected by the U.S. Bill of Rights. What schools must avoid is state sponsored and mandated practice of any particular religion.

Recommendation Three: Consider Gender Influences

Coeducation in the public schools became the norm in the United States by the end of the 19th century (Tyack & Hansot, 1990), and much activity in middle and secondary schools is organized by students, and even adults, around heterosexual expectations and conduct. Students and many parents view school—especially high school—as the site of social preparation for marriage and the family, and high school social activities vie with academics for students' attention (e.g., Best, 2000). As we suggest in the previous section, these expected patterns can be the source of conflict for Muslims and youth from some other groups, where distance and discretion characterize the relationships of boys and girls from different families. In her illuminating study of Yemeni American girls at a public school in Michigan, Sarroub (2005) shows how classrooms can be havens for interactive learning for these Muslim young women, who experienced hallways, lunchrooms, and other more public spaces as placing them under the critical male scrutiny of relatives and neighbors. Teachers, school leaders, and policymakers should be familiar with and respectful of variations in what we call gender deportment.

Sons and daughters of immigrants, of course, may or may not conform to what their parents believe to be proper behavior. Most parents, immigrant and otherwise, find their children challenging, resisting, and even overturning family expectations. Intergenerational conflict, especially between mothers and daughters, occurs in all families and has been documented as an issue faced by many Muslim families in the United States (Schur, 2005). School personnel must be educated to be aware of these differing response patterns and expect that young people under stress may need support from adults at school. Teachers, counselors, and administrators in these situations must withhold enforcing their own gender expectations on families and parents while assuring that students have an encouraging learning environment. Generational conflicts are not limited to gender issues, however, as we note in the following section.

Recommendation Four: Recognize Influences of Individualism and Collectivism

Around the world, societies value both their individual members and the groups composed of such individuals. What differs across societies and their cultures is how the relationship between individual and group is conceptualized, and the sets of values and expectations attached to individuals and communities (Spindler & Spindler, 1990). We have previously contrasted the idea of the individual as the basic social unit—an idea that developed in the West during the Enlightenment—with the idea of the family as the basic social unit, common across the Middle-Eastern region. (See Fahlman, 1983, for comments reflecting this contrast from Lebanese Muslim students in a Canadian setting and Zanten, 1997, for how the contrast plays out with Algerian Muslim immigrants in France.)

These differing notions can be a source of misunderstandings and conflict between immigrants and U.S. school personnel. School leaders, policymakers, and teachers should take these patterns into account when interacting with immigrants and their children.

For example, in their report of interviews with Muslim students and their parents in New York City, Ahmad and Szpara (2003) found that students were generally positive about their schooling, but that they believed that "misperceptions and negative stereotypes about Islam and Muslim values are pervasive in schools" (p. 298). Decisions about children's education, for example, may be influenced by what parents believe to be family priorities. These differences can also be the source of conflicts between immigrant children and their parents as they adapt to U.S. society; in her study of Yemini-American girls Sarroub (2001) demonstrates how aware these youngsters are of living in between two contrasting cultures and how they struggle to belong to both. As we emphasize at the start of this chapter, identities in the 21st century are many-faceted; they have become fluid everywhere. Immigrant children and their parents bring multiple, sometimes conflicting, identities to the challenge of the new cultural demands posed by migration.

CONCLUSION

Immigrant children from the Middle East bring many advantages to their experiences in U.S. schools that we have summarized in preceding sections. As the current focus of U.S. foreign policy and military intervention, Middle-Easterners—with the exception of Israelis—have also become vulnerable to suspicion, hostility, and stereotype. Educational policy and practice, as we have recommended, can confront and challenge negative assumptions. Sound policies and practices can also provide both native-born and immigrant children the opportunity to respectfully explore differences and share similarities.

Sources of Information

The baseline data for this book are from the 2000 Census Public Use Microdata Samples 5% (PUMS 5%), which includes 14.8 million people in the United States. The PUMS 5% dataset was drawn from the long form of the 2000 census. This long-form census survey was sent to approximately one of every six households in the United States. The universe for this book includes all children between 5 and 18 years of age living in households with parents or guardians. Our initial data analysis used a total of 2,694,000 children of all generations and 125,800 immigrant children. The terms *children* and *youth* are used throughout the book to refer to individuals from childhood to adolescence. Our data analyses exclude teenagers who are householders, spouses maintaining their own households, or parenting a child of their own in a relative's household. These young people are not children in the sense that they are probably no longer dependent on their parents and have taken on some responsibilities normally associated with adulthood.

In this section we describe the 2000 census data and the data analysis methods we have used. Census data, data collected by the National Center for Educational Statistics, and data from other sources are used for these analyses. The most comprehensive and up-to-date information comes from the 2000 census, including aggregated and individual data. We also have used other data collected by the U.S. Census Bureau, such as the Current Population Survey (CPS) 2005, 2006, and 2007, and the American Community Survey (ACS) 2004, 2005, and 2006. Our main data source for this book, the PUMS 5%, contains socioeconomic and demographic characteristic records collected from 5% of the total population and about 16% of all housing units in the United States. The PUMS 5% is a stratified subsample of the full census sample of the 2000 Census long-form survey. Census analysts have used a stratified systematic selection procedure with an equal probability of selecting subjects for the microdata samples. They have sampled housing unit by housing unit to allow a study of family relationships and housing unit characteristics.

The PUMS 5% file consists of two types of records: housing and persons. Each housing unit record is followed by a variable number of person records, one for each member of the housing unit, or none, if the housing unit is vacant. Because the sample provides data for all persons living in a sampled household, we can study how the household members' characteristics are interrelated: for example, income, educational attainment, place of birth, and citizenship and linguistic status of parents, other adults, and children. The PUMS 5% contains individual weights for each person and housing unit, which, when applied to the individual records, expand the sample to the total population. Because the census provides more details for smaller geographic areas and subpopulations than most other data sources, its accuracy is reliable. Furthermore, the 2000 census forms were translated into Spanish, Chinese, Korean, Tagalog, and Vietnamese, and "assistance guides" were provided in 49 other languages.

PUMS 5% is the largest population sample ever used in educational research, providing records for approximately 14.8 million persons and more than 6 million housing units. The dataset for our book comes from the analysis of approximately 2.7 million children and about 126,000 foreign-born children aged 5 through 18. We list the major variables we used as baseline information in three categories: characteristics of individuals, of microsystems (households), and of macrosystems (environments).

- *Individual level:* Characteristics include age, gender, race, ethnicity,[1] nationality,[2] place of birth, disability status, educational enrollment, private or public school enrollment, high school graduation,[3] oral English proficiency, ability to speak a language other than English at home, place of birth, year of immigration, immigration generational status, citizenship status, and such.

- *Microsystem level*: Cultural characteristics include household language, linguistic isolation status, parents' English proficiency, and parents' length of residence in the United States. Socioeconomic characteristics

1 Race and ethnicity are determined by combining the responses from the Hispanic origin question (whether they are Spanish, Hispanic, or Latino) and a race question (the race or races they considered themselves to be) in the 2000 census long form. See details on the question choices in our introduction.

2 We created a variable combining the responses from questions about place of birth and ancestry from the 2000 census long form.

3 Our study defines a person who did not have a high school diploma and was not enrolled in school in 2000 as a school dropout. The 1990 census was the first decennial census with questions allowing persons to report the completion of the 12th grade without receiving a high school diploma or equivalent (GED) U.S.Bureau of the Census, 1993b.

include such information as parental education and occupation, type of family arrangement, family income, poverty status,[4] and so forth.

- *Macrosystem level*: Geographic location is represented by region, division, state, and county. Communities are characterized by size and location as inner city (inside the central city), metropolitan other than central city, and nonmetropolitan areas.

All of these attributes are defined in Chapter 2 in the text or under the tables. For more detailed information and the rationales for collecting data for these variables, see *2000 Census PUMS 5% Technical Documentation* (U.S. Bureau of the Census, 2003b).

One major weakness of census data recognized by the U.S. Bureau of the Census is the problem of undercounted populations, which include urban residents, especially those in low-income, inner-city areas; people with limited English-language skills; and racial and ethnic minorities. These people are much more likely than other people to be missed by the census data collection. Recently immigrated families—particularly those that are poor, have no permanent address, are undocumented, or speak and read no English—are more likely than other people to be among the uncounted population. For example, the undercount rate is estimated at 1.4% for the entire U.S. population, but about 2.9% for the U.S. Hispanic population; approximately one million Hispanic people were missing from the 2000 census.

For more information about the 2000 census long-form questionnaire, term definitions, sample design and sampling, nonsampling errors, and undercounting, see the *Census 2000 Summary File 1 Technical Documentation* by the U.S. Bureau of the Census, listed in our reference section (U.S. Census Bureau, 2007c).

---

4 Poverty statistics are based on annual income in the calendar year immediately prior to the survey, and reflect family size. The poverty threshold for a family of four was $17,029 in 1999. See Bishaw & Iceland (2003).

References

Abraham, N., & Shryock, A. (Eds.). (2000). *Arab Detroit: From margin to mainstream.* Detroit: Wayne State University.

Acuna, R. F. (1972). *Occupied America: The Chicano's struggle toward liberation.* San Francisco: Canfield Press.

Acuna, R. F. (2003). *U.S. Latino issues.* Westport, CT: Greenwood Press.

Adelman, H. (2002, Feb.). *Refugees and boarder security post-September 11.* Paper presented at the meeting of Peacekeeping or gatekeeping: Canadian security policy after September 11, Toronto, Canada.

Ahmad, I., & Szpara, M. Y. (2003). Muslim children in urban America: The New York City Schools experience. *Journal of Muslim Minority Affairs, 23*(2), 295–301.

Ainsworth-Carnell, J. W., & Downey, D. B. (1998). Assessing the oppositional culture explanation for racial/ethnic differences in school performance. *American Sociological Review, 63,* 536–553.

Ajibode, I. (2006). *Diary of an immigrant: In pursuit of the American dream.* Lincoln, NE: Universe.

Alba, R. D. (1990). *Ethnic identity: The transformation of white America.* New Haven, CT: Yale University Press.

Alba, R. D. (2002). *Bilingualism persists, but English still dominates.* Retrieved January 1, 2007, from http://www.migrationinformation.org/Feature/display.cfm

Alba, R. D., & Nee, V. (1998). Rethinking assimilation theory for a new era of immigration. *International Migration Review, 31,* 826–874.

Alba, R. D., & Nee, V. (2003). *Remaking the American mainstream: Assimilation and contemporary immigration.* Cambridge, MA: Harvard University Press.

Albertini, V. L. (2004). Racial mistrust among immigrant minority students. *Child and Adolescent Social Work Journal, 21*(4), 311–331.

Alidou, H. (2000). Preparing teachers for the education of new immigrant students from Africa. *Action in Teacher Education, 22*(2A), 101–108.

Alvarez, J. (1992). *How the Garcia girls lost their accents.* New York: Plume.

Anisef, P. (1975). Consequences of ethnicity for educational plans among grade 12 students. In A. Wolfgang (Ed.), *Education of immigrant students* (pp. 122–136). Toronto: Ontario Institute for Studied in Education.

Arthur, J. (2000). *Invisible sojourners: African immigrant diaspora in the United States.* Westport, CT: Praeger.

Associated Press (2005). *Hate groups turn focus on Hispanic immigrants.* Retrieved January 7, 2008, from http://azbilingualed.org/News%202005/hate_groups_turn_focus_on_hi

Aswad, B. C., & Bilgé, B. (Eds.). (1996). *Family and gender among American Muslims: Issues facing Middle Eastern immigrants and their descendants.* Philadelphia: Temple University Press.

Bailey, B. H. (2001). Dominican-American ethnic/racial identities and United States social categories. *International Migration Review, 35*(3), 677–708.

Bankston, C. L., & Zhou, M. (2002). Being well vs. doing well: Self-esteem and school performance among immigrant and nonimmigrant racial and ethnic groups. *International Migration Review, 36*(2), 389–415.

Barringer, H. R., Gardner, R. W., & Levin, M. J. (1993). *Asians and Pacific Islanders.* New York: Russell Sage.

Barringer, H. R., Takeuchi, D. T., & Xenos, P. (1990). Education, occupational prestige, and income of Asian Americans. *Sociology of Education, 63*(1), 27–34.

Bartel, A. (1989). Where do the new U.S. immigrants live? *Journal of Labor Economics, 7*(4), 371–391.

Beiser, M. (1995). Migration and health: The mental health of Southeast Asian refugees resetting in Canada. *Migration World Magazine, 23*(5), 34–36.

Belanger, D. (2001). Social justice in education for undocumented families. *Journal of Family Social Work, 6*(4), 61–73.

Best, A. (2000). *Prom night: Youth, schools, and popular culture.* New York: Routledge.

Bhattacharya, G. (2000). The school adjustment of South Asian immigrant children in the United States. *Adolescence, 35*(137), 77.

Bilgé, B., & Aswad, B. W. (1996). Introduction. In B. C. Aswad & B. Bilgé (Eds.), *Family and gender among American Muslims: Issues facing Middle Eastern immigrants and their descendants* (pp. 1–16). Philadelphia: Temple University Press.

Bischoff, H. (2002). *Immigration issues.* London: Greenwood Press.

Bishaw, A., & Iceland, J. (2003). *Poverty: 1999. Census 2000 Brief,* C2KBR-19. Washington, DC: U.S. Bureau of the Census.

Bleakley, H., & Chin, A, (2004). Language skills and earnings: Evidence from childhood immigrants. *The Review of Economics and Statistics, 86*(2), 481–96.

Bloom, D. E., & Brender, A. (1993). Labor and the emerging world economy. *Population Bulletin, 48*(2), 2–40.

Boal, M. (2001, November 22). Muslim students feel the backlash. *Rolling Stone, 882,* 41–43.

Bobb, B. V. (2000). Neither ignorance nor bliss: Race, racism, and West Indian migrant experience. In H. Cordero-Guzmán, R. C. Smith, & R. Grosfoguel (Eds.), *Migration, transnationalization, and race in a changing New York* (pp. 212–239). Philadelphia: Temple University Press.

Bonacich, E. (1973). A theory of middlemen minorities. *American Sociological Review, 38,* 583–594.

Books, S. (2004). *Poverty and schooling in the U.S.: Contexts and consequences.* Mahwah, NJ: Lawrence Erlbaum Associates.

Borman, K. M., & Baber, M. Y. (1998). *Ethnic diversity in communities and schools: Recognizing and building on strengths.* Stamford, CT: Ablex.

Bowles, S., & Gintis, H. (1976). *Schooling in capitalist America: Educational reform and the contradictions of economic life*. New York: Basic Books.

Brittain, C. (2002). *Transnational messages: Experiences of Chinese and Mexican immigrants in American schools*. New York: LFB/Scholarly Publishing LLC.

Brittingham, A., & de la Cruz, G. P. (2005). *We the people of Arab ancestry in the United States. Census 2000 special reports*. Washington, DC: U.S. Census Bureau.

Bryant, J. A. (2004). Tinderbox economics, immigration, and education in a North Carolina town. *Social Education, 68*(6), 414–417.

Bryant, J. A. (2007, Apr. 1). *School-family-community partnerships: Strategies for school counselors working with Caribbean immigrant families*. Retrieved May 1, 2008, from http://www.thefreelibrary.com/School-family-community+partnerships:+strategies+for+school...-a0165235189

Butcher, K. (1994). Black immigrants to the United States: A comparison with native blacks and other immigrants. *Industrial and Labor Relations Review, 47*, 265–284.

Butterfield, S. P. (2004). Challenging American conceptions of race and ethnicity: Second generation West Indian immigrants. *International Journal of Sociology and Social Policy, 24*, 75–102

Cahan, S., & Davis, D. (2001). Age at immigration and scholastic achievement in school-age children: Is there a vulnerable age? *International Migration Review, 35*(2), 587–595.

Camarota, S. A. (2002). Immigrants from the Middle East: A profile of the foreign-born U.S. population from Pakistan to Morocco. *The Journal of Social, Political, and Economic Studies, 27*(3), 315–340.

Caplan, N., Choy, M. H., & Whitmore, J. K. (1991). *Children of the boat people: A study of educational success*. Ann Arbor: University of Michigan Press.

Capps, R. (2001). *Hardship among children of immigrants: Findings from the 1999 National Survey of American Families*. Washington, DC: The Urban Institute.

Capps, R. (2005). *The health and well-being of young children of immigrants*. Washington, DC: The Urban Institute.

Carrasquillo, A. L. (1991). *Hispanic children and youth in the United States*. New York: Garland.

Chan, C. (2007). Breadth versus depth: The treatment of Asian Americans in United States history textbooks. In C. Park, R. Endo, S. Lee, & X. L. Rong (Eds.), *Asian American education: Acculturation, literacy development, and learning* (pp. 131–154). Charlotte, NC: Information Age Publishing.

Chemerinsky, E. (2006). *Civil liberties and the war on terrorism*. Retrieved May 3, 2007, from http://www.washburnlaw.edu/wlj/45-1/articles/chemerinsky-erwin.pdf

Chinchilla, N., Hamilton, N., & Loucky, J. (1993). Central Americans in Los Angeles: An immigrant community in transition. In J. Moore & R. Pinderhughes (Eds.), *In the barrios: Latinos and the underclass debate* (pp. 51–78). New York: Russell Sage.

Chiswick, B. R., & DebBurman, N. (2004). Educational attainment: Analysis by immigrant generation. *Economics of Education Review, 23*(4), 361–379.

Choi, N.G. (2001). *Psychosocial aspects of the Asian-American experience: Diversity within diversity*. New York: The Haworth Press.

Coll, C. G., & Szalacha, L. A. (2004). The multiple contexts of middle childhood. *The Future of Children, 14*(2), 81–98.

Collier, B. P. (1987). Age and rate of acquisition of second language for academic purposes. *TESOL Quarterly, 21*, 617–641.

Collier, V. P. (1995). Acquiring a second language for school. Retrieved May 26, 2006, from http://www.ncela.gwu.edu/pubs/directions/04.htm

Conchas, G. Q. (2006). *The color of success.* New York: Teachers College, Columbia University.

Contreras, R. A. (2002). The impact of immigration policy on education reform. *Education and Urban Society, 34* (2), 134–55.

Cordero-Guzman, H., & Henken, T. (2005). Immigration. In S. Oboler, & D. J. Gonzalez (Eds.), *The Oxford encyclopedia of Latinos and Latinas in the United States.* London: Oxford University Press, Inc. (e-reference edition). Oxford University Press. University of North Carolina–Chapel Hill. Retrieved February 1, 2008, from http://www.oxford-latinos.com/entry?entry=t199.e413

Cornbleth, C., & Waugh, D. (1995). *The great speckled bird: Multicultural politics and education policymaking.* New York: St. Martin's Press.

Cortina, R., & Gendreau, M. (Eds.). (2003). *Immigrants and schooling: Mexicans in New York.* New York: Center for Migration Studies.

Crandall, J. (1998). New frontiers in education policy and program development: The challenge of the underschooled immigrant secondary students. *Educational Policy, 12*(6), 719–734.

Crawford, J. (1991). *Bilingual education: History, politics, theory and practice.* Los Angeles, CA: Bilingual Educational Services.

Crawford, J. (2000). *At war with diversity: U.S. language policy in an age of anxiety.* Tonawanda, NY: Multilingual Matters Ltd.

Crawford, J. (2006). *Making sense of Census 2000.* Retrieved May 15, 2007, from http://su.edu/educepsl/LPRU/features/article5.htm

Crowder, K. (1999). Residential segregation of West Indians in the New York New Jersey metropolitan area: The roles of race and ethnicity. *International Migration Review, 33*(1), 79–113.

Cubberley, E. P. (1909). *Changing conceptions of education.* New York: Houghton-Mifflin.

Cummings, J. (1989). *Empowering minority students.* Sacramento, CA: California Association for Bilingual Education.

CYFD (Children, Youth and Family Department, New Mexico State). (2007). What is working with undocumented and mixed status immigrant children and families. Retrieved August 17, 2008, from: http://www.cyfd.org/bestpractices/Best_Practices_Bulletin-Working_with_Immigrant_Families.pdf

D'Agostino, M. (2003). Muslim personhood: Translation, transnationalism, and Islamic religious education among Muslims in New York City. *Journal of Muslim Minority Affairs, 23*(2), 285–294.

Daniels, R. (2002). *Coming to America: A history of immigration and ethnicity in American life.* New York: Perennial.

Davis, M. P. (1990). *Mexican voices/American dreams: An oral history of Mexican immigration to the United States.* New York: Henry Holt.

Day, J.C. & Newburger, E.C. (2002). The value of a college degree. ED470038. Retrieved August 10, 2007, from http://www.ericdigests.org/2003-3/value.htm

DeWind, J. (1990). Alien justice: The exclusion of Haitian refugees. *Journal of Social Issues, 46*(1), 121–32.

DeWind, J., & Kasinitz, P. (1997). Everything old is new again? Process and theories of immigrant incorporation. *International Migration Review, 31*(4), 1096–121.

Diamba, Y. (1999). African immigrants in the United States: A socio-demographic profile in comparison to native Blacks. *Journal of Asian and African Studies, 34*(2), 210–15.

DiCerbo, P.A. (2000). *Framing effective practice: topics and issues in educating English language learners.* Retrieved May 10, 2007 from http://www.ncela. gwu.edu/pubs/tasynthesis/framing/framing.pdf

Dodoo, F. N. (1997). Among Africans in America. *Social Force, 76*(2), 527–546.

Dworkin, A. G., & Dworkin, R. J. (1999). *The minority report: An introduction to racial, ethnic, and gender relations* (3rd ed.). Fort Worth, TX: Harcourt Brace.

Ehrlich, A. (2003). *Learning through transition: Creating a health education program for African immigrant adults in the Bay area.* Unpublished monograph, Stanford University. Retrieved March 2, 2007, from http://www.stanford.edu/dept/ SUSE/ICE/monographs/Ehrlich.pdf

Espitia, M. (2004). The other "other Hispanics": South American-origin Latinos in the United States. In D. G. Gutierrez (Ed.), *The Columbia history of Latinos in the United States since 1960* (pp. 257–280). New York: Columbia University Press.

Fahlman, L. (1983). Culture conflict in the classroom: An Edmonton survey. In E. H. Waugh, B. Abu-Laban, & R.B. Qureshi (Eds.), *The Muslim community in North American* (pp. 202–211). Alberta: University of Alberta Press.

Farley, R., & Walter, R. A. (1989). *The color line and the quality of life in America.* Oxford, UK: Oxford University Press.

Farrell, J. J. (1980). *The immigrant and the school in New York City.* New York: Arno.

Feliciano, C. (2001). The benefits of biculturalism: Exposure to immigrant culture and dropout of school among Asian and Latino youths. *Social Science Quarterly, 82*(4), 865.

Fernandez-Kelly, P., & Curran, S. (2001). Nicaraguans: Voices lost, voices found. In R.G. Rumbaut and A. Portes (Eds.), *Ethnicities: Children of immigrants in America* (pp. 127–156). Berkeley, CA: University of California Press.

Ferris, E. G. (1987). *The Central American refugees.* New York: Praeger.

Fix, M., Zimmermann, W., & Passel, J. (2001). *The integration of immigrant families in the United States.* Washington, DC: The Urban Institute.

Foner, N. (1987). The Jamaicans: Race and ethnicity among migrants in New York City. In N. Foner (Ed.), *New immigrants in New York City* (pp. 131–158). New York: Columbia University Press.

Foner, N. (2001). *Islands in the city: West Indian migration to New York.* New York: New York University Press.

Fordham, S. (1988). Racelessness as a factor in black students' school success: Pragmatic strategy or pyrrhic victory. *Harvard Education Review, 58*(1), 54–84.

Fordham, S. (1996). *Blacked out: Dilemmas of race, identity, and success at Capital High.* Chicago: University of Chicago Press.

Freedman, S. G. (2004). Behind top student's heartbreak, illegal immigrants' nightmare. *New York Times, 153*(52935): B.

Fuligni, A. J., & Hardway, C. (2004). Preparing diverse adolescents for the transition to adulthood. *The Future of Children, 14*(2), 99–120.

Galen, J. V. (2007). Introduction. In J.V. Galen & G. Noblit (Eds.), *Late to class: Social class and schooling in the new economy* (pp. 1–18). Albany, NY: State University of New York Press.

Galster, G. C., Metzger, K., & Waite, R. (1999). Neighborhood opportunity structures of immigrant populations, 1980 and 1990. *Housing Policy Debate, 10*(2), 395–441.

Garcia, E. E. (2001). *Hispanic education in the United States*. Lanham, MD: Rowman & Littlefield.

Garcia, R. J. (1995). Critical race theory and proposition 187: The racial politics of immigration law. *Chicano–Latino Law Review, 17*, 118–154.

Gardner, R. W., Robey, B., & Smith, P. C. (1985). Asian Americans: Growth, change, and diversity. *Population Bulletin, 40*(4), 3-43.

Genesee, F., & Nicoladis, E. (1995). Language development in bilingual preschool children. In E. E. Garcia, & B. McLaughlin (Eds.), with B. Spokek, & O. N. Saracho, *Yearbook in meeting the challenge of linguistic and cultural diversity in early childhood education, 6* (pp. 18–33). New York City, NY: Teachers College Press.

Genesee, F., Paradis, J., & Crago, M. B. (2004). *Dual language development and disorders: A handbook on bilingualism and second language learning*. Baltimore, MD: Brookes.

Gibson, M. A. (1988). *Accommodation without assimilation: Punjabi Sikh immigrants in American high schools and community*. Ithaca, NY: Cornell University Press.

Gibson, M. A. (1991). Ethnicity, gender and social class: The school adaptation patterns of West Indian youths. In M. A. Gibson & J. U. Ogbu (Eds.), *Minority status and schooling: A comparative study of immigrant and involuntary minorities* (pp. 169–203). New York: Garland.

Gibson, M. A. (1995). Additive acculturation as a strategy for school. In R. G. Rumbaut & W. A. Cornelius (Eds), *California's immigrant children* (pp. 77–106). San Diego, CA: Center for U.S.-Mexican Studies.

Gibson, M. A. (1998). Promoting academic success among immigrant students: Is acculturation the issue? *Educational Policy, 12*(6), 615.

Gibson, M. A. (2002). The new Latino diaspora and educational policy. In S. Wortham, E. G. Murrillo, and E. T. Hamann (Eds.), *Education in the New Latino Diaspora*, (pp. 241–262). Westport, CT: Ablex Publishing.

Gilmore, J. (2000). *Faces of the Caribbean*. New York: Russell Press.

Glazer, N. (1977). Jewish Americans. In M.J. Gold, C. A. Grant, & H.N. Rivlen (Eds.), *In praise of diversity: A resource book for multicultural education* (pp. 163–175). Washington, DC: Teacher Corps, Association of Teacher Educators.

Glazer, N. (2002). The emergence of an American ethnic pattern. In R. Takaki (Ed.), *Debating diversity* (pp. 39–54). New York: Oxford University Press.

Gonzalez, A. (2003). The education and wages of immigrant children: The impact of age at arrival. *Economics of Education Review, 22*(2), 203.

Gonzalez, J. M., & Darling-Hammond, L. (1997). New concepts for new challenges: Professional development for teachers of immigrant youth. Topics in

Immigrant Education 2. Washington, DC: Center for Applied Linguistics. ERIC421018

Goodwin, A. L., Genishi, C., Asher, N., & Woo, K. A. (2005). Voices from the margins: Asian American teachers' experiences in the profession. In C. C. Park, R. Endo, & A. L. Goodwin (Eds.), *Asian and Pacific American Education* (pp. 99–120). Greenwich, CT: Information Age Publishing.

Gordon, M. M. (1964). *Assimilation in American life: The role of race, religion and national origins*. New York: Oxford University Press.

Goyette, K., & Xie, Y. (1999). Educational expectations of Asian American youths: Determinants and ethnic differences. *Sociology of Education, 72*(1), 22–36.

Grant, L., & Rong, X. L. (1999). Gender, immigrant generation, ethnicity and the schooling progress of youth. *Journal of Research and Development in Education, 33*(1), 15–26.

Grant, L., & Rong, X. L. (2002). Gender inequality. In D. L. Levinson, P. W. Cookson, Jr., & A. Sadovnik (Eds.), *Education and sociology: An encyclopedia* (pp. 289–295). New York: RoutledgeFalmer.

Guerrero, M. D. (2004). Acquiring academic English in one year: An unlikely proposition for English language learners. *Urban Education, 39*(2), 172–199.

Guthrie, L., & Guthrie, G. (2000). *Longitudinal research on AVID 1999-2000: Final report*. Burlingame, CA: Center for Research Evaluation and Training in Education.

Gutierrez. D. G. (Ed.). (2004). *The Columbia history of Latinos in the United States since 1960*. New York: Columbia University Press.

Haddid, Y. (2005). Practicing Islam in America. In J. Schur (Ed.), *The Arabs* (pp. 81–90). New York: Thomson & Gale.

Handlin, O. (1951). *The uprooted*. New York: Grosset & Dunlap.

Harris, M. (1999). *Theories of culture in postmodern times*. Walnut Creek, CA: Altamira Press.

Harwood, E. (1986, September). American public opinion and U.S. immigration policy. *Annals of the American Academy of Political and Social Science, 487*, 201–212.

Hawkins, M. (2004). *Language learning and teacher education*. Buffalo: Multilingual Matters Ltd.

Haynes, C. (1998). Muslim students' needs in public schools. *Update on Law-Related Education, 22*(1), 17–21.

Heath, S. B. (1986). Sociocultural contexts of language development. In *Beyond language: Social and cultural factors in schooling language minority students* (pp. 143–186). Sacramento, CA: State Department of Education, Bilingual Education Office.

Heath, S. B., & McLaughlin, M. W. (Eds.). (1993*). Identity and inner-city youth: Beyond ethnicity and gender*. New York: Teachers College Press.

Hernandez, D. J., & Charley, E. (Eds.). (1998). *From generation to generation: The health and wellbeing of children in immigrant families*. Washington, DC: The National Academy of Science Press.

Higman, B. W. (1997). Introduction. In B. W. Higman (Ed.), *General history of the Caribbean*. London: Unesco Pub.: Macmillan Education.

Hirschman, C., & Wong, M. (1986). The extraordinary educational attainment of Asian Americans: A search for historical evidence and explanations. *Social Forces, 65*(1), 1–27.

HMP (Hemispheric Migration Project), & CSUCA (Consejo Superior Universitario Centroamericano, Secretaria General). (1989). *Central American refugees.* Washington, DC: Georgetown University, Center for Immigration Policy and Refugee Assistance.

Holtz-Eakin, D. (2004). *A description of the immigrant population.* Retrieved June 20, 2006, from http://www.cbo.gov/sjpwdpc.cfm?index=6019&sequence=0

Hondagneu-Sotelo, P. (2004). Gender and the Latino experience in late-twentieth-century America. In D. G. Gutierrez (Ed.), *The Columbia history of Latinos in the United States since 1960* (pp. 281–302). NYC, New York: Columbia University Press.

Hondagneu-Sotelo, P. & Avila, E. (2000). "I'm here, but I am there": The meanings of Latina transnational motherhood. In K. Willis & B. Yeoh (Eds.) *Gender and Migration* (331–356). Northampton, MA: An Elgar Reference Collection.

Hook, J. V. (2003). *Poverty grows among children of immigrants in US.* Retrieved June 7, 2006, from http://www.migrationinformation.org/feature/display.cfm?ID=188 http://www.esri.com/library/whitepapers/pdfs/trends-in-multiracial-population.pdf

Howe, I. (1980). *World of our fathers.* New York: Bantam.

Hsia, J. (1988). *Asian Americans in higher education and at work.* Hillsdale, NJ: Lawrence Erlbaum.

Huntington, S. (2004). *Who are we?: The challenges to America's national identity.* New York: Simon & Schuster.

InFocus. (2005). Children in immigrant families. Retrieved July 22, 2006, from The Center for Health and Health Care in School, http://www.healthinschools.org/News-Room/InFocus/2005/Issue-1.aspx

James, T. (1987). *Exile within: The schooling of Japanese Americans 1942–1945.* Cambridge, MA: Harvard University Press.

Jargowsky, P.A. (1997). *Poverty and place: Ghettos, barrios, and the American city.* New York: Russell Sage Foundation.

Jasso, G., & Rosenzweig, M. R. (1990). *The new chosen people: Immigrants to the United States.* New York: Russell Sage.

Jayakody, R., & Chatters, L. M. (1997). Differences among African American single mothers. In R. J. Taylor, J. S. Jackson, & L. M. Chatters (Eds.), *Family life in Black America* (pp. 167–184). Thousand Oaks, CA: Sage Publications.

Jaynes, G. D. (Ed.). (2000). *Immigration and race: New challenges for American democracy.* New Haven, CT: Yale University Press.

Jencks, C., Smith, M., Acland, H., Bane, M. J., Cohen, D., Gintis, H., Heyns, B., & Michelson, S. (1972). *Inequality: A reassessment of the effect of family and schooling in America.* New York: Basic Books.

Jiobu, R. M. (1988). *Ethnicity and assimilation.* Albany, NY: State University Press of New York.

Jo, J. (2004). Neglected voices in the multicultural America: Asian American racial politics and its implication for multicultural education. *Multicultural Perspectives, 6*(1), 19–25.

Jo, J., & Rong, X. L. (2003). Historical struggles for equity: Politics of education and language policies and its implication for Asian Americans. In R Hunter & F. Brown (Eds.), *Challenges of urban education and efficacy of school reform* (pp. 25–48). London: Elsevier.

John Harvard's Journal. (2004, September-October). "Roots" and race. *John Harvard's Journal, 107*(1), 69.

Johnson, J. H., Jr., Farrell, W.C., Jr., & Guinn, C. (1997). Immigration reform and the browning of America: Tensions, conflicts and community instability in metropolitan Los Angeles. *International Migration Review, 31*(4), 1055–1095.

Johnson, X. (2001, August). *Immigration spreads throughout nation.* The Wall Street Journal-Reis.com, 2001. Retrieved June 30, 2006, from http://www.joel kotkin.com/Demographics/WSJ%20Immigration%20Spreads%20Throughout %20Nation.htm

Kalmijn, M. (1996). The socioeconomic assimilation of Caribbean American Blacks. *Social Forces, 74*, 911–930.

Kao, G., & Tienda, M. (1995). Optimism and achievement: the educational performance of immigrant youth. *Social Science Quarterly, 76*(1), 1–19.

Kasinitz, P. (1992). *Caribbean New York: Black immigrants and the politics of race.* Ithaca, NY: Cornell University Press.

Kasinitz, P., Battle, J., & Miyares, I. (2001). Fade to Black? The children of West Indian immigrants in Southern Florida. In R.G. Rumbaut and A. Portes (Eds.), *Ethnicities: Children of immigrants in America* (pp. 267–300). Berkeley, CA: University of California Press.

Kasinitz, P., Mollenkopf, J., & Waters, M. C. (2002). Becoming America/becoming New Yorkers: Immigrant incorporation in a majority minority city. *International Migration Review, 36*(4), 1020–1036.

Katz, S. R. (1999). Teaching in tensions: Latino immigrant youth, their teachers, and structures of schooling. *Teachers College Record, 100*(4), 809–840.

Kaufman, J. (2004). The interplay between social and cultural determinants of school effort and success: An investigation of Chinese-immigrant and second-generation Chinese students' perceptions toward school. *Social Science Quarterly, 85*(5), 1275–1298.

Kaufmann, K. M., & Lay, J. C. (2004). Commentary three. *The Future of Children, 14*(2), 150–154.

Kayyali, R. A. (2006). *The Arab Americans.* Westport, CT: Greenwood Press.

Kenan, S. (2005). Reconsidering peace and multicultural education after 9/11: The case of educational outreach for Muslim sensitivity curriculum in New York City. *Educational Sciences: Theory & Practice, 5*(1), 172–180.

Kent, M. M., Pollard, K. M., Haaga, J., & Mather, M. (2001). First glimpses from the 2000 U.S. Census. *Population Bulletin, 56*(2).

Kiang, P. N., & Kaplan, J. (1994). Where do we stand? Views of racial conflict by Vietnamese American high-school students in a Black and White context. *Urban Review, 26*(20), 95–119.

Kim, E. Y. (1993). Career choice among second-generation Korean-Americans: Reflections of a cultural model of success. *Anthropology and Education Quarterly, 24*, 224–248.

Kim, H. (1997). *Diversity among Asian American high school students*. (ERIC Document Reproduction Service, No. ED408388)

Kim, H., Rendon, L., & Valadez, J. (1998). Student characteristics, school characteristics, and educational aspirations of six Asian American ethnic groups. *Journal of Multicultural Counseling & Development, 26*(3), 166–176.

Kitano, H. (1976). *Japanese Americans: The evolution of a subculture*. Englewood Cliffs, NJ: Prentice Hall.

Kitano, H. H. (2001). Asian Americans in the twentieth century. In N. G. Choi (Ed.), *Psychosocial aspects* (pp. 7–18). New York: The Haworth Press, Inc.

Kitano, H., & Daniels, R. (2005). *Asian Americans: Emerging minorities* (4th ed.). Upper Saddle River, NJ: Prentice Hall.

Knight, F. W. (1997). Race, ethnicity and class in Caribbean history. In B. W. Higman (Ed.), *General history of the Caribbean* (Vol, VI, pp. 200–252). Paris, France: UNESCO Press.

Krashen, S. (1999, May 6). *Bilingual education: Arguments for and (bogus) arguments against*. Paper presented at the Georgetown University Roundtable on Language and Linguistics. Georgetown: Washington, D.C.

Kubota, R. (2004). Toward critical contrastive rhetoric. *Journal of Second Language Writing, 13*(1), 7–27.

Kuhn, D. (2006). Does the Asian success formula have a downside? *Education Week, 25*(26), 29.

Lee, E. (1966). A theory of migration. *Demography, 3*(1), 47–57.

Lee, E., & Rong, X. L. (1988). The educational and economic achievement of Asian-Americans. *Elementary School Journal, 88*, 545–560.

Lee, F. R. (2002, November 30). Why are black students lagging? *The New York Times*. Retrieved July 2, 2008, from http://www.racematter.org?whyareblack studentslaggin.htm

Lee, R. G. (2000). Fu Manchu lives! Asian Pacific Americans as permanent aliens in American culture. In P. M. Ong (Ed.), *Transforming race relations* (pp. 159–187). Los Angeles: UNLA Asian American Studies Center.

Lee, S. (1996). *Unraveling the model minority stereotype: Listening to Asian American youth*. New York: Teachers College Press.

Lee, S. (2001). More than "model minorities" or "delinquents": A look at Hmong American high school students. *Harvard Educational Review, 71*(3), 505–528.

Lee, S. (2005). *Up against Whiteness: Race, school, and immigrant youth*. New York: Teachers College.

Lee, S. & Kumashiro, K. K. (2005). *A report on the status of Asian American and Pacific Islanders in education: Beyond the "model minority" stereotype*. Washington, DC: National Education Association.

Lenneberg, E. H. (1967). *Biological foundations of language*. New York: Wiley

Lessow-Hurley, J. (2003). *Meeting the needs of second language learners*. Alexandria, VA: Association for Supervision & Curriculum Development.

Lew, J. (2006). *Asian Americans in class: Charting the achievement gap among Korean American youth*. New York: Teacher College Press.

Lewis, B. (1998). *The multiple identities of the Middle East*. New York: Schocken Books.

Li, G. (2003). Literacy, culture, and politics of schooling: Counternarratives of a Chinese Canadian family. *Anthropology & Education Quarterly, 34*(2), 182–204.

Li, G. (2007). Home environment and second-language acquisition: The importance of family capital. *British Journal of Sociology of Education, 28*(3), 285–299.

Li, J. (2001). Expectations of Chinese immigrant parents for their children's education: The interplay of Chinese tradition and the Canadian context. *Canadian Journal of Education, 26*(4), 477–494.

Li, J. (2003). Affordances and constraints of immigrant Chinese parental expectations on children's school performance. *Alberta Journal of Educational Research, 49*(2), 198–200.

Li, J. (2004). Parental expectations of Chinese immigrants: A folk theory about children's school achievement. *Race, Ethnicity, and Education, 7*(2), 167–183.

Lieberson, S. (1980). *A piece of the pie: Black and White immigrants since 1880*. Berkeley: University Press.

Lindhom-Leary, K. (2001). *Dual language education*. Buffalo, NY: Multilingual Matters.

Lingxin, H., & Bonstead-Bruns, M. (1998). Parent-child differences in educational expectations and the academic achievement of immigrant and native students. *Sociology of Education, 71*(3), 175–198.

Lobo, A. P. (2001). U.S. diversity visas are attracting Africa's best and brightest. *Population Today, 29*(5), 1–2.

Logan, J. (2001). *From many shores: Asian in Census 2000*. Albany, NY: Lewis Mumford Center for Comparative Urban and Regional Research.

Logan, J. (2003). *America's newcomers*. Albany, NY: Lewis Mumford Center for Comparative Urban and Regional Research.

Logan, J. (2004). *Resegregation in American public schools? Not in the 1990s*. Albany, NY: Lewis Mumford Center for Comparative Urban and Regional Research.

Logan, J., & Deane, G. (2003). *Black diversity in metropolitan America*. Albany, NY: Lewis Mumford Center for Comparative Urban and Regional Research.

Logan, J., Alba R. D., & Zhang, W. (2002). Immigrant enclaves and ethnic communities in New York and Los Angeles. *American Sociological Review, 67*, 299–322.

Lopez, G. R. (2001). The value of hard work: Lessons on parent involvement from an (im)migrant household. *Harvard Educational Review, 71*(3), 416–437.

Lopez, N. (2002). Race-gender experiences and schooling: Second-generation Dominican, West Indian, and Haitian youth in New York City. *Race, Ethnicity and Education, 5*(1), 67–89.

Lopez, N. (2003). *Hopeful girls, troubled boys: Race and gender disparity in urban education*. New York: Routledge.

Losen, D. J., & Orfield, G. (2002). *Racial inequity in special education*. Cambridge, MA: Harvard Education Press.

Louie, V. S. (2001). Parents' aspirations and investment: The role of social class in the educational experiences of 1.5- and second-generation Chinese Americans. *Harvard Educational Review, 71*(3), 438–474.

Louie, V. S. (2004). *Compelled to excel*. Stanford, CA: Stanford University Press.

Lucas, T. (1997). Into, through, and beyond secondary school: Critical transitions for immigrant youths. Topics in immigrant education 1. ED421017. Retrieved May 31, 2007, from http://search.ebscohost.com/login.aspx?direct=true&db=eric&AN=ED421017&site=ehost-live

Lys, D. (2007). *Dropout risk factors predicting Hispanic eighth grade students' self-perceived possibility of graduation from high school*. Unpublished Doctoral Dissertation, retrieved January 23, 2008, from http://proquest.umi.com/pqdweb?index =0&did=1320941051&SrchMode=2&sid=1&Fmt=2&VInst=PROD&VType=P QD&RQT=309&VName=PQD&TS=1212791669&clientId=15094

Ma, W. (2007). Dialoging internally: Participatory learning in a graduate seminar. In C, Park, R. Endo, S. Lee, & X. L. Rong (Eds.), *Asian American education: Acculturation, literacy development, and learning* (pp. 167–196). Charlotte, NC: Information Age Publishing.

Macias, R. F. (1993). Language and ethnic classification of language minorities: Chicano and Latino students in the 1990s. *Hispanic Journal of Behavioral Sciences, 15,* 230–57.

Martin, P., & Midgley, E. (1994). Immigration to the United States: Journey to an uncertain destination. *Population Bulletin, 49*(2).

Martin, P., & Midgley, E. (2003). Immigration: Shaping and reshaping America. *Population Bulletin, 58*(2).

Martin, P., & Midgley, E. (2006). Immigration: Shaping and reshaping America. *Population Bulletin, 61*(4).

Martin, P., & Widgren, J. (1996). International migration: A global challenge. *Population Bulletin, 51*(1), 2–47.

Martin, P., & Widgren, J. (2002). International Migration: Facing the challenge. *Population Bulletin, 57*(1).

Massey, D. S. (1993). Theories of international migration: A review and appraisal. *Population and Development Review, 19*(3), 431–466.

Matthijs, K. (1996). The socioeconomic assimilation of Caribbean American blacks. *Social Forces, 74*(3), 911-930.

McClellan, B. E. (1999). *Moral education in America: Schools and the shaping of character from colonial times to the present.* New York: Teachers College Press.

McDaniel, A. (1995). The dynamic racial composition of the United States. *Daedalus, 124*(1), 179–198.

McDonnell, L. M., & Hill, P. R. (1993). *Newcomers in American schools: Meeting the educational needs of immigrant youth.* Santa Monica, CA: RAND.

McNeil, L. M. (2005). Faking equity: High-states testing and the education of Latino youth. In A. Valenzuela (Ed.), *Leaving children behind: How "Texas-style" accountability fails Latino youth* (pp. 57–112). Albany, NY: State University of New York Press.

Melville, B. M. (1985). Salvadorans and Guatemalans. In D. W. Haines (Ed.), *Refugees in the United States: A reference handbook* (pp. 167–180). London: Greenwood.

Merchant, B. (2000). Education and changing demographics. In B. A. Jones (Eds.), *Educational leadership* (pp. 82–90). Stamford, CT: Ablex Publishing Corporation.

Midobuche, E. (2001). More than empty footprints in the sand: Educating immigrant children. *Harvard Educational Review, 71*(3), 529–535.

Mitchell, N. (2005). Academic achievement among Caribbean immigrant adolescents: The impact of generational status on academic self-concept. *Professional School Counseling, 8*(3), 209–218.

Model, S. (1991). Caribbean immigrants: A black success story? *International Migration Review, 24,* 248–276.

Moll, L. C., & Gonzales, N. (2004). Engaging life: A funds of knowledge approach to multicultural education. In J. A. Banks & C. M. Banks (Eds.), *Handbook of research on multicultural education* (2nd ed.) (pp. 699–715). San Francisco: Jossey-Bass.

Montero-Sieburth, M., & LaCelle-Peterson, M. (1991). Immigration and schooling: An ethnohistorical account of policy and family perspectives in an urban community. *Anthropology and Education Quarterly, 22*, 300–325.

Mueller, R. (2004, October). *Restricted immigration of foreign students to the United States in the post 9/11 period: Is the US loss a gain for Canada?* Paper presented at the CNS-ACSUS in Canada colloquium, Vancouver, Canada.

Muller, T. (1994, Feb. 9). Exploring the facts about immigration. *The Chronicle of Higher Education*, p. B1–B2.

Nagel, C. (2005). Introduction. In G. W. Falah & C. Nagel (Eds.), *Geographies of Muslim women: Gender, religion, and space* (pp. 1–15). New York: Guilford Press.

Nakanishi, D. T. (1995). Growth and Diversity: Introduction. In D. T. Nakanishi & T.B. Nishida (Eds.), *The Education of Asian/Pacific Americans* (pp. Xi-XX). New York: Routledge

Nakanishi, D. T., & Nishida, T. V. (Eds.) (1995). *The Asian American educational experience: A source book for teachers and students*. New York: Routledge.

Nappi, H., Harritt, C., Rong, X. L., Chang, I., Hayes, R., Jung, Y., Jackson, J., & Clark, T. (1999, November). How social studies teachers help Hispanic immigrants students succeed? Paper presented to the 1999 Annual Meeting of National Council for Social Studies, Orlando, FL.

National Center for Educational Statistics. (2005). *Education statistics quarterly, 6*(3). Washington, DC: U.S. Department of Education.

National Center for Educational Statistics. (2006). Concentration of enrollment by race/ethnicity and poverty, in *Condition of education, 2005*. Retrieved July 5, 2007, from http://nces.ed.gov/programs/coe/2006/section1/table.asp?tableID=440

National Center for Education Statistics. (2007). *2003 -2004 School and Staff Survey*. Retrieved October 4, 2007, from http://nces.ed.gov

NCELA. (2006). *Ask an expert*. Retrieved October 23, 2006, from National Clearinghouse for English Language Acquisition and Language Instruction Educational Programs Web site: http://www.ncela.gwu.edu

Neckerman, K. M., Carter, P., & Lee, J. (1999). Segmented assimilation and minority cultures of mobility. *Ethnic and Racial Studies, 22*(5), 945–965.

Neff, A. (2005). The Americanization of the first generation. In J. Schur (Ed.), *The Arabs* (pp. 64–74). New York: Thomson & Gale.

Neightingale, D. S., & Fix, M. (2004). Economic and labor market trends. *The Future of Children, 14*(2), 49–60.

Nevins, J. (2005). Deportations of Mexican-origin people in the United States. In S. Oboler & D. J. Gonzalez (Eds.), *The Oxford encyclopedia of Latinos and Latinas in the United States*. (e-reference edition). London: Oxford University Press. Retrieved February 1, 2008, from http://www.oxfordlatinos.com/entry?entry=t199.e228

Newport, E. L. (2002). Critical periods in language development. In L. Nadel (Ed.), *Encyclopedia of cognitive science*. London: Macmillan Publishers Ltd./Nature Publishing Group.

Ng, F. (1995). *The Asian American encyclopedia*. New York: Marshall Cavendish.

Nieto, S. (1995). From brown heroes and holidays to assimilationist agendas: Reconsidering the critiques of multicultural education. In C. E. Sleeter & P. L. Mclaren (Eds.), *Multicultural education, critical pedagogy, and politics of difference* (pp.191–220). Albany, NY: SUNY Press.

Nieto, S. (2000). *Affirming diversity: The sociopolitical context of multicultural education* (3rd ed.). New York: Longman.

Noguera, P. (2005). It takes more than pressure to help struggling schools. *Teachers College Record*. Retrieved May 16, 2005, from http://www.tcrecord.org

Northwest Regional Educational Laboratory. (2001). *The immigrant experience*. Retrieved June 20, 2007, from http://www.nwrel.org/cnorse/booklets/immigration/4.html

Novelli, W. D., & Goyer, A. (2004). Commentary four. *The future of children, 14*(2), 155–159.

Oboler, S., & Gonzalez, D. J. (2005). *The Oxford encyclopedia of Latinos and Latinas in the United States*. London, England: Oxford University Press.

O'Connell, J. A. (1987). Enhancing educational opportunities for Hispanic women. *The Journal of College Admission*, 116, 20–25.

Ogbu, J. U. (1978). *Minority education and caste: The American system in cross-cultural perspective*. New York: Academic Press.

Ogbu, J. (1987). Variability in minority school performance: A problem in search of an explanation. *Anthropology & Education Quarterly, 18*, 313–334.

Ogbu, J. (1991). Low school performance as an adaptation: The case of blacks in Stockton, California. In M. A. Gibson & Ogbu. J. U. (Eds.), *Minority status and schooling: A comparative study of immigrant and involuntary minorities* (pp. 249–286). New York: Garland.

Ogbu, J. (1994). Racial stratification and education in the United States: Why inequality persists. *Teacher College Record, 92*(2), 264–298.

Ogbu, J. (1999). Beyond language: Ebonics, proper English, and identity in a Black-American speech community. *American Educational Research Journal, 36*(2), 147–184.

Okutsu, J. K. (1989). Pedagogic hegemonicide and the Asian American student. *Amerasia, 15*(1), 233–242.

Olsen, L. (1997). *Made in America: Immigrant students in our public schools*. New York: The New Press.

Omi, M., & Winant, H. (1994). *Racial formation in the United States: From the 1960s to the 1990s* (2nd ed.). New York: Routledge.

Orellana, M. F. (2001). The work kids do: Mexican and Central American immigrant children's contributions to households and schools in California. *Harvard Educational Review, 71*(3), 366–389.

Orfield, G., & Yun, J. T. (1999). *Resegregation in American schools: The Civil Rights Project*. Cambridge, MA: Harvard University. Retrieved June 23, 2007, from http://www.law.harvard.edu/civilrights

Orgocka, A. (2004). Perceptions of communication and education about sexuality among Muslim immigrant girls in the U.S. *Sex Education, 4*(3), 255–271.

Ovando, C.J., & Collier, V.P. (1998). *Bilingual and ESL classrooms: Teaching in multicultural context* (2nd ed.). Boston, MA: McGraw-Hill.

Padilla, A. M., & Gonzalez, R. (2001). Academic performance of immigrant and U.S.-born Mexican heritage students: Effects of schooling in Mexico and bilingual/English language instruction. *American Educational Research Journal, 38*(3), 727–742.

Page, S. E. (2007). *The difference: How the power of diversity creates better groups, firms, schools, and societies.* Princeton, NJ: Princeton University Press.

Pak, Y. K. (2002). *Wherever I go, I will always be a loyal American.* New York: RoutledgeFalmer Press.

Pang, V. O., & Cheng, L. L. (1998). *Struggling to be heard: The unmet needs of Asian Pacific American children.* Albany, NY: State University of New York Press.

Park, R. E. (1928). Human migration and the marginal man. *American Journal of Sociology, 33*, 881–893.

Passel, J. S. (2006). *The size and characteristics of the unauthorized migrant population in the U.S. (Washington, DC: Pew Hispanic Center, March 7, 2006).* Retrieved Jan 3, 2008, from http: //www.pewhispanic.org

Passel, J. S., & Suro, R. (2005). *Rise, peak, and decline: Trends in U.S. immigration 1992–2004.* Washington, DC: Pew Hispanic Center.

Pedraza, S. (1990). Immigration research: A conceptual map. *Social Science History, 14*(1), 43–67.

Pedraza, S. (1991). Women and migration: The social consequences of gender. *Annual Review of Sociology, 17*, 303–325.

Pedraza-Bailey, S. (1985). Cuba's Exiles: Portrait of a refugee migration *International Migration Review, 19*(1), 4–34.

Peng, S. S., & Wright, D. (1994). Explanation of academic achievement of Asian American students. *Journal of Educational Research, 87*(6), 346–352.

Perez, L. (2001). Growing up in Cuban Miami: Immigration, the enclave, and the new generations. In R. G. Rumbaut and A. Portes (Eds.), *Ethnicities: Children of immigrants in America* (pp. 91–126). Berkeley, CA: University of California Press.

Perez, S. M. (2004). Shaping new possibilities for Latino children and the nation's future. *The Future of Children, 14*(2), 122–133.

Perlmann, J. (2000). Introduction: The persistence of culture versus structure in recent work. In H. Vermeulen & J. Perlmann (Eds.), *Immigrants, schooling and social mobility: Does culture make a difference?* (pp. 22–33). New York: St. Martin's Press.

Perry, M. D. (1999). *Carifuna youth in New York city: Race, ethnicity, and the performance of diasporic identities.* Unpublished master's thesis, University of Texas, Austin, TX.

Perry, T., & Delpit, L. (1998) *The real Ebonics debate: Power, language, and the education of African-American children.* Boston: Beacon Press.

Peshkin, A. (1991). *The color of strangers, the color of friends: The play of ethnicity in school and community.* Chicago: University of Chicago Press.

Pessar, P. R. (1995). *A visa for a dream: Dominicans in the United States.* Boston: Allyn and Bacon.

Pew Hispanic Center (2005). *The new Latino south: The context and consequences of rapid population growth.* Retrieved June 20, 2007, from http://pewhispanic. org/reports/report.php?ReportID=50

Pew Hispanic Center (2006). Hispanic attitudes toward learning English. Retrieved May 1, 2007, from www.pewhispanic.org

Pew Hispanic Center (2007). 2007 National Survey of Latinos: As illegal immigration issue heats up, Hispanics feel a chill. Retrieved January 5, 2008, from http://pewhispanic.org/reports/pring.php?reportID=84

Phelan, P., Davidson, A. L., & Yu, H. C. (1998). *Adolescents' worlds: Negotiating family, peers, and school.* New York: Teachers College Press.

Pierre, J. (2004). Black immigrants in the United States and the "cultural narratives" of ethnicity. *Identities: Global Studies in Culture and Power, 11*, 141–170.

Popova, M. (1999). Chasing the dog's tail. In A. Garrod & J. Davis (Eds.), *Crossing customs: International students write on U.S. college life and culture* (pp. 73–90). New York: Falmer Press.

Portes, A. (1995). Segmented assimilation among new immigrant youth: A conceptual framework. In R. G. Rumbaut & W. A. Cornelius (Eds.), *California's immigrant children* (pp. 71–76). San Diego: Center for U.S.-Mexican Studies.

Portes, A., & Hao, L. (1998). *E Pluribus Unum*: Bilingualism and language loss in the second generation. *Sociology of Education, 71*, 269–294.

Portes, A., & Hao, L. (2002). *The price of uniformity: Language, family, and personality adjustment in the immigrant second generation.* Working paper. Princeton, NJ: Center for migration and development, Princeton University.

Portes, A., & Rumbaut, R. G. (1996). *Immigrant America: A portrait* (2nd ed.). Berkeley, CA: University of California Press.

Portes, A., & Rumbaut, R. G. (2001). *Legacies: The story of the immigrant second generation.* Berkeley, CA: University of California Press.

Portes, A., & Rumbaut, R. G. (2006). *Immigrant America: A portrait* (3rd ed.). Berkeley, CA: University of California Press.

Portes, A., & Zhou, M. (1993). The new second generation: Segmented assimilation and its variants. *Annals of the American Academy of Political and Social Science, 530*, 74–96.

Portes, P. (2005). *Dismantling educational inequality: A cultural-historical approach to closing the achievement gap.* New York: Peter Lang.

Portes, R. P., & Zady, M. F. (2002). Self-esteem in the adaptation of Spanish-speaking adolescents: The role of immigration, family conflict, and depression. *Hispanic Journal of Behavioral Science, 24*, 296–318

Putnam, R. D. (2007). *E Pluribus Unum*: Diversity and community in the twenty-first century. *Scandinavian Political Studies, 30*(2), 137–174.

Ravitch, D. (1974). *The great school wars: A history of the New York City public schools.* New York: Basic Books.

Ray, B. (2002). *Immigrant integration: Building to opportunity.* Washington, DC: Migration Policy Institute.

Ream, R. K. (2005*). Uprooting children: Mobility, social capital, and Mexican American underachievement.* NYC, New York: LFB Scholarly Publishing LLC.

Reardon-Anderson, J., Capps, R., & Fix, M. (2002). *The health and well-being of children in immigrant families. New Federalism (Series B, No. B-52).* Washington, DC: The Urban Institute.

Reeves, T., & Bennett, C. (2004). *We the people: Asians in the United States (Census 2000 special reports, CENSR-17).* Washington, DC: U.S. Bureau of the Census.

Roberts, S. (2005, February 21). More Africans enter U.S. than in days of slavery. *New York Times*. Retrieved June 7, 2007, from http://mumford.albany.edu/census/othersay/02212005NewYorkTimes.pdf

Roderick, T. (2001). *Countering bias against Arab American, Muslim, and South Asian students: Suggestions for educators*. Retrieved January 18, 2008, from http://www.teachablemoment.org/high/counteringbias.html\

Rodriguez, R. (1982). *Hunger of memory: The education of Richard Rodriguez*. New York: Bantam.

Rodriguez, R. (2002). *Brown: The last discovery of America/Richard Rodriguez*. Imprint. New York: Viking, 2002.

Rogers, R. R. (2006). *Afro-Caribbean immigrant and the politics of incorporation: Ethnicity, exception, or exit*. Cambridge, England: Cambridge University Press.

Romo, H. (2005). Immigrant children. In S. Oboler, & D. J. Gonzalez, (Eds.). *The Oxford encyclopedia of Latinos and Latinas in the United States*. London, England: Oxford University Press. (e-reference edition). Oxford University Press. University of North Carolina - Chapel Hill. Retrieved February 1, 2008, http://www.oxford-latinos.com/entry?entry=t199.e411

Rong, X. L. (1988). *Immigration and education in the United States, 1880-1980*. Unpublished doctoral dissertation, University of Georgia, Athens.

Rong, X. L. (1997). Immigrant generation, gender, national origin and schooling attainment among youths of six Asian American groups. Paper presented to the 1997 Annual Meeting of American Educational Research Association, Chicago, April, 1997.

Rong, X. L. (2005a). *Immigration, language, educational attainment, and children's socio-demographic backgrounds*. (Unpublished Manuscript).

Rong, X. L. (2005b). Use sojourner strategies to create transnational social capital among Chinese immigrant children and parents. In C. Park, S. Lee, & L. Goodwin (Eds.) *Asian and Pacific American education: Learning, socialization, and identity*, (pp. 165–191) Greenwich, CT: Information Age Publishing Inc.

Rong, X. L. (2006). Immigration, urban schools and accountability. In F. Brown & R. Hunt (Eds.), *No Child Left Behind and other federal programs for urban school districts* (pp. 321–340). Boston: Elsevier's Production.

Rong, X. L., & Brown, F. (2001). The effects of immigrant generation and ethnicity of educational attainment among young African and Caribbean blacks in the United States. *Harvard Educational Review, 71*(3), 536–565.

Rong, X. L., & Brown, F. (2002). Socialization, culture and identities – educating Black immigrant children: What educators need to know and do. *Education and Urban Society, 34*(2), 247–273.

Rong, X. L., Brown, F., & Guo, X. (1996, April). *The effects of generation of U.S. residence on educational attainment among Black and White youths*. Paper presented at the annual meeting of the American Educational Research Association, New York.

Rong, X. L., & Fitchett, P. (2008). Socialization and identity transformation of Black immigrant youth in the United States: Towards greater understandings and an additive education. *Theories into Practice, 47*(1), 35–42.

Rong, X. L., & Grant, L. (1992). Ethnicity, generation, and school attainment of Asians, Hispanics, and non-Hispanic Whites. *Sociological Quarterly, 33*(4), 625–636.

Rong, X. L., & Grant, L. (1995, August). Schooling attainment of Hispanic youth: Variations by national origin, generation of U.S. residence, and gender. Paper presented at the 1995 annual meeting of American Sociological Association, Washington, DC.

Rong, X. L., & Jo, J. (2002, April). *Hitting in opposite directions? A comparison of the adaptive strategies of Chinese and Jamaican immigrant teens and their families.* Paper presentation at the annual meeting of American Educational Research Association, New Orleans, LA.

Rong, X. L. & Jo, J. (2004). More than a "Comfort Zone": The critical views within the transition and transformation of Chinese language schools in American south. Paper presented to 2004 Annual Meeting of American Educational Research Association, San Diego, April 2004.

Rong, X. L., & Preissle, J. (1997). The continuing decline in Asian American teachers. *American Educational Research Journal, 34*(2), 267–293.

Rong, X. L., & Preissle, J. (1998). *Educating immigrant students: What we need to know to meet the challenges.* Thousand Oaks, CA: Sage-Corwin Press.

Rosenbloom, S. R., & Way, N. (2004). Experiences of discrimination among African American, Asian American, and Latino adolescents in an urban school. *Youth and Society 35*(4), 420–451.

Rossell, C. H., & Baker, K. (1996). *Bilingual education in Massachusetts: The emperor has no clothes.* Boston: Pioneer Institute for Public Policy.

Roudi-Fahimi, F., & Kent, M. M. (2007, June). Challenges and opportunities—The population of the Middle East and North Africa. *Population Bulletin, 62*(2), 1–20.

Rubinstein-Avila, E. (2007). From the Dominican Republic to Drew High: What counts as literacy for Yanira Lara? *Reading Research Quarterly, 42*(4), 568–589.

Ruck, M. D., & Wortley, S. (2002). Racial and ethnic minority high school students' perceptions of school disciplinary practices: A look at some Canadian findings. *Journal of Youth and Adolescence, 31*(3), 185–95.

Ruiz-de-Velasco, J., & Fix, M. (2002). Limited English proficient students and high-stakes accountability system. In M. Piche, W. L. Taylor & R. A. Reed (Eds.), *Rights at risk: Equality in an age of terrorism* (pp. 245–261). Washington, DC: Citizens' Commission on Civil Rights.

Rumbaut, R. G. (2005, June-July). *A language graveyard? Immigration, generation, and linguistic acculturation in the United States.* Paper presented at the International Conference on the Integration of Immigrants: Language and Educational Achievement, Social Science Research Center, Berlin, Germany. Retrieved June 23, 2007, from http://jbd.sagepub.com/cgi/reprint/32/1/56

Rumbaut, R. G., & Portes, A. (2001). (Eds.). Introduction-ethnogenesis: Coming of age in immigrant America. In R.G. Rumbaut & A. Portes (Eds.), *Ethnicities: Children of immigrants in America* (pp. 1–19). Berkeley, CA: University of California Press.

Saliba, N. E. (2005). Leaving the Ottoman Empire. In J. Schur (Ed.), *The Arabs* (pp. 28–40). New York: Thomson & Gale.

Sampson, R. J., Squires, G. D., & Zhou, M. (2001). *How neighborhoods matter: The value of investing the local level. Issue Series in Social Research and Social Policy.* Washington, DC: American Sociological Association.

Sarroub, L. K. (2001). The sojourner experience of Yemini American high school students: An ethnographic portrait. *Harvard Educational Review, 71*(3), 390–415.

Sarroub, L. K. (2005). *All-American Yemini girls: Being Muslim in a public school.* Philadelphia: University of Pennsylvania Press.

Schlesinger, A. (2002). The return to the melting pot. In Ronald Takaki (Ed.), *Debating Diversity* (pp. 257–259). New York: Oxford University Press.

Schnaiberg, L. (1999) Immigrants: Providing a lesson in how to adapt. *Education Week, 18*(20), 34–35.

Schur, J. (2005). Introduction. In J. Schur (Ed.), *The Arabs* (pp. 14–26). New York: Thomson & Gale.

Schwartz, W. (1999). Arab American students in public schools. *ERIC Digest*, Number 142. (ERIC Document Reproduction Service No. ED429144).

Shannon, S. M., & Escamilla, K. (1999). Mexican immigrants in U.S. schools: Targets of symbolic violence. *Educational Policy, 13*(3), 347.

Sharabi, H. (2005). A world forever changed—Leaving Palestine. In J. Schur (Ed.), *The Arabs* (pp. 49–55). New York: Thomson & Gale.

Shavarini, M. K. (2004). *Educating immigrants: Experiences of second-generation Iranians.* New York: LFB Scholarly Publishing LLC.

Shields, M., & Behrman, R. (2004). Children of immigrant families: Analysis and recommendations. *The Future of Children, 14*(2), 4–16.

Siemens Foundation. (2007). *2006–07 Siemens Science Competition National Finalists.* Retrieved August 7, 2007, from http://www.siemens-foundation.org/en/competition/2006_winners.htm

Singer, A. (2002, April 2). *America's diversity at the beginning of the 21st century: Reflections from Census 2000.* Brookings Institution. Retrieved June 7, 2006, from http://www.brookings.edu/papers/2002/04immigration_singer.aspx

Skutnabb-Kangas, T. (2000). Linguistic human rights and teachers of English. In J. K. Hall & W. G. Eggington (Eds.), *The sociopolitics of English language teaching* (pp. 22–44). Tonawanda, NY: Multilingual Matters, Ltd.

Smith-Hefner, N. J. (1990). Language and identity in the education of Boston-area Khmer. *Anthropology and Education Quarterly, 21*(3), 250–268.

Smith-Hefner, N. J. (1993). Education, gender, and generational conflict among Khmer refugees. *Anthropology and Education Quarterly, 24*(2), 135–158.

Sowell, T. (1994). *Race and culture: A world view.* New York: Basic Book.

Spindler, G., & Spindler, L. (1990). *The American cultural dialogue and its transmission.* London: Falmer Press.

Stafford, S. B. (1987). Language and identity: Haitians in New York City. In C. R. Sutton & E. M. Chaney (Eds.), *Caribbean life in New York City: Sociocultural dimensions* (pp. 202–217). New York: Center for Migration Studies of New York.

Stanton-Salazar, R. D. (1997). A social capital framework for understanding the socialization of racial minority children and youths. *Harvard Educational Review, 67*, 1–40.

Stepick, A. (1998). *Pride against prejudice: Haitians in the United States.* Boston, MA: Allyn & Bacon.

Stepick, A., Stepick, C. D., Eugene, E., Teed, D., & Labissiere, Y. (2001). Shifting identities and intergenerational conflict: growing up Haitian in Miami. In R.

G. Rumbaut & A. Portes (Eds.), *Ethnicities: Children of immigrants in America* (pp. 229–266). Berkeley, CA: University of California Press.

Stevens, G. (1994). The English language proficiency of immigrants in the U.S. In B. Edmonston & J. S. Passel (Eds.), *Immigration and ethnicity: The adjustment of America's newest immigrants* (pp. 163–185). Washington, DC: Urban Institute.

Stewart, D. W. (1993). *Immigration and education.* New York: Lexington Books.

Stone, S., & Han, M. (2005). Perceived school environments, perceive discrimination, and school performance among children of Mexican immigrants. *Children & Youth Services Review, 27*(1), 51–66.

Suarez-Orozco, C. (2001a). Afterword: Understanding and serving the children of immigrants. *Harvard Educational Review, 71*(3), 579–589.

Suarez-Orozco, C. (2001b). *Children of immigration.* Cambridge, MA: Harvard University Press.

Suarez-Orozco, C. E., & Suarez-Orozco, M. M. (2001). *Children of Immigration.* Cambridge, MA: Harvard University Press.

Suarez-Orozco, M. M. (1989). *Central American refugees and U.S. high schools: A psychosocial study of motivation and achievement.* Stanford: Stanford University Press.

Suarez-Orozco, M. M. (2001). Globalization, immigration, and education: The research agenda. *Harvard Education Review, 71*(3), 345–365.

Suarez-Orozco, M. M., & Suarez-Orozco, C. E. (1995). The cultural patterning of achievement motivation: A comparison of Mexican, Mexican immigrant, Mexican American, and Non-Latino White American students. In R. G. Rumbaur & W. A. Cornelius (Eds.), *California's immigrant children* (pp. 161–190). San Diego, CA: Center for U.S.-Mexican Studies.

Sue, S., & Okazaki, S. (1990). Asian-American educational achievements: A phenomenon in search of an explanation. *American Psychologist, 45*(8), 913–920.

Sung, L. B. (1987). *The adjustment experience of Chinese immigrant children in New York City.* New York: Center for Migration Studies.

Sunshine, C. A., & Warner, K.Q. (Eds.). (1998a). *Caribbean connections: Moving north.* Washington, DC: Network of Educators on the Americas.

Sunshine, C. A., & Warner, K. Q. (1998b). A Primer on Caribbean Migration. In C. Sunshine & K. Warner (Eds.), *Caribbean connections: Moving north* (pp. 2–43). Washington, DC: Network of Educators on the Americas.

Suzuki, B. (1977). Japanese-American experience. In M. J. Gold, C. A. Grant, & H. N. Rivlin (Eds.), *In praise of diversity: A resource book for multicultural education* (pp. 139–162). Washington, DC: Teacher Corps, Association of Teacher Educators.

Swanson, C. B. (2004). Sketching a portrait of public high school graduation: Who graduates? Who Doesn't? In G. Orfield (Ed.), *Dropouts in America: Confronting the graduation rate crisis* (pp. 13–40). Cambridge, MA: Harvard Education Press.

Tabs, E. D. (2003). *Postsecondary attainment, attendance, curriculum, and performance: Selected results from the NELS: 88/2000 postsecondary education transcript study (PETS), 2000.* Retrieved June 4, 2007, from http://nces.ed.gov/pubs 2003/2003394.pdf

Taft, R., & Cahill, D. (1981). Education of immigrants in Australia. In J. Bhatnagar (Ed.), *Educating immigrants* (pp. 16–46). New York: St. Martin's.

Takahashi, J. (1998). *Nisei/Sansei: Shifting Japanese American identities and politics.* Philadelphia, P.A.: Temple University Press.

Takaki, R. (1998). *Strangers from a different shore* (2nd ed.). Boston, MA: Back Bay Books.

Takaki, R. (2002). *Debating diversity.* Oxford: Oxford University Press.

Takanish, R. (2004). Leveling the playing field: Supporting immigrant children from birth to eight. *The Future of Children, 14*(2), 61–80.

Tateishi, J., & Yoshino, W. (2000). *The Japanese American incarceration: The journey to redress.* Retrieved May 11, 2007, from http://www.abanet.org/irr/hr/spring00 humanrights/tateishi.html

Teranishi, R. T. (2004). Yellow and brown: Emerging Asian American immigrant populations and residential segregation. *Equity and Excellence in Education 37*(3), 255-263.

Thomas, W. P., & Collier, V. P. (1997). *School effectiveness for language minority students.* Alexandria, VA: National Clearinghouse for Bilingual Education.

Timimi, S. B. (1995). Adolescence in immigrant Arab families. *Psychotherapy, 32*(1), 141–149.

Torres-Saillant, S., & Hernandez, R. (1998). *The Dominican Americans.* Westport, CT: Greenwood Press.

Trueba, H. T. (1999). *Latinos Unidos.* Lanham, MD: Rowman & Littlefield.

Trueba, H., Jacobs, L., & Kirton, E. (1990). *Cultural conflict and adaptation: The case of Hmong children in American society.* New York: Falmer.

Tse, L. (2001). *"Why don't they learn English?": Separating fact from fallacy in the U.S. language debate.* New York, N.Y.: Teachers College Press.

Tuan, M. (1995). Korean and Russian students in a Los Angeles high school: Exploring the alternative strategies of two high-achieving groups. In R. G. Rumbaut & S. S. Cornelius (Eds.), *California's immigrant children* (pp. 107–130). San Diego: Center for U.S.-Mexican Studies.

Tuan, M. (1998) (Ed.). *Forever foreigners or honorary Whites?: The Asian ethnic experience today.* Princeton, NJ: Rutgers University Press.

Tyack, D. B. (1974). *The one best system.* Cambridge, MA: Harvard University Press.

Tyack, D., & Hansot, E. (1990). *Learning together: A history of coeducation in American public schools.* New York: Russell Sage Foundation and Yale University Press.

Tyson, K., Darity, W., & Castellino, D. R. (2005). It's not "a Black thing": Understanding the burden of acting White and other dilemmas of high achievement. *American Sociological Review, 70*, 582–605.

Uba, L. (1994). *Asian Americans: Personality patterns, identity, and mental health.* New York: Guilford Press.

Uba, L. (2002). *A postmodern psychology of Asian Americans: Creating knowledge of a racial minority (Alternatives in psychology).* Albany, NY: SUNY Press.

United Nations Development Programme Report. (2005). *Table 12.* Retrieved October 5, 2007, from http://hdr.undp.org/reports/global/2005/pdf/HDR05_HDI.pdf.

Urban Institute. (May 2006). Children of immigrants: Facts and figures. Retrieved August 2, 2007, from http://www.urban.org/uploadedpdf/900955_children_of_immigrants.pdf

U.S. Bureau of the Census. (1983). *1980 census of general social and economic characteristics, United States summary 1-63, Table 166.* Washington, DC: Author.

U.S. Bureau of the Census. (1986). *1986 current population survey.* Washington, DC: Author.

U.S. Bureau of the Census. (1989). *1989 current population survey.* Washington, DC: Author.

U.S. Bureau of the Census. (1993a). *1990 census of population, CPHL-96 (language use and English ability, persons 5 to 17 years, by state: 1990 census).* Washington, DC: Author.

U.S. Bureau of the Census. (1993b). *1990 census of population and housing—Public use microdata samples 5%.* Washington, DC: Author.

U.S. Bureau of the Census. (2001a). *Overview of race and Hispanic origin, document C2KBR/01-1.* Washington. DC: Author.

U.S. Bureau of the Census. (2001b). *Questions and answers for Census 2000 data on race.* Retrieved July 8, 2005, from http://www.census.gov/press-release/www/2001/raceqandas.html

U.S. Bureau of the Census, (2002). *2000 census population and housing.* Technical documentation, summary File 3 Retrieved May 3, 2007, from http://www.albany.edu/csda/census2000/2000data.html#SF3

U.S. Bureau of the Census. (2003a). *2000 Census of population and housing-public use microdata samples 5%.* Washington, DC: Author.

U.S. Bureau of the Census. (2003b). *2000 Census, PUMS 5% Technical Documentation.* Washington, DC: Author.

U.S Bureau of the Census. (2003c). *2000 Census summary file, Table p. 19, PCT13, and PCT14.* Washington, DC: Author.

U.S. Bureau of the Census. (2003d). *Summary tables on Language Use and English Ability: 2000 (PHC-T-20).* Washington, DC: Author.

U.S. Bureau of the Census. (2004). *The American community-Hispanics: 2004.* Document ACS-03. Washington, DC: Author.

U.S. Bureau of the Census. (2005). *The American community survey 2005.* Retrieved July 14, 2008, from http://www.iaas.umb.edu/research/acs/

U.S. Bureau of the Census. (2006). *The American community survey 2005.* Retrieved July 14, 2007, from http://factfinder.census.gov/servlet/DatasetMainPage-Servlet?_program=ACS

U.S. Bureau of the Census (2007a). *The American community-Asians: 2004.* Washington, DC: Author.

U.S. Bureau of the Census. (2007b). *The American community-Blacks: 2004.* Washington, DC: Author.

U.S. Bureau of the Census. (2007c). *Census 2000 summary file 1 technical documentation.* Washington, DC: Author. Retrieved August 6, 2007, from http://www.census.gov/prod/cen2000/doc/sf1.pdf

U.S. Bureau of the Census. (2007d). Selected historical decennial census population and housing counts. Retrieved November 2, 2007, from http://www.census.gov/population/www/censusdata/hiscendata.html

U.S. Department of Education. (1993a). *The condition of education, 1993.* Washington, DC: Author.

U.S. Department of Education. (1993b). *Digest of education statistics, 1993*. Washington, DC: Author.

U.S. Department of Education. (2003). *No Child Left Behind: A parent's guide*. Washington, DC: Office of the Secretary and Office of Public Affairs.

U.S. Department of Education. (2006a). *The condition of education, 2006*. Washington, DC: Author.

U.S. Department of Education. (2006b). *Digest of education statistics, 2006*. Washington, DC: Author.

Valenzuela, A. (1999). *Subtractive schooling: U.S.-Mexican youth and the politics of caring*. Albany: State University of New York Press.

Valenzuela, A. (Ed.). (2005). Introduction: The accountability debate in Texas: Continuing the conversation. In A. Valenzuela (Ed.), *Leaving children behind: How "Texas-style" accountability fails Latino youth* (pp. 1–32). Albany, NY: State University of New York Press.

Vasquez, M. (1982). Confronting barriers to the participation of Mexican American women in higher education. *Hispanic Journal of Behavioral Science, 4*, 147–165.

Velasco, J. R. (2005). Performance-based school reforms and the federal role in helping schools that serve language-minority students. In A. Valenzuela (Ed.), *Leaving children behind: How "Texas-style" accountability fails Latino youth* (pp. 33–55). Albany, NY: State University of New York Press.

Verdonk, A. (1982). The children of immigrants in the Netherlands: Social position and implied risks for mental health. In R. Nann (Ed.), *Uprooting and surviving* (pp. 49–70). Boston: D. Reidel.

Vermeulen, H. (2000). Introduction: the role of culture in explanations of social mobility. In H. Vermeulen & J. Perlmann (Eds.), *Immigrants, schooling and social mobility: Does culture make a difference?* (pp. 1–21). New York: St. Martin's Press.

Viadero, D. (2000). Generation gap. *Education Week, 19*(39), 28–30.

Viadero, D. (2003). Study probes factors fueling achievement gaps. *Education Week, 23*(13), 1, 12.

Viadero, D. (2007). No easy answers about NCLBs effect on "poverty gap." *Education Week, 27*(12), 14.

Vickerman, M. (1999). *Crosscurrents: West Indian immigrants and race*. Oxford, UK: Oxford University.

Villalva, K. E. (2006). Hidden literacies and inquiry approaches of bilingual high school writers. *Written Communication, 23*(1), 91–129.

Villenas, S. (2002). Reinventing education in new Latino communities: Pedagogies of change and continuity in North Carolina. In S. Wortham, E. G. Murrillo, and E. T. Hamann (Eds.). *Education in the New Latino Diaspora* (pp. 17–36). Westport, Connecticut: Ablex Publishing.

Waggoner, D. (1991). *Undereducation in America*. New York: Auburn House.

Waldinger, R., & Bozorgmehr, M. (Eds.). (1996). *Ethnic Los Angles*. New York: Russell Sage Foundation.

Wang, L. (1995). *Lau v. Nichols*: History of struggle for equal and quality education. In D. T. Nakanish & T. Y. Nishida (Eds.), *The Asian American educational experience: A source book for teachers and students* (pp. 58–91). New York: Routledge.

Waters, M. C. (1991). The role of lineage in identity formation among Black Americans. *Qualitative Sociology, 14*(1), 57–76.

Waters, M. C. (1994). Ethnic and racial identities of second-generation Black immigrants in New York City. *International Migration Review, 28*, 795–820.

Waters, M. C. (1999). *Black identities*. Cambridge, MA: Harvard University Press.

Way, N., & Chen, L. (2000). Close and general friendships among African American, Latino, and Asian American adolescents from low-income families. *Journal of Adolescent Research, 15*(20), 274–301.

Wei, D. (1986). The Asian American success myth. *Interracial Books for Children, 17*(3, 4), 16–17.

Weinberg, M. (1997). *Asian-American education: Historical background and current realities*. Mahwah, NJ: Lawrence Erlbaum Associate.

Wiley, T. G. (2002). Accessing language rights in education: A brief history of the U.S. context. In J. W. Tollefson (Ed.), *Language policies in education: Critical issues* (pp. 39–64), Mahwah, NJ: Lawrence Erlbaum Associates.

Wilson, W. J. (1987). *The truly disadvantaged: The inner city, the underclass, and public policy*. Chicago: University of Chicago Press.

Woldemikael, T. M. (1989). *Becoming Black American: Haitians and American institutions in Evanston, Illinois*. New York: AMS Press.

Wu, F. H. (2002). *Yellow race in American beyond Black and White*. New York: Basic Books.

Yeh, C. J. (2004). An exploratory study of school counselors' experiences with and perceptions of Asian American. *Professional School Counseling, 4*(5), 349.

Yosso, T. J. (2005). Whose culture has capital? A critical race theory discussion of community cultural wealth. *Race, Ethnicity and Education, 8*(1), 69–91.

Zanten, A. van. (1997). Schooling immigrants in France in the 1990s: Success or failure of the republican model of integration? *Anthropology and Education Quarterly, 28*(3), 351–374.

Zehr, M. A. (2001, March 21). The "lost boys" of Sudan find a home. *Education Week, 20*(27), 34–35.

Zhang, Y. (April, 2003). *Immigrant generational differences in academic achievement and its growth: The case of Asian American high school students*. Paper presented at the Annual Meeting of the American Educational Research Association at Chicago.

Zhou, M. (1995). *Chinatown: The socioeconomic potential of an urban enclave (conflicts in urban and regionally development)*. Philadelphia, PA: Temple University Press.

Zhou, M. (2001). Immigrants schooling and social mobility: Does culture make a difference? (Book Review). *International Migration Review, 35*(3), 932–933.

Zhou, M. (2003). Urban education: Challenges in educating culturally diverse children. *Teachers College Record, 105*, 208–225.

Zhou, M., & Kim, S. S. (2006). Community forces, social capital, and educational achievement: The case of supplementary education in the Chinese and Korean Immigrant communities. *Harvard Educational Review, 76*(10), 1–29

Zhou, M., & Sao, X. Y. (2005). The multifaceted American experiences of the children of Asian immigrants: Lessons for segmented assimilation. *Ethnic and Racial Studies, 28*(6), 1119–1152.

Zimmermann, W., & Tobin, M. (1995). *Immigration and concentrated poverty*. Washington, DC: The Urban Institute.

Index

CORWIN PRESS

The Corwin Press logo—a raven striding across an open book—represents the union of courage and learning. Corwin Press is committed to improving education for all learners by publishing books and other professional development resources for those serving the field of PreK–12 education. By providing practical, hands-on materials, Corwin Press continues to carry out the promise of its motto: **"Helping Educators Do Their Work Better."**